AMER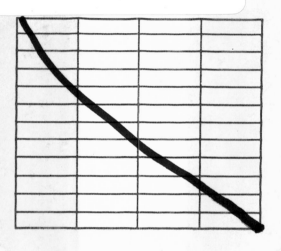TIONS

AMERICAN INTERGOVERNMENTAL RELATIONS

FOUNDATIONS, PERSPECTIVES, AND ISSUES

Second Edition

Laurence J. O'Toole, Jr., editor
University of Georgia

A Division of Congressional Quarterly Inc.
Washington, D.C.

Copyright © 1993 Congressional Quarterly Inc.
1414 22nd Street, N.W., Washington, D.C. 20037

Printed in the United States of America

Cover design: Ed Atkeson, Berg Design, Albany, New York

Library of Congress Cataloging-in-Publication Data

American intergovernmental relations: foundations, perspectives, and issues / Laurence J. O'Toole, Jr., editor. —2nd ed.
    p.   cm.
    Includes index.
    ISBN 0-87187-718-X
    1. Federal government—United States. 2. Intergovernmental fiscal relations—United States. I. O'Toole, Laurence J., 1948-
JK310.A48   1993
321.02′3′0973--dc20

                          92-30912
                          CIP

For Mary

CONTENTS

Part III
Fiscal Aspects of Intergovernmental Relations   201

Part IV
Administrative Aspects of Intergovernmental Relations

Part V
The Post-Reagan Era, the Emerging Responsibilities
of the States, and the Future of the
Intergovernmental System

PREFACE

As at other junctures in the evolution of the American system of federalism, the last several years have brought changes, challenges, and opportunities in both the study and the practice of intergovernmental relations in the United States. Today, the American intergovernmental system is a focal point of controversy. Yet the debates of the 1990s have not been unanticipated. In fact, part of the idea behind the experiment with a federal system that the founders introduced two centuries ago was to establish an adaptable structure within which issue-specific disputes could occur and competing values be engaged. Since then the framework has indeed been dramatically altered under forces of political, economic, and social modernization. These pressures have resulted in tremendously increased interdependence and complexity for all participants, whose multiple interconnections have made bargaining a fact of life. The foundations of such a system, its operations and consequences, and the issues occupying the attention of today's intergovernmental analysts and practitioners are the subjects of attention here.

The basic structure of the first edition has been retained in this second edition, as have many of the readings that continue to be pertinent. These have been supplemented with a number of new readings that suggest promising ways to understand the dynamism of the intergovernmental network and to document some of the major developments of the past decade. Among the themes and topics introduced in the second edition are a coalition-based approach for interpreting intergovernmental politics, recent developments in constitutional law affecting federalism (especially the *Garcia* and *South Carolina* cases), the altered roles of intergovernmental lobbying groups in an era of federal budgetary constraint, responses by local governments in the time of cutbacks at all levels, the increasing importance of mandates as they affect state and also local governments, and the resurgent roles and responsibilities of the states in the 1990s.

The readings have been selected to blend classic expositions with contemporary findings and controversies. To provide a broad survey of the system's foundations, perspectives, and issues—and in so doing to document the themes of complexity and interdependence—this book contains selections from many of the most important, enduring, and often controversial documents on American intergovernmental relations, as well as provocative analyses of many of today's most interesting and pressing intergovernmental issues. Criteria for selection of the individual articles have been their significance to the field, their fit with the book's scope and themes, and their contrasting perspectives.

Part I explores the roots of today's American intergovernmental system. Readings convey the ideas behind the original federal bargain, the classic interpretations of how the system has developed (with an emphasis on cooperation and conflict between governments), and some important theoretical perspectives on the modern system.

Parts II through IV explore the operations of contemporary American intergovernmental relations along political, financial, and administrative lines. Each part highlights the themes of interdependence and complexity, and the predictable tensions within and across governmental units. Readings include both analyses of the system as a whole (for example, its fiscal aspects) and explorations of the perspectives and activities of specific participants (such as governors, the Congress, or urban lobbyists).

Part V contains readings on a selection of issues and challenges, especially the future of the system and the role of the states, in the post-Reagan era. Each issue is explained from the various important perspectives in the debate and linked to the themes of interdependence and complexity developed throughout the book.

Each part opens with an interpretive essay intended to provide background and unite the selections. Discussion and study questions conclude each part and are designed to help readers test their understanding of the basic information contained in the articles, to provoke independent thought, and to expand their knowledge by encouraging integration of the various readings. The overall goal has been to give readers the opportunity to grapple with the issues and to think coherently and independently about the subject of American intergovernmental relations.

The book is designed for use as either a main or a supplementary text in upper-division undergraduate and graduate courses on federalism and intergovernmental relations. Students of state and local government and politics should also find the collection useful.

Many people helped me during the preparation of this book. First, I thank the authors and publishers of the works excerpted or reprinted here for granting permission to include the fruits of their labors. Joanne Daniels, director of CQ Press when the first edition was published, originally encouraged me to pursue this idea and later invited an updated version. The second edition has benefited from further encouragement, plus numerous suggestions and assistance on matters large and small, from Brenda Carter and Shana Wagger at CQ Press. A number of other people assisted in rendering the burden of revision more feasible and pleasant. Reviewers David R. Beam and Margaret T. Wrightson offered encouragement and also helpful suggestions at the time I began work on this revision. Richard Tobin and David Robertson evaluated an early draft of the full manuscript and contributed appropriate measures of encouragement, counsel, and critique. The finished product is better for the assistance of all these scholars. My research assistant, Letha Strothers, expedited the book's production. My family, now larger with Kathleen joining Conor and Mary, continues to sustain us all with remarkable spirit and resilience, and to tolerate the confusedly peripatetic ways of its fourth member.

AMERICAN INTERGOVERNMENTAL
RELATIONS: AN OVERVIEW

Who (if anyone) should assist America's big cities with the financial responsibility for handling a spate of ills from homelessness to Acquired Immune Deficiency Syndrome (AIDS) to attracting business investment? Should state governments be able to force localities to initiate new activities without providing the cash to cover expenses? Should the nation adopt a common and upgraded school curriculum in an effort to improve education and also economic competitiveness with other nations? Or should local districts across the wide variety of states comprising the country be permitted, even encouraged, to innovate on their own?

Should the federal government be heavily involved in the enforcement of such important policies as ensuring citizens' civil rights, encouraging equal employment opportunity, and assisting with affirmative action? Alternatively, should Washington have *any* role in the operations of local police and fire departments?

How should the people handle problems that confront one region of the United States but surpass that locale's ability to cope? When a huge oil spill devastates parts of the precious Alaskan wilderness, who should take action, and how? When a reform of national tax law creates unintendedly negative effects on the finances of the states, what should be done? When acid rain from industrial air pollution contributes to the deterioration of natural resources a thousand miles away, whose problem and responsibility should it be? All these and many more are topics of intergovernmental relations.

Intergovernmental relations is the subject of how our many and varied American governments deal with each other; and what their relative roles, responsibilities, and levels of influence are and should be. The subject is no flash-in-the-pan concern; it has generated long-standing interest, indeed constant and pervasive controversy, throughout American political and administrative history.

In fact, the establishment of the United States was itself a sort of experiment in intergovernmental relations, since an effort to create a federal system like this one had never before been attempted. Nearly

1

every major matter of domestic policy debated and decided throughout the nation's more than two hundred years has been imbued with important intergovernmental aspects. Intergovernmental issues have contributed to such significant events in American history as the Civil War, the establishment of the social-welfare state during the New Deal era, the attack on poverty in the 1960s, and the attempt to shift responsibilities to the states during the Reagan years.

But the subject is more than a collection of isolated issues. Indeed, it would be difficult to make systematic sense of policy disputes like those mentioned above without first understanding the intergovernmental system per se—its historical development as well as its current structure. To prepare for an exploration of current issues and disputes and to provide a context for the readings that follow, this chapter offers a brief overview of the intergovernmental system in the United States, emphasizing the federal government's role in the system's development.

Federalism, as the term is understood today, means a system of authority constitutionally apportioned between central and regional governments.[1] In the American system, the central, or national, government is often called the federal government; the regional governments are the states. The federal-state relationship is interdependent: neither can abolish the other and each must deal with the other. *Intergovernmental relations* is the more comprehensive term, including the full range of federal-state-local relations.

In the 1990s there are approximately 83,000 American governments—one national, 50 state, and the rest local. The latter consist of several distinct types. *Counties,* numbering some 3,000 units, are general-purpose governments originally created throughout most of the country to administer state services at the local level. Today, counties are genuine local governments providing an array of services to their citizens, and many—especially the larger, more urban ones—are increasingly involved in complex intergovernmental arrangements with other local jurisdictions, states, and the national government. *Municipalities,* numbering about 19,000, are local governments established to serve people within an area of concentrated population. The nation's largest cities and small villages alike are municipalities, although the types of powers they have and the services they offer may vary considerably. Municipalities are created to serve explicitly the interests of the local community. Through much of American history, municipalities have had extensive and often highly conflicting relationships with their "parent" states—relationships sometimes made all the more challenging from the point of view of the municipalities since they are not granted constitutionally independent status by the states, as are the states in the U.S. framework. Since the New Deal era in the 1930s and the rapid expansion of the intergovernmental system in the 1960s, municipalities—especially large cities—have dealt with Washington, as well, on many matters. And as federal cutbacks to these governments took hold beginning in the 1980s, municipalities have often developed defensive and somewhat conflictual relations with both state and national authorities—as they have also sought to develop additional revenue sources and less one-sided dependence on the other levels.

Additional local governments include:

- *townships* (approximately 17,000), which are usually sub-divisions of rural counties and are relatively unimportant except in some parts of New England and the mid-Atlantic states;
- *school districts* (15,000), which are separate governments established in many parts of the country to direct public school systems; and
- *special districts* (numbering 29,532 in a recent count), which are limited-purpose governments set up to handle one or perhaps a few public functions over a specially designated area.[2]

Special districts are currently responsible for managing public housing; building and maintaining bridges, tunnels, and roads; supplying water and sewerage services to residents; assessing and regulating air quality; and caring for the district's mass transportation needs. The creation of many of these districts over the years has been directly or indirectly encouraged by other governments—such as the states and Washington—which sought "coordinated" local action on one or another policy problem.

If given a chance to view their handiwork today, it is likely that the founders of this nation would find much to surprise them in the operations of American politics and government, especially in the intergovernmental workings. Yet intergovernmental developments over the past two centuries have been affected greatly by some fundamental choices consciously made by those early Americans.

The Founding and the Framework

The framers of the U.S. Constitution sought a way to combine the several states into a structure that would minimize "instability, injustice, and confusion," in the words of James Madison.[3] The founders were familiar with the arguments of earlier political thinkers who claimed that government protection of individual rights would have to be small-scale and cover a geographically limited jurisdiction. Yet their own experience suggested problems with such an arrangement. Under the Articles of Confederation, enacted after the Revolution, the thirteen American states had agreed on a formal arrangement that is now called a *confederation*.[4] The states were loosely joined for certain purposes, but their association fell far short of a real nation. The states retained almost all power, and the "united states" under the Articles found it virtually impossible to act with dispatch on matters of importance.

To solve this problem, the "federalists" of that period proposed to organize a nation able to act in a unified and central fashion for certain purposes. They argued that large republics, not small ones, were more likely to be able to prevent internal tyranny. They also suggested, however, that the states themselves retain independent governments with correspondingly independent jurisdictions. As a matter of fact, state autonomy was a political necessity at the time if widespread support of a new constitutional order were to be elicited. In the absence of any such historical arrangement, the new experiment in intergovernmental relations would have to develop out of the American experience.

The founders' construction of the new system virtually ensured continuing controversy about the respective roles of the national and state governments by creating sufficient ambiguity to leave many of the most important questions unresolved. As a result, later years were to see major changes in American intergovernmental relations under the influence of various political, economic, and social forces, while the basic framework remained constant.[5]

What does that framework actually stipulate? The Constitution seems to divide responsibilities between the two levels of government according to subject. Certain functions (for example, interstate commerce and national defense) are assigned to the national authorities, while many others (such as selection of presidential electors) are left to the states. Furthermore, the Tenth Amendment in the Bill of Rights asserts that "the powers not delegated to the United States by the Constitution, nor prohibited by it to the States, are reserved to the States respectively, or to the people." The states appear to have been given an advantage.

Yet the explanation cannot end here, for the same Constitution provides conflicting cues, authorizing the national Congress to "provide for the . . . general Welfare" and to "make all Laws which shall be necessary and proper" for executing this and the other powers given to the legislature. What constitutes the "general welfare" and which laws are necessary and proper are inherently political questions. Thus, it should be no surprise that the answers adopted by different people and at different times have not been consistent. The founders established a framework in which American governments would have separate but not completely independent spheres. The different levels would find it both useful and necessary to engage in conflict and cooperation; neither would be willing or able to ignore the other.

The Idea of Dual Federalism

Even in the earliest decades of the nation's existence, this tension was evident between the idea of *dual federalism* (that is, each of the two levels of government operating within its separate sphere without relying on the other for assistance or authorization) on the one hand and ambiguous overlap on the other.

The notion of dual federalism influenced the decisions of the Supreme Court at least until the early decades of the twentieth century. Furthermore, during the 1800s various presidents sometimes vetoed legislation that would have created a federal presence in policy fields such as public works construction on the grounds that the Constitution simply did not permit such national involvement in arenas reserved for the states.[6] In 1854, for example, President Franklin Pierce vetoed legislation that would have authorized federal land grants to be used for state institutions for the insane. In a number of fields, like education and social policy, dual federalism was the predominant view of federal-state intergovernmental relations.

Conflict and Cooperation in Earlier Times

Yet neither sphere was completely independent, even in the early years. Throughout the nineteenth century, the national government and the states often disagreed about the limits of their own authority. The Civil War is perhaps the prime example, but conflict occurred on other matters as well, such as policy on labor, social welfare, and economic regulation. Through the necessity of resolving jurisdictional disputes, therefore, the federal and state governments found it necessary to recognize their interdependence.

Conflict was not the only stimulus, however, for interaction. As various policy problems captured the attention of the nation's officials and citizenry, federal and state governments were sometimes able to piece together intergovernmental mechanisms to address immediate concerns. For instance, if some early national and state leaders viewed direct federal aid for internal improvements (for example, road and canal construction) as a violation of constitutional restrictions on intergovernmental arrangements, the governments *were* able to agree to cooperate in the formation of *joint stock companies,* part public and part private entities created to surmount the restrictions on direct participation by the national government. (Governments and private businesses could buy stock in a company and appoint members to its board of directors, thus indirectly supporting and influencing its operations.)[7]

Another mechanism for cooperation during the previous century, before the dramatically increased intergovernmental interdependence of recent years, was the *land grant*. Through this device, the federal government would offer some of its land (it owned plenty) to the states for specified purposes. The recipient government would be obliged to abide by certain federal requirements, but direct involvement by the national government was minimal. Land grants were intended to help achieve goals in the fields of education (thus the origins of today's nationwide set of land-grant colleges and universities), economic development, and (on a very limited scale) social welfare.

Other forms of intergovernmental cooperation, such as technical assistance from federal to state governments and informal exchanges and loans of expert personnel during peak or crisis periods, were relatively common occurrences even during the nation's first century. Nevertheless, it was not until the twentieth century that the dual federal perspective declined appreciably in significance and American intergovernmental relations developed into a system with sustained high levels of *interdependence* and consequent *complexity*. Several political, economic, and social events and trends fueled these developments.

Developments in the Early Twentieth Century

From early in the present century until recent years, federal involvement, especially financial involvement, in intergovernmental relations escalated. The Progressive era at the turn of the century brought an expanded role for government in general, as reformers argued that the society and the economy could not tolerate laissez-faire. The concentration of power in large corporations, the reluctance of some state governments to enact regulatory and other social welfare legislation (although other states were leaders in enacting farsighted and sometimes tough policy on such subjects), and the dawning recognition that the nation's natural resources were limited and would have to be conserved encouraged an expanded domestic policy role for Washington. This shift was also encouraged in many cases by the newly developing and professionalizing state bureaucracies, which saw in federal involvement opportunities for upgrading and for expanded funding; and by some interest groups that had been pushing at the state level for public attention to one problem or another. (Then, as now, organized interests—whether concerned with expanded highway construction or social services—have recognized that it is usually easier and more effective to deal with one central government on such matters than with scores of divergent ones throughout the states.)

The growing national will to attempt action in new arenas was followed by the central government's acquiring the practical wherewithal for action. The resources needed were money and clear authority; by the 1920s both had been generated.

Federal Financial Aid

In 1913 the U.S. Constitution was amended to permit the enactment of a federal income tax. Previously the national government had provided some limited financial support to the states, but the intergovernmental fiscal ties were few and far between. Until very recently, however, the passage of the Sixteenth Amendment enabled the national government to raise revenue more easily than the subnational ones. The income tax, which was "elastic" (that is, its receipts increased faster than the economy during periods of growth), has been a more politically palatable revenue source than other sources typically emphasized by the states and local governments.

This situation has changed in recent years. First, the income tax increased its bite in individuals' paychecks during the period of rapid inflation in the 1970s, resulting in a decline in its popularity and the enactment of an indexing provision to control the effects of inflation. Second, federal legislative changes during the 1980s reduced the progressiveness of the tax, that is, the extent to which it draws revenue from the affluent. And other federal taxes, especially social security, have begun to assume a larger burden. Third, most states and even some local governments enacted income taxes of their own, with formulas tied in complicated ways to various provisions of the federal tax code. The development of intergovernmental finances in recent decades therefore documents one way in which the system has been linked via complexity. Thus, with the income tax the federal government created a source of money that could be tapped repeatedly to fill needs that had not yet received the states' wholehearted attention.

The obvious mechanism of intergovernmental cooperation in many such cases was the *grant-in-aid*. By 1920 there were eleven grants-in-aid operating in the United States. Land grants and other varieties of intergovernmental assistance were never again to outstrip cash grants in importance. Because of the significance of grants-in-aid and their sustained use in the early twentieth century, it would be useful to explain at this point some of the basic implications of this kind of federal program.

A grant-in-aid is a transfer of funds from one government to another for some specified purpose. Typically the recipient government is asked by the donor to abide by certain terms as conditions of the assistance.[8] These usually include a requirement that the recipient unit match the donor's financial contribution with one of its own, as well as a series of "strings," or stipulations, as to how the funds will be utilized, how the program will be managed, and how the recipient government will report to the donor.

Starting on a small scale early in this century, and then expanding rapidly during certain periods—especially the New Deal and Great Society eras—grants-in-aid from the federal government to the states and eventually local governments became extremely important features of the intergovernmental system in the United States. States too have provided financial support to their local governments. (In 1988 total state aid amounted to $149 billion. This total includes some federal aid passed to the local units through the states.)[9] But federal aid, because of its size, relative newness, and capacity to produce large-scale alterations in the intergovernmental system, may be considered an especially significant feature of America's fiscal federalism (see Table 1).

Validation of Grants-in-Aid

As the national government began to exercise influence through the use of grants-in-aid in the early 1900s, some observers wondered if the grant mechanism was an unconstitutional federal intrusion into the affairs of the states. Armed with the doctrine of dual federalism, critics of federal grants argued that Washington's offers were actually coercive inducements and violated the notion of separate spheres for these two levels of government. In a pair of landmark decisions in 1923 the Supreme Court paved the way for major expansions in the grant system—and for tremendously increased interdependence and complexity among levels of government—in succeeding years. The Court asserted that grants were voluntary arrangements and the federal government was therefore not violating the constitutionally established separation of functions in the federal system.[10] As the years elapsed, the grant framework became a dominant feature of the American intergovernmental network; it tied thousands of governments intricately together, whatever the direction preferred or perturbations experienced from any point in the system.

Basic Types of Assistance

Grants have offered the opportunity for substantially expanded federal influence over state and local governments, and a number of important political and administrative consequences flow from this fact. Yet it is essential to recognize that while grants create chances for national involvement, they do not vitiate the pluralism of the intergovernmental system—at least not necessarily. Grants have developed as the prime instruments used to promote bargaining and jockeying for

Table 1   Federal Aid to State and Local Governments, Selected Years

Year	Amount (Billions)[a]	Amount in Constant 1982 Dollars (Billions)	Number of Grants
1902	$ .028		5
1912	—		7
1913	.039		—
1920	—		11
1922	.242		—
1932	.593		12
1934	2.4		—
1937	—		26
1940	2.1		—
1946	—		28
1952	3.1		38
1960	7.0	24.7	132
1964	10.1	33.6	—
1967	15.2	46.0	379
1975	49.8	87.1	442
1978	77.9	109.7	—
1981	94.8	100.7	539
1982	88.2	88.2	441
1984	97.6	90.2	405
1987	108.4	90.6	435
1990	133.8 (est.)	98.2	—
1992	149.4 (est.)	100.1	—

[a] 1961 dollars through 1952; otherwise, current dollars.

SOURCE: U.S. Advisory Commission on Intergovernmental Relations, *The Federal Role in the Federal System: The Dynamics of Growth—A Crisis of Confidence and Competence* (Washington, D.C.: ACIR, July 1980), 120-121; and *Revenues and Expenditures*, vol. 2 of *Significant Features of Fiscal Federalism, 1990* (Washington, D.C.: ACIR, August 1990), 42.

advantage among governments; they have frequently stimulated both cooperation and conflict among such governments. It should therefore surprise no one that the system of intergovernmental aid employed in this country has elicited ambivalent evaluations from participants and citizens alike.

Grants come in many shapes and sizes. The donor government may structure the purpose quite narrowly, offering aid for the construction of certain kinds of highways within a state. Such *categorical grants* were typical in the early part of this century. The donor may also design an intergovernmental program for a variety of purposes within a broad field such as education, community development, or social services. This type of aid, called a *block grant*, gained some prominence in more recent decades. In the early 1970s a new form of aid, *revenue sharing,* was created to enable one government to offer financial aid to another with virtually no restrictions as to its use.[11]

When enacted, all of these types of intergovernmental assistance required some rules and regulations regarding the method of distributing the aid. How is a unit selected to receive assistance and how much is it entitled to? Some grants, including all federal block grants, specify a precise formula in the legislation creating the program. Such *formula grants* include quantifiable elements, such as size of population, amount of tax effort, proportion of population unemployed or below poverty level, density of housing, or rate of infant mortality. The specified formula is a rule that tells potential recipient governments precisely how they can calculate the quantity of aid to which they are entitled under the provisions of the law, so long as the recipient qualifies for such assistance under the other stipulations of the program. Usually, the elements in a formula are chosen to reflect characteristics related to the purpose of the aid (number of school-age children for an education grant, age and/or density of residential housing for housing assistance). Some factors in the formula are also likely to have political significance since there is no such thing as a "neutral" formula—all formulas reward some states or localities more than others, depending on their relative standing given the formula specified.

However, another method of distributing aid is possible. *Project grants* allocate funding on a competitive basis, and potential recipients have no advance knowledge about the size of the grant. Instead, the authorizing legislation typically indicates the sorts of jurisdictions that are eligible to apply for aid and the criteria that will be employed to judge the merit of a government's application. Whether or not a government then receives funding depends on how strong a case it can make in its own behalf. Bureaucrats in the federal departments that supply aid determine the relative worthiness of different proposals and different jurisdictions, often by means of a detailed decision-making and evaluation system.

Why bother to make these distinctions among types of aid? The answer is that different types of grants have tended to produce different types of relationships between and among the participating governments. Much of the intergovernmental system during this century can be rendered intelligible by analyzing the consequences of different types of aid, the subject of much of the remainder of this chapter.

The Legacy of the New Deal

Most of the grant-in-aid programs developed by the national government in the early decades of the 1900s were relatively limited. They assisted primarily in fields that commanded strong political support, such as agriculture and road construction. Federal assistance, and thus national influence, was directed almost entirely toward the states rather than local governments. During this period, and until the 1960s, the system of intergovernmental aid was dominated by categorical formula grants. For the first part of the century, these were accompanied by relatively few strings, required considerable matching on the part of the recipients, and were rare enough that they did not seem to impose much of an administrative or political burden on the states.

With the New Deal in the 1930s the federal government under the leadership of President Franklin D. Roosevelt tackled the challenging economic and social problems of the Depression era. Although it would have been technically possible to establish new national-level programs to cope with the difficulties of the period, the more politically palatable method of the grant-in-aid was repeatedly used instead. Thus, while the national government's role expanded, the states and local governments retained significant leverage. Within a two-year period, categorical grants were established in such a variety of fields— free school lunches, aid to dependent children, emergency work relief, and so on—that they became the foundation for the social-welfare state in America. The first real forms of assistance to some of the nation's local governments, the cities, were initiated during this period as well. For the states and some of their local governments, then, national authorities were no longer distant or sporadically communicating entities. Instead, in many areas of domestic policy, two or three levels of government were tied together in intricate patterns of intergovernmental relations—much like a "marble cake," rather than a "layer cake" of dual federalism.[12]

Thus, the New Deal period witnessed a permanent increase in the density and importance of intergovernmental relationships in the United States, and during the next couple of decades—even during the administration of Republican president Dwight D. Eisenhower— the number of federal programs and quantity of federal aid continued to grow. Eisenhower himself was uncomfortable with the apparently prominent role of the national government in domestic policy matters, and he established the Commission on Intergovernmental Relations with the explicit charge to identify areas of federal involvement that could feasibly be "returned" to the states. But even the very modest suggestions of this commission went unimplemented. During the 1950s it seemed, as it often has since then, that the idea of separating functions by level of government was supported in the abstract, but was exceedingly difficult to execute. Concerted efforts to reduce the levels of interdependence and complexity in the intergovernmental system have, until very recently, been singularly unsuccessful. During the Reagan years, as discussed below, the federal government simplified the grant system in certain ways. Yet even these were not without costs (as some readings in this book demonstrate, intergovernmental regulations can provide policy benefits), and they introduced complicating changes as well, such as increased intergovernmental mandating in place of the grant mechanism in some policy spheres.

The difficulty experienced by American governments when they try to reduce their reliance on one another is not surprising. Since the New Deal citizens and public officials have tried to harness the national government's tremendous resources in order to attack pressing problems and redress inequities. They have at the same time attempted to retain diversity and innovation through vital state and local governments wherever possible. Shifting to some form of dual federalism, with a much less intense pattern of relationships and dependencies, could affect federal commitments in a multitude of important policy areas, like environmental protection, civil rights, income security, and education. Furthermore, such a change might entail radical shifts in the nation's tax system. And even the most carefully considered plans would have to face bewildering dilemmas about how to reduce intergovernmental interdependence without inflicting serious inequities on some states and localities.

These days, when, as in the 1950s, one hears proposals to limit the federal role in the intergovernmental system and simplify the pattern of American governments, such caveats are useful to keep in mind. While many of the states are assuming newly resurgent roles in the policy settings of the 1990s, Washington is certain to play a crucial part for the foreseeable future. It may even be asserted that creating a radically simplified intergovernmental arrangement by moving the national government out of a direct role in many important policy arenas is not a practical or responsible option. Why, then, the clamorous call for reform? Why have so many policymakers and intergovernmental experts complained about the "overloaded" pattern?[13] Later in this book, the considerable validity of a number of the criticisms will become clear. Focusing on the major developments affecting the intergovernmental system since the 1960s will be useful in understanding this controversy.

Creative Federalism and Its Implications

With Lyndon Johnson's presidency and the election of a heavily Democratic and activist Congress in 1964, a several-year period of tremendously expanded intergovernmental activities and initiatives began. Johnson proposed a "creative federalism" that would signify multiple new national commitments to assist states, localities, and private individuals and organizations in their efforts to solve many of the domestic difficulties afflicting American society. These efforts of the Johnson era were directed primarily at problems of racial discrimination, poverty, and urban and rural development. The president and the Congress responded not just with rhetoric but with hundreds of intergovernmental programs.

Indeed, the number of federal programs of grant-in-aid tripled from the beginning of the 1960s to 1975 (Table 1). Almost all of the new programs from Washington were categorical grants, and—unlike earlier times—most of them were project grants. By the late 1960s most of the grants available were project grants, although many of these were relatively small and in toto constituted a minority of the aid dollars. In addition, the amount of support aimed directly at local governments rose sharply. Many localities (especially the nation's older, larger, more fiscally strapped cities) came to consider the federal government more of an ally than their own state governments and became increasingly reliant on federal largesse. The results of these and other massive changes in the intergovernmental system enacted in such a compressed period were, as might be expected, mixed.

Intergovernmental Activism

In many respects the consequences of this major increase in intergovernmental activity were impressive. Although hampered by fiscal constraints, especially as the war in Southeast Asia drained its resources, the nation made measurable progress on a number of troubling problems.[14] The dramatic increase in federal support was especially welcome to many state and local governments, which had difficulty obtaining the resources to fund programs demanded by their citizenry; also, the emphasis on a variety of project grants meant that potential recipients could find appropriately targeted programs.

The explosion in the grants system had the further effect of encouraging or mandating the professionalization of personnel and the use of up-to-date financial procedures in the administrative agencies handling the programs in the recipient units. Intergovernmental programs became increasingly influenced by functional specialists at all levels of government. The requirements attached to many of the new grants also forced states and localities to devote renewed attention to public problems they may have overlooked in the past.

Another trend fueled by creative federalism was the growth of interest groups in the nation's capital, especially intergovernmental groups. Those concerned with specific intergovernmental programs, whether on environmental pollution or juvenile delinquency, increasingly looked to Washington as they tried to influence legislation and the implementation of regulations, to monitor the actions of the federal agency involved, and to maintain contact with other interested parties. The tremendous expansion of the grants system in the 1960s was both a result of and a stimulus for a burgeoning number of interest groups operating at the national level in intergovernmental politics. These changes, too, contributed to the growing complexity of intergovernmental policy making.

These sorts of interest groups were not the only ones to achieve a heightened national presence. As the grants process became ever more important and the system increasingly more complex, officials of state and local governments found it crucial to acquire information about the process in Washington and the decisions being made. Furthermore, state and local officials began to realize that their own interests might deserve representation in the policy process at the national level. Accordingly, several groups of state or local general-purpose officials organized for the first time, moved their operations to Washington, or upgraded their staff and expanded their activities. These groups, including entities like the National Governors' Association, the Council of State Governments, the National Association of Counties, and the U.S. Conference of Mayors, refer to themselves as public interest groups, or *PIGs*. By the 1960s they became increasingly recognized as leaders in the representation of state and local interests in national policy making. In addition to the governments that began to locate offices and representatives in Washington, other more functionally specialized groups of state and local officials, such as highway officials, budget officers, and social workers, have organized into national groups and participate in the policy process. Nowadays, and even in the midst of the financial constraints of the 1990s, any discussion of an intergovernmental issue in Congress or an administrative agency is likely to elicit concern, participation, lobbying, and debate involving many such organizations.

Thus, the Johnson era encouraged several salutary developments in intergovernmental relations and further elaborated other interesting trends. Yet, as might be expected when such massive changes are effected, difficulties and tensions also arose.

Emergent Frustrations and Tensions

The almost limitless choices made available to state and local officials because of the tremendous increase in intergovernmental programs also meant that the potential recipients could afford to shop around among programs and federal agencies to bargain for the most favorable deal. As a result of the interagency competition for clients, federal policy in a program would sometimes be loosely enforced. Recipients were more and more able to evade federal intent while absorbing federal dollars.

Conversely, the system, which now had huge numbers of partially overlapping (and often project-duplicating) grants, created vexing difficulties for officials at state and local levels. With several related programs available to assist a city in such tasks as rebuilding its sewers, a great deal of time, effort, and information went into deciding which program(s) to pursue. Grants established ostensibly for the same purpose might be housed in different federal agencies, require entirely different application and approval processes, stipulate very different matching requirements, and be implemented with conflicting schedules. Furthermore, as potential recipients of project grants scrambled to complete detailed applications for scores of grant requests on short notice, the winners were not necessarily the most competent or the most needy jurisdictions. Instead, the one who packaged proposals in the most salable fashion (exercising what has come to be called "grants-manship"), was often rewarded.

The systemic changes generated another set of tensions for state and local governments. With the multitude of programs, many of which were now funded by grants constructed with high matching ratios (that is, Washington would pay for most of the total expenses incurred under the program), state and local governments were finding it increasingly difficult either to abstain from commitments to federal aid or to make such commitments wholeheartedly. When a donor government offers a grant, this lowers the cost of the good or service provided for the potential recipient and thus renders it more attractive. However, when the number of individually appealing programs multiplies greatly, the consequence can be significant distortion in the recipient's own budget choices. Instead of spending its locally generated revenue on the public services judged most important by its own officials and citizens, a city can be encouraged to utilize a substantial portion as matching funds for programs that are, in essence, national priorities. The expansion of the aid system in the 1960s prompted complaints on this score from uneasy mayors, governors, and others who were concerned about their apparently declining ability to maintain some independence.

Such general-purpose officials had other concerns as well. Many of them believed the expanded system of categorical grants was composed of unduly narrow programs that were not easily adaptable to the needs in their own jurisdictions. Furthermore, the pattern, taken as a whole, had become so complex that it was all but impenetrable to generalists. These officials had a difficult time even discovering just how much aid was being received from federal sources. And many of the important, detailed decisions that are made as part of an intergovernmental grant bargain—for instance, determining the eligibility of clients for programs or establishing goals—were made far from the presence of the general-purpose officials. Increasingly important in the intergovernmental policy process was a great number of specialists across governmental levels—especially in administrative agencies charged with executing the program, legislative committees with responsibility for the substantive area, and pressure groups with a strong interest in the program. Intergovernmental experts, particularly those concerned about the decreasing ability of general officials to oversee and direct activities across this maze, dubbed these policy networks *vertical functional autocracies.*

In these chains of influence, it became increasingly difficult for anyone, even major officials like governors or mayors or presidents, to decipher just *who* was causing *what* to happen intergovernmentally. When responsibility is so diffused, the mechanisms of democratic government cannot readily ensure that policy reflects the will of the people or their representatives. In other words, another possible cost of such an arrangement is a decline in political responsiveness.

In short, then, the era of creative federalism brought energy and inventiveness to intergovernmental questions; but the massive changes in the system meant a significant escalation in costs and frustrations as well. It should not be surprising, therefore, that interdependence and complexity emerged as major political features during the quarter century following the Johnson era. Despite manifold differences in emphasis, approach, and impact, intergovernmental actors during the most recent period have grappled with a structure exhibiting common characteristics and daunting demands. The following pages first characterize the modern intergovernmental pattern in general terms and then explore important events and efforts during several recent national administrations.

The Modern Pattern: Interdependence, Complexity, and Intergovernmental Bargaining

In the pattern that emerged from the explosive growth of creative federalism, it became difficult for actors in the system to make rational decisions to benefit the individuals or activities for which they held responsibility. It was also difficult to design any coherent change in the system itself. These problems stemmed directly from the dominant characteristics of the intergovernmental system: its interdependence and related complexity.

It would be helpful to define these two concepts more precisely here. *Interdependence* means that power is shared among branches and layers of government, even within policy sectors. Instead of one level consistently controlling decisions about policy, nearly any change requires mutual accommodation among several levels of government. No one is in control of the system itself, and unanticipated consequences are a fact of life. *Complexity* accompanies such interdependence. Complexity means that the intergovernmental network is large and differentiated; no one participant can possibly possess enough information about its components and dynamics consistently to make rational decisions on its own or to operate in isolation from the rest.

Especially since the era of creative federalism, but also as a consequence of the framework established by the founders, many participants in the intergovernmental system have plenty of opportunities to exercise influence—particularly to delay or frustrate action to which they are opposed. It is much more difficult, however, to generate and systematically execute *positive* action in a straightforwardly rational manner.

An important result of the system's grounding in interdependence and complexity (one that became obvious in the 1960s and endures in altered form to the present day) is that the typical style of decision making in the American intergovernmental system is one of bargaining under conditions of partial conflict among the participants. The actors in the system, including the various governments involved, have different interests to serve and objectives to seek; yet they cannot succeed by acting unilaterally. They may join together into one or more loose coalitions aimed at achieving some intergovernmental objective.[15] But they must perforce negotiate as a nearly ceaseless activity if they are to have any chance of defending themselves or achieving even some of their goals.

Of course, bargaining under conditions of partial conflict is a very abstract notion and encompasses many different types of situations. The bargaining between governments in a project-grant structure differs in predictable and important ways from the bargaining activity likely with a formula grant: the former setting typically provides more influence to bureaucratic actors associated with the donor government, those who write the rules and evaluate the competitive applications from potential recipients. The fact of bargaining and its pervasiveness throughout the system, however, is important to keep in mind. Bargaining is typical even during the 1990s, a time when grant programs will not grow at nearly the pace of earlier periods and when other, ostensibly more controlling, or unilateral, or regulatory ties have become prominent between the federal and other governments. As readings in this book document, recent years have brought national judicial decisions that challenge the constitutional and fiscal bases of state autonomy; and unfunded mandates (rather than grants) have become increasingly utilized as a mechanism of coordination across governments. Yet these shifts do not unambiguously signify a new centralization. In some ways, also documented later in this volume, the states are now able to initiate more action, or to resist more, than in the previous period. And federal officials may have fewer levers to enforce their own efforts at intergovernmental influence when the grant mechanism is absent from, or less prominent in, the bargaining arena. It may be concluded, therefore, that the shifts of the past decade or more have altered the *types* of bargaining and the issues subject to negotiation. The fact of bargaining nevertheless remains crucial to an understanding of American intergovernmental dynamics.

Some of the tensions inherent in such an interdependent and complex system became visible in the 1960s and have escalated since. Red tape, which is the continuation of intergovernmental negotiation and conflict by other means, is one manifestation. The federal government has usually viewed the requirements it imposes on its grants as essential to ensure a program's integrity. Yet recipient units claim that the burdens have become excessive. (Localities also blame the states in part for their red-tape burden.) Federally created intergovernmental mandates have escalated sharply since 1975 and have become the bête noire of state and local officials.

Two general points emerge. First, the problems and tensions in the modern system are not primarily the product of ill will or ignorance, nor can they be traced primarily to one level of government. Rather, the American intergovernmental system was founded on ambivalent principles and built to establish arenas for conflict and controversy. A second and related point is that changing the particular pattern of intergovernmental relationships or reforming certain aspects of the system—for example, through the enactment of spending and policy shifts such as Ronald Reagan sought during the 1980s—would have important consequences but could hardly resolve the value conflicts of a complex and interdependent system. At this point, accordingly, we should examine some of the developments in the American intergovernmental system since the period of creative federalism. Many of these are made comprehensible by an awareness of the difficulties just surveyed, and many, in turn, presage some of the topics of current interest and controversy.

Nixon's New Federalism

A number of the difficulties outlined above were obvious by the close of the Johnson administration. Richard Nixon reacted to the tensions in the changing system by proposing reforms ostensibly aimed at increasing the influence of general-purpose (especially elected) officials at all levels, shifting power away from Washington and toward federal field offices and state and local governments, reducing the control exercised by functional specialists, and trimming intergovernmental red tape. (This direction was maintained, though with somewhat diminished effort and effectiveness, by his successor, Gerald Ford.) Nixon's efforts were undoubtedly fueled by a desire to shift policy away from the social activism of the Johnson years.

Of what, exactly, did Nixon's "new federalism" consist? He proposed a series of initiatives: revenue sharing, block grants, and administrative proposals.

1. *Revenue sharing.* One of Nixon's most ambitious suggestions was the establishment of a program of revenue sharing from the federal level to state and local governments. Revenue sharing (also called "general revenue sharing") had acquired a certain currency for several reasons: it seemed to meet the demands of state and local governments for more discretion, it was attractive to the most financially hard-pressed jurisdictions, it could shift some influence to the general-purpose elected officials and away from the functional specialists in state and local governments, and (for those, like Nixon, who were looking for politically acceptable mechanisms of reducing categorical support) it might permit the simultaneous trimming of more narrowly targeted programs. In 1972 the State and Local Fiscal Assistance Act was passed with the support of much of the Democratic leadership in Congress and of the major PIGs of state and local officials. This law established a revenue-sharing program of approximately $6 billion per year for five years. All state governments and all general-purpose local governments were eligible for aid, which was to be allocated on the basis of complicated formulas. The program was extended, with modifications, in 1976, and again in 1980. In 1984 revenue sharing was reenacted for localities alone, as the federal budget tightened. And in 1986, following several efforts, the program was ended because Congress found itself facing an increasingly severe national deficit. During its tenure, revenue sharing helped many governments—too many, thought some observers, who believed that aid should be targeted more carefully to needy jurisdictions. But even at its peak of support and funding, it constituted only a small fraction of total federal assistance for the larger recipient governments.

2. *Block grants.* Another major proposal that would have a significant effect on the intergovernmental system did not originate with Nixon, although the idea is most closely identified with him. Block grants began during the Johnson administration, as intergovernmental

analysts searched for mechanisms to alleviate some of the problems discussed above. Before the Nixon era, two block grants (one in health care, one in law enforcement) were created. Each was formed by combining a series of closely related categorical grants into a broader, formula-based package. Nixon then suggested a set of enactments in six policy sectors. These stimulated considerably more antagonism than did the general revenue-sharing proposal. Defenders of the categoricals, including members of the vertical functional autocracies, resisted; their concerns would have no statutory protection once a block grant was put into place. Although the general-purpose officials at the state and local levels were favorably inclined toward the *idea* of block grants, they were skeptical of some of the Nixon proposals, which would have reduced the overall level of intergovernmental funding. Ultimately, only three additional block grants emerged from this period: in employment, social services, and community development. Yet some of these programs have had a major impact on intergovernmental affairs, and they have been followed by additional block grants enacted during the Reagan years.

3. *Administrative initiatives.* Nixon encouraged the implementation of administrative reforms by supporting a series of efforts to alter the grant application and review process. By both legislation and executive order, potential recipient governments were allowed to expedite their applications by combining several related requests. In certain cities chief executives were granted increased control over some categorical funds. Also, a number of donor agencies reduced their decision-making time. The emphasis on block grants was designed in part to relieve administrative burdens. However, some of the alterations were just palliatives. The strength of the political forces responsible for the development of categorical programs has meant that block grants established with few restrictions tend over time to acquire more.

Despite all these changes, the intergovernmental system was not radically altered. For one thing, the more traditional categorical grant was by no means disused. Indeed, such programs and the amount of aid going to support them increased even through the Nixon years. In 1975 the intergovernmental apparatus was larger than it had been during the Johnson years (Table 1). For another, the return to formula-based grants eased certain difficulties (year-to-year funding uncertainties for recipients) but exacerbated others (such as interregional and interjurisdictional tensions because a formula would establish a set of clear winners and losers in legislation). Also, administrative and regulatory difficulties in the system proved to be more tenacious than many had anticipated.

In short, at the end of the Nixon-Ford period the intergovernmental system was larger than ever. Impressively complex and interdependent, it continued to face criticism from nearly everyone.

The Carter Period

President Jimmy Carter was not the activist in intergovernmental matters that Nixon was—or, for that matter, that his successor was. But, as a former governor familiar with the concerns of general political executives and of state and local units, Carter worked at developing communication links with the PIGs and with state and local governments, tried to advance some of the administrative reforms from the Nixon-Ford years, and paid special attention to economic problems facing the cities. He pushed passage, for example, of the Urban Development Action Grant (UDAG) program during a severe economic recession in the late 1970s. UDAG is representative of the way grant politics has developed in the modern era: Democrats have tended to emphasize urban constituencies (part of their standard coalition) as recipients of national support, while Republicans have sought shifts toward state assistance, partly as a way to channel aid to counties and thus to their suburban constituencies.

Yet Carter proposed no overall plan for reform of the system, nor did he recommend any major changes in the pattern of intergovernmental aid. Two developments in the late 1970s exacerbated some of the difficulties faced by policymakers and managers. First, a combination of sour economic conditions, federal budget difficulties, and Carter's fundamentally conservative fiscal instincts placed stringent limits on any efforts to increase federal aid. Federal spending increases slowed and in 1978 reversed direction. Yet the tensions that had come to mark the modern period of intergovernmental relations were, if anything, increased; for federal aid was being limited at a time when many units of government had come to depend on it. Second, during this period of strained resources, the federal government, especially Congress, did not easily loosen its hold on other units of government; instead, Washington sought to accomplish its intergovernmental goals via direct requirements, frequently including some that were mandated across many different programs. Although Carter typically sought deregulation, he did consent to the addition of significant new requirements in a number of programs.

Reagan's Attempted Revolution, and Its Aftermath

The first part of Ronald Reagan's term in office saw perhaps the most systematic, if not the most sustained, effort to remake the American intergovernmental system since the New Deal. Like Carter,

Reagan had served as a governor and understood some of the consequences of complexity and interdependence for many participants in the intergovernmental network. However, unlike Carter, he believed that the United States had been created as a system in which national powers and jurisdiction were severely limited, and in which the states had the strongest, most vital governments, with the broadest jurisdiction over domestic matters.

Furthermore, Reagan supported tax reductions for wealthier Americans as part of his "supply side" approach to fiscal questions. Popular resistance to higher taxes coupled with a Reagan-encouraged buildup in military expenditures in the 1980s meant that budget constraints became especially tight for domestic programs. Given the popularity of the most expensive federal entitlement programs, intergovernmental aid became vulnerable to significant cuts. Meanwhile, pressures by citizens and interest groups to address a whole set of policy issues at state and local levels did not abate. The stage was set for higher levels of fiscal tension and conflict in the intergovernmental system.

As a major part of his program early in the first term, Reagan offered several ideas for a massive restructuring of the intergovernmental system. In brief, Reagan's proposals, for which he adopted Nixon's term, the "new federalism," were as follows:

1. *An additional series of block grants.* In his first year in office, Reagan proposed that more than one hundred categoricals be combined into a handful of broadly based block grants with very few regulations. Congress complied with several of these initiatives.

2. *A dramatic simplification of the system of intergovernmental aid.* Program responsibilities were to be shifted to single levels of government and away from the "marble cake" intergovernmental configurations. Despite Reagan's backing, the plan attracted only spotty support among the PIGs and virtually none among the program advocates in the nation's vertical functional autocracies. Congress made no real move to approve the plan, and Reagan's attention was diverted from this contentious issue.

3. *A devolution of responsibilities for many policies from the national level to the states.* Reagan suggested that scores of intergovernmental programs involving federal participation, including most of the remaining expensive ones, be turned over to the states in their entirety and that an appropriate quantity of revenue be shifted to the states as well. No action was taken on this proposal. Yet several years after Reagan had left office, some of the intent behind this idea was nevertheless being fulfilled. One reason was a choice in Washington simply not to enforce or even to monitor the states regarding certain

programs. Another had to do with the looming budget problems at the national level and the refusal of presidents Reagan and then Bush to advocate federal tax increases. By the early 1990s new policy initiatives that might involve substantial new expenditures from Washington had thus become nearly impossible under these constraints. Meanwhile many states, which were being pressed by interest groups and the citizenry to address daunting public problems like health care, infrastructure financing, education, and economic development, had become centers of more policy activism than had been seen in years outside of the nation's capital.

4. *Administrative simplification.* The president worked to trim red tape and lighten the putative burden of federal mandates. In this regard, Reagan scored his "successes," as did his predecessors. Yet many complained about the abdication of federal responsibility for important national goals, and others felt the reforms did not go nearly far enough. Several years after Reagan's departure from the White House, the evidence accumulated that mandates from Washington have increased overall.

Reagan's efforts to restructure the intergovernmental system were challenged not only by proponents of increased national authority and advocates of strong categorical initiatives, but also by many who have traditionally sought more influence for the state and local governments. While the nation's governors and mayors were often delighted with the idea of reducing the red tape and mandate requirements, they could hardly have been expected to rejoice in other features of the Reagan program. The fact that Reagan accompanied his suggestions with significant budget reductions in many of the most important programs meant that he was giving these officials more discretion while reducing the size of the pie. (The cutbacks in federal aid under Reagan were far more severe than those experienced under Carter; see Table 1.) Also, the president's proposals to trade responsibilities and devolve many programs created quite a stir. Urban leaders were concerned that the federal assistance they had been receiving would end if funding decisions were moved to state capitals. And many states and localities were convinced that, ultimately, they would be the financial and political losers once governmental responsibilities were sorted out. By the second half of Reagan's first term, the most ambitious proposals had been set aside in favor of further grouping of categorical programs into block grants. Even these suggestions encountered hostility or indifference in Congress. The conflict between executive and legislative branches vis-à-vis intergovernmental assistance revealed another dimension of the politics of grants. Congress and the presidency, controlled by different parties, pursued divergent strategies to assist somewhat different constituencies. Thus the theme of divided government *within* the national structure—a prominent topic in recent political discussions—has had practical consequences in the intergovernmental system *across* levels of government as well.

Furthermore, in the latter portion of the Reagan era additional signals from the federal government suggested to states and localities that any effort toward independent action on their part might need to be tempered by an emerging set of new conditions emanating from the center. In a set of important decisions by the Supreme Court regarding the scope of state authority, especially in the now-famous *Garcia* case of 1985, federal judicial authorities determined that the main protector of the states' status as vital decision-making entities in the system would have to be the clout of states in the political institutions of the national government itself, rather than constitutional safeguards like the Tenth Amendment, enforceable by the Court.[16] States, in short, would have to look out for themselves, politically speaking, by lobbying in Washington against possible national intrusions into their domain. Thus in the 1990s, even as the federal judiciary developed a reputation for stricter constitutional construction, it seemed to pose the potential of eroding some of the formal underpinnings of the established intergovernmental order.

Nevertheless, the impact of the Reagan administration's efforts, though complicated, was far from incidental. The signs of change in the intergovernmental network of the 1990s are multiple. States have picked up some of the policy initiatives that heretofore had largely been controlled by Washington, although some observers are concerned that states will use their energies to benefit the most privileged interests. Local governments have scrambled to replace national funding for some of their programs with state aid and via alternative sources. The PIGs, which in earlier decades had organized into nationally important forces with the onset of large-scale federal assistance, struggled to define new roles of comparable influence in the emerging era of budgetary constraint. Limited now in its ability to stimulate complex shifts in policy via generously funded new grant programs, the federal government nevertheless seeks day-to-day influence through the channels of the hundreds of existing ones, persisting in attempts to control intergovernmental action through the instrument of mandates. All these participants clearly do not want to relinquish their influence in the interdependent, complex, and now fiscally strained system. How will this intricate interplay of political forces unfold is an important but presently unanswerable question. There are now many signs of renewed state governmental strength and creativity. But there are also numerous threats to the jurisdiction and to continued competence of many of these same units. Unproductive interstate competition for economic development thus remains a real prospect. Big cities are, in some cases, in even more desperate circumstances than ever. At the same time, however, mayors and city managers have succeeded in developing innovative financing arrangements, regional cooperative ventures, and partnerships with the private sector to address staggering social problems. Washington meanwhile continues to exert great, even intrusive, influence as national financing for new intergovernmental challenges recedes. The upshot is a set of challenges and crosscutting pressures.

The dizzying transformations of the 1980s, then, have resulted in an intergovernmental arrangement that differs in key respects from the one in place at the dawn of the Reagan period. And yet any vision of radical simplification, of a dual federalism that could meet the challenges of the country's twenty-first-century needs and aspirations, can be seen as chimerical. Indeed, the efforts of the Bush administration on intergovernmental matters have been devoted largely to maintaining the shape of the pattern inherited from the Reagan years rather than either asserting a new direction or, somehow, implementing the thoroughgoing ideas suggested in the "new American revolution" proposed by Reagan at the outset of his term in office. Despite the major developments of the last several years, the most fundamental aspects of American intergovernmental relations, including the strengths, weaknesses, frustrations, and dilemmas of the pattern, have remained prominent.

There is no denying that the form of the system has changed considerably since the nation's founding. Political, economic, and social forces have stimulated major changes in the overall scope of governmental activity, in the mix of values that intergovernmental arrangements are meant to serve, in the relative influence of the different governments, and in their degree of reliance on one another. Far from preserving a simple, stratified pattern, the choices made centuries ago created opportunities for dramatic shifts toward new forms of interdependence and complexity in the intergovernmental network.

Notes

1. Thus the term *federal* has two meanings in contemporary usage. One refers to a system of governance that employs a constitutional partitioning of authority between central and regional units. The other is as a synonym

for the national government. Both notions are employed in this chapter and in various readings throughout the book. The meaning should be clear from the context.

2. U.S. Bureau of the Census, *1987 Census of Governments*, vol. 1, no. 1, *Governmental Organization* (Washington, D.C.: U.S. Government Printing Office, 1988), v.

3. Federalist No. 10, *The Federalist Papers,* ed. Clinton Rossiter (New York: New American Library, 1961), 77.

4. At the time, the term *federation* had a meaning close to that of *confederation* today. See Martin Diamond's essay in this volume. The meaning changed after the initiation of the American experiment in federated government.

5. The concepts of federalism (in the first sense mentioned in n. 1) and intergovernmental relations are linked but not identical. The former refers to certain aspects of the dealings between national and regional governments, while the latter is meant to encompass relations among all governments within a nation. Intergovernmental relations are considerably affected but not completely determined by federalism. This book examines federalism but focuses broadly on intergovernmental relations. Nevertheless, interstate and interlocal relations receive relatively less attention because of space limitations.

6. One example is Madison's veto of a bill to authorize construction of roads and canals in the states. See Daniel J. Elazar, *The American Partnership: Intergovernmental Co-operation in the Nineteenth Century* (Chicago: University of Chicago Press, 1962), 15.

7. Ibid.

8. The terms *recipient* and *donor* are borrowed from Jeffrey L. Pressman, *Federal Programs and City Politics* (Berkeley and Los Angeles: University of California Press, 1975).

9. U.S. Advisory Commission on Intergovernmental Relations, *Significant Features of Fiscal Federalism, 1990, Vol. 2, Revenues and Expenditures* (Washington, D.C.: ACIR, August 1990), 48.

10. The cases were *Massachusetts* v. *Mellon* and *Frothingham* v. *Mellon* 262 U.S. 447 (1923).

11. As explained later in this chapter, this experiment proved temporary. Federal financial constraints during the Carter and Reagan administrations persuaded Congress to follow presidential recommendations; the program was ended for state and then local governments, respectively.

12. See Morton Grodzins's classic essay in Part I of this volume.

13. For example, David B. Walker, *Toward a Functioning Federalism* (Cambridge, Mass.: Winthrop, 1981); and see Deil S. Wright, *Understanding Intergovernmental Relations,* 3d ed. (Pacific Grove, Calif.: Brooks/Cole, 1988), 94.

14. See Norman Furniss and Timothy Tilton, *The Case for the Welfare State: From Social Security to Social Equality* (Bloomington: Indiana University Press, 1977); and John E. Schwarz, *America's Hidden Success: A*

Reassessment of Twenty Years of Public Policy (New York: Norton, 1988).

15. Thomas Anton, *American Federalism and Public Policy: How the System Works* (Philadelphia: Temple University Press, 1989).

16. *Garcia* v. *San Antonio Metropolitan Transit Authority,* 469 U.S. 552 (1985).

Part I

HISTORICAL AND THEORETICAL PERSPECTIVES

American governments exhibit an impressive variety and complexity. This rich intergovernmental world is best understood by learning something of American history. We would also benefit from learning more about the theoretical perspectives that experts have used to analyze, explain, and predict intergovernmental events.

In the field of intergovernmental relations, history and theory have typically been closely linked. To clarify this point, let us first define what is meant by *theory*. A theory is a coherent set of statements describing and explaining the relationships and underlying principles of some aspect of the world. A useful (although somewhat oversimplified) distinction may be made between two kinds of theory: normative theory seeks to explain and justify how the world *ought* to be; empirical theory offers explanations and predictions for how some part of the world actually *is* or *will be*.

These two types of theory are directed at quite different goals. In the field of intergovernmental relations, however (and, typically, in analyses of the related topic of American federalism), efforts to explain an intergovernmental system are often bound up with attempts to persuade others that certain forms of intergovernmental relations are preferable. One obvious and understandable example was the founders' attempt to design a basic framework and then persuade the public to accept it. Madison, Hamilton, and the others tried to construct powerful normative arguments in support of certain goals (such as the preservation of freedom), yet they also had to use empirical theories to help determine which governmental—and intergovernmental—structures were likely to result in the preferred outcomes. In other words, many intergovernmental theories have been both normative and empirical.

As was noted in the introductory chapter, dramatic changes have taken place in intergovernmental relations (despite stability in the overall framework) during the course of American history. A clear understanding of these developments is essential because, first, knowing the nature and significance of such changes can alert one to some of the most important features of the current system; second, history can explain some of today's apparently haphazard or irrational intergovernmental patterns; and third, because many discussions about intergovernmental relations are highly normative, modern debates and proposals often use history to justify certain courses of action. Thus, Lyndon Johnson and his advisers did this to bolster some of their innovative notions of intergovernmental cooperation; similarly, the administration of Ronald Reagan used historical events to explain and defend its contrasting efforts to move the nation closer to a dual federal structure.

The selections in Part I describe the historical evolution of intergovernmental relations and further explain its twofold theoretical aspects. Several articles in later parts of this book also contain useful theoretical perspectives and historical interpretations, although these are typically directed more at a limited aspect of the system or a more truncated historical period. The readings in the present part include a number of classic expositions with which any serious student of the subject should be familiar. As the reader will see, however, the experts are hardly in complete agreement on either history or theory. Also, it may be useful as one examines other material later in this book to consider the extent to which the evidence from the current operations of the American intergovernmental system supports or undermines the arguments developed in this set of classic readings.

The first selection in this part is *The Federalist*, Number 39. *The Federalist* was actually a series of political tracts published as newspaper letters near the time that the Constitution was being considered for adoption. The papers, signed "Publius," were written by James Madison, Alexander Hamilton, and John Jay, three well-known supporters of the new Constitution, and were intended to persuade citizens to support the proposal. In the paper included here, Madison characterizes the American structure as one that combines national *and* federal characteristics. Although more than two hundred years have passed since the essay was first penned, it remains one of the most explicit discussions of what the founders had in mind. Pay particular attention to Madison's use of key terms, the complexity of the political structure he describes, and his argument in defense of the new American experiment in intergovernmental relations.

In the second selection, Martin Diamond explains what the founders were attempting to build and how they sought to justify the governmental structure. He emphasizes the link between the founding and certain important values, such as liberty and the preservation of representative government.

Whereas the first two readings concentrate on the period of the founding and on the basic structure within which American intergovernmental relations would have to develop, the next three cover some important aspects of historical and modern intergovernmental relations in practice.

In a selection from his book *The American Partnership*, a study of intergovernmental relations in the nineteenth century, Daniel J. Elazar presents what is probably the most well-known case that cooperation rather than conflict has marked intergovernmental affairs in this country throughout its history. Elazar points to the many pragmatic, cooperative arrangements from an earlier era, thus suggesting that theories based on notions of dualism and conflict have never had empirical support. His essay also offers some explanation for how intergovernmental dynamics have stimulated the bureaucratization and professionalization of American government.

Elazar was a student of Morton Grodzins, whose essay excerpted here is perhaps the most widely quoted argument in intergovernmental relations. Employing the now-famous images of layer cakes and marble cakes, Grodzins aptly describes the intergovernmental interdependence and complexity that were beginning to attract attention in the mid 1960s. Grodzins's essay is worth reading for a number of other reasons as well. For instance, he explains the ties so often developed on intergovernmental matters among administrators, legislators, and interest groups, and he analyzes the link between intergovernmental relations and the structure of American political parties, at least as they developed prior to today's emphasis on television campaigns, direct mail, and political action committees. Grodzins's overall goal, as he explains in a part of the essay not included here, is to describe the American system as one of "decentralization by mild chaos," which he labels "an important goal for the American federal system."

By way of contrast, Harry Scheiber critiques and rejects the historically based claims of both Elazar and Grodzins that sharing and cooperation, not conflict, have been more prevalent in American intergovernmental relations. He also explains why such interpretations of intergovernmental history may have an important effect on the course of contemporary intergovernmental policy-making.

Deil Wright is one of the most prominent experts on intergovernmental matters in the United States today. His interest is explicitly American intergovernmental relations and management rather than federalism because he regards intergovernmental themes as more accurate and inclusive in the contemporary context. For him, the "hallmarks of this system" of "increased complexity and interdependency" are "(1) the number and variety of governmental units; (2) the number and variety of public officials involved; (3) the intensity and regularity of contacts among the officials; (4) the importance of the officials' actions and attitudes; and (5) the preoccupation with financial policy issues." [1] In the reading taken from his major text, Wright sketches three models of intergovernmental relations, surveys the evidence available to support each, and chooses one model as particularly appropriate to explain and describe contemporary intergovernmental activity.

The last two readings in Part I offer an implicit contrast to much of the other material. William Riker, a leading empirically oriented political scientist and student of federalism as it has developed around the world, critiques the "moral evaluation" and "ideology" frequently employed to defend federalism as a basic element of intergovernmental structure. In the first piece, written a number of years ago, Riker argues that while policy consequences do derive from the choice to maintain a federal structure, many of the usual virtues claimed on behalf of federal (especially American federal) government are spurious. In the second, written more recently, he reexamines his earlier views and offers a brief interpretation of his *own* evolving ideology. Riker's analysis suggests that intergovernmental experts should inject more empiricism and less ideology into their historical and theoretical work.

Note

1. Deil S. Wright, *Understanding Intergovernmental Relations,* 3d ed. (Pacific Grove, Calif.: Brooks/Cole, 1988), 14.

1. FEDERALIST NO. 39

James Madison

The last paper having concluded the observations which were meant to introduce a candid survey of the plan of government reported by the convention, we now proceed to the execution of that part of the undertaking.

The first question that offers itself is whether the general form and aspect of the government be strictly republican. It is evident that no other form would be reconcilable with the genius of the people of America; with the fundamental principles of the Revolution; or with that honorable determination which animates every votary of freedom to rest all our political experiments on the capacity of mankind for self-government. If the plan of the convention, therefore, be found to depart from the republican character, its advocates must abandon it as no longer defensible.

What, then, are the distinctive characters of the republican form? Were an answer to this question to be sought, not by recurring to principles but in the application of the term by political writers to the constitutions of different States, no satisfactory one would ever be found. Holland, in which no particle of the supreme authority is derived from the people, has passed almost universally under the denomination of a republic. The same title has been bestowed on Venice, where absolute power over the great body of the people is exercised in the most absolute manner by a small body of hereditary nobles. Poland, which is a mixture of aristocracy and of monarchy in their worst forms, has been dignified with the same appellation. The government of England, which has one republican branch only, combined with an hereditary aristocracy and monarchy, has with equal impropriety been frequently placed on the list of republics. These examples, which are nearly as dissimilar to each other as to a genuine republic, show the extreme inaccuracy with which the term has been used in political disquisitions.

From *The Federalist Papers,* ed. Clinton Rossiter (New York: New American Library, 1961), 240-246.

If we resort for a criterion to the different principles on which different forms of government are established, we may define a republic to be, or at least may bestow that name on, a government which derives all its powers directly or indirectly from the great body of the people, and is administered by persons holding their offices during pleasure for a limited period, or during good behavior. It is *essential* to such a government that it be derived from the great body of the society, not from an inconsiderable proportion or a favored class of it; otherwise a handful of tyrannical nobles, exercising their oppressions by a delegation of their powers, might aspire to the rank of republicans and claim for their government the honorable title of republic. It is *sufficient* for such a government that the persons administering it be appointed, either directly or indirectly, by the people; and that they hold their appointments by either of the tenures just specified; otherwise every government in the United States, as well as every other popular government that has been or can be well organized or well executed, would be degraded from the republican character. According to the constitution of every State in the Union, some or other of the officers of government are appointed indirectly only by the people. According to most of them, the chief magistrate himself is so appointed. And according to one, this mode of appointment is extended to one of the co-ordinate branches of the legislature. According to all the constitutions, also, the tenure of the highest offices is extended to a definite period, and in many instances, both within the legislative and executive departments, to a period of years. According to the provisions of most of the constitutions, again, as well as according to the most respectable and received opinions on the subject, the members of the judiciary department are to retain their offices by the firm tenure of good behavior.

On comparing the Constitution planned by the convention with the standard here fixed, we perceived at once that it is, in the most rigid sense, conformable to it. The House of Representatives, like that of one branch at least of all the State legislatures, is elected immediately by the great body of the people. The Senate, like the present Congress and the Senate of Maryland, derives its appointment indirectly from the people. The President is indirectly derived from the choice of the people, according to the example in most of the States. Even the judges, with all other officers of the Union, will, as in the several States, be the choice, though a remote choice, of the people themselves. The duration of the appointments is equally conformable to the republican standard and to the model of State constitutions. The House of Representatives is periodically elective, as in all the States; and for the period of two years, as in the State of South Carolina. The Senate is elective for the period of six years, which is but one year more than the period of the Senate of

Maryland, and but two more than that of the Senates of New York and Virginia. The President is to continue in office for the period of four years; as in New York and Delaware the chief magistrate is elected for three years, and in South Carolina for two years. In the other States the election is annual. In several of the States, however, no explicit provision is made for the impeachment of the chief magistrate. And in Delaware and Virginia he is not impeachable till out of office. The President of the United States is impeachable at any time during his continuance in office. The tenure by which the judges are to hold their places is, as it unquestionably ought to be, that of good behavior. The tenure of the ministerial offices generally will be a subject of legal regulation, conformably to the reason of the case and the example of the State constitutions.

Could any further proof be required of the republican complexion of this system, the most decisive one might be found in its absolute prohibition of titles of nobility, both under the federal and the State governments; and in its express guaranty of the republican form to each of the latter.

"But it was not sufficient," say the adversaries of the proposed Constitution, "for the convention to adhere to the republican form. They ought with equal care to have preserved the *federal* form, which regards the Union as a *Confederacy* of sovereign states; instead of which they have framed a *national* government, which regards the Union as a *consolidation* of the States." And it is asked by what authority this bold and radical innovation was undertaken? The handle which has been made of this objection requires that it should be examined with some precision.

Without inquiring into the accuracy of the distinction on which the objection is founded, it will be necessary to a just estimate of its force, first, to ascertain the real character of the government in question; secondly, to inquire how far the convention were authorized to propose such a government; and thirdly, how far the duty they owed to their country could supply any defect of regular authority.

First.—In order to ascertain the real character of the government, it may be considered in relation to the foundation on which it is to be established; to the sources from which its ordinary powers are to be drawn; to the operation of those powers; to the extent of them; and to the authority by which future changes in the government are to be introduced.

On examining the first relation, it appears, on one hand, that the Constitution is to be founded on the assent and ratification of the people of America, given by deputies elected for the special purpose; but, on the other, that this assent and ratification is to be given by the people, not as individuals composing one entire nation, but as composing the distinct and independent States to which they respectively belong. It is to be the assent and ratification of the several States, derived from the supreme authority in each State—the authority of the people them-selves. The act, therefore, establishing the Constitution will not be a *national* but a *federal* act.

That it will be a federal and not a national act, as these terms are understood by the objectors—the act of the people, as forming so many independent States, not as forming one aggregate nation—is obvious from this single consideration: that it is to result neither from the decision of a *majority* of the people of the Union, nor from that of a *majority* of the States. It must result from the *unanimous* assent of the several States that are parties to it, differing no otherwise from their ordinary assent than in its being expressed, not by the legislative authority, but by that of the people themselves. Were the people regarded in this transaction as forming one nation, the will of the majority of the whole people of the United States would bind the minority, in the same manner as the majority in each State must bind the minority; and the will of the majority must be determined either by a comparison of the individual votes, or by considering the will of the majority of the States as evidence of the will of a majority of the people of the United States. Neither of these rules has been adopted. Each State, in ratifying the Constitution, is considered as a sovereign body independent of all others, and only to be bound by its own voluntary act. In this relation, then, the new Constitution will, if established, be a *federal* and not a *national* constitution.

The next relation is to the sources from which the ordinary powers of government are to be derived. The House of Representatives will derive its powers from the people of America; and the people will be represented in the same proportion and on the same principle as they are in the legislature of a particular State. So far the government is *national,* not *federal.* The Senate, on the other hand, will derive its powers from the States as political and coequal societies; and these will be represented on the principle of equality in the Senate, as they now are in the existing Congress. So far the government is *federal,* not *national.* The executive power will be derived from a very compound source. The immediate election of the President is to be made by the States in their political characters. The votes allotted to them are in a compound ratio, which considers them partly as distinct and coequal societies, partly as unequal members of the same society. The eventual election, again, is to be made by that branch of the legislature which consists of the national representatives; but in this particular act they are to be thrown into the form of individual delegations from so many distinct and coequal bodies politic. From this aspect of the government it appears to be of a mixed character, presenting at least as many *federal* as *national* features.

The difference between a federal and national government, as it relates to the *operation of the government,* is by the adversaries of the plan of the convention supposed to consist in this, that in the former the powers operate on the political bodies composing the Confederacy in their political capacities; in the latter, on the individual citizens composing the nation in their individual capacities. On trying the Constitution by this criterion, it falls under the *national* not the *federal* character; though perhaps not so completely as has been understood. In several cases, and particularly in the trial of controversies to which States may be parties, they must be viewed and proceeded against in their collective and political capacities only. But the operation of the government on the people in their individual capacities, in its ordinary and most essential proceedings, will, in the sense of its opponents, on the whole, designate it, in this relation, a *national* government.

But if the government be national with regard to the *operation* of its powers, it changes its aspect again when we contemplate it in relation to the extent of its powers. The idea of a national government involves in it not only an authority over the individual citizens, but an indefinite supremacy over all persons and things, so far as they are objects of lawful government. Among a people consolidated into one nation, this supremacy is completely vested in the national legislature. Among communities united for particular purposes, it is vested partly in the general and partly in the municipal legislatures. In the former case, all local authorities are subordinate to the supreme; and may be controlled, directed, or abolished by it at pleasure. In the latter, the local or municipal authorities form distinct and independent portions of the supremacy, no more subject, within their respective spheres, to the general authority than the general authority is subject to them, within its own sphere. In this relation, then, the proposed government cannot be deemed a *national* one; since its jurisdiction extends to certain enumerated objects only, and leaves to the several States a residuary and inviolable sovereignty over all other objects. It is true that in controversies relating to the boundary between the two jurisdictions, the tribunal which is ultimately to decide is to be established under the general government. But this does not change the principle of the case. The decision is to be impartially made, according to the rules of the Constitution; and all the usual and most effectual precautions are taken to secure this impartiality. Some such tribunal is clearly essential to prevent an appeal to the sword and a dissolution of the compact; and that it ought to be established under the general rather than under the local governments, or, to speak more properly, that it could be safely established under the first alone, is a position not likely to be combated.

If we try the Constitution by its last relation to the authority by which amendments are to be made, we find it neither wholly *national* nor wholly *federal*. Were it wholly national, the supreme and ultimate authority would reside in the *majority* of the people of the Union; and this authority would be competent at all times, like that of a majority of every national society to alter or abolish its established government. Were it wholly federal, on the other hand, the concurrence of each State in the Union would be essential to every alteration that would be binding on all. The mode provided by the plan of the convention is not founded on either of these principles. In requiring more than a majority, and particularly in computing the proportion by *States,* not by *citizens,* it departs from the national and advances toward the *federal* character; in rendering the concurrence of less than the whole number of States sufficient, it loses again the *federal* and partakes of the *national* character.

The proposed Constitution, therefore, even when tested by the rules laid down by its antagonists, is, in strictness, neither a national nor a federal Constitution, but a composition of both. In its foundation it is federal, not national; in the sources from which the ordinary powers of government are drawn, it is partly federal and partly national; in the operation of these powers, it is national, not federal; in the extent of them, again, it is federal, not national; and, finally in the authoritative mode of introducing amendments, it is neither wholly federal nor wholly national. PUBLIUS

2. WHAT THE FRAMERS MEANT BY FEDERALISM

Martin Diamond

... Relatively little serious attention has been given to the Framers' own view of federalism, because something confidently called "modern federalism" has been understood to have superseded the original version. It is the contention of this essay that the recovery of the Framers' view of federalism is necessary to the understanding of American federalism. In what follows, an attempt is made to indicate what the Framers meant by federalism, as that is revealed in the proceedings of the Federal Convention.

I

The American Republic has been regarded by nearly all modern observers as *the* example of a federal government. Indeed the various modern definitions of federalism are little more than slightly generalized descriptions of the American way of governing. ...

According to these typical definitions, the essential federal characteristic is the "division of political power," a division of supremacy (sovereignty, as used to be said) between member states and a central government, each having the final say regarding matters belonging to its sphere. There is a corollary to this sort of definition which has also come to be generally accepted. All college students are now taught that, in this respect, there are three kinds of government—confederal, federal, and unitary (national)—and that the United States exemplifies the middle term. This familiar distinction illuminates the definitions of federalism. In this view, a confederacy and a nation are seen as the extremes. The defining characteristic of a confederacy is that the associated states retain all the sovereign power, with the central body entirely dependent legally upon their will; the defining characteristic of a nation is that the central body has all the sovereign power, with the

Author's note: This paper was written while the author was enjoying a fellowship year at the Center for Advanced Study in the Behavioral Sciences.

From Robert A. Goldwin, ed., *A Nation of States* (Chicago: Rand McNally, 1974), 25-41. Reprinted by permission, Kenyon Public Affairs Conference Center.

localities entirely dependent legally upon the will of the nation. In this view, then, federalism is truly the middle term, for its defining characteristic is that it modifies and then combines the best characteristics of the other two forms. A *federal* system combines states which *confederally* retain sovereignty within a certain sphere, with a central body that *nationally* possesses sovereignty within another sphere; the combination is thought to create a new and better thing to which is given the name federalism.

Now what is strange is this. The leading Framers viewed their handiwork in an entirely different light. For example, *The Federalist*, the great contemporary exposition of the Constitution, emphatically does not regard the Constitution as establishing a typically federal, perhaps not even a primarily federal system of government. *The Federalist* regards the new American Union as departing significantly from the essentially federal character. The decisive statement is: "The proposed Constitution, therefore, is, in strictness, neither a national nor a federal Constitution, but a composition of both." [1] As will become clear, our now familiar tripartite distinction was completely unknown to the men who made the Constitution. They had a very different understanding than we do of what federalism is. For them, there were but two possible modes: confederal or federal as opposed to unitary or national. They had, therefore, in strictness, to regard their Constitution as a composition of federal and national features. We now give the single word federal to the systems the Framers regarded as possessing both federal and national features. This means we now regard as a unique principle what they considered as a mere compound.

Consider Tocqueville's opinion: "Evidently this is no longer a federal government, but an incomplete national government, which is neither exactly national nor exactly federal; but the new word which ought to express this novel thing does not yet exist." [2] For good or ill, the word that came to express the novel thing turned out to be the old word federal. It is no fussy antiquarianism to assert the necessity to understand the Constitution the way its creators did, as possessing both federal and national features. In order to understand the system they created for us and how they expected it to work, we must be able to distinguish the parts that make up the whole, and see the peculiar place of each in the working of the whole. Now they regarded certain parts as federal and certain parts as national, and had different expectations regarding each. To use the word federal, as we do now, to describe both the "federal" and "national" features of their plan is to lump under one obscuring term things they regarded as radically different. It becomes thus difficult if not impossible to understand their precise intentions.

This is a sufficient reason to do the job of recovering precisely what they meant by federalism.

Federalism meant then exactly what we mean now by confederalism: "a sort of association or league of sovereign states.". . . A brief consideration of the Articles of Confederation will further reveal what men meant then by a federal arrangement, especially when comparison is made to the Constitution.

In recent years we have come to think of the Articles as having created too weak a central government. This is not precise enough. Strictly speaking, neither the friends nor the enemies of the Confederation regarded the Articles as having created any kind of *government* at all, weak or otherwise. Article III declared that "the said states hereby enter into a firm *league of friendship* with each other.". . . Men referred then to the Articles as a kind of treaty, and, no more than any other treaty organization is thought to create a government, was it thought that the Articles had created one. The language of the Articles makes this clear. The word government never appears in that document, whereas the Constitution speaks repeatedly of the Government, the Treasury, the Authority, the Offices, the Laws of the United States. There are no such terms in the Articles; there could be none because it was fatally a federal arrangement, a league not a government.

Article I declared that "the stile of this confederacy shall be 'The United States of America.'" Twice more at the outset that capitalized expression occurs. But on every subsequent occasion (about forty times) the term is given in lower-case letters as the "united states." That is, as a mere league, the Confederacy was not a governmental being to which a proper name could be strictly applied. In the Constitution, on the contrary, the term United States is invariably capitalized. Indeed, the formal language of the Articles makes clear that the Confederacy had no real existence save when the states were formally assembled. When speaking of its duties or functions, the Articles invariably refer to the Confederacy as "the united states *in Congress assembled.*" All men seem to have referred to the Confederacy in this exact phrase. It must be remembered also that the word "Congress" did not then mean an institution of government. As an ordinary word it meant then simply a "meeting," especially "an assembly of envoys, comissioners, deputies, etc. from different courts, meeting to agree on terms of political accommodation." [3] Under the Articles the United States had no being; its existence consisted solely in the congregation of envoys from the separate states for the accommodation of certain specified matters under terms prescribed by the federal treaty. The slightest glance at the Constitution, of course, shows that it refers to the duties and powers of the government of a country.

The Founding Fathers, like all other men at the time and perhaps all other men up to that time, regarded federalism, not as a kind of government, but as a voluntary association of states who sought certain advantages from that association. For example, at the very outset of the Convention, it became necessary for the delegates to state openly their understanding of the nature of the federal form. Gouverneur Morris "explained the distinction between a *federal* and *national, supreme* government; the former being a mere compact resting on the good faith of the parties; the latter having a complete and *compulsive* operation." [4] The entire Convention, with the single exception of Hamilton, in one remark, concurred in this view of the nature of federalism.[5]

From this view it followed that any federal arrangement would be characterized by certain ways of doing things. As one delegate put it, "a confederacy supposes sovereignty in the members composing it and sovereignty supposes equality." [6] That is, when forming a league, the member states retain their political character, i.e., sovereignty; and, each being equally a political entity, each state participates in the league as an equal member. That is, each state has one equal vote in making the league's decisions; moreover, because the league is a voluntary association of sovereign states and rests upon the "good faith" of the members, extraordinary or even unanimous majorities are to be preferred. Compare the Articles which called for at least a majority of nine of the thirteen states in all important cases. From this view of federalism it further followed that a league had no business with the individual citizens of the member states, the governing of them remaining the business of the states. In its limited activities, the central body was to deal only with *its* "citizens," i.e., the sovereign states.

According to the Framers, then, a federal system was federal in three main ways. First, the member states were equals in the making of the central decisions. Second, these central agreements were to be carried out by the member states themselves. Third, the confederal body was not to deal with the vast bulk of political matters; governing, for all practical purposes, remained with the member states. Given this view of the meaning of federalism, we can readily see why the Framers could not possibly regard the new Constitution as merely a federal system, but rather regarded it as a "composition" of both federal and national elements.

II

The Federal Convention began its work by considering the detailed plan carefully prepared in advance and presented to it by the Virginia delegation. The Virginia plan proposed the creation of a powerful government which it throughout described by the shocking term *national*. It clearly went far beyond the common understanding that the Convention was only to propose amendments to the existing Confederacy. The great issue so abruptly placed before the Convention was made perfectly explicit when Governor Randolph, at the suggestion of Gouverneur Morris, proposed a substitution for the initial clause of the Virginia Plan. The original formulation was: "Resolved that the articles of Confederation ought to be so corrected and enlarged, as to accomplish the objects proposed by their institution; namely, common defense, security of liberty and general welfare." [7] The substitute formulation left no possible doubt about how far the Virginia Plan went. Resolved "that a Union of the States merely federal will not accomplish the objects proposed by the articles of Confederation, namely common defense, security of liberty and general welfare"; and resolved further "that a *national* Government ought to be established consisting of a *supreme* Legislative, Executive and Judiciary." [8]

Randolph said, in short: by the Articles we meant to insure our defense, liberty and general welfare; they failed; no system of the merely federal kind will secure these things for us; we must create a supreme, that is, national government.

Discussion centered on the resolution proposing a national and supreme government. Oddly enough, the resolution was almost immediately adopted, six states to one. At this moment the Convention was pointed to a simply national government, and not the "composition" which finally resulted. But the matter was not to be so easily settled, not least because several small state delegations, which happened to be federally minded, subsequently arrived. Despite the favorable vote on the Randolph resolution, the Convention had not yet truly made up their mind. Too many delegates remained convinced federalists. They would have to be persuaded to change their minds or the final plan would have to be compromised so as to accommodate the wishes of those who would not go so far as a straightforwardly national plan. Therefore, as specific portions of the Virginia Plan were discussed in the ensuing weeks, the fundamental issue—a federal versus a national plan—came up again and again.

The most important feature of the discussions is the following. The Convention had originally squared off on the issue of federalism *versus* nationalism, the true federalists regarding nationalism as fatal to liberty, the nationalists regarding confederalism as "imbecilically" incompetent. Compromise would have been impossible across the gulf of two such opposed views. One or the other of the two original views had to be modified so that the distance between the two could be bridged by compromise. And that is precisely what happened. After three weeks of discussion, the issue had subtly changed. The opponents of a purely national government found themselves unable to defend the pure federal principle. The simple nationalists remained such in principle, while the pure federalists implicitly found themselves forced to acknowledge the inadequacy of the federal principle. Now the question was between those still advocating a purely national plan and those who, having abandoned a purely federal scheme, were determined only to work some federal features into the final outcome. Thus the famous compromise, the "composition" which finally resulted, was a compromise between the simple nationalists and half-hearted federalists, i.e., federalists who were themselves moving toward the national principle. Only because of this underlying victory of the simple nationalists was the issue finally made capable of compromise.

This does not mean that the pure federalists yielded easily or completely. The ideas which led them to their federalist position had a powerful hold over their minds. A fundamental theoretical issue, as we shall see, had to be raised before they could be made substantially to retreat from their federalist position. And, even then, important concessions had finally to be made to the unconvinced and only partially convinced. Moreover, the ideas supporting that federalist position have long retained their vitality in American politics; and the federal elements which finally found their way into the Constitution have always supplied historical and legal support to recurring expressions of the traditional federalist view. It is necessary to acknowledge the survival of this view and the grounds for its survival. But it is impossible to understand the work of the Convention without seeing that the view survived only after having first been shaken to its very root, and hence that it survived only in a permanently weakened condition.

How this happened is perfectly revealed in a notable exchange between Madison, straightforwardly for the national plan at that point, and Sherman of Connecticut, one of the intelligent defenders of the federal principle.

> The objects of Union [Sherman] thought were *few*. 1. defence against foreign danger. 2. against internal disputes & a resort to force. 3. Treaties with foreign nations. 4. regulating foreign commerce, & drawing revenue from it. These & perhaps a few lesser objects *alone rendered a confederation of the States necessary.* All other matters civil & criminal would be much better in the hands of the States. *The people are more happy in small than in large States.*[9]

Whereas Madison

> differed from the member from Connecticut in thinking the objects mentioned to be all the principal ones that required a National

Government. Those were certainly important and necessary objects; but he combined with them the necessity of providing more effectually for the security of private rights, and the steady dispensation of Justice. Interferences with these were evils which had more perhaps than anything else, produced this convention. Was it to be supposed that republican liberty could long exist under the abuses of it practised in some of the States.[10]

Madison was skillfully pressing a sensitive nerve. Not only were the delegates concerned with the inadequacy of the Confederacy for "general" purposes, but nearly all were also unhappy with the way things had been going in the states themselves since the Revolution. Above all, the delegates agreed in fearing the tendency in many of the states to agrarian and debtors' measures that seemed to threaten the security of property. The Shays' Rebellion, for example, had terrified many of the delegates. Sherman had himself, after the passage quoted above, adverted to this dangerous tendency, and had, moreover, admitted that "too small" states were by virtue of their smallness peculiarly "subject to faction." Madison seized upon this.

The gentleman had admitted that in a very small State, faction & oppression would prevail. It was to be inferred then that wherever these prevailed the State was too small. Had they not prevailed in the largest as well as the smallest tho' less than in the smallest; and were we not thence admonished to enlarge the sphere as far as the nature of the Government would admit. This was the only defence against the inconveniencies of democracy consistent with the democratic form of Government.[11]

Sherman, the defender of the federal principle, considered the ends of union to be few. Madison, the defender of the national principle, considered the ends of union to be many. Sherman would leave the most important matters of government to the individual states. Madison would place the most important matters—e.g., "security of private rights, and the steady dispensation of justice"—under a national government. Sherman believed that the people would be happiest when governed by their individual states, these being the natural dwelling place of republicanism. Madison believed that republican liberty would perish under the states and that therefore the people would be happiest when under a national government; only such a government made possible the very large republic which in turn supplied the democratic remedy for the inconveniences of democracy.

Madison, then, argued with Sherman and the other defenders of the federal principle in two ways. First, he appealed to the delegates to acknowledge that they really wanted very much more from union than Sherman admitted. . . . the Convention's decisive action turned on just this issue. The fact that nearly all the delegates, themselves included, wanted a very great deal from union became *the* stumbling block to the defenders of a federal plan. . . . the explicit endorsement of a national plan dramatically followed the most powerful showing of how much was wanted from union and how little could be supplied by the federal principle. But it would not have sufficed merely to demonstrate the incompatibility of federalism and a union from which much was desired. The delegates could still have done what any man can do who has two equal and contradictory desires. They could have abandoned their preference for the federal principle in favor of firm union, as Madison wished, or they could have abandoned a firm union in favor of the federal principle, as Madison emphatically did not wish. Madison therefore had also to give the delegates a reason to choose only one of the two incompatible alternatives, namely, a firm union under a national government. This meant persuading the delegates to renounce their attachment to federalism. And that is precisely what Madison attempted. He sought to undermine that attachment by supplying a new solution to the problem for which federalism had been the traditional answer.

The best men, like Sherman, who defended the federal principle at the Convention, and those, like R. H. Lee, who subsequently opposed adoption of the Constitution, did not defend federalism for its own sake. Who could? They defended the federal principle against the plan of a national or primarily national government because they thought they were thereby defending a precious thing, namely, republican liberty. They saw a connection between republicanism and federalism. They regarded federalism as the sole way in which some of the advantages of great size could be obtained by those who wanted to enjoy the blessings of republicanism. . . .

The true federalists rested their case on the proposition that only the state governments, and not some huge national government, could be made or kept truly free and republican. In this they were following the very old belief, popularized anew in the way men understood Montesquieu, that only small countries could enjoy republican government. The reasoning that supported the belief ran something as follows. Large countries necessarily turn to despotic rule. For one thing, large countries need despotic rule; political authority breaks down if the central government does not govern more forcefully than the republican form admits. Further, large countries, usually wealthy and populous, are warlike by nature or are made warlike by envious neighbors; such belligerency nurtures despotic rule. Moreover, not even the best intentions suffice to preserve the republicanism of a large country. To preserve their rule, the people must be patriotic, vigilant, and informed. This requires that the people give loving attention to public things, and that the affairs of the country be on a scale commensurate with the people's understanding. But in large countries the people, baffled and rendered apathetic by the complexity of public affairs, at last become absorbed in their own pursuits. Finally, even were the citizens of a large republic able to remain alert, they must allow a few men actually to conduct the public business. Far removed from the localities and possessed of the instruments of coercion, the necessarily trusted representatives would inevitably subvert the republican rule to their own passions and interests. Such was the traditional and strongly held view of the necessity that republics be small. . . .

It is clear, then, that Madison had to persuade the delegates, as it were, that they could have their cake and eat it, too. That is, they could have the firm union that would supply the blessings they wanted, *without* sacrificing the republicanism for which they had hitherto thought federalism was indispensable. Federalism was indispensable only so long as men held to the small-republic theory. And that is the theory Madison tried to demolish. Nothing is more important to an understanding of both the theoretical and practical issues in the founding of the American Republic than a full appreciation of Madison's stand on behalf of the very large republic. . . .

Madison turned the small-republic argument upside down. On the contrary, he argued, *smallness* was fatal to republicanism. The small republics of antiquity were wretched nurseries of internal warfare, and the Convention itself had been "produced" by the fear for liberty in the "small" American states. "Was it to be supposed that republican liberty could long exist under the abuses of it practised in some of the States. . . . Were we not then admonished to enlarge the sphere as far as the nature of the Government would admit." Smallness is fatal to republican liberty. Only a country as large as the whole thirteen states and more could provide a safe dwelling-place for republican liberty. Republicanism not only permits but requires taking away from the states responsibility for "the security of private rights, and the steady dispensation of Justice," else rights and justice will perish under the state governments.

This was the great and novel idea which came from the Convention: a large, powerful republic with a competent national government regulated under a wise Constitution. . . .

Notes

1. *Federalist* 39, p. 250. All references are to the edition of Henry Cabot Lodge, introduction by Edward Mead Earle (New York: Modern Library, 1941).
2. *Democracy in America,* ed. Phillips Bradley (New York: Alfred A. Knopf, 1945), I, 159.
3. Samuel Johnson, *Dictionary of the English Language* (2 vols.; Heidelberg: Joseph Englemann, 1828).
4. *Documents Illustrative of the Formation of the Union of the American States,* ed. C. C. Tansill (Washington, D.C.: U.S. Government Printing Office, 1927), p. 121. Italics supplied.
5. *Ibid.,* p. 216.
6. *Ibid.,* p. 182.
7. *Ibid.,* p. 116.
8. *Ibid.,* p. 120.
9. *Ibid.,* pp. 160-61. Italics supplied.
10. *Ibid.,* pp. 161-62.
11. *Ibid.,* p. 162.

3. THE SCOPE OF CO-OPERATION

Daniel J. Elazar

... The American federal system has been fundamentally a co-operative partnership of federal, state, and local governments since the early days of the Republic. Within a dualistic structural pattern, the governments of the United States have developed a broadly institutionalized system of collaboration, based on the implicit premise that virtually all functions of government must be shared by virtually all governments in order to fulfill the demands of American democracy for both public service and private access. More specifically, the evidence presented [earlier in Elazar's book] indicates that the relative balance between the federal government and the states has not significantly shifted over the past one hundred seventy-five years. The two levels of government have played the same respective roles in the system from the first, and these roles have not been significantly altered, despite the great changes that have taken place within the United States and in the world. Consequently, the pattern of American federalism in practice, in so far as it differs from the classic theory of American federalism, has certain fundamental implications in the context of American history and in the context of democratic theory.

Programs and Policies: A Review

From the first days of American independence, the controversy as to the scope of national vis-à-vis state powers has been part and parcel of the American political scene. While the controversy has continued to rage unabated, the American people have by and large endeavored to use both federal and state governments as means to achieve specific ends, rather than as ends in themselves. When problems arose, solutions were sought that would harmonize with the reality of the times, involving government whenever and wherever necessary, generally at every level. Out of these attempts to solve

---

From *The American Partnership: Intergovernmental Co-operation in the Nineteenth-Century United States* (Chicago: University of Chicago Press, 1962), 297-305. Reprinted by permission of the author.

actual problems, there evolved a series of co-operative relationships between all levels of government.

As the new nation began to expand under the Constitution, expansion came to center primarily around movement westward, the conquest of the continent. Out of this expansion arose a number of major problems that required governmental consideration. Among them, three major categories stand out: internal improvements, education, and disposition of the public domain. A fourth major category centering around the slavery issue reached national prominence and forced the ultimate conflict as a result of problems arising from territorial expansion westward and the attempt to spread slavery to the land frontier. It should be noted that each of these major categories has its counterpart in the twentieth century, which has required governmental action just as its forerunner did.

The term "internal improvement" covered a multitude of specific problems, all basically concerned with facilitating the geographic and material expansion of the American people, while at the same time binding the various sections of the country more closely together as one political and economic system. Roads, canals, railroads, harbors, public buildings and institutions, river improvements, land reclamation, mineral production and extraction, agricultural development, and the creation of a banking system to finance all these projects, constituted the internal improvement programs of the day. All demanded a share of the interest, energy, and money, both public and private, of the expanding nation. Internal improvements provided a major portion of the intergovernmental programs that emerged during the century, simply because they provided a major portion of all governmental activity.

While much attention was directed toward material progress, no less was given to the development of a responsible and capable citizenry, particularly in the newly settled areas of the Midwest and Far West. The dominant educational problems were to provide a basic foundation for productive citizenship through the common schools and to advance intellectual, agricultural, and mechanical training of young men and women in colleges and universities. As the frontier advanced, so did the desire for education. Population groups demanded government programs to fill needs that the struggling pioneers could not meet alone. Once again, the use of co-operative government programs provided the vehicle whereby such aid could be rendered within the framework of the federal system.

Since our nation is dedicated to the task of providing opportunity for each individual to engage in the pursuit of happiness in a manner as nearly approaching his own definition of that goal as socially possible, the disposition of the major national resource, the public domain, in a manner consistent with that high purpose continued to be a leading problem. As the nation evolved a policy for the solution of the problem, the tension between public and private interests brought forth increasingly greater efforts on the part of all levels of government. From these efforts emerged the federal land grants to the various states for a multitude of purposes, ranging from veterans' benefits to railroad construction; the direct federal land grants for transportation and development companies; and finally, the land grants to individual settlers under the various homestead and pre-emption acts. Even before the adoption of the Constitution, it was determined that the disposition of the public domain would provide the means whereby the other problems were to be attacked, with land serving in place of cash as the substance of federal grants-in-aid.

Several basic patterns for the actual implementation of co-operative federalism developed in the nineteenth century. Informal relationships developed, primarily in the field, where officials of the federal government, the states, and the localities exchanged information or co-operated to solve specific problems. Examples of this informal co-operation cover the range of governmental activities. In relations with the Indians, the federal government theoretically held exclusive jurisdiction. Actually, federal authorities in any specific situation consulted with officials of the state and locality concerned, and often relied upon their co-operation to implement a policy or subdue hostiles.[1] The co-operative relations between the second Bank of the United States and the various states in the development of a national monetary system were semiformal, based on national needs. Co-operation between the United States Army Corps of Engineers and state and local authorities in the construction and maintenance of river and harbor improvements made that program a shared one *de facto* long before such sharing was officially recognized in law. The localities contributed financial, material, and technical aid amounting to at least one-fifth of the cost of any Corps of Engineers project.[2] Problems of law enforcement also led to a number of informal co-operative relationships, both in routine law enforcement matters in which local police and United States marshals worked together and in more specialized fields such as control of smuggling and immigration.[3] Wherever the military was stationed, a series of informal co-operative relationships grew up, which covered a number of governmental functions; some were temporary reactions to emergency situations, and others ongoing relationships that continued for many years.

Other co-operative relationships that were never formalized grew up around federal programs designed to dispose of the public domain, which officially made no reference to the states and localities. These included the various homestead and reclamation programs, such as the homestead and pre-emption acts, the tree-culture acts, the town-site selection acts, and some parts of the desert lands and reclamation acts. As a general rule, whenever a federal program affected the citizens of a state, the state governments concerned became unofficial parties to, and even agents in, its administration.

For various reasons that were dealt with in previous chapters, a number of internal improvement programs were initiated through the federal government only. Certain western roads and railroads were constructed by the federal government or with direct federal aid generally because the regions they traversed were predominantly in the territorial stage of government. Little time elapsed before even these programs were incorporated into the co-operative system, originally with territorial and local authorities and ultimately with the state governments once they had been formed.[4] Collaboration in these programs was almost always quasi-formal even from the outset, since any portion of the road or railroad that was to be built within an existing state forced the builders to obtain the approval of the state legislature, as required by the terms of the Congressional grant, and the legislature would often demand tailoring of the planned improvement to meet the needs of the state. In almost every case, co-operation had to evolve because every program involved some issues of interest to each level of government. The choices that confronted the political leaders were such that the alternatives to co-operation would have produced at best unmanageable chaos and at worst disunion.

Another by no means separate form of intergovernmental co-operation involved formally co-ordinated relationships. Programs in this category did not involve the exchange of money, land, or personnel, but instead action was co-ordinated pursuant to statutory provisions enacted by Congress and the participating state legislatures. Under such programs, the federal government and each participating state undertook to implement parts of a jointly produced nationwide or state-federal plan without sharing the costs for individual projects. This is the type of co-operation which the United States Constitution provides for the administration of national elections.

The master plan for an internal transportation and communications system designed by the United States Army Corps of Engineers in co-operation with the boards of public works in the various states in the early nineteenth century was of this nature. The public works that emerged from that joint endeavor still form part of the pattern of the twentieth-century American highway and railroad system. The sequence of national banking programs, which were designed to establish a national banking system with a stable nationwide currency, frequently provided examples of this form of intergovernmental co-operation.

Many times, a co-operative program would be initiated as a co-ordinated activity only to be expanded as a formal federal-aid program at a later date. The inland waterways system designed by Albert Gallatin and others in Jefferson's administration fits into this category. The history of the Dismal Swamp Canal is illustrative of the tenuous line that often existed between co-ordinated and formal federal-aid programs. Intergovernmental co-operation in the field of education was exceptional in that it moved in the other direction, beginning as a federal-aid program in most states and later becoming almost entirely transformed into a co-ordinated activity until the mid-twentieth century.

Midway in scope between co-ordinated and formal grant-in-aid programs were some quasi-grant programs, which developed particularly in cases in which the federal government had to reimburse various states for money spent on its behalf for "national defense." While the reimbursement could not be earmarked for specific purposes under federal law, it was almost universally used by the state leadership as an opportune way to establish or supplement funds for the promotion of education. This general use of reimbursement funds for educational purposes was instrumental in obtaining Congressional and executive approval for many reimbursements that would otherwise not have been granted. The administration entailed in the transfer of funds for such reimbursements was of necessity co-operative. Other illustrative quasi-grant programs included the exchange of documents and scientific specimens, which were not grants so much as they were attempts to facilitate academic, legal, and cultural interchanges within the Union.

The most significant formal co-operative programs were generally those which involved federal grants of land, money, and services to the states. These programs can be divided into two categories: those that included both financial aid and the contacts with federal personnel necessary to implement the federal aspects of the program (grants-in-aid), and those that made only personnel available (services-in-aid). . . .

Grants-in-aid in the nineteenth century took the form of land grants, grants of materials, cash grants based upon land sales, and direct cash grants, with land grants the most prevalent. Land grants were made to the states for education (common schools, colleges, and special educational institutions), internal improvements (roads, canals, river and harbor improvements, railroads), public purposes (public buildings, salt springs), reclamation (desert lands, swamp lands), veterans (bounty lands), and welfare (public institutions). Cash grants based on land sales were made for internal improvements and conservation. Direct cash grants were made for defense (the militia grants),[5] internal improvements (transportation and banking), veterans (soldiers' homes), education (land-grant-college supplementary aid), and agriculture (agricultural experiment stations). Materials grants included construction materials on public lands, plants, seeds, fish, publications, scientific specimens, and weights and measures. Services-in-aid included the sending of federal personnel to co-operate with state officials (road and canal construction, waterway improvements, agriculture); the sending of federal officials to prepare the groundwork for state programs (road, canal, and railroad surveying); and the lending of federal experts to the states for specific projects (road, railroad, and canal construction).

All these forms of intergovernmental co-operation involved considerable administrative interaction between federal, state, and local officials. This interaction was carried on through established departments and bureaus on the federal level and, usually, through boards and commissions generally comprised of ex officio elected officials on the state and local levels. The forms of this administrative interaction were quite fluid, since the entire system of co-operative relationships had to be developed through trial and error for each program.

While day-to-day operations rested largely with the various administrative bodies in the executive branches of several levels of government, the members of the legislative assemblies—and particularly the representatives of the states and localities in Congress—were alert and active in overseeing the numerous programs. The role of these politicians was an interstitial one. In a real sense, they provided the cement that held the bricks together and enabled the programs to function with a maximum of local control. Although this study could not deal with their activities in proper depth, in every program that involved federal action, they were continuously present and involved, always prepared to question an administrator's action, enlarge or decrease an appropriation, and contact the appropriate bureau on behalf of a public or private constituent. All this was in addition to the fundamental authority of Congress to establish the programs in the first place.

In addition to the formal administrative arrangements and the traditional role of the legislature, a spirit of professionalism arose among the officials implementing a particular program. Although it varied in intensity from program to program, where the spirit of professionalism was strong, it was strong at all levels of government. This spirit led to the development of a professional interest in the implementation and expansion of each program, which meant that the professionals involved in it would strive to increase the amount of federal-state co-operation as an effective vehicle for the expansion of their own functions. Often, when political pressures formally lessened the amount of intergovernmental action in a given program, the professionals involved would find ways to continue the program in a manner closely approximating its previous level. There were times when existing programs were expanded and even new programs initiated by devoted professionals after Congress had hesitated to grant formal authorization. Often the federal professionals were abetted in this by the cabinet secretary under whom they served.

It might be said that the evolution of a co-operative system was the result of a considerable effort on the part of a number of men who, along with the founding fathers, may justly be termed the architects of the American federal system. These men could be found at all three levels of government (they usually served at more than one level during their public careers) and in all three branches of government. Some of them were prominent figures as well in their day, others were hardly known outside of their immediate circles. . . . All were indispensable in the evolution of the American partnership.

Co-operative Federalism: The Alternate Hypothesis

On the basis of the evidence presented in the previous chapters [in Elazar's book], and summarized in this one, it would seem necessary to develop a different theory to explain the nature of the American federal system and its character over time. Any new theory must take into account the continuous existence of an amount of intergovernmental collaboration equal to, and in fact greater than, the amount of separation (as traditionally defined) in the federal system. More precisely, the amount of intergovernmental collaboration in the nineteenth century in relation to the total amount of governmental activity in American life (what may be termed the velocity of government) was no less than, or substantially different from, the amount of intergovernmental collaboration that exists in the mid-twentieth century in relation to the total velocity of government. Co-operative—not dual—federalism has been the mode since the establishment of the Republic, in the nineteenth century as well as in the twentieth. . . .

In a sense, a substantial share of the history of American government has been the search for methods to provide for the necessary collaboration of the various units of the federal system while at the same time preserving and strengthening those units as separate bases for such collaboration. It has been shown that much of what historians have mistaken for the rejection of intergovernmental co-operation in the nineteenth century was, in reality, the rejection of certain methods of interaction as failing to meet one or both of the above criteria.

Notes

1. For a few of the many examples of this, see records in the Thomas Gilcrease Institute of American History and Art, Tulsa, Oklahoma; the Indian Archives in the Oklahoma Historical Society Library, Oklahoma City, Oklahoma (these archives are themselves a grant from the federal government to the state of Oklahoma); the National Archives, Washington, D.C.; and "Miscellaneous Papers and Documents Relating to the Ute Uprising, 8/16/1887-5/28/1889" (microfilm) in the Colorado State Archives, Denver, Colorado.
2. This figure is based on calculations made for specific projects selected at random from materials in the U.S. Army Corps of Engineers records, National Archives.
3. William E. Burke, *Federal Finances* (Chicago: F. J. Schultze and Co., 1891). The enforcement of the federal fugitive slave laws provides an excellent example of both the operation and breakdown of intergovernmental co-operation in law enforcement. The laws not only took such co-operation between federal and state law enforcement officials for granted, but were based on such co-operation to attain any real effectiveness. When antislavery sentiment in the North forced the state and local lawmen to desist from aiding in the apprehension and return of fugitive slaves, the entire program broke down. For a view of the constitutional impact of this problem, see Carl Brent Swisher, *American Constitutional Development* (Boston: Houghton Mifflin, 1943), pp. 236-38.
4. See W. Turrentine Jackson, *Wagon Roads West* (Berkeley: University of California Press, 1956), for a discussion of the integration of wagon roads constructed by the federal government into the co-operative system.
5. Federal grants to arm and equip the state militias were initiated in 1808 as the first federal cash grants-in-aid to the states on record. An obvious example of co-operative federalism, the case of the militia has not been dealt with at any length in this volume dedicated to the "hard case." Information on intergovernmental co-operation in maintaining the militia in the nineteenth century is available in William H. Riker, *Soldiers of the States* (Washington, D.C.: Public Affairs Press, 1957).

4. THE FEDERAL SYSTEM

Morton Grodzins

Federalism is a device for dividing decisions and functions of government. As the constitutional fathers well understood, the federal structure is a means, not an end. The pages that follow are therefore not concerned with an exposition of American federalism as a formal, legal set of relationships. The focus, rather, is on the purpose of federalism, that is to say, on the distribution of power between central and peripheral units of government.

I
The Sharing of Functions

The American form of government is often, but erroneously, symbolized by a three-layer cake. A far more accurate image is the rainbow or marble cake, characterized by an inseparable mingling of differently colored ingredients, the colors appearing in vertical and diagonal strands and unexpected whirls. As colors are mixed in the marble cake, so functions are mixed in the American federal system. Consider the health officer, styled "sanitarian," of a rural county in a border state. He embodies the whole idea of the marble cake of government.

The sanitarian is appointed by the state under merit standards established by the federal government. His base salary comes jointly from state and federal funds, the county provides him with an office and office amenities and pays a portion of his expenses, and the largest city in the county also contributes to his salary and office by virtue of his appointment as a city plumbing inspector. It is impossible from moment to moment to tell under which governmental hat the sanitarian

Author's note: This paper is the product of research carried out in the Federalism Workshop of the University of Chicago. I am indebted to the workshop participants, particularly Daniel J. Elazar, Dennis Palumbo, and Kenneth E. Gray, for data they collected. I profited greatly in writing Part III of the paper from Mr. Elazar's prize-winning dissertation, "Intergovernmental Relations in Nineteenth Century American Federalism" (Chicago, 1959).

From The Report of the President's Commission on National Goals, The American Assembly, *Goals for Americans* (Englewood Cliffs, N.J.: Prentice-Hall, 1960), 265-282.

operates. His work of inspecting the purity of food is carried out under federal standards; but he is enforcing state laws when inspecting commodities that have not been in interstate commerce; and somewhat perversely he also acts under state authority when inspecting milk coming into the county from producing areas across the state border. He is a federal officer when impounding impure drugs shipped from a neighboring state; a federal-state officer when distributing typhoid immunization serum; a state officer when enforcing standards of industrial hygiene; a state-local officer when inspecting the city's water supply; and (to complete the circle) a local officer when insisting that the city butchers adopt more-hygienic methods of handling their garbage. But he cannot and does not think of himself as acting in these separate capacities. All business in the county that concerns public health and sanitation he considers his business. Paid largely from federal funds, he does not find it strange to attend meetings of the city council to give expert advice on matters ranging from rotten apples to rabies control. He is even deputized as a member of both the city and the county police forces.

The sanitarian is an extreme case, but he accurately represents an important aspect of the whole range of governmental activities in the United States. Functions are not neatly parceled out among the many governments. They are shared functions. It is difficult to find any governmental activity which does not involve all three of the so-called "levels" of the federal system. In the most local of local functions—law enforcement or education, for example—the federal and state governments play important roles. In what, *a priori,* may be considered the purest central government activities—the conduct of foreign affairs, for example—the state and local governments have considerable responsibilities, directly and indirectly.

The federal grant programs are only the most obvious example of shared functions. They also most clearly exhibit how sharing serves to disperse governmental powers. The grants utilize the greater wealth-gathering abilities of the central government and establish nationwide standards, yet they are "in aid" of functions carried out under state law, with considerable state and local discretion. The national supervision of such programs is largely a process of mutual accommodation. Leading state and local officials, acting through their professional organizations, are in considerable part responsible for the very standards that national officers try to persuade all state and local officers to accept.

Even in the absence of joint financing, federal-state-local collaboration is the characteristic mode of action. Federal expertise is available to aid in the building of a local jail (which may later be used to house federal prisoners), to improve a local water purification system, to step up building inspections, to provide standards for state and local personnel in protecting housewives against dishonest butchers' scales, to prevent gas explosions, or to produce a local land use plan. States and localities, on the other hand, take important formal responsibilities in the development of national programs for atomic energy, civil defense, the regulation of commerce, and the protection of purity in foods and drugs; local political weight is always a factor in the operation of even a post office or a military establishment. From abattoirs and accounting through zoning and zoo administration, any governmental activity is almost certain to involve the influence, if not the formal administration, of all three planes of the federal system.

II
Attempts to Unwind the Federal System

Within the past dozen years there have been four major attempts to reform or reorganize the federal system: the first (1947-49) and second (1953-55) Hoover Commissions on Executive Organization; the Kestnbaum Commission on Intergovernmental Relations (1953-55); and the Joint Federal-State Action Committee (1957-59). All four of these groups have aimed to minimize federal activities. None of them has recognized the sharing of functions as the characteristic way American governments do things. Even when making recommendations for joint action, these official commissions take the view (as expressed in the Kestnbaum report) that "the main tradition of American federalism is the tradition of separateness." All four have, in varying degrees, worked to separate functions and tax sources.

The history of the Joint Federal-State Action Committee is especially instructive. The committee was established at the suggestion of President Eisenhower, who charged it, first of all, "to designate functions which the States are ready and willing to assume and finance that are now performed or financed wholly or in part by the Federal Government." He also gave the committee the task of recommending "Federal and State revenue adjustments required to enable the States to assume such functions." [1]

The committee subsequently established seemed most favorably situated to accomplish the task of functional separation. It was composed of distinguished and able men, including among its personnel three leading members of the President's cabinet, the director of the Bureau of the Budget, and ten state governors. It had the full support of the President at every point, and it worked hard and conscientiously. Excellent staff studies were supplied by the Bureau of the Budget, the White House, the Treasury Department, and from the state side, the Council of State Governments. It had available to it a large mass of research data, including the sixteen recently completed volumes of the Kestnbaum Commission. There existed no disagreements on party lines within the committee and, of course, no constitutional impediments to its mission. The President, his cabinet members, and all the governors (with one possible exception) on the committee completely agreed on the desirability of decentralization-via-separation-of-functions-and-taxes. They were unanimous in wanting to justify the committee's name and to produce action, not just another report.

The committee worked for more than two years. It found exactly two programs to recommend for transfer from federal to state hands. One was the federal grant program for vocational education (including practical-nurse training and aid to fishery trades); the other was federal grants for municipal waste treatment plants. The programs together cost the federal government less than $80 million in 1957, slightly more than two per cent of the total federal grants for that year. To allow the states to pay for these programs, the committee recommended that they be allowed a credit against the federal tax on local telephone calls. Calculations showed that this offset device, plus an equalizing factor, would give every state at least 40 per cent more from the tax than it received from the federal government in vocational education and sewage disposal grants. Some states were "equalized" to receive twice as much.

The recommendations were modest enough, and the generous financing feature seemed calculated to gain state support. The President recommended to Congress that all points of the program be legislated. None of them was, none has been since, and none is likely to be.

[In a section omitted here, Grodzins surveys some of the history of intergovernmental cooperation in the United States, raising points made by Elazar in the previous essay.—Ed.]

IV
Dynamics of Sharing: The Politics of the Federal System

Many causes contribute to dispersed power in the federal system. One is the simple historical fact that the states existed before the nation. A second is in the form of creed, the traditional opinion of Americans that expresses distrust of centralized power and places great value in the strength and vitality of local units of government. Another is pride in locality and state, nurtured by the nation's size and by variations of regional and state history. Still a fourth cause of decentralization is the sheer wealth of the nation. It allows all groups, including state and local governments, to partake of the central government's largesse, supplies room for experimentation and even waste, and makes unnecessary the tight organization of political power that must follow when the support of one program necessarily means the deprivation of another.

In one important respect, the Constitution no longer operates to impede centralized government. The Supreme Court since 1937 has given Congress a relatively free hand. The federal government can build substantive programs in many areas on the taxation and commerce powers. Limitations of such central programs based on the argument, "it's unconstitutional," are no longer possible as long as Congress (in the Court's view) acts reasonably in the interest of the whole nation. The Court is unlikely to reverse this permissive view in the foreseeable future.

Nevertheless, some constitutional restraints on centralization continue to operate. The strong constitutional position of the states—for example, the assignment of two senators to each state, the role given the states in administering even national elections, and the relatively few limitations on their law-making powers—establish the geographical units as natural centers of administrative and political strength. Many clauses of the Constitution are not subject to the same latitude of interpretation as the commerce and tax clauses. The simple, clearly stated, unambiguous phrases—for example, the President "shall hold his office during the term of four years"—are subject to change only through the formal amendment process. Similar provisions exist with respect to the terms of senators and congressmen and the amendment process. All of them have the effect of retarding or restraining centralizing action of the federal government. The fixed terms of the President and the members of Congress, for example, greatly impede the development of nationwide, disciplined political parties that almost certainly would have to precede continuous large-scale expansion of federal functions.

The constitutional restraints on the expansion of national authority are less important and less direct today than they were in 1879 or in 1936. But to say that they are less important is not to say that they are unimportant.

The nation's politics reflect these decentralizing causes and add some of their own. The political parties of the United States are unique. They seldom perform the function that parties traditionally perform in other countries, the function of gathering together diverse strands of power and welding them into one. Except during the period of nominating and electing a president and for the essential but non-substantive business of organizing the houses of Congress, the American parties rarely coalesce power at all. Characteristically they do the reverse, serving as a canopy under which special and local interests are represented with little regard for anything that can be called a party program. National leaders are elected on a party ticket, but in Congress they must seek cross-party support if their leadership is to be effective. It is a rare president during rare periods who can produce legislation without facing the defection of substantial numbers of his own party. (Wilson could do this in the first session of the sixty-third Congress; but Franklin D. Roosevelt could not, even during the famous hundred days of 1933.) Presidents whose parties form the majority of the congressional houses must still count heavily on support from the other party.

The parties provide the pivot on which the entire governmental system swings. Party operations, first of all, produce in legislation the basic division of functions between the federal government, on the one hand, and state and local governments, on the other. The Supreme Court's permissiveness with respect to the expansion of national powers has not in fact produced any considerable extension of exclusive federal functions. The body of federal law in all fields has remained, in the words of Henry M. Hart, Jr., and Herbert Wechsler, "interstitial in its nature," limited in objective and resting upon the principal body of legal relationships defined by state law. It is difficult to find any area of federal legislation that is not significantly affected by state law.

In areas of new or enlarged federal activity, legislation characteristically provides important roles for state and local governments. This is as true of Democratic as of Republican administrations and true even of functions for which arguments of efficiency would produce exclusive federal responsibility. . . . A large fraction of the Senate is usually made up of ex-governors, and the membership of both houses is composed of men who know that their re-election depends less upon national leaders or national party organization than upon support from their home constituencies. State and local officials are key members of these constituencies, often central figures in selecting candidates and in turning out the vote. Under such circumstances, national legislation taking state and local views heavily into account is inevitable.

Second, the undisciplined parties affect the character of the federal system as a result of senatorial and congressional interference in federal administrative programs on behalf of local interests. Many aspects of the legislative involvement in administrative affairs are formalized. The Legislative Reorganization Act of 1946, to take only one example, provided that each of the standing committees "shall exercise continuous watchfulness" over administration of laws within its jurisdiction. But the formal system of controls, extensive as it is, does not compare in importance with the informal and extralegal network of relationships in producing continuous legislative involvement in administrative affairs.

Senators and congressmen spend a major fraction of their time representing problems of their constituents before administrative agencies. An even larger fraction of congressional staff time is devoted to the same task. The total magnitude of such "case work" operations is great.... Special congressional liaison staffs have been created to service this mass of business, though all higher officials meet it in one form or another....

The widespread, consistent, and in many ways unpredictable character of legislative interference in administrative affairs has many consequences for the tone and character of American administrative behavior. From the perspective of this paper, the important consequence is the comprehensive, day-to-day, even hour-by-hour, impact of local views on national programs. No point of substance or procedure is immune from congressional scrutiny. A substantial portion of the entire weight of this impact is on behalf of the state and local governments. It is a weight that can alter procedures for screening immigration applications, divert the course of a national highway, change the tone of an international negotiation, and amend a social security law to accommodate local practices or fulfill local desires.

The party system compels administrators to take a political role. This is a third way in which the parties function to decentralize the American system. The administrator must play politics for the same reason that the politician is able to play in administration: the parties are without program and without discipline.

In response to the unprotected position in which the party situation places him, the administrator is forced to nurse the Congress of the United States, that crucial constituency which ultimately controls his agency's budget and program. From the administrator's view, a sympathetic consideration of congressional requests (if not downright submission to them) is the surest way to build the political support without which the administrative job could not continue. Even the completely task-oriented administrator must be sensitive to the need for congressional support and to the relationship between case work requests, on one side, and budgetary and legislative support, on the other. "You do a good job handling the personal problems and requests of a Congressman," a White House officer said, "and you have an easier time convincing him to back your program." Thus there is an important link between the nursing of congressional requests, requests that largely concern local matters, and the most comprehensive national programs. The administrator must accommodate to the former as a price of gaining support for the latter.

One result of administrative politics is that the administrative agency may become the captive of the nationwide interest group it serves or presumably regulates. In such cases no government may come out with effective authority: the winners are the interest groups themselves. But in a very large number of cases, states and localities also win influence. The politics of administration is a process of making peace with legislators who for the most part consider themselves the guardians of local interests. The political role of administrators therefore contributes to the power of states and localities in national programs.

Finally, the way the party system operates gives American politics their over-all distinctive tone. The lack of party discipline produces an openness in the system that allows individuals, groups, and institutions (including state and local governments) to attempt to influence national policy at every step of the legislative-administrative process. This is the "multiple-crack" attribute of the American government. "Crack" has two meanings. It means not only many fissures or access points; it also means, less statically, opportunities for wallops or smacks at government.

If the parties were more disciplined, the result would not be a cessation of the process by which individuals and groups impinge themselves upon the central government. But the present state of the parties clearly allows for a far greater operation of the multiple crack than would be possible under the conditions of centralized party control. American interest groups exploit literally uncountable access points in the legislative-administrative process. If legislative lobbying, from committee stages to the conference committee, does not produce results, a cabinet secretary is called. His immediate associates are petitioned. Bureau chiefs and their aides are hit. Field officers are put under pressure. Campaigns are instituted by which friends of the agency apply a secondary influence on behalf of the interested party. A conference with the President may be urged.

To these multiple points for bringing influence must be added the multiple voices of the influencers. Consider, for example, those in a small town who wish to have a federal action taken. The easy merging of public and private interest at the local level means that the influence attempt is made in the name of the whole community, thus removing it from political partisanship. The Rotary Club as well as the City Council, the Chamber of Commerce and the mayor, eminent citizens and political bosses—all are readily enlisted. If a conference in senator's office will expedite matters, someone on the local scene can be found make such a conference possible and effective. If technical information is needed, technicians will supply it. State or national professional organizations of local officials, individual congressmen and senators, and not infrequently whole state delegations will make the local cause their own. Federal field officers, who service localities, often assume local views. So may elected and appointed state officers. Friendships are exploited, and political mortgages called due. Under these circumstances, national policies are molded by local action.

In summary, then, the party system functions to devolve power. The American parties, unlike any other, are highly responsive when directives move from the bottom to the top, highly unresponsive from top to bottom. Congressmen and senators can rarely ignore concerted demands from their home constituencies; but no party leader can expect the same kind of response from those below, whether he be a President asking for congressional support or a congressman seeking aid from local or state leaders.

Any tightening of the party apparatus would have the effect of strengthening the central government. The four characteristics of the system, discussed above, would become less important. If control from the top were strictly applied, these hallmarks of American decentralization might entirely disappear. To be specific, if disciplined and program-oriented parties were achieved: (1) It would make far less likely legislation that takes heavily into account the desires and prejudices of the highly decentralized power groups and institutions of the country, including the state and local governments. (2) It would to a large extent prevent legislators, individually and collectively, from intruding themselves on behalf of non-national interests in national administrative programs. (3) It would put an end to the administrator's search for his own political support, a search that often results in fostering state, local, and other non-national powers. (4) It would dampen the process by which individuals and groups, including state and local political leaders, take advantage of multiple cracks to steer national legislation and administration in ways congenial to them and the institutions they represent.

Alterations of this sort could only accompany basic changes in the organization and style of politics which, in turn, presuppose fundamental changes at the parties' social base. The sharing of functions is, in fact, the sharing of power. To end this sharing process would mean the destruction of whatever measure of decentralization exists in the United States today. . . .

Note

1. The President's third suggestion was that the committee "identify functions and responsibilities likely to require state or federal attention in the future

and . . . recommend the level of state effort, or federal effort, or both, that will be needed to assure effective action." The committee initially devoted little attention to this problem. Upon discovering the difficulty of making separatist recommendations, i.e., for turning over federal functions and taxes to the states, it developed a series of proposals looking to greater effectiveness in intergovernmental collaboration. The committee was succeeded by a legislatively based, 26-member Advisory Commission on Intergovernmental Relations, established September 29, 1959.

5. THE CONDITION OF AMERICAN FEDERALISM: AN HISTORIAN'S VIEW

Harry N. Scheiber

... Debate has been colored lately by differences of opinion concerning the actual historic tradition of American federalism. The long-standing view was that throughout the 19th century, and in most respects until the New Deal, "dual federalism"—in which the functions of the three levels of government were well delineated and in which their administrative activities were kept separate and autonomous—was the prevailing system. Only in the 20th century did there emerge a new order, termed "cooperative federalism," in which all the levels of government became "mutually complementary parts of a *single* governmental mechanism all of whose powers are intended to realize the current purposes of government according to the applicability of the problem at hand." [1]

Now there has become popular a new historical view, associated mainly with the late Morton Grodzins, that dual federalism never characterized the American political system. From the beginning, it is asserted, there was a high degree of intergovernmental activity, involving shared functions and responsibilities; indeed, there was "as much sharing" in the period 1790-1860 as there is today.[2] Surprising as it may seem, this historical construct has gained wide currency among political scientists and bids fair to become the new conventional wisdom about American federalism.[3] ...

I. The Fallacy of Continuity

The model of "cooperative federalism" portrays the present-day federal system as one in which most of the important functions of government are shared. Professor Grodzins argued that the system does not resemble a layer cake "of three distinct and separate planes" so much as a marble cake: "there is no neat horizontal stratification," for

From a study submitted by the Subcommittee on Intergovernmental Relations Pursuant to S. Res. 205, 89th Congress, to the Committee on Government Operations, U.S. Senate, October 15, 1966 (Washington, D.C.: U.S. Government Printing Office). Reprinted by permission of the author, Harry N. Scheiber, University of California, Berkeley. All rights reserved.

both policy-making and administrative functions are shared by Federal, State, and local governments. Grodzins went further, declaring that the marble-cake analogy was applicable no less to American federalism in the 19th century than it is today. "There has in fact never been a time," he wrote, "when Federal, State, and local functions were separate and distinct. Government does more things in 1963 than it did in 1790 or 1861; but in terms of what government did, there was as much sharing then as today." [4]

This historical construct has enormous potential in terms of its political impact. For it lends the weight of historical authority and precedent to the *status quo,* or indeed to any centralization of power that is accompanied by arrangements for the sharing of administrative functions. It has the further advantage of discrediting those who might fear centralization because they attribute the historic strength of representative government in America to the tradition of dual federalism. "One cannot hark back to the good old days of State and local independence," Grodzins declared, "because those days never existed." This refrain was echoed, with good political effect, by Lyndon Johnson during his 1964 Presidential campaign. . . .

Grodzins himself provided little evidence on which to judge his version of historic federalism. He asserted, *ex cathedra,* that "whatever was at the focus of State attention in the 19th century became the recipient of national grants" in the form of cash aid, land grants, or loans of technical personnel. To support such contentions, Grodzins relied heavily on the historical research of his student Daniel Elazar. Elazar in turn has asserted (1) that when government assumed responsibility in specific functional fields, government at all levels "acted in concert"; and (2) that "Federal funds provided the stimulus for new programs throughout the nineteenth century." In his research, he has found that "virtually every domestic governmental program involved intergovernmental cooperation in some form." [5]

There are three main flaws in the Grodzins-Elazar construct. First, it does not cover systematically the whole spectrum of State policy concerns and administrative activities to prove the contention that "whatever was at the focus of State attention" received Federal aid. The Grodzins-Elazar argument can be upheld, in short, only if one accepts a tautological definition of "the focus of State attention"; those programs which *did* receive Federal aid must be viewed as at "the focus." [6]

Second, Grodzins and Elazar do not establish plausible criteria as to what was trivial and what important in the field of "intergovernmental cooperation." Thus they treat the most superficial administrative contacts (for example, State libraries' exchange of legal volumes with

Federal agencies, or loan of surveying instruments to the States by the U.S. Coast Survey) as evidence of viable cooperation.[7]

Finally, and most centrally, they do not consider the basic issue of power as it was distributed relatively among levels of government. Indeed, they do not even consider power as it was exercised at different levels in the few State programs that *were* aided with Federal grants of cash, personnel, or land.

The question of Federal cash grants in the 19th century can be disposed of readily: they were of negligible importance by any quantitative measure.[8] The first cash-grant program on a continuing basis, aside from cash aid for maintaining pensioned Civil War veterans in State homes, came in 1887, when the Hatch Act provided $15,000 per year to the States in aid of agricultural research. As late as 1902, less than one per cent of all State and local revenues came from the central government, by contrast with perhaps 20 per cent in 1934 and 14 per cent in 1963. Obviously there was *not* "as much sharing then as today," measured either by the relative magnitude of Federal grants in total State-local financing or by the proportion of State-local policy concerns affected by Federal cash aid. Loans of Federal technical personnel were even less important, comprising mainly the services of the Army Engineers for the brief period 1824 to 1838.[9]

The Federal land grants to the States comprise the only substantial evidence for the Grodzins-Elazar historical construct. These grants were mainly for two purposes: education and transportation.[10] In the field of education, there were two land-grant programs of importance, the cession of portions of the Federal land in public-land States of the West for support of common schools; and the Morrill-Act cessions of 1862, granting scrip receivable for public lands to the States in proportion to their population, for support of agricultural and mechanical colleges.

Neither program, however, comprised genuine sharing comparable to that which characterizes the modern grant-in-aid programs—for neither significantly narrowed the range of policy-making discretion enjoyed by the States. In common education, the States continued to have exclusive control over professional and certification standards, over determination of levels of total support, over curriculum structure and content, and the like. There was no matching formula operative; there were no administrative contacts with agencies of the Federal government charged with policy or administrative functions (the U.S. Office of Education was not even established until 1867); and there was no auditing nor inspection by Federal officials.[11]

Federal grants for transportation offer somewhat more persuasive evidence of genuine "sharing" of 19th century policy-making functions.

The grants to the States and to private railroad companies did affect vitally the pace and location of new transport construction. However, supportive and subsidy activity was only one aspect of policy-making in this field. Equally important was regulation of rates and operating practices on the lines of transport. One cannot find government at all levels "acting in concert" (Elazar's phrase) in this policy area. It was the States alone that established basic corporation, property, taxation, and eminent-domain law under which transportation facilities were built, financed, and operated. From the 1830's on, the States had control over railroad charges; and the Granger laws of the 1870's had ample precedent in State regulatory legislation of the preceding decades.[12] Not until 1887, when it established the Interstate Commerce Commission, did Congress first assert its power in the regulatory field. The relative distribution of power over transport costs in the national economy cannot, moreover, be judged alone by reference to statutes and court decisions. For in their administrative operations, the States exercised real control over the ostensibly free internal-transport market. As owners and operators of basic lines of internal transport in the canal era, 1825-1850, the States blatantly evaded Constitutional limitations on their power to regulate interstate commerce. In every major canal State, the public authorities levied discriminatory tolls that favored their own producers at the expense of those located out of State. As a result, the State canal tolls until 1850 constituted a web of effective barriers to free internal trade.[13]

In sum, even if one takes into account the cash value of Federal land ceded to the States, the 19th-century Federal grants did not involve pervasive sharing of policy-making powers. Intergovernmental administrative contracts were casual at best: even in the major land-grant programs, the Federal administrative role was limited mainly to the bookkeeping operations of the General Land Office. It requires tortured semantics and neglect of the critical issue—relative power—to argue basic continuity in the history of the 19th- and 20th-century federalism on evidence such as Grodzins and Elazar have adduced. If this historical construct of cooperative federalism is fallacious, what, then, is the record?

The federal system may be rather understood as having gone through four major stages of power distribution. The basic pattern of intergovernmental relations has been redefined and reformulated in each of these stages—and the "creative federalism" advocated by President Johnson must be comprehended in a context of successive transformations rather than as a mere variant of a timeless theme.

[The author continues, offering a detailed summary of these historical developments. Scheiber's views on the stages of American federalism are most clearly stated in another article, from which the next seven paragraphs are excerpted.—Ed.]*

The first stage, the era of dual federalism and rivalistic state mercantilism, runs from 1789 to 1861. This is a period when the behavior of the federal system conformed closely to the juridical model of dual federalism. The Supreme Court generally supported dualism in the responsibilities of the central and state governments, and Congress refrained from making innovative policy in many areas formally opened to it by the Court. Moreover, the relatively decentralized character of the economy meant that the states' geographic jurisdiction was congruent with decentralized promotional and regulatory powers.

The second stage, 1861-1890, was one of transitional centralization. Amendment of the Constitution, together with vast expansion of the policy responsibilities of the national government and an increase in the jurisdiction of the federal courts, meant significant centralization of real power. In 1887 Congress undertook national regulation of the railroads, and three years later the Sherman Act marked the beginning of general business regulation. Meanwhile, the Supreme Court's activism was itself a centralizing force, albeit along lines that served to attenuate state initiatives or federal civil rights laws.[14]

The years 1890-1933 constitute the third stage, accelerating centralization. Successive federal laws advanced national regulation; World War I brought intensive, if temporary, centralization; and the Supreme Court continued to "censor" state legislation with a heavy hand. Modern grants-in-aid originated in this period, although on only a small scale.

A residue of dual federalism from the antebellum era was evident in the area of civil rights, as Southern blacks were left virtually helpless against private coercion, state action, and often terrifying violence; the states continued to have almost exclusive control over labor policy, and they have also retained control over such traditional areas as education, family law, and criminal law.

The New Deal inaugurated the fourth stage, which brought the well-known "Constitutional Revolution" and the transformation of the American political economy. Increases in both the extent and intensity of federal regulation, the establishment of regional planning in the Tennessee Valley, federalization of labor policy, the reorganization of agriculture as a managed sector, and expansion of welfare programs all combined with the adoption of Keynesian fiscal policy and contempo-

---

* From "Federalism and Legal Process: Historical and Contemporary Analysis of the American System," *Law & Society Review* 14 (Spring 1980): 679-681. Reprinted by permission of the Law and Society Association.

rary income and estate taxation policy. It was in this broad context of quick and intensive centralization that Cooperative Federalism emerged as a style or technique of intergovernmental relations.

The fifth phase is the post-World War II era, in which modern centralized government spawned the Creative Federalism of Johnson and the New Federalism of Nixon and Ford while the Warren Court validated enormous extensions of national power in the fields of race relations, criminal justice, and structural reform. Many areas of policy for which state and local government were responsible before 1933 have now become strongly centralized.

Again recognition must be given to vestiges of dual federalism, both in the law and in the dynamics of politics. Thus there is continuing rivalry among the states in the competition for industrial development; there is regional division on some major issues; and the Supreme Court has made some cracks even in the monolithic powers derived from the Commerce Clause (*National League of Cities* v. *Usery*, 426 U.S. 833, 1976). As Lowi has written, however, the system is now a "modern, positive national state," if also "the youngest consolidated national government," among the large modern nation-states.[15]

[Here Scheiber's Senate subcommittee study resumes.—Ed.]

The American political system has undergone a revolution since 1933, and another major departure appears in process now. This retrospective view suggests, first, a warning that behind us is no homogeneous history of cooperative federalism, and that the Great Society may bring changes no less pervasive than those produced by the New Deal. It may be comforting to assume that cooperative federalism dates from 1790, just as it is comforting to assume that the real power of State-local government has recently grown more rapidly than the Federal Government's, or that issues of relative power are now irrelevant. But such assumptions will foreclose meaningful discussion of how shifts in power distribution (which are not automatically negated by mere administrative sharing) will in the future affect the federal system and the welfare of the Nation. If cooperative federalism from 1933 to the 1960's differs from the projected creative federalism of Lyndon B. Johnson, either in style or specific functional arrangements, the historical record suggests the perils of performance falling short of promise. It also indicates the importance of understanding what changes in power distribution we are prepared to accept—as matters of necessity or matters of choice.

James Madison wrote in 1787:

> Conceiving that an individual independence of the States is utterly irreconcilable with their aggregate sovereignty, and that a

consolidation of the whole into one simple republic would be as inexpedient as it is unattainable, I have sought for a middle ground which may at once support a due supremacy of the national authority, and not exclude the local authorities wherever they can be subordinately useful.[16]

We might do well to recall that purpose; for now that creative federalism is focusing on the problems basic to the quality of American life, the stakes are high and the possibility of either failure or stifling uniformity is appalling.

Notes

The author acknowledges with thanks the support of the Public Affairs Center of Dartmouth College during course of research for this study. Prof. Frank Smallwood contributed invaluable criticism and generously shared his own ideas with the author during each stage of the work. Prof. Gene M. Lyons, director of the Public Affairs Center, offered suggestions and criticism, and also a forum: for the paper was first read at the Orvil E. Dryfoos Conference on Public Affairs, Dartmouth College, Hanover, New Hampshire, May 21, 1966. Professors James A. Maxwell of Clark University, Roger H. Brown of American University, and Henry W. Ehrmann of Dartmouth also provided helpful suggestions and criticism.

1. Edward S. Corwin, "The Passing of Dual Federalism," in R. G. McCloskey, ed., *Essays in Constitutional Law* (New York, 1957), p. 205.
2. Morton Grodzins, "Centralization and Decentralization," in R. A. Goldwin, ed., *A Nation of States* (Chicago, 1963), p. 7.
3. For example, in a recent symposium on "Intergovernmental Relations in the U.S.," *Annals*, Vol. 359 (May 1965), many of the contributors quote Grodzins approvingly on the alleged historical continuity of American federalism.
4. Grodzins in *Nation of States*, pp. 3-4, 7.
5. Grodzins, "The Federal System," *Goals for Americans* (President's Commission on National Goals, New York, 1960), p. 270; Elazar in *Annals*, Vol. 359, p. 11; Elazar, *The American Partnership* (Chicago, 1962), p. 338.
6. For a decisive argument supporting the alternative view that power distribution in the American federal system changed markedly over the 19th century, cf. William H. Riker, *Federalism* (Boston, 1964), esp. p. 83.
7. Elazar, *Amer. Part., passim.*
8. Up to 1860, only $42 million in cash was granted by the Federal Government to the States and localities, of which two-thirds comprised the 1837 distribution of the Treasury surplus, a one-time, unique effort. (This was in addition to Federal assumption of State debts in 1790.) Paul

B. Trescott, "The U.S. Government and National Income, 1790-1860," in National Bureau of Economic Research, *Trends in the American Economy in the 19th Century* (Princeton, 1960), pp. 337-61. Elazar's own analysis of Minnesota State finance, 1860-1900, supports my contentions. Federal cash payments constituted one-third total State receipts in 1863, a unique instance; all other years computed show Federal payments as 1 to 2 per cent of receipts at most *(Amer. Part.,* p. 280).

9. Forest Hill, *Roads, Rails, and Waterways: The Army Engineers and Early Transportation* (Norman, Okla., 1957).

10. Minor programs of aid—measured in terms of personnel and/or funds involved—many of them dating only from the 1890's, are given in Elazar, *Amer. Part.,* pp. 302-303n. Both Grodzins and Elazar treat "19th century origins" of intergovernmental programs in a loose temporal framework, often emphasizing the significance of Federal grants that originated only in the nineties. This, together with their emphases on trivial data (measured in terms of policy-making powers actually shared or in terms of cash magnitudes involved), is distortive, I think, of the actual evolution of techniques and principles at issue.

11. Harry Kursh, *The Office of Education* (Phila., 1965). Elazar views post-1900 changes as mere "routinization of sharing procedures" *(Amer. Part.,* p. 337). As will become evident, I consider the changes so designated as far more substantive and important in terms of power relationships than Elazar suggests.

12. On early regulation, see Robert S. Hunt, *Law and Locomotives* (Madison, 1958), a study of Wisconsin, and similar studies for other states; also, Frederick Merk, "Eastern Antecedents of the Grangers," *Agric. Hist.,* 23:1-8 (1949).

13. H. Scheiber, "Rate-Making Power of the State in the Canal Era," *Political Sci. Quar.,* 77:397-413 (1962).

14. Laurence Tribe, *American Constitutional Law* (Mineola, N.Y., 1978), p. 5; Harry N. Scheiber, "Federalism and the American Economic Order, 1789-1910," *Law and Society Review,* 10: 100-118 (1975).

15. Theodore Lowi and Alan Stone (eds.), *Nationalizing Government: Public Policies in America* (Beverly Hills, Calif., 1978), p. 25.

16. James Madison, *The Forging of American Federalism,* ed. S. K. Padover (Torchbook edn., N.Y., 1965), p. 184 (letter to Geo. Washington, April 16, 1787).

6. MODELS OF NATIONAL, STATE, AND LOCAL RELATIONSHIPS

Deil S. Wright

... We can now formulate some simplified models of IGR [intergovernmental relations]. Figure [1] represents visually three models of authority relationships among national, state, and local jurisdictions in the United States. These models, like most simple models, fall far short of displaying the complexities and realities of governance in several respects, for example, numbers and types of entities, numbers and variations in personnel, different types of programs and functions, varying fiscal resources, and so on. The models depict three generic types of authority: coordinate authority (autonomy), dominant or inclusive authority (hierarchy), and equal or overlapping authority (bargaining). Despite its simplicity, each model, by concentrating on the essential features of a possible IGR arrangement, guides us in formulating hypotheses. (No two models, of course, generate identical sets of hypotheses.) By testing these hypotheses, we can discover which model best fits the U.S. political system as it operates today.[1]

Coordinate-Authority Model

In the coordinate-authority model of IGR sharp, distinct boundaries separate the national government and state governments. Local units, however, are included within and are dependent on state governments. The most classic expression of state-local relations is Dillon's Rule, named after the Iowa judge who asserted it in the 1860s, which summarizes the power relationships between the states and their localities:

1. There is no common-law right of self-government.
2. Local entities are creatures of the state, subject to creation and abolition at the unfettered discretion of the state (barring constitutional limitations).

3. Localities may exercise only those powers expressly granted.
4. Localities are "mere tenants at the will of the legislature." [2]

For more than a century Dillon's Rule has been a nationwide guidepost in legal and constitutional relations between the states and their local governments. Hidden behind its seeming simplicity is a central issue in IGR and in the models of figure [1]: Who should govern? This fundamental philosophical question clearly cannot be answered by the model, nor has Dillon's Rule succeeded in resolving it. But the model has helped frame a significant question, and that is one positive result from constructing models.

What does the coordinate-authority model imply concerning national-state power relationships? It implies, again, that the two types of entities are independent and autonomous; they are linked only tangentially. This model received implicit endorsement in the 1880s from Lord Bryce, an eminent Briton who visited the United States and observed its political system. . . . Bryce's analogy was drawn from observation and experience, but he could have cited an 1871 U.S. Supreme Court decision for a stamp of approval. In *Tarbel's Case* the Court stated:

> There are within the territorial limits of each state two governments, restricted in their sphere of action, but independent of each other, and supreme within their respective spheres. Each has its separate departments, each has its distinct laws, and each has its own

Figure 1 Three Models of Intergovernmental Relations in the United States

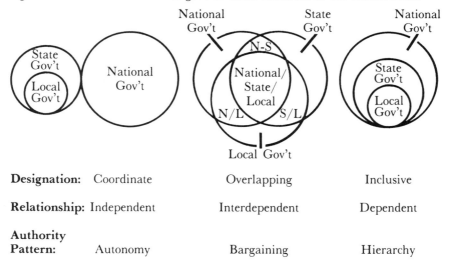

Designation:	Coordinate	Overlapping	Inclusive
Relationship:	Independent	Interdependent	Dependent
Authority Pattern:	Autonomy	Bargaining	Hierarchy

tribunals for their enforcement. Neither government can intrude within the jurisdiction of the other or authorize any interference therein by its judicial offices with the action of the other.[3]

Both an impartial foreign observer and the institution charged with interpreting the Constitution agreed, then, that *each* of the two units—the national and the state—governs within its respective sphere of authority.

What happened when the respective spheres of authority put the national government and a state in conflict, when they ceased to be tangential and clashed directly? The result is well known to students of U.S. federalism. The Supreme Court became the arbiter of national-state relations.[4] For several decades the Supreme Court, operating on the premise of the coordinate-authority model, attempted to set distinct, insulated spheres of national and state powers. But Court decisions in the 1930s necessitated substantial rethinking of how this model did (or did not) describe the operation of the U.S. political system.

Two scholars, Morton Grodzins and Daniel Elazar, extensively explored the coordinate-authority model and found it woefully wanting, not simply for the present and recent past but for the nineteenth century as well.[5] ... Indeed, many students of constitutional law and history look back at Supreme Court decisions from the 1860s to the 1930s and loudly applaud the discrediting of the so-called dual federalism (or what we are calling the coordinate-authority) model. Many U.S. and state courts seemed determined to impose that model on a growing industrial society of increasingly complex and interdependent units.

IGR model builders are probably in near-unanimous agreement that the coordinate-authority model is obsolete, addressed as it is to nonexistent social and political conditions. Before dispatching the model to oblivion, however, consider the Supreme Court decision of June 24, 1976. In *National League of Cities v. Usery* the Court, in sweeping language, ruled that Congress did not have the authority to require that either the states or their local governments observe minimum-wage and maximum-hour laws. In a 5-4 decision declaring unconstitutional a 1974 federal law extending wage-and-hour requirements to state and city employees, the Court said the legislation violated the "attributes of sovereignty attaching to every state government which may not be impaired by Congress."[6] The Court concluded:

> Congress has sought to wield its power in a fashion that would impair the States' ability to function effectively in a federal system. ... We hold that insofar as the challenged amendments operate to directly displace the States' freedom to structure integral operations in areas of traditional governmental

functions, they are not within the authority granted Congress [by the commerce clause].[7]

The decision in the *Usery* case was widely hailed as a significant revival of state-local prerogatives and protection based on three elements of judicial reasoning in the majority opinion by Justice [William] Rehnquist. First, it reasserted the relevance of the Tenth Amendment in guarding state (and local) interests from the otherwise unrestrained exercise of national (congressional) power, in some respects like the First Amendment guarantees to protect individual rights. Second, it defined those Tenth Amendment limitations based on state and local governments' "integral operations" in activities that involved "traditional functions." Third, the Court looked carefully at the 1974 amendments to the Fair Labor Standards Act involving minimum wages and extra payment for overtime hours worked by municipal employees, for example, police officers, firefighters. The majority found these "integral" and "traditional" activities were impaired by the congressional statute based on the commerce clause. The legislation, according to the Court, resulted in an unconstitutional infringement on state-local legislative options to control and direct governmental operations.

The legal legacy of the *Usery* case between 1976 and 1985 cannot and need not be reviewed. Suffice it to say that hopes for a continued and even expanded judicial endorsement of the coordinate-authority model failed to materialize. Indeed, the trend in case law went in the opposite direction, culminating in 1985 in an explicit overruling of the *Usery* opinion in *Garcia v. San Antonio Metropolitan Transportation Authority*. In this 5-4 decision, delivered by Justice Harry Blackmun, the Court majority rejected "as unsound in principle and unworkable in practice, a rule of state immunity from federal regulation that turns on a judicial appraisal of whether a particular governmental function is 'integral' or 'traditional'." [8]

One effect of the *Garcia* determination, according to the language of the opinion, is a withdrawal of the Court from a role in defining the authority of, or jurisdictional boundaries between, the national and state governments—as the coordinate-authority model implies. On this point the Court majority was explicit about how state (or local) interests may be protected. "State sovereign interests ... are more properly protected by procedural safeguards inherent in the structure of the federal system than by judicially created limitations on federal power." [9] In other words, the Court said in *Garcia* that effective restraints on Congress's use of the commerce power could and should be achieved through political rather than judicial processes.

The *Garcia* decision set alarm bells ringing in state and local personnel offices and in legislative chambers across the nation. Compliance costs, particularly for overtime pay (above forty hours) involving public-safety personnel, were variously estimated at $2-4 billion. Congress, under pressure from state and local officials, enacted legislation in 1985 that clarified and eased implementation of the Court decision. Passage of the legislation, some argued, confirmed that the Court majority assessment that federalism hinges on the political process was an astute conclusion. Others, particularly dissenting Justices Lewis Powell and Sandra Day O'Connor, challenged the majority's view.

> JUSTICE POWELL: The State's role in our system of government is a matter of constitutional law, not of legislative grace.
> Despite some genuflecting in the Court's opinion to the concept of federalism, today's decision effectively reduces the Tenth Amendment to meaningless rhetoric when Congress acts pursuant to the Commerce Clause. [10]
> JUSTICE O'CONNOR: In my view, federalism cannot be reduced to the weak "essence" distilled by the majority today. [11]

Commentary on *Garcia*, pro and con, has been extensive, even voluminous, but the complexity and the merits of the views expressed are not directly pertinent to the main point we are discussing: the nature of the coordinate-authority model. The *Usery* case suggested that this model of national-state-local relationships persisted in the attitudes and actions of IGR participants until very recently. Furthermore, the model was rejected by the Supreme Court with only the slimmest majority. Changes in Court composition or in legal philosophy could renew the relevance of this model.

Inclusive-Authority Model

The inclusive-authority model is represented in figure [1] by concentric circles diminishing in size from national to state to local. Let us suppose that the area covered by each circle represents the proportion of power exercised by that jurisdiction with respect to the others. Suppose also that the national government wants to expand its proportion of power in relation to states and localities. Two strategies are possible. One reduces the various powers of either the states or localities or both; the other enlarges the national government's circle with or without enlarging the state and/or local circles. For obvious reasons this second strategy is often called "enlarging the pie."

Both strategies can be understood by means of game theory: a systematic way of studying behavior in decision-making situations. The theory assumes that all participants strive to optimize their behavior, each trying to maximize gains and minimize losses within the limits of allowed behavior (hence the analogy with games). The outcomes depend not only on the behavior of any one participant but on the responses of other participants as well.

The first strategy above, Type I, is the classic case of a three-person, zero-sum game, like poker. The sum of the players' winnings equals the sum of their losses. An illustration of this in the IGR context occurs in the *Usery* and *Garcia* cases on the legislation requiring state and local units to meet minimum-wage and maximum-hour requirements. The national government exercised (expanded) its power at the expense of state and local powers. The gain in national power equaled the power lost by state and local units. The Supreme Court validation of the law required states and local governments to pay increased labor costs. Thus, national gains equaled state and local losses.

In game theory the second strategy above, Type II, or "enlarging the pie," is called a non-constant-sum game. All participants in this type of game can "win" or make gains. Perhaps the best IGR illustration of the Type II non-constant-sum strategy is fiscal: the conditional grant-in-aid. The national sector can expand by raising more money to offer as grants to states and localities. The funds can be offered with conditions ("losses") imposed on the recipients, but the benefits ("winnings") are so attractive that they appear to outweigh the attached constraints. From these examples of the two strategies we would expect national IGR policies to lean far more toward Type II strategies (such as grants-in-aid) than toward Type I.

Type II strategies assume, however, that the total resources ("winnings") *can* be expanded. That assumption is less likely in a period of fiscal and other resource constraints similar to that experienced since 1978 and predicted for the late 1980s and 1990s. Indeed, the phrases "cutback management" and "doing more with less" have become common partially as a result of Proposition 13 "fever," federal aid cutbacks, and the size of the federal deficit. It would not be surprising, then, to see more movement from Type II to Type I strategies in national-state-local relationships. Examples of zero-sum or polarized IGR relationships seem likely to persist and perhaps increase in fields such as energy, environment, and social regulatory arenas. More specific illustrations include nuclear waste storage, hazardous waste siting, abortion, drinking age, and school prayer issues.

The inclusive-authority model serves uses other than allowing predictions of IGR policies. It also conveys the essential hierarchical nature of authority. The dependency relationships imply power patterns that are similar to Dillon's Rule for state-local relations, that is, states and localities would be mere minions of the national government with insignificant or incidental impact on U.S. politics and public policy. To the question of who governs, this model provides an unequivocal answer: the national government.

How well (and in what areas) does the inclusive-authority model describe the realities of present-day U.S. politics, policy, and administration? Curiously enough, conservative and liberal observers alike see this model dominant in many aspects of our public life. Barry Goldwater, Reagan, and other conservatives see a powerful federal engine rolling over weakened and supine states and localities.

On the liberal side Senator Joseph Clark, as early as 1960, saw with approval the inception of a "national federalism": the national government not only was in charge (according to Clark) but *should* be in charge.[12] A more extensive and thoughtful elaboration of the same idea appeared in practitioner-scholar James Sundquist's *Making Federalism Work*.[13] Writing in 1969, in the wake of the Great Society programs, Sundquist highlighted the following:

1. "The nation for decades has been steadily coalescing into a national society" (p. 10).
2. "The Great Society was, by definition, one society; the phrase was singular, not plural" (p. 12).
3. There was "centralization of objective-setting" (p. 13).
4. "Somewhere in the Executive Office must be centered a concern for the structure of federalism—a responsibility for guiding the evolution of the whole system of federal-state-local relations, viewed for the first time as a *single* system" (p. 246).

Sundquist left little doubt that the national government should be in charge, but he was not convinced that it controlled a single, hierarchical system.

Other observers, especially those who have focused on the capabilities or incapacities of the states, have also concluded that the states and their localities are governing entities in name only; hence, the choice of the term *nominal* or *centralized federalism*. This conclusion has been reached by four approaches.

One approach, the power-elite perspective, sees the ship of state guided by a select and cohesive corps of national leaders at the helm. State and local governments and their political leaders are carried along like barnacles on a hull.[14] They are insignificant and powerless to affect important political or societal choices. The most recent (fourth) edition of *Who's Running America* completely omits any state or local officials as part of an elite 6,000-7,000 persons who guide the nation.[15]

A second approach, the technocratic-pluralist position, identifies the dispersal of decision-making power into quasi-public or even private economic fiefdoms that are national in scope. The states or other entities, singularly or collectively, cannot counteract these powerful private-interest groups. This approach argues, for example, that organized medicine and the health industry control the health of the nation despite the "policy power" of the states to control the health, welfare, morals, and safety of their citizens.[16]

A third approach, which might be called economic federalism, has some views in common with the power-elite and technocratic-pluralist points of view. This facet of the inclusive model can be summarized by excerpts from an extensive 1958 essay on the subject by Arthur S. Miller.

> I do not mean to focus upon the administrative agency, but upon the recipient of economic power—the large corporate enterprise or factory community—probably the most important of the groups in American society. These are the functional units of economic federalism and the basic units of a system of private governments.
>
> . . .
>
> It takes no fanciful mental gymnastics to say that the factory community operates as the recipient of delegated power to carry out important societal functions. It is the economic counterpart—and superior, be it said—of the unit of political federalism, the forty-eight state governments. It is the basic unit of functional federalism. It is a private governmental system, performing some of the jobs of government.[17]

A fourth approach to the conclusion that states and localities enjoy only a nominal existence is the administrative orientation. The states, it is argued, are little more than administrative districts of the national government, making state governors, in effect, "chief federal systems officers." . . . In the early 1950s L. D. White, in "The March of Power to Washington," wrote that the states were then well on the way to becoming hollow shells.[18] By the late 1950s Miller reported the district concept as an established fact.

> So far as the traditional federal system is concerned, the implications of this change are clear. Chief among them is that, to a large extent, states today operate not as practically autonomous units, but as administrative districts for centrally established policies. It is doubtless inaccurate to think of them as hollow political shells, but it does seem to be true that the once-powerful state governments have been bypassed by the movement of history. Save for "housekeeping" duties, they have little concern with the main flow of important decisions. When new problems arise, eyes swivel to

Washington, not to the state capitol—where eyes also turn to the banks of the Potomac.[19]

The administrative district charge was vigorously challenged by William Anderson on the basis of his and his associates' empirical investigations in the 1940s and 1950s. Specifically addressing the grant-in-aid issue, Anderson contended that the states gained as much as the national government from the fund transfer.

> In short, as administrators of federal programs under grants-in-aid the state governments have acquired something in the nature of an added check upon the national administration. Political power, like electricity, does not all run in one direction.[20]

Whatever the past state of affairs in IGR, another writer, Ferdinand Lundberg, predicts a fully fused and centralized system in the twenty-first century. He contends that all state and local governments will be operated from a U.S. version of the United Kingdom's Home Office, such as a department of internal affairs. More specifically, he foresees:

> City managers and state executives will probably be appointed or declared eligible from civil service lists by the national government, although there may still be vestigial elections of purely symbolic governors, mayors, and town councilmen.
>
> Each of the present American states, it seems evident, is destined to become pretty much of an administrative department of the central government, just as counties and cities will be subdepartments.[21]

The hallmarks of the inclusive-authority model should now be clear. One is the premise that state and local governments depend totally on decisions that are nationwide in scope and arrived at by the national government, or by powerful economic interests, or by some combination of the two. A second premise is that non-national political institutions such as governors, state legislators, and mayors have approached a condition of nearly total atrophy. A third premise is that the functions formerly performed by these now-vestigial organs have been fused into a centralized, hierarchical system.

To what degree or extent is the hierarchical, inclusive-authority model present in the United States today? We cannot say with certainty because our measures of power relationships are poorly calibrated, and the immense body of data required to arrive at such a global conclusion is simply not available. There has been movement toward this model through court decisions, congressional statutes, and administrative regulations. . . .

[Wright then presents three cases. The first shows how the national government can acquire leverage via the "strings" on grants-in-aid. The second describes how the U.S. Department of Justice and federal courts intervened to regulate whether San Antonio, Texas, could annex some adjoining territory, the national concern being the effect the annexation decision had on political representation of Hispanics. The third case suggests that the U.S. Supreme Court has upheld the use of national legislation to require that states use certain criteria and procedures in setting rates for electricity generation and distribution.—Ed.]

Do these three examples confirm that the inclusive-authority model best summarizes the contemporary state of IGR in the United States? Despite their close approximation of the hierarchical model, we think that these examples are not fully representative of the broad spectrum and dominant pattern of IGR in the United States. Instead, we look to a third model.

Overlapping-Authority Model

The inclusive-authority and coordinate-authority models of IGR are at opposite ends of a spectrum. In the first, hierarchy prevails; in the second, the national and state governments are equal and autonomous. The past, present, or future applicability of either model for IGR in the United States has been sharply challenged. Although there are occasional instances of such hierarchical and autonomous IGR patterns, the weight of academic research suggests that these two models inadequately and inaccurately describe how the bulk of governmental operations are conducted in the United States.

The third and most representative model of IGR practice is the overlapping-authority model (see figure [1]). The overlay among the circles conveys three characteristic features of the model:

1. Substantial areas of governmental operations involve national, state, and local units (or officials) simultaneously.
2. The areas of autonomy or single-jurisdiction independence and full discretion are comparatively small.
3. The power and influence available to any one jurisdiction (or official) is significantly limited. The limits produce an authority pattern best described as bargaining.

Bargaining is used in the common dictionary sense of "negotiating the terms of a sale, exchange, or agreement. Wide areas of IGR involve exchanges or agreements. For example, the national government offers scores of assistance programs to states and localities in *exchange* for their *agreement* to implement a program, carry out a project, or pursue any one of a wide variety of activities. Of course, as part of the bargain the recipient of assistance must usually agree to conditions such as the providing of matching funds and the satisfaction of accounting, reporting, auditing, and performance requirements.

[Wright then presents several illustrations of bargaining and exchange in intergovernmental relations. These are "aimed at illustrating several of the combinations and permutations of interjurisdictional connections": city annexation of county territory in Virginia, an example of local-local mediation; the use of the negotiated investment strategy to allocate more than $30 million in Social Service Block Grant funds in Connecticut, a case of state-local interaction; the Annual Arrangements and the Urban Development Action Grants processes used by the U.S. Department of Housing and Urban Development in the early 1970s and the mid 1980s, respectively, instances of local-national bargaining; and the first-term Reagan administration's unsuccessful effort to achieve "decongestion," or a sorting out of functional responsibilities by level of government, a case of national-state relations.—Ed.]

The prospects as well as the problems involving intergovernmental change seem sharply and clearly exposed when looked at from a bargaining-negotiation standpoint. It is as if we are looking at fundamental cell structures, like the DNA double helix, under a microscope when we look at IGR from the perspective of this model. A recent book, *Successful Negotiating in Local Government*, captured the essence of this approach to IGR.

> Past efforts to reform the intergovernmental system have been repeatedly hampered by the reformer's inability to appreciate the fact that while there is cooperation within the system, there is also competition, conflict, and even coercion among the various governmental levels. And while negotiations among government agencies are not uncommon, parties often come to and leave the negotiations with very different objectives. Thus, there is an obvious need for a process that facilitates recognition of the complex nature of intergovernmental relations and allows for developing a core of common objectives.[22]

It is appropriate in drawing this discussion to a close to highlight the chief characteristics of the overlapping-authority model. These are:

- limited and dispersed power
- modest and uncertain areas of autonomy
- high degree of potential or actual interdependence
- simultaneous competition and cooperation

- bargaining-exchange relationships
- negotiation as a strategy for reaching agreement

The analysis and interpretation of the overlapping-authority model, as approached here, have a clear bias in the direction of cooperation and negotiated settlement. An alternative overlapping-authority model could also be applied from a competitive, quasi-market, public-choice approach. That is, the presence of multiple entities (and actors) operating as providers (and consumers) of public services could function more like an economic market as the basis for exchange relationships.

Numerous examples of market-type models could be cited. Only a generalized description of one approach is provided. An early (1961) formulation of this line of analysis was by Ostrom, Tiebout, and Warren; they argued that metropolitan areas, such as Los Angeles, were polycentric political systems.[23] The production and provision of public goods could be viewed as public service industries in which different cities, counties, and special districts (as well as the state and national governments) offered different "packages" of service levels to citizen-consumers. This public-choice view of the overlapping model was further elaborated by Bish and Ostrom.[24] One paragraph from their analysis captures the themes of this alternative interpretation of the overlapping model.

> Intergovernmental relationships are especially important in a public economy composed of a multiplicity of overlapping governmental jurisdictions. Tax competition and coordination, fiscal transfers, and service contracts can facilitate mutually productive intergovernmental cooperation. Courts, legislatures, and informal arrangements are also available for the resolution of intergovernmental conflicts. Multiple agencies serving the same people with different bundles of public goods and services can be viewed as multiple firms in *public service industries.* Constrained competition between multiple "firms" operating in different public service industries can create relatively efficient and responsive systems of government in metropolitan areas.[25]

There is a major difference between the negotiated-agreement approach to the overlapping model and this latter, public-choice approach. The difference centers on the degree to which there is, can be, and should be a common interest served in spite of the conflicting and even chaotic character of IGR conditions. The public-choice approach is much less inclined to see, expect, and promote a basic aim or shared aims in an IGR situation.

Notes

1. The models discussed in this section have been used in two sharply contrasting investigations. One deals with the perceptions of state legislators about responsibilities for various functions: Robert D. Thomas, "Florida Legislator Attitudes toward Inter-Jurisdictional Policy Responsibilities," *Publius: The Journal of Federalism* 9 (Summer 1979): 119-33. The second uses the models to examine the changing nature of authority patterns within the Democratic and Republican parties: Gary D. Wekkin, "Political Parties and Intergovernmental Relations in 1984: The Consequences of Party Renewal for Territorial Constituencies," *Publius: The Journal of Federalism* 15 (Summer 1985): 19-38. For a contrasting urban-focused policy approach to intergovernmental policy implementation, see Paul E. Peterson, *City Limits* (Chicago: University of Chicago Press, 1981), 268 pp.

2. *City of Clinton v. Cedar Rapids and Missouri River Railroad,* 24 Iowa 455 (1868). For a recent analysis of Dillon's Rule from a policy orientation, see John G. Grumm and Russell D. Murphy, "Dillon's Rule Reconsidered," *The Annals* 416 (November 1974): 120-32.

3. *Tarbel's Case,* 13 Wall. 397 (1872).

4. John R. Schmidhauser, *The Supreme Court as Final Arbiter in Federal-State Relations, 1789-1957* (Chapel Hill: University of North Carolina Press, 1958).

5. [Morton] Grodzins, *The American System: A New View of Governments in the United States,* Daniel J. Elazar, ed. (Chicago: Rand McNally, 1966); Elazar, *The American Partnership: Intergovernmental Cooperation in the Nineteenth-Century United States* (Chicago: University of Chicago Press, 1962).

6. *National League of Cities v. Usery,* 426 U.S. 833 (1976), at 845. See also *Wall Street Journal,* 25 June 1976, p. 1.

7. 426 U.S. 852.

8. 469 U.S. 546 (1985).

9. Ibid., at 552.

10. Ibid., at 560, 567.

11. Ibid., at 580.

12. Joseph Clark, "Toward National Federalism," in *The Federal Government and the Cities: A Symposium* (Washington, D.C.: George Washington University, 1961), pp. 39-49.

13. James L. Sundquist, with David W. Davis, *Making Federalism Work* (Washington, D.C.: Brookings Institution, 1969).

14. C. Wright Mills, *The Power Elite* (New York: Oxford University Press, 1956); G. William Domhoff, *Who Rules America?* (Englewood Cliffs, N.J.: Prentice-Hall, 1967); G. William Domhoff, *The Higher Circles: The Governing Class in America* (New York: Random House, Vintage, 1970).

15. Thomas R. Dye, *Who's Running America? The Conservative Years,* 4th ed. (Englewood Cliffs, N.J.: Prentice-Hall, 1986).

16. Grant McConnell, *Private Power and American Democracy* (New York: Knopf, 1966), especially pp. 166-95; Theodore J. Lowi, *The End of Liberalism: Ideology, Policy, and the Crisis of Public Authority* (New York: Norton, 1969).
17. Arthur S. Miller, "The Constitutional Law of the 'Security State'," *Stanford Law Review* 10 (July 1958): 620, 629, 634, 637 (footnotes omitted). Copyright 1958 by the Board of Trustees of the Leland Stanford Junior University.
18. Leonard D. White, *The States and the Nation* (Baton Rouge: Louisiana State University Press, 1963), p. 3.
19. Miller, "The Constitutional Law of the 'Security State'," p. 629.
20. William Anderson, *The Nation and the States, Rivals or Partners?* (Minneapolis: University of Minnesota Press, 1955), p. 204.
21. Frederick Lundberg, *The Coming World Transformation* (Garden City, N.Y.: Doubleday, 1963), p. 18.
22. Christine Carlson, "Negotiated Investment Strategy: Mediating Intergovernmental Conflict," in *Successful Negotiating in Local Government, National Forum: The Phi Kappa Phi Journal* 63, no. 4 (Fall 1983), 28-29.
23. Vincent Ostrom, Charles M. Tiebout, and Robert Warren, "The Organization of Government in Metropolitan Areas: A Theoretical Inquiry," *American Political Science Review* 55 (December 1961): 831-42. See also Robert Warren, "A Municipal Services Model of Metropolitan Organization," *American Institute of Planners Journal* 30 (August 1964): 193-204.
24. Robert L. Bish and Vincent Ostrom, *Understanding Urban Government: Metropolitan Reform Reconsidered* (Washington, D.C.: American Enterprise Institute, 1973), 111 pp.
25. Ibid., pp. 1-2.

7. FEDERALISM

William H. Riker

... Much of the discussion of federalism, like the discussion of all institutions, is moral evaluation. More accurately, it is straightforward ideology in the sense that it is the justification of the advantage of some advantaged interest. Sometimes the moral evaluation or ideology masquerades as science, though of course its nonscientific character is fairly evident, even to the common reader. . . . [As] a guide to the reader through that intellectual morass, I offer a brief survey of the ideological issues.

The Beneficiaries of Federalism

Who benefits from federalism? This is the first question one must answer before one can understand the ideology. By its nature, ideology is the justification of an interest served by an institution. To understand an ideology, therefore, it is first necessary to understand who the beneficiary of the institution is. But the identification of who benefits is not easy, largely because the beneficiaries vary over time.

When federations are relatively new, the practical issue in their politics is: Shall the federal system continue to exist or shall it be broken up into the constituent units? When that is the issue, then it is readily apparent that the beneficiaries of the continued existence of the system are those who wanted federalism in the first place. I have earlier argued that those who want it are those who are especially conscious of the need for defense against either external or internal enemies or those who would use the big government of federalism for aggression. For convenience let us call these military beneficiaries "nationalists."

Nationalists are by definition those who put military and police security at the top of their priority list of political goals. Their opponents—for convenience, call them "antinationalists," for they are

From "Federalism," in Fred I. Greenstein and Nelson W. Polsby, eds., *Handbook of Political Science, Volume 5: Governmental Institutions and Processes* (Reading, Mass.: Addison-Wesley, © 1975), 151-159 (portions only). Reprinted with permission.

not necessarily localists—are those who are less concerned about military security and more concerned about other goals such as questions of the distribution of wealth or religious, linguistic, or racial equality.

For example, in the early history of the United States the Federalists were those who first of all wanted to put their house in order against the possible reopening of the war—it was on that basis that Washington could bring together two nationalist politicians like Hamilton and Jefferson whose secondary goals were so diverse. The Antifederalists, on the other hand, were those who were so especially concerned about political democracy and questions of distribution that they were willing to chance weakness in war to achieve these other goals. . . .

Given this division of politics, at the beginning of a federation, into nationalist and antinationalist impulses, one can say that the initial beneficiaries of federalism are the nationalists, whatever and however contradictory their secondary goals may be.

But the initial circumstances of a federalism do not last forever. In the shifting scene of alliance, both domestic and international, politics make strange bedfellows. Former enemies become friends and former friends become enemies. And these circumstances change the nature of political problems and lead people to reorder their priorities, just as within a couple of years after 1789 Jeffersonians began to become very like the original Antifederalists. On a longer time scale, the circumstances that call forth the original nationalist impulse can even reverse themselves. Thus the United States was formed to fight Great Britain, but in the second century of the American Union it fought two gigantic wars to save England from its political and military mistakes.

With the change in issues, the continued existence of the federation becomes an accepted political premise. It is, of course, possible that the question of existence be reopened, as it was in the United States in 1860 or as it has been recently in Canada or Nigeria. But, aside from such reopening, in mature federations the political issue is no longer whether or not the nation will continue to exist. Rather, political issues are the ordinary nonfederal issues that characterize the politics of any nation: questions of distribution, group influence, racial and religious and linguistic differences, economic policy, etc.

And when these ordinary questions dominate politics, who benefits from federalism then? The answer is, of course, that various minorities benefit. The fact that two levels of government are able to make policy on the same subjects . . . means that the government at one level need not behave the same as the government at another level. If they do behave the same way, then the minority that makes a different policy in a province or state would not be able to make that policy. Federalism permits, indeed guarantees, that there will be some subjects on which policy is made locally. Hence it guarantees also the possibility that such policy may differ from national policy. And if it does, then a minority benefits. . . .

So the question of who benefits from federalism varies with the degree of nationalism and the internal political structure of the federal system. When there is barely enough nationalism to keep the federation going, then the beneficiaries are nationalists, who of course may be of almost any ideological hue. Thus, the victors in the American Civil War contained radical abolitionists and economic conservatives. Or, in Canada, now that the issue of continued existence has been raised to the central position in politics, the beneficiaries of federalism are the English-speaking Canadians and those French-speaking ones who are opposed to a free Quebec. When, however, national feeling is sufficiently strong to guarantee the continued life of the federalism, then the beneficiaries are those who can use constituent governments to enforce minority policies.

Just who these minorities are varies with the political structure of the federalism. . . .

United States. The United States became sufficiently centralized after the Civil War that the issue of continued existence was no longer raised. In the subsequent century the main beneficiaries of federalism have undoubtedly been southern whites, who could use their power to control state governments to make policy on blacks that negated the national policy. It is possible also that business interests used federalism to evade regulation in the era from 1890 to 1935. . . , although it is not clear that a national intention to regulate business in that period ever existed. Clearly, however, in the United States, the main effect of federalism since the Civil War has been to perpetuate racism. Now that race has become a national issue, however, state governments can no longer make policy on race and federalism is irrelevant to racial issues. For the moment the chief significance of federalism in the United States seems to be the protection of some business interests against the juggernaut of the "liberal" bureaucracy in Washington.

. . . One could go on through a list of all well-established federations, but the amount learned would hardly justify the space taken. It is sufficient to conclude with the observation that in every federation there are identifiable beneficiaries and that one can begin to understand the ideology of federalism by identifying these beneficiaries.

It is important to note, however, just what the beneficiaries of a mature federalism get. Since, as I have already shown, the constitutional and administrative features of federalism are accidental rather than essential, it should follow that these do not make a profound difference in political life. And this is indeed the case. Nothing happens in a federation because of the federal constitutional arrangements that could not happen otherwise in fundamentally the same way. One can never blame federalism for a political outcome, for outcomes are the consequences of the preferences of the population. One can only blame federalism for facilitating an emphasis in popular preference. Thus one does not blame an unlocked window for a burglary; the culprit is the burglar. The role of the unlocked window is simply to facilitate entry. So it is with federalism. Federalism itself was never the culprit in American racism, for the real cause of racist behavior is the preferences of whites. All that federalism ever did was to facilitate the expression of racist beliefs and the perpetuation of racist acts. As long as whites strongly prefer racist institutions, one can expect institutions to be racist regardless of whether the country is federal or unitary. But when the preference for racist institutions weakens, then federalism helps racism by rendering difficult the enforcement of an antiracist policy on the minority of white racists. So we can say that the beneficiaries of federalism get only marginal benefits on policy, but marginal or not, they are undoubtedly real.

The Ideology of Federalism

The ideologists of federalism do not, of course, utter arguments justifying the benefits that accrue to these beneficiaries. To do so would be to admit that not everyone gets something out of the institution of federalism. Yet it is the nature of ideology to be a claim of universal benefit ... the ideology of federalism consists of a claim that everyone gets such and such a benefit from it. Since we know, however, from the examination of beneficiaries just completed, that in fact some people, often a majority, do not benefit at all, it is easy enough to spot an ideology, because it is presented as a claim that everybody gets something good from the institutions of federalism. Let us look at some of these claims.

1. *That federalism promotes democratic polity.* It should be abundantly clear, just from looking at the list of federal governments, that not all of them are democracies or even pretend to be democracies, although their claim to be federations is indisputable. Mexico is one example, Yugoslavia is another. Nigeria was a third, before its civil war. To find an association between federalism and democracy is, on the face of it, absurd. ... A particularly extreme form of this ideological claim is the argument that the process of federalism, by providing opposition, leads to pluralism. ... But there does not seem to be much

pluralism in the Soviet Union. [This was written before the upheavals in Yugoslavia and the Soviet Union.—Ed.]

2. *That federalism promotes democracy by promoting an interest in state government.* ". . . local government is more responsive to public opinion and more responsible to the people" *(Federalism as a Democratic Process,* 1942, p. 82) is a typical form of this argument, which has been repeated ad nauseam in the ideological literature. Fortunately, this particular claim is subject to direct investigation. One question is whether or not state governments actually are responsive to democratic control. The recent series of studies initiated by Dawson and Robinson (1963) and brought to a considerable conclusion by Dye (1966) and reviewed by Jacob and Lipsky (1968) generally support the proposition that state governments are more influenced in their actions by the state of their economies than by the demands of their citizens (for a different view see Samberg, 1971). Regardless of the apparent lack of responsiveness of the states, which may be an artifact of measurement, it is clearly the case that governments cannot be democratically controlled if citizens know less and care less about state governments than about any other kind: national, local, or international. Jennings and Ziegler (1970) have shown on the basis of survey research that citizens simply do not follow state politics very well. And when people do not know what a government is doing, they cannot hold it responsible. And if they cannot hold it responsible, it can hardly be particularly democratic, especially by comparison with national and local governments, which are more visible.

In general, one would expect that the greatest interest of the citizens would be centered on that level of government that does the most important things. Thus, in a centralized federation one would expect interest to center on the national government, while in a peripheralized federation one would expect the interest to focus on the constituent governments. The evidence from the United States is thus what one would expect from a centralized federalism. Owing to the paucity in the contemporary world of peripheralized federalisms it is difficult to determine if states are more salient in them than is the central government. Perhaps Nigeria before the Biafran revolt is a case of truly peripheralized federation, however. If so, the fact that the main political leaders there preferred state to national office suggests that the states were more salient. . . .

3. *That federalism maintains individual freedom.* This is by far the most popular of the ideological arguments in favor of federalism. . . . Freedom is the right to make rules as one chooses. Rules in turn impose constraints on all those who would not by preference have made exactly those rules. We speak of the person who is constrained by

rules as one who has an external cost imposed on him or her. The ideal of freedom is then to minimize the external costs suffered by some person in the society. In an aristocratic society one minimizes the external costs of the well-born; but in the equalitarian society of today, presumably one minimizes the external costs of some representative citizen chosen at random from the whole. The best way to minimize costs for such a citizen is to have policy made by the largest relevant unit of government. For all issues of national concern, then, maximum freedom is attained when policy is made nationally. Conversely, for all issues of local concern, maximum freedom is attained when policy is made locally. . . . Federalism interferes with making policy on national issues nationally. But the converse is not true: nonfederal governments do not necessarily interfere with local policymaking on local issues. Federalism is thus a real barrier to good distribution of the authority to make policy. States' rights guarantee minority governing on national issues, if the minority differs from the majority in significant ways. That is, federalism permits minorities to impose very high external costs on the majority. Thus, for example, in the United States, states' rights from 1890 to 1960 meant that the southern states could develop a tyrannical government that created several generations of poor and uneducated blacks whose maintenance was a charge on the rest of the nation. All this to satisfy the preferences of southern white racists.

In Tarlton (1965), it is argued that federalism works better when the constituent units are alike, "symmetric" is Tarlton's word. The reason for this is that states' rights in an asymmetrical system impose high external costs on national majorities. In general, therefore, in any federal system, but especially in asymmetrical ones like the United States, federalism weakens freedom. So the claim of the ideologists of federalism that the system strengthens freedom is thus false. Indeed federalism . . . weakens freedom. . . .

Moral Evaluation of Federalism

It has so far been shown that the beneficiaries of centralized federalism are those minorities that are permitted to make policy locally on national issues. The contrary assertions of ideologists, that everybody benefits, have been shown to be false. But to show that minorities benefit does not settle the question of moral evaluation. Even if federalism typically hurts a majority, it may well be that a majority might decide to maintain it, especially if the hurt is only marginal.

There are at least two reasons why a majority harmed by federalism might decide to keep it. One reason is that the costs it imposes are relatively low. If, whenever a majority is strongly in favor of a policy, states' rights are overridden, then federalism is only a minor cost on the majority. This well may be the situation in the United States, where in the last generation or so racist states' rights have been fairly consistently denied by a not-very-determined majority in favor of a single national policy on civil liberties. If states' rights can be maintained only when the majority doesn't much care, then the costs of federalism, while greater than the costs of other kinds of government, are not relatively great. In short, then, nations may choose to remain federal simply because federalism doesn't mean very much one way or another. If this is so, then one might well make the moral judgment that federalism is not worth bothering about.

Another reason for keeping a harmful federation is that it might cost too much to get rid of it. To have federalism may be more costly than not having it; yet getting rid of federalism may still be more costly than keeping it. That is, in descending order of cost, the following alternatives may exist for a nation with federal government:

1. dissolving the federation
2. changing (by, e.g., civil war) to a unitary government
3. maintaining the federation
4. maintaining a unitary government.

In such case the *status quo* is preferred, not out of any absolute moral judgment, but out of an instrumental judgment that it is the least expensive of immediate alternatives.

Both these reasons seem to be important in the evaluation of centralized federal governments today. In a federation like Australia the institutions are a minor nuisance and hence not very costly. In a federation like Canada, which may be becoming peripheralized, the costs of transforming to a unitary government may be so great that no one has seriously considered doing so for a generation. In the case of the United States, probably both judgments are relevant.

Both these judgments on federalism are a way of saying that it is not very significant as an institution. Whether or not this statement is factually correct seems to me the most important subject for research on federalism. It would indeed be interesting to know if so much concern for moral evaluation has been wasted on an institution that does not have much effect on political life. . . .

References

Dawson, Richard, and James Robinson (1963). "Inter-party competition, economic variables, and welfare policies in the American states." *Journal of Politics* 25:265-89.

Dye, Thomas (1966). *Politics, Economics, and the Public: Policy Outcomes in the American States*. Chicago: Rand McNally.

Federalism as a Democratic Process: Essays by Roscoe Pound, Charles H. McIlwain, Roy F. Nichols (1942). New Brunswick, N.J.: Rutgers University Press.

Jacob, Herbert, and Michael Lipsky (1968). "Outputs, structures, and power: an assessment of changes in the study of state and local politics." *Journal of Politics* 30:510-38.

Jennings, M. Kent, and Harmon Ziegler (1970). "The salience of American state politics." *American Political Science Review* 64:523-35.

Samberg, Robert (1971). "Conceptualization and measurement of political system output." Ph.D. dissertation, University of Rochester.

Tarlton, Charles D. (1965). "Symmetry and asymmetry as elements of federalism: a theoretical speculation." *Journal of Politics* 27:861-74.

8. A NOTE ON IDEOLOGY

William H. Riker

... This collection of chapters [comprising a set of Riker's essays on American federalism] spans more than thirty years. It would be strange indeed if, during that entire time, I had maintained exactly the same ideological stance. And ... I have not.

In the half-century after the first world war the world was flooded with statist confidence in the beneficence of powerful government, e.g., communism, fascism, welfare statism, peronism, etc., which in the United States took the form of, first, the New Deal, and, later, the "great society." In the last two decades, however, disillusionment with big government has set in, with a revival of nineteenth-century liberal values, or at least with a recognition that government is as likely to be a force for evil as for good. My own ideological migrations have been much in spirit with the age: from New Dealer in the fifties to liberal antistatist in the eighties.

These ideologies have quite different implications for federalism: the statism of the New Deal implies that the national government should be unfettered. Since federalism restrains the national government by setting the scene for conflicts between the states and the nation, the appropriate stance for a New Dealer is to seek to eliminate federalism. On the other hand, the liberal goal of protecting rights from governmental attack justifies restraints like federalism and separation of powers that occasion intergovernmental and interbranch deadlocks.

Given my ideological shift, I have also changed my evaluation of federalism. Initially I regarded it as an impediment—minor, perhaps—but still an impediment to good government. Now I regard it as a desirable, though still minor, restraint on the leviathan. (Of course, however, I have always regarded it as a necessary condition of nationhood in 1787 and hence a feature that must, as a practical matter, be accepted with the Constitution as a whole.)

From William H. Riker, *The Development of American Federalism* (Boston: Kluwer Academic Publishers, 1987), preface.

The variation in my ideological judgment has been reinforced by a fundamental change—during the 1960s—in the political significance of federalism. Prior to that time, the moral meaning of federalism was ambiguous. It was liberal as a restraint on statism. But it was profoundly illiberal because the main local value it protected was, initially, slavery, and, later, legal disabilities for blacks. Thus liberals might oppose federalism on racial grounds (like the Radical Republicans from the 1850s to the 1880s) or favor it on politico-economic grounds (like the Supreme Court that, partially in the name of federalism, struck down the most extreme statism of the New Deal). Conversely, statists might oppose federalism on politico-economic grounds (like the original New Dealers who formed national cartels) or favor it on racial grounds (like the southerners who composed a good third of the New Deal coalition).

The civil rights reforms of the 1960s removed this ambiguity by eliminating the protection for local repression. With the racial dimension of judgment thus removed, it became possible, for the first time in American history, to value federalism unambiguously as a deterrent to statism, a deterrent that liberals could readily support and that statists might believe restrictive and unpleasant.

This political clarification, of course, helped me to reverse my ideological judgment. But ... my description of federalism and of its historical variations remains pretty much the same, despite shifts in ideology. So the description itself is consistent—a practical refutation, I believe, of the claim by opponents of social science that moral premises preclude useful generalization.

Part I

REVIEW QUESTIONS

1. What did the founders of the American system mean by such key concepts as republican government, federalism, and nation? How did they link these ideas together? How has the meaning of federalism altered over time in the United States?

2. Discussions of American intergovernmental relations frequently include a discussion of federalism. Compare and contrast the two notions of intergovernmental relations and federalism.

3. For the founders, even the office of the U.S. presidency represented an arrangement meant to ensure vitality for both national and state governments. Explain how this could be the case. Identify other institutions in the structure of the national government that were designed by the founders to perform similar functions. Do you believe they do so today? Why or why not? (Take note of the discussions by both Diamond and Riker in this regard.)

4. Basic decisions made in the early years of the nation created substantial ambiguity and opportunities for increased intergovernmental interdependence in later years. Bearing this in mind, explain how Madison's position in his argument with Sherman (summarized in Diamond's essay) could be used to justify substantial expansion of national authority on such policy matters as civil rights.

5. Imagine a debate between Elazar (or Grodzins) and Scheiber on American intergovernmental cooperation and conflict. What would be the major points of agreement and disagreement? Which arguments would be more convincing to you?

6. A friend of yours asserts that history is irrelevant to contemporary events, that it doesn't matter what the founders thought or planned, and that it is a waste of time to try to determine what forms of

intergovernmental arrangements were most prominent in earlier times. Can you rebut these claims? (Take special note of Scheiber's discussion here.)

7. Grodzins's essay is properly treated as a classic, but even in 1960 some of his assertions were controversial. It is clear, for instance, that he is far from neutral toward the system he examines. Is his positive evaluation warranted? What problems can you see with the "easy merging of public and private interests at the local level"?

8. When Grodzins wrote more than thirty years ago, a dissenting footnote was appended to his essay by two other intergovernmental analysts, John A. Perkins and Emmette S. Redford. They argued, in part, that

> the present system of shared responsibility confuses rather than fixes responsibility. Ascertainable responsibility for policy, administrative performance, and financing is an essential feature of effective self-government. The possibility of achieving it needs to be explored. . . . The chaos of party processes itself impairs leadership for national functions and national aims. Mr. Grodzins's conclusion that the costs of this chaos are tolerable may be drawn too easily.[1]

Looking back on developments in the intergovernmental system during the last three decades (the introductory chapter in this volume may give you some ideas), do you find that these criticisms have been substantiated? Why or why not? (It may be a good idea to review this question again after you have completed readings in later sections of this book.)

9. Consider Grodzins's essay in the light of modern political realities. Do you think that today's increasingly *nationally* based party institutions, organized around such activities as fundraising and widespread use of the electronic media, weaken the political hold of federalism? Do parties today seem to encourage or discourage "leadership for national functions and national aims," a goal desired by Perkins and Redford (see the quotation excerpted in question 8)?

10. Which model does Wright identify as the most useful for explaining today's intergovernmental relations? Is his case persuasive? In what ways is this model consistent with the historical descriptions

of Elazar and Grodzins? Of Scheiber? Of the introductory chapter of this book?

11. Given the cutbacks in federal aid that have occurred since the late 1970s, do you think that there has been a corresponding shift in the most appropriate model (from Wright's analysis) for describing the intergovernmental system? In some policy fields, at least?

12. How and why does Riker link American federalism with racism? with business interests? How does he see the connection with racism changing during recent decades? How do you see political ideology related to people's support for or distrust of federalism as a structure of government?

13. Could or should the United States consider abolishing the system of federalism? What, if any, would be the costs of abolishing it? Would such a change be likely to affect the practice of intergovernmental relations in this country? Why or why not?

Note

1. *Goals for Americans* (Englewood Cliffs, N.J.: Prentice-Hall, Inc., 1960), 282.

Part II

POLITICAL ASPECTS OF
INTERGOVERNMENTAL RELATIONS

The American intergovernmental network is fundamentally a *political* system, or a complex of such systems. As the readings in Part I have suggested, the structure was designed to establish opportunities for different government units representing differing interests to stake out positions and exercise influence while also seeking accommodation with one another. Part II focuses on the question of how that influence is distributed and used. The readings in the following pages examine political aspects of intergovernmental relations; however, as many of the essays make clear, any attempt to analyze separately the political, fiscal, and administrative aspects of the current functioning of the system must be somewhat artificial. Politics and administration are inextricably linked and financial resources are cause and effect of events in both spheres. Nonetheless, these three categories do help to organize some of the basic perspectives and issues of importance for the system.

A comprehensive study of the political aspects of American intergovernmental relations must analyze the roles, behavior, and interconnections of a long list of actors who can substantially influence intergovernmental decisions. This complexity, after all, is one of the hallmarks of the intergovernmental pattern.

Among those likely to be politically important in the system are, of course, the major national governmental institutions: the presidency, the Congress, and the federal court system. In addition, as the opening chapter of this volume indicated, the national bureaucracy is often an especially significant participant. Also important are public interest groups (PIGs), whether centered on function or representing state and local governments or general-purpose public officials. Political parties can exert their effects on intergovernmental decisions, as can more specialized advisory bodies such as the Advisory Commission on Intergovernmental Relations. The national executive, legislature, courts, bureaucracy, interest groups, and parties all have their counterparts at the state level. And here there are numberless institutions and political organizations operating among the various types of local governments. City and county executives and other locally powerful interests are *very* active in intergovernmental politics. Furthermore, an array of coordinating bodies—councils of government, regional planning bodies, and functionally specific interlocal units (for example, those assisting in transportation planning)—exchange information and sometimes affect policy directly.

Because the participants in intergovernmental politics are too numerous and their relationships too complex to be covered in depth here, Part II offers an overview, organized into three related yet distinct kinds of readings.

The first two excerpts concentrate not on specific intergovernmental actors and their political relations per se but rather on important features of the context within which politics develop in the system: public opinion, plus the diversity of governmental structures in the system and the implications stemming from the involvement of many different kinds of governments. These two readings suggest that diversity is likely to be a hallmark of the system and influence the development of politics.

The first piece (no. 9), which is excerpted from a study conducted by the U.S. Advisory Commission on Intergovernmental Relations (ACIR), indicates that people harbor widely differing views about the relative efficacy and fairness of various governments and taxing methods. One subject of special note in the ACIR study is the difference between opinions of white and nonwhite Americans on some fundamental aspects of the intergovernmental system. The second (no. 10) is by Robert Reischauer, a researcher who is currently director of the Congressional Budget Office. He presents an interesting and somewhat disturbing analysis of the effects of diversity in the network. He documents specific policy consequences and demonstrates that the formal structure *does* make a difference. He asserts that it is impossible to achieve any coherent goal via an intergovernmental grant without encountering considerable problems as well. Although some of the specific data used by Reischauer in his illustrations would be slightly different now, all his basic points remain valid.

The next six articles examine some of the specific actors in intergovernmental politics. Three of these (nos. 11-13) cover some frequently underexamined institutions or actors in the network: the PIGs and the governors. The fourth (no. 14) examines how these and other actors build themselves into broader coalitions to press their interests and goals in the political realm. Then two additional selections (nos. 15-16) highlight the role and impact of an increasingly important actor: the federal courts.

Donald Haider (no. 11) conducted an extensive empirical study of the PIGs at the time of their emergence in the 1970s. His research centered especially on those units that represent state and local executives, as these organizations sought to influence federal decisions in Washington. Haider generalizes, on the basis of several cases, on the operations and the political strengths and weaknesses of the PIGs. Haider's study is particularly valuable in explaining the different roles these groups have been known to take on various kinds of issues, and in exploring alliances and cleavages among them. Although some of the specific policy issues alluded to by Haider have been resolved or superseded by events, his analysis remains perceptive and useful.

Still, as the introductory essay in this volume indicates, several years of tight budgets at the national level have substantially affected the ability of the PIGs, as well as individual state or local governments, to wield power. Jonathan Walters (no. 12) offers an update to Haider's description of political strategy and tactics among the PIGs. It is clear from his discussion that many of the most important political representatives of state and local government in Washington currently are having to rethink the most appropriate ways by which they can assist their member governments and direct their influence. This example shows how closely related are the fiscal and political aspects of intergovernmental relations.

Thad Beyle (no. 13) describes the role of the governor in the system, especially on the matter of policy innovation. Like other actors who experience the stress of governmental interdependence, the governor feels pressure as someone "in the middle." Given the systemic changes of recent years and the states' newly dynamic efforts to deal with myriad policy issues, governors have become more important than ever. The gubernatorial level in the system may well be the locus for a great deal of policy alteration in the future. This article documents especially well a portion of gubernatorial activity: that devoted to "lateral" innovation, or policy change developing via interstate or regional links rather than through the vertical ties across levels of government.

The selection from Thomas Anton's book-length study of intergovernmental relations and public policy (no. 14) suggests the complexity of the shifting alliances formed when these and other actors seek influence in the system. His analysis shows how widespread, and complicatedly linked, are the beneficiaries clustering around planned or existing programs. Anton demonstrates that political coalitions for intergovernmental programs can be much larger and more heterogeneous than most analysts have realized. His characterization helps to explain in more tangible terms some of the sources of interdependence and complexity discussed in general fashion earlier in this volume.

Two readings in this part of the book are devoted to an infrequently studied but increasingly important channel of indirect political influence. Flawed though the court system may be, the federal judiciary has generally been an institution more receptive than the overtly political branches of government to well-argued claims of disadvantaged (or any other) citizens. George Brown (no. 15) discusses the growing significance of this institutional actor—especially with regard to the grant system—and incidentally highlights the complexity of the multichannel system.

Yet not all judicial influence on the intergovernmental network stems from the importance of the grant system. And ever since the heyday of the ideas of dual federalism, advocates of some degree of state autonomy from federal reach have relied on the courts and their enforcement of the Tenth Amendment to the U.S. Constitution, which would seem to give states primary jurisdiction in any policy field not directly assigned to national authorities. In a most important case decided by the Supreme Court in 1985, the *Garcia* outcome may have altered this balance. Thus, ironically, as states and their local governments have become increasingly important in responding to the policy problems facing the nation, their independent constitutional status seems to have been called into question, at least in the eyes of some observers. A. E. Dick Howard, a leading expert in constitutional law, is one such analyst. Howard's article (no. 16) explains the *Garcia* decision and critiques the Court's reasoning and its implications. Whether or not one agrees with Howard's concerns on this issue, the essay should make clear how important judicial actors can be in helping to determine the most basic political aspects of the system and define the terms of political debate.

Finally, the last pair of readings in Part II focus not on individual actors in intergovernmental politics but on their interrelationships, through which they exercise influence. While intergovernmental theory was one emphasis of Part I, this group of readings also contains profound theoretical insights. In contrast to the political rhetoric suggesting that the national government has usurped all power in the intergovernmental system, the final two selections of Part II offer more careful, restrained, and subtle analyses.

Jeffrey Pressman's study (no. 17) of federal-city relations in Oakland, California, claims that intergovernmental disputes do not always, or even usually, point to inadequate communication and coordination. Rather, it is the structure of the interaction—that is, the roles people fill and the ways they must deal with one another—that generates persistent conflict. This piece is valuable in a number of respects. Pressman summarizes donor and recipient positions, discusses the problems involved in establishing productive bargaining arenas, and convincingly documents some of the ties between politics and administration in intergovernmental relations.

The final reading in this part is an excerpt (no. 18) from Martha Derthick's seminal book-length case study of one grant program as it was implemented in one state. Derthick's research on public assistance in Massachusetts covered decades of the program's operation in great detail. Her analysis touches on the strategies and tactics of many participants in the intergovernmental system. In this selection she sketches the patterns of influence primarily between the federal government and the state and, secondarily, between state and local— and federal and local—governments. Derthick covers the dynamics of intergovernmental influence, including the key roles of the bureaucracies, the limitations on state legislatures, and the possibilities of and limitations on national control as these are exhibited in the modern system. She also raises some intriguing questions about accountability and democratic government. Her analysis is especially valuable since grants continue to be the central mode of intergovernmental ties, despite the recent prominence of alternative forms of intergovernmental influence aside from financial aid. (The emergence of mandates is treated in detail in Part IV of this book.) Understanding how grants serve to persuade actors in the system, therefore, remains of the utmost importance.

In general, then, the essays in Part II discuss intergovernmental politics as the interaction of citizens, principal actors and their coalitions, and institutions. In these excerpts several features of American intergovernmental relations are illuminated: important details of interdependence and complexity, the scope of intergovernmental bargaining processes, some broadly systemic tendencies, and at least a few normative implications of today's intergovernmental politics.

9. PUBLIC ATTITUDES ON
GOVERNMENT AND TAXES

U.S. Advisory Commission on Intergovernmental Relations

This is the 19th annual public opinion survey commissioned by the Advisory Commission on Intergovernmental Relations (ACIR). . . .

From 1972 to 1989, ACIR asked citizens to choose the tax they considered to be the worst, that is, the least fair, from among the federal income tax, state income tax, state sales tax, and local property tax. . . . From 1972 to 1978, the local property tax was cited as the worst tax five times. From 1979 to 1988, respondents consistently rated the federal income tax as the worst tax. In 1989 the local property tax was selected as the worst tax—by 32 percent, up from 28 percent—and the percentage of respondents choosing the federal income tax dropped from 33 to 27.

In 1988, ACIR also introduced a modified version of this question, adding the Social Security tax as a response. . . . Including Social Security, 26 percent chose the federal income tax as worst in 1988, and 21 percent chose it in 1989. . . . To date, the inclusion of the Social Security tax has had no effect on the relative rankings of the other four taxes.

In 1990, using only the question including Social Security, the percentages of respondents who perceive the local property tax and the federal income tax as least fair are about the same: 28 percent for the local property tax and 26 percent for the federal income tax. . . . The proportion of respondents selecting the federal income tax as worst increased from 1989 to 1990 by 5 percent (from 21 to 26 percent). Interestingly, despite the recent increases in the Social Security tax and the attention focused on the Social Security tax burden and fund surplus in early 1990, only 15 percent of the respondents cited this tax as worst (compared to 18 percent in 1989).

Interesting regional variations emerged in the responses to this question. While respondents in three of the four regions (Northeast, North-Central, and South) picked the local property tax as the least

---

From *Changing Public Attitudes on Governments and Taxes 1990* (Washington, D.C.: ACIR, 1992), 3-4, 6-13. Reprinted by permission.

fair, those in the West more frequently chose the federal income tax, by 31 to 18 percent. . . .

Analysis of prior results . . . shows that regional differences in attitudes are more than isolated occurrences, that worst-tax responses fluctuated by region from 1988 through 1990, but tended to maintain their direction. For example, respondents in the northeastern and north-central states have been relatively steadfast in their dislike of the local property tax. Likewise, citizens in the western states have consistently expressed greater dissatisfaction with the federal income tax. Responses in the South, however, shifted after 1988. In that year, southerners identified the federal income tax as the worst; in 1989 and 1990, they chose the local property tax. Additional subgroups in 1990 that believe the federal income tax is the least fair include people making over $40,000 per year (33 percent), and white collar, sales, and clerical workers (32 percent). . . .

Subgroups that feel most negatively toward the local property tax include respondents over age 65 (33 percent), retired people (37 percent), and individuals living in the north-central states (33 percent). The relatively high negative reaction to the local property tax among retired individuals may be attributable to the fact that many retirees live on lower incomes, and their income taxes and Social Security taxes are either nonexistent or markedly lower than when they were working. White collar, sales, and clerical workers are among those least likely to believe the local property tax is worst; only 21 percent of this group identified the property tax as the worst tax. Contrary to the conventional wisdom that homeowners dislike the local property tax more than renters, respondents who own their homes are not markedly more likely than those who rent to view the local property tax as the worst tax (30 and 25 percent, respectively).

Of those choosing the Social Security tax as worst, the subgroups that most often cited that tax as the worst are white collar, sales, and clerical workers (25 percent) and persons aged 25 to 34 (21 percent). Groups that least often cited the Social Security tax as the worst are individuals who did not complete high school (10 percent), unemployed persons (10 percent), and retired persons (10 percent).

From Which Level of Government Do You Feel You Get the Least for Your Money?

ACIR asked this question in 1989 and 1990. It is a variation of a question that has been asked since 1972: "From which level of government do you feel you get the *most* for your money?" The long-term trend in responses to the "most for your money" question has been interesting. . . . From 1972 through 1978, respondents said the federal government gave them the most for their money. This pattern was broken in 1979, the year after funding levels for federal aid programs peaked as a percentage of federal outlays and of state and local revenues. Since that time, respondents have alternately judged the federal and local governments as giving them the most for their money, often with a very small margin separating them.

Changing the wording of this question from "most" to "least" appears to have had a significant effect on the responses. One generally would expect individuals who say that a particular government gives them the most for their money to identify another government as giving them the least. However, in 1989, when both versions of this question were asked, similar pluralities of respondents believed that the federal government gave them the most for their money (33 percent . . .) and the least for their money (36 percent . . .). . . .

The results of the 1990 "least for your money" question suggest increased dissatisfaction with federal taxing and spending policies. This year, a larger plurality (41 percent) responded that the federal government gives them the least for their money than in 1989 (36 percent). . . . Respondents choosing state government remained about the same (26 percent in 1990 and 25 percent in 1989), while 21 percent chose local government, down from 25 percent a year earlier.

Individuals 35 to 44 years old were particularly likely in 1990 to say that the federal government gives them the least for their money (47 percent). . . . Those most likely to say that state government gives them the least for their money were blacks (38 percent) and individuals from the Northeast (33 percent). Those most likely to say that local governments give them the least for their money were people with incomes of $15,000 to $24,999 per year (27 percent).

There was a sharp difference in the responses of blacks and whites to this question. Whites were almost twice as likely to feel that the federal government gives them the least for their money (43 percent of whites to 23 percent of blacks). Blacks, on the other hand, were more likely to respond that their state government gives them the least for their money (38 percent of blacks to 24 percent of whites).

To the Extent That Government May Be Involved, in Which Level of Government Do You Have the Most Trust and Confidence to Handle Each of the Following Problems?

As in 1989, respondents to the 1990 ACIR poll were asked in which government they had the most trust and confidence to handle a variety of problems. . . . This year's set of six problems included foreign and domestic issues.

The responses varied considerably from subject to subject. For example, [survey evidence] reveals that the public most often places its trust and confidence in the federal government to provide services to immigrants and attract foreign investment and trade, and in state government to maintain highways and bridges. Responses were more mixed for the other three problems (health care for the disabled, poor, and elderly; child care; and job training).

Although pluralities of those asked said they trust the federal government most to provide health care for the disabled, poor, and elderly, and state government to provide job training and child care, substantial numbers of respondents selected all three types of government as the one they trust most to handle each of these three problems.

Following is some additional detail about the poll results on these six functions of government.

Services to Immigrants

A majority of citizens polled (60 percent) said they trust the federal government most to provide services to immigrants ..., compared to 15 percent for state government and 6 percent for local government.

In the Northeast, North-Central and South regions, the majority expressed most trust and confidence in the federal government (69 percent, 67 percent, and 57 percent), compared to a substantially lower 49 percent in the West. Fully 25 percent of respondents living in the West indicated the most trust and confidence in state government to handle services to immigrants. Occupationally, 72 percent of professionals, managers, and owners of businesses trust the federal government most to supply these services, as do 56 percent of blue-collar workers and 57 percent of retired persons.

Attraction of Foreign Investment and Trade

Beyond the finding that a majority of respondents (58 percent) has the most trust and confidence in the federal government to handle the attraction of foreign investment and trade, two other findings about this question are interesting. ... First, the majority for the federal government held in every subgroup except one; still, blacks chose the federal government at least three times as often as the other choices. ... Second, the percentage of individuals answering "don't know/no answer" (13 percent) was more than twice as great as those selecting local government (5 percent) and about the same as those designating state government (17 percent). The unusually high proportion of respondents opting for the "don't know" category suggests that the public is not as familiar with or as interested in this issue as in the others.[1]

Health Care for the Disabled, Poor, and Elderly

A plurality expressed the most trust and confidence in the federal government to handle health care for the disabled, poor, and elderly (36 percent), followed by 28 percent for state government. . . . Only 18 percent of those surveyed said they most trust local government.

Subgroup variations in age and region are distinct. The federal government was chosen over state and local governments two to one by individuals over 65 years of age (41 percent to 21 percent and 17 percent, respectively) and by people from the Northeast (47 percent to 22 percent and 18 percent). Westerners chose state government about as frequently as the federal government to provide health care to these groups (34 to 31 percent), and individuals under 35 years of age selected either government equally (35 percent each). Of those choosing local government to provide health care, it did best with individuals in the North-Central region (20 percent) and with those who have attended but not completed college (26 percent). . . .

Child Care

Thirty-four percent of those asked said they trust the state government most to provide child care . . . , and 29 percent chose local government. Only 16 percent selected the federal government for child care (its lowest figure for any of the six problems included this year).

A number of subgroups exhibited sharp variations. For example, those most likely to need child care (respondents under 35 and between 35 and 44 years of age) trusted state government most to provide this service (41 and 35 percent, respectively). Individuals over 65 years of age, on the other hand, said they trust local government most (33 percent).

A plurality of both "total employed" and "employed females" also expressed trust in the state government to provide child care (38 and 36 percent, respectively). In contrast, a plurality of both "total not employed" and "not employed females" chose local government most (32 and 33 percent). Whether employed or unemployed, respondents selected either state or local government more than twice as often as the federal government.

Additionally, . . . a plurality of respondents with children under age 18 expressed most confidence in state government to provide child care (37 percent), while respondents with no children divided fairly equally between state and local government (30 to 32 percent, respectively).

Job Training

More Americans surveyed trust state government to handle job training (37 percent) than the federal or local governments (24 and 23 percent, respectively), with a plurality for state government in every region of the country. . . . Also, respondents from the Northeast were more likely (31 percent) than those from the other three regions to select the federal government over local governments (17 percent).

Given that unemployed individuals are often the intended beneficiaries of government job training programs, their views on this question are of special interest. Similar pluralities of both employed (38 percent) and unemployed (34 percent) said they trust state government most to provide job training. Unemployed respondents, however, were twice as likely as employed respondents to respond "don't know/no answer."

Maintenance of Highways and Bridges

A 57 percent majority expressed the most trust and confidence in state government to handle the maintenance of highways and bridges . . . , compared to only 17 percent for the federal government, and 11 percent for local government. A majority in every category but one said it trusts state government most. Forty-eight percent of blacks chose the state, still a wide plurality over the other choices made by blacks. . . . Those most likely to pick state government were individuals making $40,000 or more (64 percent). Twenty-four percent of college graduates considered the federal government most trustworthy, as did 23 percent of professionals, managers, and owners of businesses, 21 percent of retired workers, and 22 percent of people living in the Northeast. Local government fared best with white-collar, sales, and clerical workers (17 percent) among those choosing local government. The responses to this question were remarkably similar in metropolitan and non-metropolitan areas, as well as in cities and suburbs.

Overall, How Would You Grade the Performance of Each of the Following Governments?

The performance question is new this year. The results indicate moderate satisfaction with all three types of government. [The evidence] shows that a plurality of Americans rated the performance of all three governments as satisfactory, with the state receiving the highest satisfactory score (46 percent), followed closely by local government (45 percent) and the federal government (43 percent).

Thirty-two percent of respondents rated the performance of local government as excellent or good, compared to 29 percent for the federal and state governments. Conversely, 23 percent of the respondents viewed the federal government's performance as unsatisfactory or a failure, compared to 20 percent for state government and 19 percent for local government.

To express the findings another way, each government was assigned a grade-point average (GPA).[2] This calculation was made by considering the "excellent" response an A, the "good" a B, the "satisfactory" a C, the "unsatisfactory" a D, and the "failure" an F, and by assigning each letter grade a numerical value ranging from 4 for an A to 0 for an F. The resulting overall GPA for each government is surprisingly similar: all three receive a C.

This finding is especially interesting following the results of the question asking respondents to identify the government that gives them the least for their money. With 41 percent of the respondents perceiving the federal government as giving them the least for their money, one might expect more respondents to assign it a relatively lower overall performance rating. There is not significant difference in the performance ratings for any of the governments as measured by the grade-point averages.

There were only a few variations by subgroup concerning the performance of the three types of government.... Most interesting, perhaps, is the finding that rural residents (36 percent) were significantly more likely than either urban or suburban residents (25 percent) to rate the federal government as excellent or good.

Overall, How Would You Grade the Ability of the Federal, State, and Local Governments to Cooperate and Work Together Today?

A plurality of respondents believes all three governmental partners are able to cooperate and work together satisfactorily (40 percent for local, and 43 percent each for state and federal ...). Twenty-nine percent of those polled said local government's ability to cooperate and work with the two other governmental partners is excellent or good, followed by state government with 27 percent and the federal government with 24 percent. Consistently, a lower percentage of respondents said that the state or local governments' ability to cooperate is unsatisfactory or a failure (21 percent each). Individuals 18 to 24 years of age were most likely to rate each government's ability to cooperate as excellent or good, and least likely to rate them as unsatisfactory or a failure. . . .

Notes

1. These findings are interesting in light of responses to related questions in earlier polls. The 1988 poll asked respondents if they thought state offices in foreign countries and foreign trips by governors and mayors to promote trade were a good use of public funds. That year, the public expressed mixed feelings on both questions. For the complete test of these questions, responses, and analysis, see *Changing Public Attitudes on Government and Taxes: 1988* (S 17), p. 7. For more information on state and local activity in international affairs, see the Summer 1990 issue of *Intergovernmental Perspective* and the forthcoming ACIR report, *State and Local Roles in Intergovernmental Affairs.*
2. To obtain an overall GPA for each of the governments, the DK/NA category was dropped and the corresponding percentage of respondents was subtracted. Hence, the subsequent GPA is based on an N of 1,108 rather than the overall N of 1,166. Also, the percentage of respondents in each response category was converted to the actual number of respondents and then multiplied by a corresponding value of 4 for an "A," 3 for a "B," 2 for a "C," 1 for a "D," and 0 for an "F." The figures for each government were: 2.25 for local, 2.17 for state, and 2.15 for federal. . . .

10. GOVERNMENTAL DIVERSITY: BANE OF THE GRANTS STRATEGY IN THE UNITED STATES

Robert D. Reischauer

... The tremendous diversity of governmental arrangements in the United States ... is inherent in the structure of American federalism and makes virtually impossible designing, generating support for, and implementing effective domestic grant programs.

Significant Aspects of Government Diversity

In a nation as physically large and populous as the United States, it is not surprising that subnational units of government are faced with very different sorts of problems, public service demands, and costs. It is surprising—but certainly not unique in federal systems—that the institutional arrangements that have evolved for providing public services are so diverse. Six basic types of government are found in the United States: states, counties, municipalities, townships, school districts, and special districts. From the perspective of the federal government, which is forced by Constitutional constraints to operate through existing governmental institutions rather than revise these structures, a number of characteristics of this diversity are important.

First, none of these governmental types is found everywhere in the nation. Residents of the District of Columbia are not served by a state government. County governments do not exist in two states (Rhode Island and Connecticut) and in 102 separate geographic areas in 21 other states. Municipal governments, which typically provide most local public services in closely settled areas, are nonexistent in rural areas as well as in some urban territories where strong county governments prevail. Townships—a type of local government that, like counties but unlike municipalities, exists to serve residents of geographic areas without regard to population concentration—are found throughout only one state (Indiana) and in parts of only 20 others. Separate independent school districts are the exclusive providers of elementary and secondary education in 30 states, do not exist in 5 others, and

From *The Political Economy of Fiscal Federalism,* ed. Wallace E. Oates (Lexington, Mass.: D.C. Heath, 1977), 115-127.

provide education in only parts of the remaining 15. Finally, special district governments, which generally have been created to perform a single governmental function, such as the conservation of natural resources or the provision of fire-protection services, are not found at all in one state (Alaska) and are lacking in parts of all others.

The second aspect of the structure of subnational government that has implications for a federal grants policy is the vast numbers of governments, their difference in scale, and their overlapping nature. . . .

A third, and by far the most important, aspect of this diversity is that the service and fiscal responsibilities imposed on various types of governments differ tremendously both among and within states. The most important state and local public service, elementary and secondary education, illustrates the variation in governments charged with providing a single service. In Hawaii, the state government alone provides elementary and secondary education, while in Maine schooling is provided in some areas by the state and in others by municipalities, townships, or separate school districts. A wide variety of other patterns exists elsewhere. . . . Education is by no means an isolated case. Welfare-related programs are provided in some areas by state governments and in others by counties or by counties and municipalities; within different areas of some states police services are provided by the state, county, municipal, or township government.

The diversity in the provision of services is matched by the diversity of responsibilities for supplying financial support. The existence of large amounts of intergovernmental grants means that often the jurisdiction responsible for providing a particular service is not the one responsible for its fiscal support. For example, elementary and secondary education in both New Hampshire and Alabama is provided exclusively by local governments, but in Alabama less than one-fifth of the costs are borne by local governments, while in New Hampshire nine-tenths of the support is provided by localities. Similarly, welfare (AFDC) [Aid to Families with Dependent Children] checks are written by local governments in both New York and Iowa, yet local governments in New York must provide over one-fourth of the funds needed to cover these checks, while local governments in Iowa must supply less than one-tenth of the funds.

Differences in service and fiscal responsibility translate into differences in the relative importance of the various types of governments. For example, state government is very important in Hawaii, where it is responsible for 89 percent of the state's direct service expenditures and 77 percent of its revenues; in Nebraska, where the similar percentages are 29 and 36, the state is not anywhere near as important a factor. Among local governments, counties are extremely important in North Carolina, where they are responsible for 70 percent of local government spending, but not so in Massachusetts, where 3 percent of such spending is in their hands. Municipalities and townships are responsible for 94 percent of local-government spending in Connecticut, but only 22 percent in Nebraska, for example.

A final critical aspect of the diversity of subnational government structure in the United States is the variation with respect to both the scope of government activity and the instruments used to raise revenues to support public services. No simple accepted view exists of the proper domain of state and local governments. Most, if not all, services provided by these governments are also available privately. In some areas, private vendors are the primary providers of such services as hospitals, fire protection, sanitation, housing, libraries, public transportation, higher education, and utilities (water, gas, and electricity) that elsewhere are supplied exclusively by the government sector. In general, a mixed situation prevails, but the level of services provided publicly varies tremendously. To take some simple examples: welfare payments per recipient vary by over 6 to 1 among the states; California's system of public higher education provides twice as many slots per high school graduate as that of New Jersey; levels of elementary and secondary public-school services—as measured by per pupil spending—vary by a factor of 10 to 1 within nine states and by over 2 to 1 within all but seven.

The revenue sources relied upon by similar types of governments also vary widely. . . .

The Implications of Governmental Diversity

For a nation that has emphasized grants-in-aid as a mechanism for solving domestic problems, the diversity of governmental structure and policy makers' lack of understanding of this diversity have a number of important implications.

First, the federal government is faced with a dilemma in choosing the appropriate governments with which it should interact when it wishes to act on a particular domestic problem area. One option is to deal exclusively with one type of government: states, counties, municipalities, etc. However, this results in certain areas of the nation not being served by the grant program, because the type of government chosen does not exist there.

More serious is the possibility that in some parts of the country the chosen type of government may lack the experience, ability, or even the legal authority to carry out the intent of the grant program. This situation has occurred to some extent in the new manpower (CETA) and community-development block-grant programs that explicitly designate urban county governments as the recipient governments—all urban areas except within the largest cities. In some regions, these counties have had little or no previous experience with manpower or community-development programs. When faced with the new grant, they tend to create a new, and sometimes duplicative, service structure rather than turn the resources over to another type of government that previously was responsible for providing such programs within that particular geographic area.

Another option for the federal government is to deal with whatever government is responsible for the particular service. This approach also has a number of problems. First, a decision must be made as to whether responsibility is to be judged in terms of providing or of financially supporting the service. In many areas, a focus on service delivery would require interaction between the federal government and local governments; an emphasis on financial support would call for the federal government to interact with state authorities. The former might appear to be more logical if the federal government is concerned with augmenting services directed at a certain problem, but it is of course possible for the states to change their own local grant strategy to blunt, if not negate, the impact intended by the federal government. This approach may also have the drawback of requiring the federal government to deal with an extremely diverse group of governments with different legal powers, constraints, and capacities. In many service areas, it may be impossible to design a grant program that would fit the needs and limits of all, or even a majority, of the governments responsible for providing the particular service in each part of the nation. In fact, in some geographic areas duplicate services are provided by overlapping jurisdictions.

Such considerations partially explain the prevalence of "project grants," which require that the governments interested in a program and capable of providing the specified service apply for part of the resources of federal grant programs. This method allows the federal government to deal with the limited number of governments that have the appropriate responsibility, and it avoids the need to know which governments have this authority. Furthermore, the project method allows the grant to be tailored individually to the resources, legal authority, and experience of the applicant government, whether it is a county, municipality, special district, or whatever. While the "project grants" approach may circumvent some problems posed by the diversity of governmental structure, it has been severely criticized in recent years for several reasons: subjective elements can enter into the distribution of resources; a great deal of red tape is necessarily generated; small and unsophisticated jurisdictions have difficulty competing for projects; and the process leaves considerable control in the hands of federal administrators.

A final option for the federal government is to deal only with the states, relying on them to handle any necessary distribution to lower levels of governments. Until recently, this was the strategy followed by most federal grant programs. . . .

This option may circumvent the problems of diversity and be more constitutionally correct, since local governments are creations of the states and not of the national government. But some suspect it is an option that guarantees that the objectives of a grant program will not be achieved. Many domestic problems brought to the Congress for action in recent years revolve around the distribution of income and the provision of public services to persons who have low incomes and/or who live in declining core cities. Generally, the affected local governments are too poor to tackle the problems alone or cannot deal with them because of the open nature of local economies. In many cases, state governments could deal with the problems but are unwilling to do so. In such instances, providing federal aid to the state for distribution to the appropriate local governments may be like asking the fox to guard the chicken coop. . . .

Dissatisfaction with the "project grant" approach and with the option of leaving federal grants in the hands of state governments has led recently to an increased effort to design mechanisms for dealing directly with the local governments that deliver services in the problem area. These efforts have met several obstacles caused by the diversity of governmental structure. First, the sheer numbers of governments involved make even the most simple programs difficult to administer. . . . Grants for a specific purpose—such as education or police protection—to a vast number of governments would probably swamp the bureaucracy with problems, questions, and demands from the recipient governments. A related issue involves program design. If thousands of small, unsophisticated jurisdictions are included as recipients, complex demands cannot be placed on them. Nor, given the diversity of governmental arrangements, can the program be too specific in what it requires recipients to do, because they may not have the power to conform. Even the general revenue-sharing program ran into this difficulty: in Illinois, many recipient townships were not empowered to engage in many of the activities required by the law; they spent as much as they deemed appropriate on services that were legal under the revenue-sharing law and their own charters but found it difficult to spend all the money granted to them.

A second obstacle to dealing directly with local governments is the difficulty in developing reasonable methods for allocating grant funds among their large numbers. The kinds of data needed to develop a sensible distribution formula are often unavailable. Considerable costs would have to be incurred to generate data that would allow the federal government to allocate grant funds to local governments in a way that followed the objectives of most programs. Faced with this situation, the federal government has taken a number of approaches. In some cases, clearly inadequate, but available, data have been used to distribute federal grants. This partially explains the use of population to allocate grants for such purposes as law-enforcement assistance, drug-abuse treatment, and other areas where the "need" or magnitude of the problem is correlated only weakly with population size. In other instances, hopelessly out-of-date information is used. For example, in the early 1970s the major federal grant for elementary and secondary education was being distributed according to data gathered in the 1960 census. A more recent approach has been to reduce the number of eligible jurisdictions to a manageable number for which data are available or can be generated at a reasonable cost. . . . While this solution is reasonable, it threatens to undermine the political coalition supporting some grant programs. Governments cut out of direct participation are less willing to fight for larger appropriations or even continuation of the program because the benefits are uncertain from their perspective.

In recent years, increasing concern has been expressed about interjurisdictional fiscal disparities. Many think that these disparities, as they are manifested in the "urban fiscal crisis," will be one of the major domestic problems of the next decade. Preliminary attempts to resolve this problem have been stymied not only by political forces but also by the difficulties posed by the diversity of government structures. While a general consensus can be reached that the amount of aid received by each government under an equalization program should relate positively to the jurisdiction's needs and inversely to its fiscal capacity, there is little agreement on the operational meaning of these terms in a nation where service responsibilities and revenue instruments vary tremendously from jurisdiction to jurisdiction. If all governments relied on similar sources of revenue, a relatively non-controversial "fiscal capacity index" could be constructed based on a weighted average of the various revenue bases. However, methods of raising revenue are diverse, so such an index necessarily would include revenue sources not used by some jurisdictions either by choice or by lack of legal authority. As a result, federal grant programs have fallen back on the use of per capita income as a crude measure of the relative fiscal capacity of different jurisdictions. In a nation where a relatively small fraction of state and local government revenue is derived directly from income taxes and where states and localities understandably try to export as much of their tax burden as possible, this solution is clearly unsatisfactory. In some local areas, there is no correlation between income and fiscal capacity as measured by revenue sources utilized by the jurisdictions. . . .

The same situation exists with respect to service requirements. Lacking a uniform set of services that are provided by all governments, "needs" have generally been measured by some gross proxy such as population. However, it is clear that the services provided by state and local governments and those which are supported by most grant programs are directed at very specific subgroups of the population—and these are not distributed among jurisdictions in proportion to the general population. . . .

Conclusion

In concluding this discussion, two corollaries of the thesis that the diversity of American governmental structure dooms the grants strategy to failure should be pointed out. The first corollary is that intergovernmental frustration levels tend to rise rather than fall as grant levels increase. From the federal perspective, more is being done to solve a problem when grant levels increase; but, from the standpoint of the recipient jurisdiction and the public at large, the constraints imposed by the government structure may render the programs ineffective. The response of the federal government to the criticism that "things aren't working" is to tighten up the administrative control of the program, then blame the states for mismanagement. This, in turn, increases hostility at the state and local levels. The second corollary is that the federal government will increasingly tend to rely on what is called the *incomes strategy.* Faced with its inability to use grants to solve domestic problems and a reluctance to demand structural changes, national policy makers will tend to design programs in which the federal government deals directly with citizens rather than dealing through intermediary state and local governments. This will reinforce the tendencies toward centralization already apparent in American federalism.

11. THE GOVERNMENT GROUPS IN THE POLICY-MAKING PROCESS

Donald H. Haider

... This chapter goes beyond ... immediate cases to probe the rich variety of tactics and strategies employed by the government groups in influencing government decisions.

General Roles

The government groups confront the usual panoply of external constraints found in the constitutional and political setting of the American federal system. They contend with separation of powers, broad national legislative and appropriative powers, noncentralized governments, interest groups and political parties with their often local bias, and news media focused upon Washington as the center of all things political. They deal with an active court system whose policies have vastly influenced existing relations among government levels. Also, state and local executives, like their federal counterparts, are buffeted by many of the same pressures and forces in their external environment—forces which have significant consequences for government programs and expenditure patterns. Elections, changes in government, and conditions of the national economy affect those inside government as well as those outside, making each susceptible to forces that neither may readily control.

For the government interest groups, their general activities are directed at securing substantial increases in amounts of federal aid made available for distribution by general-purpose governments. Translated into group policy, this means the reduction of federal categorical grants within broad flexible areas (block grants ... and ... revenue sharing) to be returned to states and localities on a regular, incremental basis with minimum restrictions as to use and maximum discretionary control by elected officials, especially chief executives. These objectives are the cause, quite obviously, of considerable friction between chief executives and the alliances between Congress, the

Reprinted with the permission of The Free Press, a Division of Macmillan, Inc., from *When Governments Come to Washington* by Donald H. Haider. Copyright © 1974 by The Free Press.

bureaucracy, and interest groups. Federal executive agencies and bureaus as well as their state-local counterparts view the government interest groups' objective essentially as threats to their jurisdiction over "their" programs. Congressional committees and subcommittees tend to respond with much the same hostility toward loss of influence and control. Most of the program-oriented interest groups surrounding an intergovernmental program also react negatively to these proposed changes. Hence, competition and conflict among these actors is built into their relations.

Each government interest group pursues independently the cultivation of direct federal relations in funding and programmatic support. However, no single government group is self-sufficient in its influence to make decisions or require decisions of others. Every major federal policy involving the groups is consequently the product of mutual accommodation among them. What one group wants is typically desired or held by another, and what all the groups advocate in common is usually what segments of Congress and the bureaucracy have claim upon as well.

In this environment the groups' influence-oriented activities lead them to assume various roles in bargaining for improved position in the intergovernmental decision process. These roles—initiator, facilitator, and obstructor—are not mutually exclusive and often overlap with one another as the groups' strategies and tactics undergo adjustment. Roles are based essentially on expectations of behavior, internally generated and externally imposed. These roles are outgrowths of the groups' institutional and constitutional positions: state and local officials rather than federal; elected, not appointed; generalists as opposed to specialists; and governed by federal-state-local statutes rather than federal exclusively. They also emerge from interorganizational needs, past group experiences, and their relations with other actors in a wide variety of policy areas. Previous outcomes—gains and losses—shape these expectations and strategical choices.

The government interest groups may be the source of new policies and programs. However, diverse constituencies and membership cleavages typically impede them from performing this initiator role, though exceptions are frequent. Membership participation is sustained largely as a consequence of the groups' size and the immediate advantages that accrue from dealing with their federal constituency on this basis. Members pursue immediate payoffs from their activities, leaving to other groups the concern for long-term strategy and future planning. Members have tangible stakes in most policy outcomes, which moderates their activities to an extent and often makes them cautious in their behavior. They are highly protective of previous gains, seeking to expand upon these achievements rather than leap to new programs or policies where outcomes and consequences may be unclear.[1] The groups seek stability in the policy arenas in which they interact, balancing their autonomy as political actors on the one hand with the necessity to form alliances with other claimants on the other. To maintain group consensus, they move deliberately and incrementally, which often prevents them from responding decisively to disruptions in the policy arenas in which they operate.

The groups represent state and local governments as an interest which, in aggregate, means the incorporation of nationwide cleavages and factions within their organizations. Narrow, precise claims, therefore, are often more difficult to generate than broader, more encompassing ones. From a systems perspective the groups provide general demands upon federal actors and institutions. Their initiator and advocacy roles may be diffuse rather than specific. They are protective of the autonomy, fiscal viability, and integrity of the particular level of government they speak for. They are defenders of the interests and prerogatives of political executives. Federal policy makers, on the other hand, perform certain conversion functions by translating group demands into tangible policies and programs. They, too, assume various roles as mediators of group conflict, arbitrators of their differences, brokers for their demands, proponents and opponents of their claims. . . .

. . . another aspect of the groups' advocacy roles [is that] they were united by the common goal, that of greater chief executive control over federal grant programs. . . .

The government interest groups are stimulated into action by public officials as much as they, in turn, stimulate them. The impact of their lobbying effort is generally to reinforce public officials' attitudes and behavior more than to change it.[2] Typically the groups function as facilitators, constantly adapting their agenda and actions in response to stimuli from a well-established network of actors. They seek common grounds for resolution of outstanding differences between them and actors whose assistance they require. The National Association of Counties (NACO) and the National League of Cities (NLC) redirected their activities to the highway program in late 1967, for example, when they expected that the American Association of State Highway Officials' (AASHO's) preliminary report on the future highway program might become a working blueprint for the Federal Highway Administration and the House Public Works Committees. The mayors' most notable legislative achievements in housing are largely attributable to their ability to join with large coalitions which have organized in support of omnibus programs. The United States Conference of

Mayors-National League of Cities (USCM-NLC) assisted Congress in drafting strong air and water pollution programs, and later in ensuring that federal funds were available to aid state and local governments in meeting federal standards. . . .

In a highly complex lobbying network, the relation between lobbyists and policy makers frequently is a transactional one. Who is doing what to whom is often blurred. . . .

Groups' roles, as previously argued, are often structured on a routine basis, largely by outside forces. The legislative pace of Congress also affects group roles and the planning of strategies and tactics. While the groups seek to structure the political environment in which they operate to their immediate advantage, more typically they must respond to the workings of Congress and the executive. The groups' carefully articulated national policies, adopted at their annual meetings, may turn out to be a "shopping list" rather than a concrete agenda for daily action. Each group monitors perhaps twenty or so specific legislative items in an average session, but it gives its top priority to substantially less. On programs coming up for renewal or congressional review, the groups may have ample time to plan lobbying activities. On the other hand, where the pace of legislation quickens or the congressional agenda is abruptly changed, the groups may have inadequate lead time to respond or to build a unified group position.

During the prolific 89th Congress, with its major programs in poverty, rent supplements, Model Cities, education, and the like, congressional committees looked to the government groups for detailed responses. The groups had considerable difficulty reacting to a host of new and controversial items of domestic legislation, which fostered organizational disruptions and often indecisiveness. Organizational leaders and staff may find themselves supportive of new legislation, but commitment of the entire association to policies which have not been fully discussed is another matter. In contrast, the 92nd Congress was distinguished by presidential vetoes over major domestic spending programs passed by Congress. In light of the Nixon administration's budgetary stringency and retrenchment in many domestic areas, Congress called upon the government groups to respond in defending these programs and selecting priorities among them.

The mayors' restraint from an all-out attack on the initial OEO legislation stemmed in a large measure from their own divided membership. Several prominent large-city mayors—Lee, Cavanagh, and Houlihan [their cities were, respectively, New Haven, Connecticut; Detroit, Michigan; and Oakland, California—Ed.]—had served as consultants to the Office of Economic Opportunity (OEO) task force and had actively participated in the Ford Foundation's "Grey Areas" program, the precursor to the federal antipoverty effort. A dozen governors and mayors also had testified favorably before congressional committees in gaining its passage, which neutralized opposition to the program from within their own ranks. The 1966 Model Cities program, with its new towns provisions, supported strongly by the League and opposed by the USCM, sparked divisions within the mayors' ranks, as did the rent supplements program in 1965. The Republican-sponsored block grant amendment to the Elementary and Secondary Education Act of 1967, which would have replaced categorical grants directly to localities with block grants to be administered by the states, placed governors on both sides of the amendment. State and local executives were divided on the issue of removing tax exemptions from industrial aid bonds, eventually opposing removal more out of fear of the precedent it would set than the issue itself. In the 92nd and 93rd Congresses, in contrast, the groups often reverted to protectionist strategies, anticipating the Nixon administration's budget cuts and planning their defensive moves accordingly. The agenda of one Congress was heavily oriented toward new programs and increased federal expenditures, that of another geared toward program elimination and budget cutting.

What this suggests is how the groups take their cues from Congress and the administration regarding immediate priorities and agenda. Whether acting as facilitators or initiators, they must first build internal consensus for action, which often raises insuperable problems for group leaders. Strong opposition may develop, lead time for response may be lacking, and alternative positions may be wanting. Administration officials are keenly aware of the groups' consensus-building difficulties and thus may seek to co-opt or neutralize the groups for short-term partisan advantages. The Nixon White House staff, for example, frequently played upon group cleavages, disrupting consensus-building operations within the groups, among them, and between them and agency-congressional actors. Indeed, several of the Nixon programs set mayors against governors and pitted county officials against mayors. One major indication of the rising importance of the government groups from the White House's perspective is the number of prominent administration officials that frequent the groups' annual gatherings. These officials seek to lobby the groups, neutralize opposition, and play upon partisan cleavages when it is necessary to do so.

Obstructionist or veto roles can be more characteristic of group responses, particularly where the costs, benefits, and possible consequences of policies are not easily discernible. Group leaders generally avoid rendering opinions on new programs or policies in advance of concrete cases or actual legislative proposals. They may specify general guidelines and conditions which would be acceptable to members, but they cautiously await final details, lest the group be recorded supportive of programs that prove unacceptable in the flesh. New legislative proposals are carefully screened with an eye toward details governing implementation, administration, authorizations, and expectations concerning a program's likely funding. Governors and mayors ask the all-important questions of whether this new program will mean less, the same, or more funds for their governments than existing programs. Will it be complementary to, supportive of, or a substitute for existing programs? How long will it take to get it going, what are the start-up costs, and how will they be paid for? What will the transition from one program or policy to another involve? Who are the intended and unintended beneficiaries of the program and how does this relate to other programs in the area? Will its passage preclude consideration of other pending programs the groups might feel more strongly about? Can existing legislation be amended to incorporate the principal concepts or benefits of the proposed program?

The questions the government interest groups and their members ask are not categorically different from those that the congressmen consider. However, they do differ in priorities, emphases, and concerns. Legislators generally give greater attention to the politics of "program passage," while state-local executives are far more preoccupied with the politics of taxes and administration. Legislators may value highly the public credit accrued from sponsoring new programs or the benefits attained from new constituencies. They can blame poor administration or inadequate funding when the programs they sponsor fall or go astray. Chief executives, on the other hand, typically concern themselves with revenue acquisition, service delivery, and program administration. Thus the basic differences in views, responsibilities, and electoral needs may lead not only to conflict among them but also to the assumption of contrasting roles.

Considering the innumerable veto points in the policy-making process, distinctive advantages are often gained by those who seek to prevent rather than initiate action. Every major policy change, whether legislative or administrative, entails the fear of costs for some participants as well as the hope of gain for proponents. The legislative process is so structured that defenders of the status quo can block, frustrate, and delay changes more easily than advocates of new proposals can marshal sufficient resources to overcome these pitfalls. The government groups are rarely recorded in opposition to new proposals initially, instead withholding support in the expectation that congressional leaders, committee members, or executive officials will bargain with them to gain their support. Such negotiations may occur within an executive agency in the prelegislative stage. They may begin just after the introduction of legislation and prior to congressional hearings, as occurred in the case of the 1968 Highway Act. Usually, however, the center of bargaining exchanges and accommodation emerges in congressional committees and subcommittees, as in the cases of Model Cities, Juvenile Delinquency, Mass Transit programs, and the Safe Streets amendments of 1970. When demands are not accommodated at this juncture, the groups may resort to the floor stage, where debates and amendments can assist them in attaining their objectives. The governors, for example, were successful at this stage in the crime bill and—to an extent—the poverty program as well. . . .

In the case of general revenue sharing, a supportive coalition of the government groups took several years to form as a consequence of the veto posture one or more exerted in early negotiations. The formulas for distributing federal revenue sharing among states and local governments were constantly being redrawn by the White House and Congress as each sought to reward particular constituencies. In the meantime the groups were hopelessly divided as to which bill offered the greatest potential for building consensus among them. President Nixon first proposed that $500 million be divided roughly 70-30 between states and local government, while Congressman [Wilbur] Mills responded with a version that allocated funds only to local governments. The President countered with a version that divided payments equally between the states and local governments and eventually settled for Congress's alternative, which essentially allocated one-third to the states, with the remainder going to counties and municipalities. It was the latter version that brought the mayors and county officials together. . . .

. . . the government interest groups withhold support or maintain an opposition posture to enhance their bargaining leverage in final outcomes. The line between a facilitator and an obstructionist role is often obscured by the fact that the groups may move from one role to another as the situation dictates. A negative stance may be a delaying tactic to allow the situation to clarify, for alternatives and compromises to emerge, or for consensus to form. Such a stance also may be the last extreme where viable options fail to materialize and compromise disintegrates. Once again, no single group is self-sufficient or powerful enough to require decisions of others unilaterally. All cases where the groups were successful in opposition, in fact, involved a coalition of groups and supportive congressional allies.

Fiscal incentives may be the strongest and most compelling justification for policy changes. The governors' reversal on the national highway program in the 1950s from a state-run and financed program to a federal one is no more remarkable than the mayors' turnabout on the poverty program. The governors were relieved of the greater costs in highway financing and thus readily shifted positions with the enticement of federal financing. The mayors were able to cope both with the poverty program and Model Cities, becoming the principal support group of the former and major clientele of the latter. The mayors also reversed themselves on the earmarking of OEO appropriations in the changeover from the Johnson to Nixon administrations. The case against earmarking was predicated on the advantages to cities and their mayors where OEO administrators had flexibility in apportioning funds among various programs. However, under the Nixon administration, Congress's failure to earmark OEO funds into separate categories would likely have led to even further executive impoundment, and hence the mayors reversed their earlier position against earmarking.

The President, Congress, and federal agencies frequently use such fiscal inducements to gain group support. The USCM, for example, was far more enthusiastic about President Johnson's proposed Model Cities legislation in 1966, once the administration agreed to substantial increases in urban renewal authorizations lest this new program threaten to cut into the renewal program's allocations. Once President Nixon proposed to raise the base figure for revenue sharing from $1 billion during the first year to $5 billion, the government groups were prepared to subordinate their outstanding differences in building a strong supportive alliance on the program's behalf.

Thus, in reviewing the groups' record, one finds that their roles are somewhat flexible, susceptible to change, and undergo constant adjustment to new situations. Organization policy provides a bargaining stance, while accommodation to the shifting political arena occurs from program initiation to implementation. It is next important to inquire how the organization and structure of Congress and the executive affect group activities, strategies, and tactics.

Spatial Concerns and Vested Interests

The age-old administrative problem—area and function as competing bases of organization and governance—confronts the groups in their Washington lobbying. The scope of immediate concerns to the government interest groups is influenced by geopolitical boundaries. Policies and problems tend to be defined largely within the context of a spatial setting determined by city, county, and state lines. But since Congress and its committee structure are organized along functional and not geographic lines, the government interest groups confront a chronic and overriding problem. That is, they seek the imposition of spatial concerns on functionally oriented and structured institutions. Not only are committee work groups organized along such functional patterns as agriculture, armed services, public works, education, and the like, but most congressional members' perceptions of public policy tend to coincide with established boundaries between functional programs and committee jurisdictions. Many of the bills to which Congress devotes a large proportion of its time fall easily into what Fred Cleaveland terms "issue contexts." These he defines as the way members of Congress perceive a policy proposal that comes before them, how they consciously or unconsciously classify it for study, and what group of policies they believe it is related to.[3] Such issue contexts strongly influence legislative outcomes because their structure helps determine the approach for analysis, statutory review, and revision, as well as the advice and expertise that enjoys privileged access.

The similarities between the functional organization of Congress and that of the executive reinforce the interdependence and mutual interests which bring together agency officials, congressional committee members, and interest group leaders. They are all concerned with the same area of government activities and programs. The legislative committee-executive agency structure, and attendant policies which link them, often defines, once a bill is introduced and assigned to a committee, the frame of reference guiding policy makers' view of that policy and the arena of action for interest group activity.[4] Therefore, the great majority of bills introduced in Congress fall traditionally into readily identifiable and predictable issue contexts. The entire process can be quite predictable in terms of previous experience, interested parties, sources of support and opposition, agency relations with overseeing committees, steps in passage or defeat, and eventual results. New committee-subcommittee chairmen, party alignments, executive reorganization, and other changes may alter this process. So too, media focus, public investigations, and cataclysmic events may move policy concerns into broader, more inclusive arenas of decision making. But such events and actor realignment are the exception rather than the rule. Their impact may be immediate, but their long-term effect is likely to lead to incremental policy adjustments. Thus the functional organization of Congress and its ties with executive agencies and interest groups are crucial not only to understanding group behavior but also to an explanation of the groups' activities.

As previously noted, most government interest groups' policies tend to be worded in a spatial context. They call for a greater role or participation of one level of government as opposed to another—for the expansion of certain programs and benefits. However, as a matter of practice, general group policies are amended to conform to what is realistically attainable in the legislative process. Spatial issues may, deliberately, not even be raised so as not to arouse vested functional interests. Groups have the alternative either to adapt their objectives to the limits fixed by institutional structures and competing claimants or to seek to mold the environment toward acceptance of their objectives.[5] The groups do both, yet they invest greater efforts in the former within the permissible limits of previous policy commitments. Initially the mayors cooperated with the highway lobby interests rather than fighting them. By doing so, the mayors were able to gain highway lobby support for using Highway Trust Funds for "highway related" purposes like fringe parking areas, special bus lanes, and traffic control. They also gained their help in lobbying for separate mass transit appropriations and operating subsidies for mass transit systems. From the mayors' perspective they gained their short-run objectives, while the highway lobby felt that the more funds Congress directly appropriated for mass transit the less pressure there would be for breaking open the HTF for mass transit uses.

The governors, of course, have historical and structural advantages over the other groups. The Senate already is organized on the basis of equal state representation and, in spite of the natural rivalry which flares between governors and senators, a substantial basis exists for accommodating federal programs to state interests. As Matthews observed of the Senate, most lobbyists believe that the best argument for most senators most of the time is in terms of advantage to the senator's state. Quoting a powerful Washington lobbyist, "A Senator won't go along with us because of friendship, or persuasiveness. . . . The real argument is that the bill will do something worthwhile for his state." [6]

Thus the primary advantage the governors have over local government interest groups stems from the historical tendency for allocative programs to be channeled through the states. For the major part of the nation's history, this has been the case. The federal government dealt with the states from the perspective of structure, potential federal influence and leverage, accountability, and tradition. The states were thereby used wherever necessary to deal with their corporate creations—local governments. This had been the case at least with nearly all categorical grant programs including agriculture, welfare, unemployment, higher education, mental health, highways, and conservation.

Because Congress and executive agencies are organized primarily along functional lines, they have a certain bias in doing business with the states. Mayors and their urban allies often must compensate for this by accommodating their strategies to the positions of other actors, previous programs, and the arenas in which they seek benefits. Moreover, the search for political constituencies is frustrated by the complexity of overlapping jurisdictions at local levels. These entail congressional districts, counties, and special district lines which criss-cross city maps and state boundaries and rarely correspond to metropolitan problems. Policy for urban areas often emerges indirectly as a result of pursuing other objectives. Public housing programs began, for example, primarily as an employment palliative and stimulant for the building trades, while federal aid to airport construction was adopted to promote civil aviation. Both are considered urban programs with benefits distributed primarily to urban residents.

The government groups also seek geographic inclusion in programs regardless of their original scope and intended beneficiaries. Group admission often requires skillful bargaining and negotiation. Federal investment programs designed to meet specific problems of the inner city are invariably broadened by congressional amendment to include rural areas, while programs targeted to specific rural needs are enlarged to include metropolitan areas. Schultze terms this process "functional logrolling" to point out how trade-offs emerge on a strictly functional basis among urban and rural interests to broaden a program's benefits and expand its constituency.[7] Trade-offs rarely occur across functional lines, though increased rural, suburban, and urban cleavages within Congress may change this. Such characteristic trade-offs also suggest the difficulty in enacting programs, especially those of a public investment nature, that are targeted to a specific geographically limited problem.

... Thus the government interest groups share with the President the problem of dealing with a policy-making process which involves agencies and congressional committees, their constituency orientation as well as functional structures.

Moreover, the government groups generally compete at a disadvantage with more well-established claimants, who tend to be more cohesive and possess greater expertise in special areas of public policy. Guilds and functional support groups, organized at all levels, operate with maximum visibility, and usually with maximum effectiveness. They help shape public policy by assisting government agencies and bureaus in developing support groups. Depending on an agency's need for these groups, it may allow these groups considerable freedom in negotiating arrangements with other guilds and allies that benefit directly or indirectly from the agency's programs. Indeed, governors and mayors discover not only the enormous problems they have in gaining admission to policy systems dominated by guild groups but also the fact that they must often rely upon them as interpreters and implementers of public policy. Guild leaders can be found leading and misleading political executives in their relations with higher government levels.

State-local executives have been known to rely on guild leaders for dealing with Washington and may even follow their lead in lobbying. Such dependency has led many an outside observer to wonder exactly who is leading whom. The governors, for example, almost blindly followed state highway officials in advocating more funds for highways—winning the applause of rural and suburban constituents— without much concern for the program's overall impact. The mayors tended to depend upon their housing experts, the National Association of Housing and Redevelopment Officials, for shaping much of their housing policy. The USCM initially echoed NAHRO's opposition to President Johnson's rent supplements program in 1965, which produced a tremendous uproar among many of the mayors' allies inside and outside of Congress. "How could the mayors follow the public housers in opposing this new program," some asked, "when it offered an opportunity to expand housing specifically and provided a strategy for dealing with urban density generally?" Once again, numerous cases could be cited illustrating the dependency of the government groups upon guilds, which was far more characteristic of group behavior prior to 1968 than after.

Notes

1. See Theodore J. Lowi, *The End of Liberalism,* Norton, New York, 1969.
2. See Raymond A. Bauer, Ithiel de Sola Pool, and Lewis A. Dexter, *American Business and Public Policy,* Atherton, New York, 1963; and Lewis A. Dexter, "The Representative and His District," in Robert Peabody and Nelson W. Polsby (eds.), *New Perspectives on the House of Representatives,* Rand McNally, Chicago, 1963, pp. 2-29.
3. Frederic N. Cleaveland (ed.), *Congress and Urban Problems,* Brookings Institution, Washington, D.C., 1969, pp. 359-360.
4. Ibid., p. 359.
5. See V. O. Key, *Politics, Parties, and Pressure Groups,* 5th ed., Crowell Co., New York, 1964, p. 130.
6. Donald R. Matthews, *U.S. Senators and Their World*, Random House, New York, 1960, p. 182.
7. Charles L. Schultze, *The Politics and Economics of Public Spending,* Brookings Institution, Washington, D.C., 1968, p. 134.

12. LOBBYING FOR THE GOOD OLD DAYS

Jonathan Walters

At 1313 E. 60th St. on Chicago's South Side, at the edge of the University of Chicago campus, stands a chunky, gray stone building that has been there since the turn of the century. Its mass reflects the stolid, unpretentious work that once went on inside. It was the headquarters of the Public Administration Clearinghouse, established in the early 1920s to help mayors, city councils, governors and state legislatures to do a better job.

"Thirteen-Thirteen" was a heartland headquarters for a grass-roots cause. It was the birthplace of the National League of Cities and housed the organizations from which the National Governors' Association and the National Conference of State Legislatures eventually sprang.

Today the work of such groups, and the setting of some of them, has changed dramatically. The National Governors' Association sits at the foot of Capitol Hill in Washington, in the Hall of the States, a marble and glass monument to the NGA's shift in focus from simple membership service to monitoring and lobbying the federal government. Just a few blocks away is the new glass-enclosed headquarters of the National League of Cities, equidistant between the Capitol and the White House and likewise well-positioned to wield influence. Visitors enter a two-story main lobby dominated by the group's name spelled out in gigantic block letters sweeping along a central staircase. The effect is impressive, bespeaking power and importance.

Among members of those organizations, however, a debate is going on about just how powerful and important they really are, and whether it is time for some institutional soul-searching. In the past decade, as federal grant programs have been slashed and more governmental work—and cost—has been dumped back onto states and localities, the influence of their government interest groups over Washington has waned considerably. Many of their past leaders—and

From *Governing* 4 (June 1991): 33-37. Copyright © 1991, *Governing* magazine. Reprinted with permission.

some who are active now—argue that this is the time to embark on a major shift and return to their roots, to the role they once played at 1313 E. 60th St., providing the information and the ideas that helped members do their jobs.

George Latimer, former mayor of St. Paul, Minnesota, completed his term as president of the National League of Cities in 1984. He was convinced by then that the group was facing in the wrong direction. "It struck me," he says, "that the shift away from Washington was occurring, and that it had been since about 1978. We never really responded to that curve. We continued to act as though all the action was in Washington."

One hears similar complaints from the rank-and-file. Tom Jones, information officer for Shelby County, Tennessee (Memphis), insists that what counties need most is information about how other counties are solving their problems. He wants his organization, the National Association of Counties, to provide it. But it doesn't. He worries that its staff has been mesmerized by the federal government: "They see Washington as the center of the universe."

The leaders of these groups have heard all those arguments. "We are an urban advocacy organization," says Tom Cochran, executive director of the United States Conference of Mayors, one of the most ardently Washington-focused government interest groups in the city. In Cochran's view, it is the primary job of the conference to keep Washington's feet to the fire and alert members to federal action.

The debate over this issue is more intense among the local interest groups than among the ones speaking for states. The governors' association has always been shaped as much by the personalities of its 50 members as by its Washington presence. The National Conference of State Legislatures has never had more than a mild case of Potomac Fever; its national headquarters is in Denver. But as the era of federal disengagement enters its second decade, the question of purpose is one that all these groups, state as well as local, are having to confront. Should Washington remain the center of their universe when the federal government is all but ordering them to solve their own problems with their own money?

To those who argue for a shift in focus, there is no better symbol of the problem than the past decade of effort by cities and counties to resurrect federal revenue sharing. The critics consider it a long and futile run at the federal treasury that has done little more than drain the groups' resources while sticking them with a "tin-cup" reputation. The National League of Cities still lists revenue sharing as a category of domestic spending in some current documents. Former Phoenix Mayor Terry Goddard, who was president of the league in 1989, argues that the organization has lost precious years clamoring for the return of revenue sharing, for example, when it probably should have been teaching cities how to cope with the loss.

Meanwhile, as a string of other programs, such as Urban Development Action Grants and Comprehensive Employment Training Act public jobs, were eliminated, the interest groups merely turned up the decibel level and poured new resources into trying to get the programs back. The programs have not come back. League of Cities figures show that federal grants to local government have declined from about $50 billion to about $19 billion in the past 10 years. Meanwhile, the interest groups have been unable to make any progress on some important Washington issues that do not involve any cost to the federal government, such as re-regulation of cable TV (which holds out the prospect of higher licensing fees to cities) and taxation of interstate mail order sales, which is money waiting to be put in the bank for states and localities.

A glance through the pages of *Nation's Cities Weekly*, *County News* or *U.S. Mayor* provides some unmistakable clues to what the interest groups are interested in. There are articles about federal defense spending, about the details of the Gramm-Rudman law, about the effort to reduce capital gains taxes. *County News* recently ran a front-page story showing President Bush signing a declaration of "National County Government Week," to celebrate the job counties do in governing. Inside the paper, story after story discussed ways in which the administration is actually forcing counties to do their governing with less and less federal support.

A recent front-page story in *Nation's Cities Weekly* relates league president Sidney Barthelemy's trip to Washington "to meet with President George Bush" on the president's "America 2000" education plan. In fact, there was no private meeting. Barthelemy was just one of the crowd assembled to hear the president lay out a tentative plan for abstract educational goals that mean little to those running schools right now. There is little in any of these papers about how localities are coping with their current problems or on new solutions they might want to try.

The mayors' conference, true to its current and unrelenting assault-on-Washington approach, has always been based in the nation's capital. It was founded there in 1932 with the encouragement of Franklin D. Roosevelt, who wanted to cement his relationship with the big-city political machines that helped elect him.

But the other interest groups have a different history. They did not start out obsessed with the federal government. They were drawn in gradually as the federal role in state and local political life kept expanding. In 1954, the National League of Cities (originally the American Municipal Association) moved to Washington from Chicago, to be followed soon after by the National Association of Counties. The states held off longer. It was not until 1967 that the National Governors' Association arrived, splitting off from the Council of State Governments, which remains as an apolitical, technical assistance and research group based in Lexington, Kentucky.

There is still a great deal going on in Washington for these groups to be concerned with. The federal government will funnel more than $130 billion to states and localities this year, and continues to impose new and burdensome mandates, often without the funds to implement them. None of the major government interest groups could afford not to have a Washington presence. But increasingly, their influence is at the margins: pushing to avoid decimation of existing programs and fighting for delays in the implementation of environmental and health-related mandates. "It's been a rear-guard action," Terry Goddard concedes.

Goddard, Latimer and other critics say the governmental entity that localities ought to be most concerned about these days—and lobbying hardest—is states. Total state aid to localities increased more than 60 percent between 1982 and 1988, from $88 billion to nearly $143 billion, according to the National Association of State Budget Officers. The number of people on state staffs increased from 3.5 million in 1978 to more than 4.2 billion in 1988. Annual state expenditures, meanwhile, rose from nearly $204 billion in 1978 to almost $585 billion in 1988. In the process, states have taken on an ever-expanding menu of responsibilities.

John Thomas, who recently resigned as executive director of the National Association of Counties and how heads the American Society for Public Administration, thinks this is the crucial issue. "County governments live and die at the state legislature," he says. "What Congress does to us is irrelevant in many ways."

Latimer, likewise, believes national organizations should offer localities more advice and technical assistance in dealing with state legislatures and state bureaucracies. "Even with all the complexity of Washington," he says, "it's still simpler working there than trying to take on 50 states. So I think the tendency of national staff is to leave the states alone. I think that is altogether a mistake, that we could have more influence if they focused on state and local activities."

There are clear reasons why the league, the mayors' conference and the counties' association have a hard time seeing it that way. They were the groups that arrived in Washington first; they were the big winners when federal programs for urban redevelopment started up in earnest in the 1960s. After decades as political creatures of the states, dependent on legislatures for their livelihood and their very existence, localities suddenly found themselves participants in the world of domestic policy, treated as seriously by Washington as the states in whose shadow they had always lived.

President Nixon delivered an added bonus to the local organizations in the 1970s when he turned to them for help in implementing the grant programs. Millions of dollars were funneled to the league, the mayors' conference and the counties' association for research and technical assistance. The money was used by the groups to help localities come up with ideas and programs for using the federal money, and to help them stay true to the strings that were attached to it.

The era of urban programs had less effect on the state organizations. Both the governors' association and the National Conference of State Legislatures spent most of the Johnson and Nixon years going about their regular business of helping their membership succeed at state government. These groups did score heavily with the passage of federal revenue sharing to states in 1972. They expanded their Washington operations and began devoting more of their resources to mining the federal government for funds.

Proportionately, though, it was the local organizations that were changed the most by federal assistance. So it was that when the cuts came in the 1980s, it was not only the localities that were hurt—it was the groups representing them. In the early 1980s, the Washington staff of the National Association of Counties went from 140 to 60. The National League of Cities cut back from about 120 to 65; the mayors' conference from 120 to about 75.

All three groups insulated their lobbying operations from the cutback. Lobbyists would be needed, after all, to recoup the losses. The mayors' conference has the same number of lobbyists today that it did when federal funding was at its peak. "It was technical services that got cut," says Tom Cochran, the executive director.

To the extent that the National Governors' Association developed a Washington focus in the '80s, it was not built around the quest for federal help. It was built around the effort to create a personal showcase in national politics and policy debate for its 50 members, and especially for its chairmen, who became the object of increasing media attention during their single-year terms. Lamar Alexander, chairman of the governors' association in 1986, inaugurated the practice of having the association specialize in research on a single topic each year; his topic was education. The effort helped give Alexander publicity and prestige he has carried with him ever since and also helped make him Secretary of Education earlier this year.

By the mid-1980s, the states, like the cities and counties, were comfortably ensconced in Washington headquarters buildings that bespoke the importance of the federal connection. But the connection was not quite the same for the states as it was for the localities. When it came to federal aid, the balance was tilting further toward the states every year. Even programs aimed ultimately at benefiting the localities were increasingly funneled through the states. In 1980, 25 percent of total federal grants went to localities, 75 percent to states. By 1988 it was 15 and 85.

That may or may not be one reason why the Washington organizations of the states have been considerably more muted during recent years in their denunciations of the federal aid cutbacks. Both Bill Pound, executive director of the state legislators' conference, and Ray Scheppach, executive director of the governors' association, like to point out that their groups were favoring a reduced federal deficit while the local organizations were clamoring for more federal aid. This is not an easy attitude for many of the locals to accept, as it was the localities that were most directly affected by the cuts and had to deal most directly with the consequences.

The whole situation has clearly left the organizations that represent the localities in a tough position: Should they accept the assumption that their members need to be more self-sufficient, and return to the role they once played in Chicago, when the first priority was providing services to their members, or should they continue to be the "urban advocacy" organizations Tom Cochran is determined to maintain at all costs?

The staying power of that latter view was demonstrated in March [1991] at the winter meeting of the National League of Cities in Washington. Mayor Barthelemy of New Orleans, the league president, called on the federal government to declare an operation "Urban Storm" to save the nation's cities. Many of the mayors present, big-city and smaller-city alike, approved of the strategy. "I don't call us 'whiners,'" said Mayor Steve Hettinger of Huntsville, Alabama. "I say we're the dreamers; we try to reflect a vision of what should be." From the anti-Washington faction, however, the reaction was one of sarcasm. "It's always the national agenda," said George Latimer, "even when there is no agenda."

Donald J. Borut, executive director of the league, has said since the start of his tenure last year that he wants his organization to become a showcase for "ideas that work," and to celebrate entrepreneurial local government. He sends at least 20 letters a week to members soliciting examples for such celebration. There has been no organized effort, however, to become a force for generating new ideas, or to be the place where they are given a hard look for real value or transferability. Borut says developing such an analytical capability would be too expensive. Rather, he says, the group is going to concentrate on acting as a conduit for all ideas.

Meanwhile, the traditional Washington focus is symbolized by Frank Shafroth, the league's indefatigable top lobbyist, who since the days of the big federal budget cuts has taken to calling himself "Dr. Doom." Shafroth has never given up his conviction that the federal government has the resources to help troubled cities, if only it had the desire. "We are on course now to spend more than $500 billion to bail out the S&L industry," Shafroth says. "It is clear in this country that where we have the will, dollars are irrelevant."

At the mayors' conference, it is full speed ahead for the traditional priorities—Community Development Block Grants, federally assisted public housing and federal aid for transportation. Cochran says his organization has no real choice but to lobby for those programs. "The governors can go to Hilton Head," he says, "and come up with five-year education plans. But I'm sitting here and the phone is ringing every day and someone has to deal with what is going on with AIDS and drugs. That's the difference in being a mayor and a governor."

Expressed that way, the debate over strategy sounds like an either-or affair. It does not have to be. Tucson Mayor Thomas Volgy, who is active within both the league and the mayors' conference, is looking for ways in which those groups can pursue both missions. He cites, for example, the local economic crises set off by military base closings. "That's a classic situation," Volgy argues, "where the league and the conference need to attack the issue at the federal level, but also provide technical services, to assess the nature of the problem, find local solutions."

In Volgy's view, the local groups have done a good job on this one issue. But he concedes that the resources may not be there to do it on more than a few subjects at the same time. "You need to provide that in 35 different categories, beg, borrow or steal," he says. "We're doing it well on about two. We still have 33 to go."

There are those who think that localities cannot afford to wait, however, and that the groups need to shift their resources accordingly. Among them is John Mercer, former mayor of Sunnyvale, California, now minority counsel to the U.S. Senate's Committee on Governmental Affairs. As a mayor, he says, he was routinely frustrated by the lack of good information available at the local level through the national organizations, and by the lack of evaluation and analysis of those ideas that were passed along. Typical, he says, was a conference session put on several years ago by the National League of Cities entitled "14

Ways to Raise Revenues." The session drew a standing-room-only crowd. Then the summary of the session was handed out: a list of 14 taxes that localities could increase. "That's not exactly what we had in mind," says Mercer. What Mercer and his colleagues wanted was to learn, for example, how some cities use ground leases of underutilized public property to attract business, "not how to raise taxes," he says.

Terry Goddard, whose term as president of the league ended two years ago, conceded Mercer's point. Even under his own tenure, Goddard says, "the league put out pamphlets that I thought were pretty worthless: everything everyone's ever said about a particular issue," without evaluation or analysis. "What works in Phoenix might fall flat on its face in Des Moines."

Mercer's experience as a mayor has prompted him to push for legislation in Congress creating an Office for Federalism, to act as a clearinghouse for good state and local government ideas. The point, he says, is to create a center that does more than simply pass ideas along for what they are worth. Those that did not hold up under scrutiny would be jettisoned; those that proved out would be packaged in such a way that they could be easily applied. At the other end, the legislation would give states and localities an opportunity to comment to the office on the effects of federal mandates.

Much stands in the way of such an idea, however, including lukewarm support on the part of some of the state and local government interest groups. Don Borut, speaking for the league, formally opposed the Mercer proposal in a letter to the Senate. "I laud and promote any effort that will bring more information to local officials," Borut says, "but it's an issue of credibility. . . . One of the things that is really important is a sense of trust in the source of information. [City officials] look to their peers and colleagues. They will tend to put greater faith in information from another mayor."

There is also, however, a question of pride and political turf. Agreeing to such a clearinghouse represents tacit agreement that the government interest groups are not doing an adequate job of providing services, and perhaps agreement as well that states and localities ought to start counting on the federal government more for ideas than for money.

The idea of a federal information clearinghouse may or may not be the answer. But the opposition to it reflects the difficulty that is likely to confront any organized effort to change the focus of the state and local interest groups. All these groups are staffed at top levels by people who have spent their professional lives learning to understand and operate in Washington. It is not going to be easy to persuade them to face in a different direction. "When these groups are interviewing people for jobs," says John Mercer, "they're not saying: 'Do you have expertise in municipal management?' No, it's: 'What do you know about the Hill?' "

But it is not just the staffs in Washington that are resistant to change. It is, in many cases, the membership as well. They, too, have learned to view the American political system as dominated by the federal government. John Thomas learned that lesson as director of the National Association of Counties. "People in county governments know that the states are where the action is," he says, "but they don't like to admit that. They see their national organization as the way to play in the Washington ball game."

13. THE GOVERNOR AS INNOVATOR IN THE FEDERAL SYSTEM

Thad L. Beyle

It was not too long ago that the American states were character-ized as indecisive, antiquated, ineffective, unwilling to face their problems, unresponsive, and not interested in the problems of their cities. Luther Gulick delivered the eulogy: "The American State is finished. I do not predict that the States will go, but affirm they have gone." [1]

Where did the problems supposedly lie in the states? Most reformers pointed to the state legislatures. James Bryce observed in 1888 that the "real blemishes in the system of state government are all found in the composition or conduct of the legislatures." [2] [Almost eighty] years later, Frank Trippett of *Newsweek* wrote: "Anyone writing of the state as an instrument of government must write of the legislature. To indict the states is to indict the legislatures." [3]

The legislatures, however, were not alone in being blamed for the states' plight. Several governors had been indicted for criminal acts while serving as governor; others had been indicted after their tenure for activities conducted while serving as governor. [4] There were also critics of gubernatorial ability and performance. In 1949, Robert Allen complained that "there are some enlightened, honest, and well-intentioned governors ... but they are pathetically few in number." [5] Trippett argued a decade and a half later that few governors "possess the personal force, the wit or will" to serve as leaders of their state and legislature. [6]

Yet, as any sage observer might note, these negative views of the states and their governors were all based on the notion of the half-empty cup rather than the half-full cup. The states were probably not as bad as the critics argued, nor should all states have been tarred with the same brush.

[A section documenting this evaluation, contained in the original article, is omitted in this book.—Ed.]

Reprinted with permission from *Publius: The Journal of Federalism* 18 (Summer 1988): 131-152.

Reform and the Performance of
Governors as Innovators

Over the past few decades there has been a spate of reform throughout the states. The general goals of reform have been to enhance gubernatorial and legislative abilities to lead state government and politics in more progressive directions. According to Sabato, these reforms have made the governor "truly the master of his own house, not just the father figure." [7] However, not all these reforms have achieved the goals sought, and some reforms conflict with others. The best example of the latter is seen in the series of gubernatorial-legislative conflicts over state budgets, policy, and administration in which both sides are able to fight a "better" war against the other branch as the reforms have enhanced each branch's capabilities. It is sometimes unclear to the citizen if the reforms have indeed "reformed" their state governments and made them more responsive to citizen needs.

Several specific reforms have given governors a better chance to gain control of the state's policy process, from formulation to administration. A few examples make the point.

1. Since 1955, the number of governors able to serve four-year rather than two-year terms has increased from 29 to 47, a change that allows governors to spend more time on policy and administration concerns and less on reelection politics. [8]

2. Since 1955, the number of governors precluded from being able to succeed to a second term has declined from seventeen to three, while those states allowing a governor to serve two consecutive terms has increased from six to twenty-four. Twenty-two states have no constitutional limit on the number of terms a governor can serve. These changes potentially allow a governor a longer time to spend on policy and administrative concerns if the voters decide to return the governor to office for another term. [9]

3. Since 1965, nearly two-dozen state governments have undergone comprehensive reorganization, and nearly all states have had partial reorganizations. In each case of comprehensive reform, the executive branch has been consolidated to varying degrees under the control of the governor. These reforms usually enhance the governor's span of control and bring under the governor's reach programs and agencies previously outside gubernatorial control. Most partial reorganizations bring under one departmental or agency roof the many specific programs and agencies working in the same functional area which may have been spread throughout state government. Some partial reorganizations have been most prevalent in

the areas of environmental protection, transportation, and human services.[10]

Process, Not Structure, Counts the Most

However, for the governor who wishes to develop innovative approaches and programs, the most important reforms are those within their own office and in the processes surrounding the initiation, adoption, and administration of policy—budgeting, planning, and policy analysis. Some examples of these changes follow.

1. The size of governors' offices has grown rapidly over the past decades. Coleman Ransone reported an average size in 1956 of eleven staff members, with a range from three to forty-three.[11] In 1976, the National Governors' Association (NGA) found that the average was twenty-nine, with a range of seven to 245. Ten years later, the average was forty-eight, with a range of seven to 215.[12] More staff means more flexibility and support for the governor in the many roles he or she must fulfill, or, to the cynic, more positions for patronage appointments and greater chance for confusion.

However, there appears to be a continuum for staffing the governor's office, running from the personal to the institutional, which correlates closely with the size of the state. . . .

2. State budget offices have moved closer to the governor, often into the governor's office, and away from their earlier preoccupation "with the custodial functions of auditing and accounting . . . [by] undertaking new and conceptually rich systems of management decision making."[13] . . . As of 1985, forty-four states had an executive budget system.[14]

3. The policy-planning function has evolved very rapidly over the last few decades to become an important part of the arsenal of weapons available to the governor's policy and management roles. . . .

4. Since the 1970s, these planning offices have further evolved to become "state policy and planning offices" with the broader set of activities and responsibilities that such a change in title or identification suggests. All but five states now have such offices to assist the governor. . . .

Governors now have a broader range of institutions and systems to assist them in their administration than did most of their predecessors. If a governor wishes to adopt an innovative course of action, these organizations and processes can provide valuable support. The informational and analytic capacity they possess represents a considerable step forward from what those outstanding governors of the early twentieth century had at their disposal.

Governors and Recent Policy Innovation

. . . we will examine innovations governors have undertaken in the last several decades. First, some caveats on innovations and states: the notion that innovativeness is a trait is a matter of considerable debate. No state is consistently innovative in every area, in the same direction, or at all times.[15] Nor are those actions or programs which are described as "innovative" always innovative. Second, many of the innovations described were nominated by governors as being innovative; we will take them at their word with the above caveats in mind.

Studies of policy innovation in state government have found that there are patterns in the level of innovativeness among the states, ranging from the most innovative (N.Y., Mass., Calif.) to the least (Miss.). States with large populations, more wealth, more urbanization, and a more industrialized economy tend to be the most innovative. Although these states also tend to have better apportioned and more professional legislatures, and a competitive party system, economic factors clearly dominate the explanation.[16] More recent studies add another set of variables to the explanation—the professionalization of the state bureaucracies and the rise of professional associations that facilitate the communication and diffusion of innovations among the states.[17]

Where are the governors in these explanations? Perhaps they are not in the equation sufficiently to make them part of the explanation, but more likely they provide a qualitative aspect to an explanation based on quantitative variables. In other words, it is difficult to measure the personal impact of a governor and his or her staff vis-à-vis other more easily measured variables. Yet most observers of state government and its processes understand the critical role a governor plays in the policy process, both good and bad.

Reaching Outside the State

In recent decades, governors have increasingly turned their attention outside of their own boundaries, in part, because it has become clear that some of the problems and concerns of the states cannot be handled by each state government acting on its own. Some problems require regional approaches rather than a single-state or a fifty-state national approach. The clearest example is public higher education, which has traditionally been the responsibility of the states.

The southern states, not being of great wealth or having major industrial capacity or strong economies, were for years finding the provision of higher education to their citizens to be onerous. Many leaders in these states knew that education was the key to unlocking the restraints of the past and moving their state's economy, society, and citizens into the mainstream of American life; however, higher education is expensive, especially the specialized training necessary for many professions. For each southern state to develop its own professional school or program across the wide range of professional needs was fiscally impossible.

Therefore, in 1948, led by their governors and legislatures, fifteen southern states joined in a regional compact to help provide higher education for their citizens. Over the years since the Southern Regional Education Board (SREB) has been in existence, these states have shared their scarce resources with each other by allowing citizens of other states to attend their schools by paying in-state tuition rather than the normally higher out-of-state rate. This fiscal policy was especially important at the professional-school level because individual states could specialize in a particular type of education or training, which could then be made available to citizens throughout the region. This policy was also singularly important for minority students in these states because they gained access to Meharry Medical College in Nashville, Tennessee, and to other specialized programs.

As former North Carolina Governor Terry Sanford argued, the "more important result [of having the SREB] may be that money is not spent for competing faculty, duplicate facilities are not built in neighboring states, and therefore funds go further in upgrading higher education all over the South." [18] Now as these southern states have developed and are more able to afford their own professional schools and programs, this feature of the SREB program is not as significant as it once was. In fact, the lack of competition that Sanford praised has been replaced by competitiveness.

Nevertheless, these southern states are finding that they have a multi-state policy and planning organization in place, with a history of working for each state on an array of higher education concerns, plus a staff with a multi-state, regional perspective. Governors, legislative leaders, and other leaders in other regions of the country have noted this and developed similar multi-state arrangements, such as the Western Interstate Compact for Higher Education (1951) and the New England Board of Higher Education (1959).

The concept of approaching educational issues and concerns on a multi-state basis was extended nationwide when the governors and legislative leaders adopted the Compact for Education in the mid-1960s to create the Education Commission of the States (ECS). ECS grew from the idea of James B. Conant who "felt that education was too important to be left to the haphazard chance of unconnected local and state efforts and too complex to be left to a single guiding national hand."[19] ECS serves as a nationwide or multi-state, not national, policy and planning organization for the governors and legislators who must make educational policy decisions in each of the states.

Similar cases of interstate cooperation led by governors and supported by the state legislatures could be cited in such diverse areas as mental health, river basins, juveniles, corrections, libraries, taxes, fisheries, growth policies, international trade, energy, and fire protection.[20] The point is straightforward: governors, along with their legislatures, have taken innovative steps to solve policy problems. These innovations often lead to the development of multi-state policy and planning organizations. These organizations can, and some have, become important parts of the policy initiation, policymaking, and policy administration processes in the states.

There were also significant steps taken to revitalize and redirect old multi-state organizations during the last decade. Foremost among these changing organizations is the National Governors' Association (NGA). The organization originated in a call by President Theodore Roosevelt in 1908 for the governors to meet with him at the White House to discuss one of his favorite subjects, conservation.

The governors' meetings soon became more regular and the agendas broader, and a sense of an organization developed with the Council of State Governments (CSG) serving as secretary. During the mid-1960s, as federal grant-in-aid programs were proliferating and the federal presence was intruding further into the states, the governors saw the need for a more permanent organization to be located in Washington to press upon the federal government the views, concerns, and needs of the states. The Washington staff was increased in size, capability, and versatility, and housed in the Hall of the States on Capitol Hill along with state offices of governors, the National Conference of State Legislatures, which was undergoing similar changes as NGA, and other state organizations.

By 1983, Carol Weissert noted that the NGA "has gone from serving primarily as a social event to providing information, technical assistance, and research needed for responsible state leadership; from shying away from taking issue stands to assuming leadership in charting a national policy course; from having no Washington presence to spearheading a strong Washington lobbying effort."[21] Sabato argues that the governors have used NGA as their vehicle to assert themselves at the "national level in an unprecedented and surprisingly effective manner . . . revolutionized from the hollow shell of yore to a bustling, professional lobby that can achieve results (and overcome the serious handicaps to effectiveness inherent in a high-powered constituency such as the governors)."[22]

There were similar movements in the regional governors' groups. Again, the trend was to leave the old social gathering approach to become more involved in policy concerns. Some of the policy concerns flowed naturally from the region involved: energy and natural resources in the West; agriculture in the Midwest; race and economic development in the South. These regional organizations became most active on the national political and policy scene in the mid-1970s, when the so-called "Snowbelt-Sunbelt" conflict over the allocation of federal funds broke out.[23]

Although the results of these activities and organizations vary, what is important here is that the governors of the fifty states and the several regions did band together and become part of the national policymaking process in order to overcome the decisions (or lack of decisions) made by those who supposedly represented their states in the Congress, namely, their U.S. senators and representatives. In a word, the governors have had to undertake new and innovative steps to provide their states with representation in the national policy process.

Innovations Within States

Beginning in 1974, the governors of the states, through NGA, began to stress the concept that innovations were occurring in all fifty states, and that they, the governors, were at the forefront of these innovations. This portrayal of the governors as innovators was part of an overall argument that the states were no longer the missing link in the federal system, but instead, were a vital, if not the most significant, partner in the system—and that it was the governors who were strengthening the states. The truth of this argument is for others to judge; the point is that the governors wanted this to be the perception of what they were about.

To do this, NGA collected individually nominated innovations by the governors and published them in book form in 1974 and 1980.[24] In the 1980s, the NGA and its affiliate, the Council of State Planning Agencies, conducted two surveys of governors and their staffs on innovations they have undertaken.[25] Surveys with questions of this nature obviously elicit information useful in public relations for the governors; consequently, the veracity of their claims and the actual impact of the innovations are difficult to measure. Nevertheless, these surveys can develop ideas helpful to other governors, and can stimulate governors and their staffs to consider just what have they done that is "innovative.". . .

In total, these gubernatorial respondents nominated 490 separate innovations in their states. Nearly 30 percent of these were administrative in nature, both fiscal and non-fiscal, suggesting that the governors were most interested in developing new ways of "running" state government. The specific policy areas they were most interested in were: the environment, natural resources, and energy (17 percent); economic development (15 percent); human resources or services (13 percent); education (7 percent); transportation (6 percent); and criminal justice and corrections (5 percent). There were few regional differences: southern governors were considerably more likely to work on educational innovations, reflecting the great needs to upgrade public education in those states. Western governors were less likely to work on education and transportation innovations, and midwestern governors were more likely to report innovations in the areas of criminal justice and corrections than their counterparts of other regions. . . .

A New Approach for the Mid-1980s

Beginning with the 1985-1986 NGA chairmanship of Governor Lamar Alexander (Tenn.-R, 1979-1987), the governors as an organization may have taken another significant step to further their impact on public policy. Instead of continuing the series of "show and tell" reports on their particular administration's innovations, under the guidance and prodding of Alexander, the governors of the fifty states conducted a fifty-state assessment of education. Governors chaired seven separate subcommittees assessing the various components of educational policy: readiness, parent involvement and choice, teaching, school facilities, college quality, technology, and leadership and management. The NGA report, *Time for Results: The Governors' 1991 Report on Education*,[26] set an agenda for each governor and state to follow in education. Through 1991, the governors will report at their annual meeting on the specific steps they are taking in their individual states to achieve education reform. This is more of a focused and directed "show and tell" than they have had in the past.

During the 1986-1987 chairmanship of Governor Bill Clinton (Ark.-D, 1979-1981, 1983-), the focus of the governors was on economic development and job creation. NGA "devoted virtually its entire annual midwinter meeting to the issue" of welfare reform. The governors, with but one dissenting vote, adopted a welfare reform concept that called for "a mandatory education and training program for able bodied welfare recipients," which would make "work more attractive than welfare." The dean of the fifty governors in tenure, fourth-termer Jim Thompson (Ill.-R, 1977-), said "I've never seen such unity on the end to be achieved." [27]

At their annual meeting in the summer of 1987, the governors issued and discussed their report, *Making America Work: Productive People, Productive Policies*, which was based on the work of six task forces focusing on two separate components, "Jobs, Growth and Competitiveness" and "Bringing Down the Barriers." [28] The governors also made the first of their annual reports on education reform.

The third year-long study, 1987-1988, will be conducted under the chairmanship of Governor John Sununu (N.H.-R, 1983-) and will focus on the changing balance in the federal system. [Sununu later served for a time as White House chief of staff during the presidency of George Bush.—Ed.] Three parallel efforts will be undertaken by the governors: "to identify the changes in federal rules that would enable state governments to operate more effectively"; "to examine existing federal laws affecting states"; and an NGA Task Force on Federalism that will "develop a broad, direct, overall approach to restoring the balance of power." [29]

To some governors, this process and its ensuing reports provided a road and idea map to follow; to other governors, it was a way to measure the progress in their state; and to other governors, such as Alexander, it was a way to provide leadership to all the states in an important policy area. Again, it is of significance that all the governors were involved in a common study of a specific concern.

To some outside observers, however, things at governors' conferences have changed.[30]

> The National Governors' Conference just ain't what it used to be. All the governors seem to talk about anymore are serious, important issues like education, welfare reform and competitiveness. It's a hell of a note. . . . The conferences undoubtedly are worthwhile. They just aren't as much fun anymore.

Conclusion

Innovation means change, and for many decades, to remain a successful state politician, especially a governor, meant to subscribe to the status quo. Change was not a goal to be sought or argued for because it could be politically dangerous to those controlling state government. The history of the last two or three decades in the states indicates that this philosophy is no longer dominant. Governors and others in the states have undertaken changes in institutions, processes, and policies in order to achieve the results they feel are necessary for their states and citizens. Undertaking innovative approaches, and bragging about them, has become a way of political life for the governors. Whether the changes or innovations actually work and achieve the goals sought is not always certain, and is difficult to measure.

Whether these actions and programs are truly innovative is always a question. As one incumbent governor advised the newly elected governors of 1982, there "is not such thing as a new idea. Be willing to copy, borrow, and freshen up the old ideas." [31]

Now as the national government is reducing its commitment to domestic policy concerns, the states will be forced to step in and increase their commitment to these concerns. State leaders appear not afraid to do so, and in doing so to attempt what they feel are new and innovative approaches to public policy and public service.

Notes

1. Luther Gulick, "Reorganization of the State," *Civil Engineering* 4 (August 1933): 420-421.
2. James Bryce, *The American Commonwealth* (rev. ed.; London and New York: The Macmillan Company, 1906), Vol. I, p. 550.
3. Frank Trippett, *The States—United They Fell* (New York: World Publishing, 1967), p. 2.
4. The governors who were indicted while in office or who resigned from office under the threat of indictment were: James E. "Pa" Ferguson, 1917 (Texas 1915-1917), impeached but resigned from office one day before conviction and later indicted on misuse of state funds; Warren T. McCray, 1924 (Indiana 1921-1924), resigned after being convicted of mail fraud; Edward Jackson, 1927 (Indiana 1925-1929), indicted on bribery charges but acquitted as the statute of limitations had expired; William Langer, 1934 (North Dakota 1932-1934, 1937-1939), was disqualified by the state supreme court following charges that he solicited funds from state and federal employees—he was cleared and served as governor again; Richard Leche, 1939 (Louisiana 1936-1939), resigned under threat of impeachment for corruption, later convicted of graft; Marvin Mandel, 1977 (Maryland 1969-1977), convicted of racketeering but served 2 days in 1979 upon reversal of the court decision; Arch Moore, 1975 (West Virginia 1969-1977, 1985-[1989]), acquitted of extortion charges in 1975; and Edwin Edwards, 1985 (Louisiana, 1972-1980, 1984-[1988, 1992-]), indicted on a series of charges but not convicted. Henry Horton, 1931 (Tennessee 1927-1933) was impeached but not convicted for manipulation of state funds. Several other governors were indicted and convicted after leaving office for conduct while in office: Otto Kerner, 1973 (Illinois 1961-1968), after leaving office and while serving as a federal judge was convicted of corruption in the purchase and sale of racetrack stock while serving as governor; Spiro Agnew, 1973 (Maryland 1967-1969), resigned the vice presidency after pleading no contest to charges of tax evasion in not reporting illegal payments from contractors while serving as governor; David Hall, 1976 (Oklahoma 1971-1975), after leaving office was convicted of extortion and bribery; and Ray Blanton, 1981 (Tennessee 1975-1979).

Blanton's normal departure from office at the end of his term was advanced by three days due to his activities in selling pardons and commutations of sentences in the latter months of his administration. This led to a popular Nashville country song, "Pardon Me Ray" and according to his successor, Lamar Alexander, the early transition "seemed like something that might happen in Latin America." *Steps Along the Way: A Governor's Scrapbook* (Nashville: Thomas Nelson, 1986), p. 25.

At this writing, Evan Mecham (Arizona 1987-1988) has been impeached by the state's House of Representatives, subjected to a successful citizens' petition recall effort, and indicted by a grand jury for an array of actions. This "triple-hit" may be unique in U.S. history. [Mecham was convicted by the Arizona Senate in April 1988 and thus removed from office. In June of that year he was acquitted by a jury on a charge of failing to disclose a $350,000 campaign loan.—Ed.]

5. Robert Allen, *Our Sovereign State* (New York: Vanguard Press, 1949), p. xi.

6. Trippett, *The States*, p. 166.

7. Larry Sabato, *Goodbye to Good-time Charlie: The American Governorship Transformed* (2nd ed.; Washington, D.C.: CQ Press, 1983), p. 57.

8. U.S. Advisory Commission on Intergovernmental Relations, *The Question of State Government Capability* (Washington, D.C.: ACIR, January 1985), p. 129.

9. Ibid.

10. Ibid., pp. 144-147.

11. Coleman B. Ransone, Jr., *The Office of the Governor in the United States* (University: University of Alabama Press, 1956), p. 44.

12. Table 2.3, "The Governors: Compensation," *The Book of the States, 1986-1987* (Lexington, Ky.: Council of State Governments, 1986), p. 35.

13. Lynn Muchmore, "Planning and Budgeting Offices: On Their Relevance to Gubernatorial Decisions," *Being Governor: The View from the Office*, eds. Thad L. Beyle and Lynn Muchmore (Durham, N.C.: Duke University Press, 1983), p. 174.

14. Table 2.4, "The Governors: Powers," *The Book of the States, 1986-1987* (Lexington, Ky.: Council of State Governments, 1986), pp. 37-38. Changes from that table occurred in Mississippi following adoption of a constitutional amendment and in North Carolina following a court suit.

15. See, for example, "Policy Diffusion in a Federal System," Special Issue of *Publius: The Journal of Federalism* 15 (Fall 1985).

16. Virginia Gray, "Why States Achieve Goals in Different Ways," *Politics in the American States*, eds. Virginia Gray, Herbert Jacob, and Kenneth Vines (4th ed.; Boston: Little, Brown, 1983), p. 19.

17. George W. Downs, Jr., *Bureaucracy, Innovation, and Public Policy* (Lexington, Mass.: Lexington Books, 1976), and Richard D. Bingham, Brett W. Hawkins, John P. Frendreis, and Mary P. LeBlanc, "Professional Associations as Intermediaries in Transferring Technology to City Governments," Executive Summary prepared for the National Science

Foundation (Milwaukee, Wis.: Department of Political Science, University of Wisconsin at Milwaukee, 1978).

18. Terry Sanford, *Storm Over the States* (New York: McGraw-Hill, 1967), p. 113.

19. Ibid., p. 115. See also James Bryant Conant, "Shaping Educational Policy," *State Government* 38 (Winter 1965): 34-38.

20. For a more extended discussion of states and interstate compacts, see David C. Nice, "State Participation in Interstate Compacts," *Publius: The Journal of Federalism* 17 (Spring 1987): 69-83.

21. Carol Weissert, "The National Governors' Association: 1908-1983," *State Government* 56 (1983): 52.

22. Sabato, *Goodbye to Good-time Charlie*, 2nd ed., p. 180.

23. For a discussion of this conflict see Deil S. Wright, *Understanding Intergovernmental Relations* (2nd ed.; Monterey, Calif.: Brooks/Cole, 1982), pp. 171-175.

24. National Governors' Conference, *Innovations in State Government* (Washington, D.C.: NGC, 1974), and Center for Policy Research, National Governors' Association, *Governors' Policy Initiatives: Meeting the Challenges of the 1980s* (Washington, D.C.: NGA, 1980).

25. 1982 survey conducted by the National Governors' Association, the Council of State Planning Agencies, and the Governors' Center at Duke University. 1983 survey conducted by the Council of State Planning Agencies.

26. National Governors' Association, *Time for Results: The Governors' 1991 Report on Education* (Washington, D.C.: NGA, 1986).

27. Julie Rovner, "Governors Jump-Start Welfare Reform Drive," *CQ Weekly Report* 45 (28 February 1987): 376.

28. National Governors' Association, *Making America Work: Productive People, Productive Policies* (Washington, D.C.: NGA, 1987).

29. "Sununu Presents Agenda as New NGA Chairman," *Governors' Weekly Bulletin* 21 (7 August 1987): 1-2.

30. Jack W. Germond and Jules Witcover, "Once-Wild Governors' Conference Now a Tame Show," *News and Observer* (Raleigh, N.C.), 30 July 1987, p. 19A.

31. Thad L. Beyle and Robert Huefner, "Quips and Quotes from Old Governors to New," *Public Administration Review* 43 (May/June 1983): 268.

14. FEDERAL COALITIONS FOR
FEDERAL PROGRAMS

Thomas J. Anton

Understanding policy development requires understanding the coalitions that come together to define, support, and sustain public benefit programs. In the American polity, these coalitions necessarily are federal in focus and operation. . . .

The Structure of Access

Beneficiaries with Interests

By definition, the objects or actions produced by various police, welfare, highway, and other public programs are *benefits;* that is, they are valued by some individual or group of individuals. Individuals for whom program products are benefits may be said to have an interest in the program both because they value the products and because they are often implicated in the generation of the products. At a minimum, once they have begun, program beneficiaries prefer that benefits be continued into the indefinite future. More typically, beneficiaries prefer that benefits be improved across time in order to increase their value. For any given program, therefore, there are individuals who have a continuing and often growing interest in the program. Individual interest, multiplied many times to account for the thousands of programs delivering benefits to millions of beneficiaries, provides both a motivation and a mechanism for access.

Who are the individuals whose interests motivate a quest for access? Conventional analysis tends to emphasize a single group, citizens who receive something from government, and a single benefit, cash or an equivalent in-kind payment (such as food stamps or means-tested housing assistance). This is assuredly a large group, encompassing retirees who receive social security or pension checks, workers who receive unemployment compensation or disability checks, families who

From Thomas J. Anton, *American Federalism and Public Policy: How the System Works* (New York: Random House, 1989), 76-82, 97-99. Reproduced with permission of the author and of McGraw-Hill, Inc.

receive child assistance or welfare payments, farmers who receive payments for crops that are grown or not grown, and many other primary beneficiaries. But the beneficiary group is much larger than many people suppose, for it includes many individuals who benefit from the processes of delivering government benefits to other individuals. We may think of these persons as secondary beneficiaries.

One prominent group of secondary beneficiaries is government employees—some 15 million of them. . . .

A less visible, thus often overlooked, group of secondary beneficiaries includes employees of the private sector and nonprofit organizations that participate in government programs. Banks that charge fees for processing government loans, or that profit from packaging such loans for sale in other markets, are direct economic beneficiaries. Hospitals that derive much of their revenue from Medicaid and Medicare are direct economic beneficiaries. Corporations that profit from defense and other government contracts, universities that impose fees on government-sponsored research, nursing homes whose revenue is derived from social service programs, are all examples of organizations whose employees benefit directly from government programs. . . .

The task becomes even more difficult when we consider the cash benefits derived from our tax system. All the benefits mentioned to this point are derived from direct government spending: Some public agency pays a salary, buys something, or mails a check to an individual or firm. The benefit, in other words, is provided by the dollar paid out. Precisely the same benefit can be achieved by *not taking* a dollar from an individual or firm that otherwise would pay a dollar in taxes to the government. Such benefits, technically referred to as *tax expenditures*, have become increasingly important as government has attempted to accomplish more and more goals through tax rather than expenditure policies. At the national level, for example, tax expenditures have increased much more rapidly than the budget as a whole during the past decade (Anton et al., 1980). . . .

It is apparent that national tax policies are extremely generous to both corporations and middle- to upper-income individuals. . . . Clearly, our system offers better rewards by far to "them that has." But the important point is that both the haves and the have-nots are recipients of public largesse. Whether it is the one-third of all American families who participate in means-tested assistance programs, or virtually all other individuals and corporations that profit from both spending and tax programs, Americans today live in a society in which government benefits are an important part of the fabric of everyday life.

The comprehensiveness of these government benefit programs is an enormously important political fact: Since so many people and organizations receive benefits, the number of individuals who are active in the development of program benefits is quite large. Since secondary beneficiaries are as interested as primary beneficiaries in the flow of benefits, the constituencies available to support programs are much larger than is often perceived. Farmers and manufacturers of processed food products are interested in programs such as Food Stamps or Child Nutrition (Hadwiger and Talbot, 1982); local banks and financiers are interested in the loans made available by the Small Business Administration (Rozoff, 1985); hospital administrators, manufacturers of medical supplies, nurses, doctors, and social workers are all interested in Medicaid (Morone and Dunham, 1984); contractors, real estate developers, and bankers are all interested in UDAGs [Urban Development Action Grants] (Rich, 1985); and so on. The comprehensive and pervasive presence of government benefits in American life motivates both a need and a search for access across a broad spectrum of social and economic groups.

Barriers to Access

The search for access is constrained by the two dominant principles of government organization in the United States: territoriality and fragmentation. By organizing several layers of public authority according to different territorial boundaries, the American system provides several points of initial access, depending on the type of program. As we have seen, the various territorial authorities are to some extent specialized in the programs they carry out. Citizens and others seeking access are able to use that specialization to select the agencies and officials to be contacted.... The territorial system is structured tightly enough to allow interested parties to choose appropriate targets of influence, but loosely enough to fit many targets within the "appropriate" range.

No territorial authority, of course, is a unified governmental system. Instead, public authority is normally fragmented among two or three separate branches for any given jurisdiction, and the branches are often fragmented among subunits. The result is a profusion of potential access points, divided among various bureaucratic, legislative, and judicial agencies. In addition to a choice among levels, therefore, individuals seeking access can choose among types of officials....

These *multiple cracks,* as they have been called, imply a certain confusion in the system of access. But here too there are organizing principles at work, of which the most significant are program and jurisdiction. Program-based access organizes influence around the benefits distributed by some program. Since so many programs are joint products of several governmental levels, program-based access often assumes a decidedly vertical form. Program administrators and beneficiaries at one level interact primarily with beneficiaries at higher and lower levels, rather than with other program beneficiaries at the same level of government. Repeated across a number of programs, from education to highways to health, this vertical form links functional constituencies in what some writers have called "picket fence federalism" (Wright, 1982).

Cross-level political interactions allow localized constituencies to become allies of state and national program managers in campaigns to increase resources, and they also allow national or state officials to become allies of beneficiaries in pursuit of localized policy goals. Pursuit of vertical influence requires knowledge of many different local environments, as well as state and national policies regarding program benefits. Program-based access patterns, accordingly, have led to a vast increase in the number of officials and other beneficiaries who reside in a local jurisdiction but who are equally at home in Washington or various state capitals. These can truly be called "federal" politicians.

Jurisdiction-based access organizes influence horizontally, around the benefits distributed by a single level of government. This form of access is more typical, in part because different levels emphasize characteristically different kinds of services, and in part because many of the services that require multilevel coordination are operationally focused at a single level. For example, the national government provides funding for many programs—Community Development Block Grants [are] an example—whose day-to-day operations are entirely in the hands of state or local officials.

Horizontal access is not necessarily focused on a single government unit, however. It is common for several separate governments, such as a school board, city, town, or sewer district, to exercise jurisdiction in the same territory. Moreover, contractual service agreements between such jurisdictions are becoming more common. Two or more cities, for example, may agree by contract to jointly support a common library, or school system, or policy services. Jurisdiction-based access may be focused on a single unit, but it is equally likely that horizontal access patterns will include multiple jurisdictions.

The Concept of Coalition

Defining Terms

Those who use these various access points typically are organized into *coalitions*, by which I mean two or more individuals, each of whom represents some other individuals who agree to promote and support some benefit program or programs. . . .

... The definition is focused on benefit programs, rather than social structures. Although it is true that individuals often share interests with many other individuals of similar social position, it is also true that similarly situated persons often have very different interests, and that individual interests change. The result is nicely summarized in the popular saying "Politics makes strange bedfellows." Labor and management, whose views differ on so many issues, may come together on the desirability of import quotas to protect jobs and profits. Food manufacturers and poor people, so different in economic status and political outlook, may come together on the desirability of food programs to promote sales and reduce hunger. Insurance companies and consumer groups, at odds on so many issues, may come together on the desirability of air bags for automobiles. These examples are common enough to suggest that a definition of coalition based on the characteristics of members is likely to overlook much behavior that is important in understanding public programs. For that reason, the definition offered here is based on what individuals want from government, rather than who they are. In this sense too, the definition is open-ended, allowing for any combination of partners that emerges to support some particular government benefit. . . .

Using the Coalition Concept

Horizontal and Vertical Dimensions. American governments are all partially autonomous in the sense that they can take certain actions without consulting other governments. But they are also entwined with higher and lower governments that can constrain their behavior. How can the coalition concept help us to understand policy development in such complex systems of interaction?

The answer is implicit in the previous discussion. If policy is a product of coalition behavior and governments are defined by the policies they pursue, then governments themselves can be viewed as coalitions of individuals pursuing government benefits. Benefits derived from those programs in which a government has autonomous control are pursued by coalitions that can be thought of as horizontal; that is, their activities focus on a single level of government. Benefits derived from programs jointly controlled by several levels of government are pursued by vertical coalitions; that is, their activities focus on the several levels of government involved in delivering the benefit. It is generally agreed that vertical coalitions are more numerous today than ever before because of the vast expansion of national government assistance programs during the 1960s and 1970s. Increasingly, however, state and local governments have been setting policies in areas long thought to be national responsibilities—local "nuclear free" zones or state government "treaties" with other nations to promote state exports are prominent recent examples. Pressures from both top and bottom have therefore expanded the number of vertical coalitions without eliminating the horizontal ones. Fortunately, we know enough about both kinds of coalition behavior to generate useful insights into federal program development. . . .

. . . Coalitions that are strong enough at one level of government to achieve their desired benefits operate primarily at that level. Coalitions that are too weak to achieve the desired benefits at one level, however, have other options. By seeking allies at higher or lower levels, these coalitions can gain sufficient strength to achieve some or all of the benefits they seek—often in the form of financial grants from a higher- to a lower-level unit. Financial aid often helps to avoid political problems by expressing agreements in dollars rather than clear statements of purpose. Political disagreements over purpose are replaced by agreements on dollar sums, leaving recipients of the dollars relatively free to use grants for their own purposes, while allowing contributing governments to claim credit for their "responsive" allocation of funds. Financial assistance programs are thus built on coalitions whose dimensions are both vertical, to aggregate the interests of multiple levels of government, and horizontal, to integrate those interests into a politically acceptable program. Problems that arise in the implementation of such programs often can be traced to inadequate consideration of one or both of these dimensions (Nathan, 1983).

For many years, scholars and journalists described the most common form of coalition as an iron triangle, sometimes referred to as a subgovernment. Triangular relationships among administrative agencies, congressional committees, and clientele groups controlled many federal programs for long periods of time, protecting both benefits and beneficiaries from interference. Although the iron triangle model continues to be relevant, newer forms of coalition have emerged in recent years. Single-issue coalitions, often using new communications and computer technologies, have become significant forces in setting the national political agenda.

As public policies have become more numerous and more complex, professional and technical experts from academia, law firms, and consulting firms have been drawn into the policy process, forming loosely structured issue networks or policy communities. Perhaps more important from a federal policy point of view, new coalitions of public officials have developed, some organized around local or state jurisdictions, others organized around geographically defined regions of the country. Originally stimulated by perceived imbalances in the flow of federal expenditures between the so-called Sunbelt and the Snowbelt, regional and jurisdictional coalitions have become established in national policymaking. Indeed, the professional and information resources available to these new coalitions, including sophisticated computer technology, now easily rival the resources available to national government agencies.

The spread of information processing capacity has dramatically reduced the costs of coalition formation. Information about the current or projected consequences of policy proposals is now routinely gathered by agencies such as the National Governors' Association and distributed to state and local governments. Depending on whether the projected consequences are good or bad, states and their localities can determine their political strategies, including whether or not to seek allies to promote or prevent some policy. Since policies affect states in very different ways, coalitions can be very different from one issue to another.

More accurate and easily available information fuels the fluidity of federal policy coalitions by revealing distributional differences that can promote a search for new allies for each new issue. Thus, while there is clearly a new regionalism in federal policy coalitions, there is also a new sophistication, driven by new information technology, that promotes a state-centered coalition process. Tension between region and state, no less than tension between region and nation, continues to provide a strong source of political cleavage in the American polity.

References

Anton et al., 1980. Thomas J. Anton, Jerry P. Cawley, and Kevin L. Kramer. *Moving Money.* Cambridge, Mass.: Oelgeschlager, Gunn and Hain.

Hadwiger and Talbot, 1982. Don F. Hadwiger and Ross B. Talbot. *Food Policy and Farm Programs.* New York: The Academy of Political Science.

Morone and Dunham, 1984. James A. Morone and Andrew Dunham. "The Waning of Professional Dominance: DRGs and the Hospitals." *Health Affairs* 3 (Spring):73-87.

Nathan, 1983. Richard P. Nathan. "State and Local Governments: A Political Analysis."*National Tax Journal* 13 (March): 1-16.

Rich, 1985. Michael J. Rich. "Congress, the Bureaucracy and the Cities: Distributive Politics in the Allocation of Federal Grants-in-Aid for Community and Economic Development." Ph.D. dissertation, Northwestern University.

Rozoff, 1985. Jonathan M. Rozoff. "The United States Small Business Administration: Reaction and Redundancy." B.A. thesis, Brown University.

Wright, 1982. Deil S. Wright. *Understanding Intergovernmental Relations.* Monterey,Calif.: Brooks/Cole.

15. THE COURTS AND GRANT REFORM: A TIME FOR ACTION

George D. Brown

Beyond a doubt there is a "law" of federal grants. Its most obvious manifestation is the hundreds—probably thousands—of federal court decisions concerning the award or administration of federal financial assistance. Indeed, the judiciary has assumed such a substantial role in the operation of the intergovernmental aid system that it would seem difficult to understand the functioning of that system—let alone reform it—without an appreciation of what the courts are doing, and why.

Yet, the current intergovernmental reform efforts devote little or no attention to the judicial role. The same is true of many analyses of the grant system and its problems. This article raises the question of whether such "benign neglect" is sound public policy, especially during a period of intense interest in grant issues. Is not the law of federal grants too important to be left to the lawyers (and the courts)? Should not those who design, work with, and analyze grant programs recognize the phenomenon and seek to influence it? . . .

[The author "begins with an analysis of three salient questions in grant law," namely, "Can grantees overturn grant conditions, who can sue to enforce conditions, and what remedies are available?" Then, in the sections reproduced here, he discusses "the volume, causes, and possible impacts of grant litigation" and then renders "some modest proposals for change and for future study."—Ed.]

Grant Litigation: Volume, Causes, and Impacts

Grant law—more precisely, grant litigation—is clearly a "hot" area. The growing volume of cases involves issues which are highly complex and significant to the operation of the grant system.

"A Veritable Explosion"

The rising tide of lawsuits generated by federal grant programs and their administration has been documented. As early as 1972, Professors Frank Michelman and Terrance Sandalow reported a

From *Intergovernmental Perspective* 7 (Fall 1981): 6-14. Reprinted by permission of ACIR.

"veritable explosion" in grant challenges by third parties.[1] . . . Others have described and analyzed the growing judicial role in grant programs.

However, it was not until 1979 that an attempt was made to compile and classify all reported grant decisions.[2] . . .

Even this effort was not comprehensive, however. The authors themselves acknowledged that

> the document is not complete and that there are areas of grant law which are not fully covered. Our intent when this project began was to collect all of the caselaw relating to federal grant programs. Our best estimate was that there were no more than 200 cases in the area. When we ended our search, we had discovered over 500 cases, and we estimate that there are still more to be discovered.

It is probably impossible to calculate with any precision the number of decided grant cases, let alone those that are filed but settled or otherwise disposed of along the way. For example, many important district court cases are simply not reported at all. Nonetheless, . . . it seems . . . clear that the number of cases is increasing.[3]

Why are grantors, grantees, and third parties turning, in ever increasing numbers, to the federal courts for resolution of grant disputes? A simple explanation of the phenomenon might be that as the volume of grant dollars increased, a parallel increase in grant-related suits was to be expected, especially in a litigious society such as ours. The real reasons are somewhat more complex, however. They can be found, to some extent, in changing doctrines of federal jurisdiction, which have expanded judicial access generally. Other causes lie within the grant system itself.

Judicial Developments and the Grant Litigation Explosion

The judicial doctrinal developments have received considerable attention in the legal literature and will be dealt with only briefly. The important point here is that the three traditional judicial constraints or barriers—standing, right of action and exhaustion of remedies—have in recent years been relaxed considerably. As a result, the floodgates of grant litigation have been opened even wider.

Standing. Standing is a flexible—some might say manipulable—concept. To have standing to sue in federal court a plaintiff must demonstrate harm, causal nexus between that harm and the defendant's conduct, and some likelihood that judicial intervention will alleviate the situation. In the mid-1970s the Court appeared to be turning standing into a formidable barrier, particularly for litigants who complained of harm at the hands of someone other than the defendant. However, recent Supreme Court decisions have taken a much less restrictive approach, requiring, for example, only that a favorable ruling be "likely" to benefit the plaintiff.[4] The lower courts have generally followed the Court's lead in grant suits and other contexts.

Right (or Cause) of Action. In the late 1970s, this obstacle also became a good deal less threatening, as courts were frequently willing to imply a right to sue from the underlying statute. The principal cause of this development is the Supreme Court's 1975 decision in *Cort* v. *Ash.*[5] The Court laid out four factors which determine whether to imply a private right of action: whether the statute creates particular benefits or rights in favor of the plaintiff; the bearing, if any, of legislative history; the effect of private suits on enforcement of the statute; and whether the subject matter is federal or one traditionally left to state law. The lower courts have applied *Cort* very liberally in the grant context, primarily because of the wide range of benefits and rights which grant programs and cross-cutting conditions create. . . . The decision in *Thiboutot [Maine* v. *Thiboutot,* 100 S. Ct. 2502 (1980)] appeared to remove even the need for this inquiry. . . .

Exhaustion of Remedies and Primary Jurisdiction. These interrelated doctrines express a judicially created preference for the administrative process as the first point of recourse when a plaintiff's claims are either against an agency or lie within an agency's special expertise. It might be expected that courts would invoke them frequently in third-party challenges to grantee practices. By and large, this has not been the case. A principal reason has been the Court's view that the grievance procedures offered to third parties are inadequate. The Supreme Court in *Cannon [Cannon* v. *University of Chicago,* 441 U.S. 667 (1979)] emphasized the fact that the complainant could not participate in the process. The courts seem to feel that requiring recourse to the administrative process would defeat the purpose of allowing a private, third-party suit. It is not clear why this should be so, especially if the grantor agency does have something to contribute. No doubt agency ambivalence on this issue has influenced the judges in this direction.

Other elements contributing to the upsurge in grant litigation include judicial and legislative relaxation and ultimate abolition of the $10,000 minimum in federal question cases, and the growing availability of attorney's fees in grant cases. Still, it is also necessary to consider changes within the grant system itself.

The Evolving Grant System as Generator of More Litigation

The major change which is most clearly related to grant litigation is the proliferation of the cross-cutting or national policy conditions.

These create substantial new clusters of interests—and interest groups—with which a grantee must reckon. Members of these interest groups—such as the handicapped and environmentalists—are frequently well organized and both willing and able to take judicial action. Frequently, they have the assistance of highly specialized "back-up centers" with great expertise in the relevant area. Third-party challenges based on asserted violations of the cross-cutting conditions are probably the biggest single growth area within the overall field of grant litigation. At the same time, the rapid growth of these cross-cutting conditions may well be a principal cause of current dissatisfaction with the system. If so, the availability of the federal courts as enforcers has important systemic consequences.

The volume of third-party challenges based on program specific conditions, which prescribe how the money is to be spent, is growing as well. A good example is the body of caselaw under the *Education for All Handicapped Children Act*, based primarily on the act's condition that participating states provide all children a "free, appropriate public education." Thus, it is the case that an increase in grant *programs*—as opposed to grant dollars—will generate more litigation. The point is that here—as in the case of the cross-cutting conditions—Congress has created new interests which can claim judicial protection.

As far as the rise in grantor-grantee disputes is concerned, Prof. Richard B. Cappalli cites the following factors, in addition to judicial developments:

> (1) the change in thinking about the grant from the concept of a gift to that of an entitlement; (2) the ever increasing complexity of the grant, as Congress adds more "strings". . . ; (3) tremendous expansion of the world of grantees, primarily through the extension of various grants to thousands of local governments and special districts; (4) movement away from discretionary grants to formula entitlements, thereby lessening grantor leverage over grantee behavior . . . .[6]

The first and fourth factors are perhaps the most significant, in terms of grantee willingness to "fight back." The earlier, highly discretionary grant system was exceedingly one-sided and contained the potential for unbridled exercises of discretion relatively immune from judicial scrutiny. The present system, dominated by formula-based programs, creates a sense of entitlement; and since federal funds are an increasingly significant component of state and local budgets, any potential loss is now likely to be contested vigorously.

In sum, the judicial and systemic developments have interacted: Congress has created a plethora of new rights during a period when the federal courts have been increasingly receptive to the assertion of claims based on federal law. The obvious result has been the explosion of grant litigation. What is not obvious is what the effects of this explosion may be on the operation of the system itself.

Impacts of the Explosion

Attempts at an across-the-board assessment of the impact of grant litigation must be somewhat judgmental and subjective. In any given case it may be possible to identify specific results, but the state of the art does not permit empirically based general conclusions. Nonetheless, the subject would appear to warrant *some* consideration, if only because of the pervasive presence of the courts as actors in the operation of grant programs.[7] Since the systemic consequences of grantor-grantee suits may be quite different from those of third-party suits, the effects will be considered separately.

Grantor-Grantee Litigation. Some analysts view the recent increase in grantor-grantee litigation as unhealthy. For example, the Office of Management and Budget has stated that "the number of disputes between federal assistance agencies and recipients is growing apace with the growing importance and complexity of federal assistance. Not only is this costly, it is disrupting what should be partnerships to get things done." [8] In a similar vein, Prof. Cappalli has argued that the judicial forum is inadequate, noting that the decision may at best involve a remand, and that suits are costly and time-consuming.[9] He concludes that the "ultimate disadvantage is the hostility which litigation engenders," and expresses a strong preference for the administrative process.

On the other hand, one can make the case that going to court is perhaps only another step, albeit a painful one, in an ongoing relationship and that the ability of grantees to sue obviously introduces an element of equalization into the relationship. The ACIR appears to have accepted this position as early as 1964;[10] and a number of federal statutes authorize appeals by grantees from adverse financial decisions.[11] Availability of the judicial forum is particularly important in cases where the grantee is attacking the grantor's interpretation of the statute itself.

Third-Party Challenges. The arguments in favor of suits by third parties attacking the award or administration of federal grants appear to be substantially stronger. Justice Harlan's opinion in *Rosado* v. *Wyman* [397 U.S. 397 (1970)], suggests two purposes which such suits further: making certain that Congress's will is not ignored by grantees, and protecting the individual beneficiaries of federal aid programs. These justifications overlap but can be examined separately.

Congress attaches conditions to federal aid in order to achieve what it perceives as national objectives. The very presence of any string—program specific or cross-cutting—represents a potential displacement of the grantee's freedom to choose, in that the grantee might well not have chosen to follow the course of conduct "mandated" by the string. That is why Congress imposed the condition in the first place. Yet the grantee may wish to evade or disobey grant conditions due to a desire to cut costs, a legitimate disagreement over how best to operate a program, or an outright desire to convert federal dollars to uses other than those intended by Congress. Thus, allowing third parties to sue to enforce grant conditions is an essential tool to help keep the grantee honest.

It is also important to focus on the types of person likely to bring such suits. In many instances, they will be individuals or groups with little clout in the grantee's political processes. Examples include welfare recipients such as the *Thiboutot* plaintiffs, racial minorities, classes such as the handicapped, low-income persons generally, or those promoting a locally unpopular cause such as environmental protection. A fundamental premise which underlies much of the present grant system is that state and local governments cannot be counted on to respond adequately to such interests. Thus, third-party grant suits represent one more instance of the federal courts serving as "the primary and powerful reliances for vindicating every right given by the Constitution, the laws, and treaties of the United States." [12]

On the other hand, it may be that third-party suits contribute to the "overload" which ACIR has identified as a principal problem of the present grant system. The Commission argues that problems of effectiveness, efficiency, costliness, and accountability are widespread. Third-party suits can contribute to the cost of participating in grant programs. There are the costs of defending the suit, increased project costs in case of delays, possible attorneys' fees, and even damages. Third-party suits also contribute to the complexity and uncertainty of administering federal aid programs. Grantees are likely to insist on elaborate federal guidance and refrain from innovation out of fear of being hauled into court. Accountability issues also emerge, increasing the opportunity for finger pointing and buck passing. To the extent that participation in grant programs becomes more and more unattractive, the phenomenon of opting out is likely to increase.

Grant suits can also frustrate the achievement of program goals. Take the case of an economic development project involving federal, local, and private funds, which is attacked on the grounds of inadequate citizen participation. If the court agrees with plaintiffs and grants an injunction, the resultant delay will drive up costs. The public funds may no longer be sufficient. The developer may pull out. Which would Congress have preferred: the project without the participation, or the participation without the project? The court is not in any position to make such trade-offs. It must enforce the grant conditions as they are written.

In sum, grant litigation, of whatever variety, raises serious institutional questions. Are the various forms of judicial involvement a good thing? Until now the question has largely been unasked, perhaps because many of those working on grant reform are not lawyers and are understandably perplexed by arcane concepts of federal jurisdiction. Yet the role of the courts seems too important not to be addressed.

The Courts and Grant Reform: A Time for Action

One can argue that a conscious decision should be made *not* to address the issue of courts and grant reform—to leave it to the lawyers and the courts after all. Indeed, cases such as *Pennhurst [Pennhurst State School and Hospital* v. *Halderman,* 101 S. Ct. 1531 (1981)] indicate the possibility of judicial self-correction. However, if the system is in need of reform—a point generally conceded—that effort ought to at least consider the role of this important, and relatively new, actor: the federal judiciary. (Although the recently enacted block grants may alter the fiscal and political landscape, there is no indication that the judicial role will be significantly altered.)

Short of congressional action, the grantor agencies might develop accessible and workable grievance procedures. Agency practice in this area varies tremendously but, in general, the administrative avenues available are not viewed as adequate. (Plaintiffs sometimes "exhaust" them anyway, just to be on the safe side.) The availability of such procedures might lead to the resolution of a large number of disputes in a forum more susceptible to negotiation and mediation than a lawsuit. Moreover, the courts would be far more willing to invoke the doctrines of primary jurisdiction and exhaustion of remedies than they are at present.

Still, the primary responsibility rests with Congress. It would be virtually impossible to address the issue of the role of the courts in any across-the-board legislation. The grant programs are simply too varied, and the disputes they generate too dissimilar. Block grants present different issues than categorical programs. It makes a difference whether one is talking about suits to enforce the cross-cutting conditions, or program-specific strings. Many different, and difficult, value judgments have to be made. Allegations of racial discrimination in a grant program are more serious candidates for federal judicial review than claims by disappointed vendors that the grantee has violated contractual obligations, while claims of insufficient citizen participation lie somewhere in between. At the moment it is the courts which make these judgments on an *ad hoc* basis.

Ideally, the role of the courts ought to be addressed specifically each time the Administration and the Congress deal with restructuring or reauthorizing each grant program. It should be possible to identify in advance the types of third-party disputes which a given program will generate. Policymakers could then decide which should be insulated from judicial review, which should receive limited judicial review, and which should receive whole-scale review of the sort awarded in most third-party suits as things stand now. For example, citizen participation issues might be resolved using agency forums, while complaints of racial or sexual discrimination would still be able to be heard in the courts, perhaps after exhaustion of administrative remedies. So far, this has happened only occasionally. The most notable example is the General Revenue Sharing Amendments of 1976, which created an elaborate citizens' suit provision including a complaint mechanism and an exhaustion requirement.

As a first step, then, those who deal with grant reform must add the role of the courts to the agenda, recognizing it as a new item. Empirical research is needed to bring to light the judicial impact on categories and subcategories of grant disputes.

The ultimate policy decisions will no doubt rest primarily on a balancing of the relative values accorded to the programmatic and federalism goals to be served by any federal grant statute, and the rights and interests of the individuals affected by such programs. The task is not easy; the trade-offs are difficult. Nonetheless, these issues have been simmering just beneath the surface for some time now. An honest dialogue will be necessary to arrive at an adequate resolution. At the very least, it is time for the dialogue to begin.

Notes

1. Frank I. Michelman and Terrance Sandalow, *Government in Urban Areas*, Supplement, St. Paul, Minn.: West Publishing, 1972, p. 275.
2. Office of Management and Budget, *Managing Federal Assistance in the 1980s, Working Paper A-7*, "Study of Federal Assistance Management Pursuant to the Federal Grant and Cooperative Agreement Act of 1977 (P.L. 95-224)," Washington, D.C.: U.S. Government Printing Office, 1979.
3. Thomas Madden, "The Law of Federal Grants," in Advisory Commission on Intergovernmental Relations, *Awakening the Slumbering Giant:*

Intergovernmental Relations and Federal Grant Law, M-122, Washington, D.C.: U.S. Government Printing Office, 1980, pp. 9-10.

4. E.g., *Regents of University of California* v. *Bakke,* 438 U.S. 265 (1978).
5. 422 U.S. 66 (1975).
6. Richard Cappalli, "Federal Grant Disputes: The Lawyer's Next Domain," *Urban Lawyer,* 11, Summer 1979, pp. 377-88.
7. The role which courts play in establishing the Constitutional parameters of grant programs . . . has received considerable attention.
8. Office of Management and Budget, *Managing Federal Assistance in the 1980s,* Washington, D.C.: U.S. Government Printing Office, 1979.
9. Richard Cappalli, *Rights and Remedies Under Federal Grants,* Washington, D.C.: Bureau of National Affairs, 1979, pp. 169-71.
10. Advisory Commission on Intergovernmental Relations, *Statutory and Administrative Controls Associated with Federal Grants for Public Assistance,* A-21, Washington, D.C.: U.S. Government Printing Office, 1964, pp. 81-83, 93-95.
11. E.g., 31 U.S.C. Section 1245 (revenue sharing).
12. *Steffel* v. *Thompson,* 415 U.S. 452, 464 (1974) (Brennan, J.).

16. *GARCIA*: FEDERALISM'S PRINCIPLES FORGOTTEN

A. E. Dick Howard

Two centuries ago, the framers who met at Philadelphia labored to produce a Constitution crafted to the needs of a free people living in a republic of extended territory. Drawing on the lessons of history, they sought to give the central government sufficient authority to deal with such national concerns as commerce among the states, while dispersing power in such a way as to protect individual liberty and local self-government—two of the ends for which the war of independence had been waged.

A linchpin of that constitutional order is federalism. One has but to read the text of the Constitution—which refers to the states at least fifty times—to realize how central the concept of federalism was to the founders' thinking. Indeed, it was a concern about the potential power of the new federal government that led to the adoption of the Bill of Rights.

In the nineteenth century, that perceptive French traveler, de Tocqueville, lavished praise on American federalism in his *Democracy in America*. On the link between self-government and liberty, he commented, "A nation may establish a free government, but without municipal institutions it cannot have the spirit of liberty."

As Americans prepare to celebrate the Constitution's bicentennial, the Supreme Court appears to have forgotten both the framers' intent and the teachings of the nation's history. In February, the Court decided *Garcia v. San Antonio Metropolitan Transit Authority*. Five justices joined in a majority opinion concluding, in effect, that if the states "as states" want protection, within the constitutional system they must look to Congress, not to the courts. The "principal means," Justice Blackmun wrote, by which the role of the states in the federal system is to be ensured "lies in the structure of the Federal Government itself."

The states and localities, to be sure, will survive the impact of *Garcia*'s immediate holding, which involves the application of the *Fair*

From *Intergovernmental Perspective* 11 (Spring/Summer 1985): 12-14.

Labor Standards Act to a municipally owned mass transit system. The holding is bound to be both burdensome and expensive, but most local governments will find ways to adjust, as they have done to other fiscal and legal vicissitudes. But far more than labor laws and bus drivers' pay is at stake in *Garcia*.

Garcia raises fundamental questions about the role of the Supreme Court as the balance wheel of the federal system. *Garcia* abdicates a function which history, principle, and an understanding of the political process argue strongly that the federal judiciary should undertake. For those who care about the health of American constitutionalism— including, but not limited to, federalism—*Garcia* should be an unsettling decision.

Although the ultimate reach of *Garcia* is unclear, the decision adopts a variation on a theme asking the Court to hold its hand when a litigant claims that a federal action is beyond the authority of the federal government in that the action encroaches upon some protected right of the states. Final resolution of such claims, this thesis runs, should be left to the political branches of the government.

Such a position reads an important part of the founders' assumptions out of the constitutional order. One may debate—though the point has long since been academic—whether the founders intended the Supreme Court to have the power of judicial review. But assuming the legitimacy of that doctrine, it is hard to escape the conclusion that the founders assumed that limiting national power in order to protect the states would be as much a part of the judicial functions as any other issue.

James Madison, in *Federalist* No. 39, was explicit: there must be a tribunal empowered to decide "controversies relating to the boundaries between the two jurisdictions." The nature of the ratification contest—especially the Federalists' need to reply to the anti-Federalist charges—supports the conclusion that the proponents of the Constitution saw the necessity that federalism be among the institutional arrangements to be protected in the constitutional system.

The principle of the rule of law adds force to what this history teaches. A basic tenet of Anglo-American constitutionalism is that no branch of government should be the ultimate judge of its own powers. The principle that one cannot be a judge in one's own cause is of centuries' standing. This principle is stated by Sir Edward Coke in *Dr. Bonham's Case* (1610) and, in our own time, has been reinforced by *United States v. Nixon*. The principle is especially important in a system which, in addition to being federal, looks to checks and balances and the separation of powers to restrain arbitrary government.

A further flaw in *Garcia* is its resting upon erroneous suppositions about the ways in which the nation's political process actually works. Essential to any argument that the Court should abstain from adjudicating limits on national power *vis-à-vis* the states, is the notion that the states have ample protection in the processes of politics.

This assumption has two dimensions. One is institutional—that the states have a major part in structuring the national government. The other is political—that the ways in which the process actually works (such as in the political parties and in Congress) focus on the states. In fact, neither branch of the argument reflects current realities.

There was a time when the states had considerable influence over the shape of federal politics. Under the original Constitution, U.S. senators were elected by the legislatures of their respective states. The Constitution did not set federal standards for congressional elections; the states controlled the franchise. And it was up to the state legislatures as to how to draw the boundaries of congressional districts.

All this has changed. The Seventeenth Amendment (adopted in 1913) brought direct election of senators. Judicial decisions (such as that striking down the poll tax) and acts of Congress (notably the *Voting Rights Act of 1965*) have federalized much of the law respecting the franchise. The 1965 statute, for example, requires preclearance (by the Attorney General or the District Court for the District of Columbia) of voting changes in areas covered by the *Act*. State power to apportion congressional seats has been circumscribed by decisions such as the Supreme Court's 1964 opinion in *Wesberry v. Sanders,* requiring that congressional districts be based on population.

Accompanying these significant shifts in institutional arrangements has been a palpable decline in the "political" safeguards. Political parties, especially at the state level, no longer are the force they once were. Increased use of primaries and the impact of "reforms" have had the unintended consequence of encouraging the development of alternative institutions. Most striking has been the rise of PACs (political action committees), which now number in the thousands.

The "nationalization" of campaign finance has led to the weakening of the federal lawmakers' loyalties to constituents. Special interest politics have tended to replace consensus politics. Moreover, the explosive growth of the federal government in modern times has brought the emergence of the "iron triangle"—the convergence of bureaucrats, interested legislators (often powerful committee chairmen), and lobbyists to determine the shape of federal programs.

In defense of having the Court abdicate Tenth Amendment questions, as it did in *Garcia,* one sometimes hears the argument that the Court cannot resolve empirical questions. Thus, it is argued, assessing the facts of a given case so as to "balance" competing state and federal interests requires the Court to undertake a mode of inquiry that more properly belongs to legislators. Yet in other areas of constitutional litigation the Court resolves empirical questions as a matter of course. Every case involving claims that a state act burdens commerce requires the resolution of economic and other such data, but the Court does not shirk this task.

Another objection to the Court's having a role in Tenth Amendment cases is that the justices cannot draw workable distinctions, such as deciding (as precedents before *Garcia* had sought to do) what is and what is not a "traditional governmental function" (and hence entitled at least to some presumptive measure of protection against federal intrusion). Such line-drawing is, of course, difficult. But its being difficult does not mean that it should not be undertaken, any more than the conceptual difficulties of deciding what constitutes "speech" or "religion"—the thorniest of problems—are grounds for not deciding First Amendment cases.

Whatever the tangles confronting the Court, there are even graver reasons to question Congress's competence or willingness to make considered judgments on constitutional questions—especially when the question is that of the limits of Congress's own power. The judicial process may have its flaws, but it aspires to a degree of rationality, including analytical reasoning, that one does not associate with the legislative process. The limits of time, the pressures of lobbyists, the temptations of expediency, undue reliance on staff, and other distractions often have more to do with the final shape of legislation than any thinking about constitutional issues. Martin Shapiro makes the point well: "The nature of the legislative process, combined with the nature of constitutional issues, makes it virtually impossible for Congress to make independent, unified, or responsible judgments on the constitutionality of its own statutes."

Still another argument for the Court's leaving the states and localities to the tender mercies of Congress is that the Court needs to husband its scarce political capital. This argument raises the spectre of a return to "dual federalism"—the *ancien regime,* before 1937, when the Supreme Court often derailed federal social and economic legislation in the name of states' rights.

Such a risk is chimerical. For the court to play a role in protecting the states as states under the Tenth Amendment, as the majority set out to do in the Court's 1976 decision in *National League of Cities v. Usery* (overruled in *Garcia*), raises no question about Congress's power over the *private* sector.

As to keeping the Court out of unnecessary controversies, most of the debate over "judicial activism" in recent decades has involved such issues as school prayer, criminal justice, and abortion. Federalism cases may provoke academic debate—and, of course, matter enormously to state and local officials—but they stir little outrage in the country at large. It is individual-rights decisions that, by and large, stir passions. One doubts that the partisans of *Garcia* would be content to see individual-rights matters, because they may be controversial, left likewise to the political process.

Garcia betrays a glaring disregard of a basic truth about American constitutionalism: that institutional rights, under our Constitution, are a form of individual rights. Even such basic guarantees as those in the Bill of Rights and the Fourteenth Amendment do not secure absolute personal rights. The protection created is against governmental (that is, institutional) actions, not against infringements by private parties. Thus, for individual rights to be secured requires assurances as to the stability of the institutional safeguards explicit or implicit in the Constitution.

The individual American—as the heir to those who brought the Constitution into being and agreed to its adoption—has a fundamental entitlement to living under the form of government spelled out in the Constitution. The separation of powers is not to be abandoned simply because it may be inconvenient. Likewise, one of the predicates of the constitutional order is that the Supreme Court adhere to the values of federalism as manifestly implicit in the Constitution.

Federalism may be an elusive idea, but it is no mere abstraction. And, while it was essential to the adoption of the original Constitution, it is more than simply a political compromise adopted to get the Constitution underway. Federalism is linked with individual liberty and with the health of the body politic.

It is through participating in government at the local level that the citizen is educated in the value of civic participation. A robust federalism encourages state and local governments as schools for citizenship. Moreover, federalism both reflects and encourages pluralism, allowing individual idiosyncrasies to flourish. One often hears Justice Brandeis quoted on the states' serving as "laboratories" for social and economic experiments. The states are more than mere laboratories; to the extent they encourage pluralism, the states are handmaidens of the open society.

Ultimately, the case for federalism rests on a concern to preserve the right of choice—the essence of political freedom. States and local governments have, of course, often trampled this very right, for example, when they have denied the vote because of one's race. The remedies for such abuses lie in vigorous judicial enforcement of constitutional guarantees and in Congress's power to protect civil rights. But the need to guard against trespasses by states or localities on individual liberties does not undermine the conclusion that federalism as such can operate as part of the very matrix of protection for individual liberties.

In refusing to enforce the Tenth Amendment—to play the role they regularly undertake in respect to other provisions of the Bill of Rights—the *Garcia* majority leaves an important constitutional sentry post unmanned. What recourse do those who care about the health of federalism have?

There are other opportunities for courts to vindicate the underlying values. Federal statutes may be interpreted in light of their impact on state and local governments. For example, the Court's 1981 *Pennhurst* decision lays down the salutary rule that federal grant conditions, to be binding on state and local governments, must be clearly identified as such when grant funds are accepted. Notions of comity can come into play when reviewing lower courts' use of their equity powers to reform state institutions (such as prisons) or when deciding how far a federal court may go in intervening in state court proceedings (as in the Court's 1971 decision in *Younger v. Harris*).

Ultimately, one may hope for the undermining or demise of *Garcia.* The majority decision stops short of saying that under no circumstances could the constitutional structure impose affirmative limits on federal actions affecting the states. A more favorable fact situation than that in *Garcia,* one entailing a more serious intrusion on the states and a more marginal federal interest, might furnish the occasion to begin the movement away from that unfortunate decision.

Early and outright reversal of *Garcia* should not lightly be predicted, even assuming new justices are appointed to the Court. Reversals typically come only after a precedent has been robbed of vitality. The Court decided *Gideon v. Wainwright* (1963), requiring states to appoint counsel for felony defendants unable to afford a lawyer, only after 20 years of experience under *Betts v. Brady* proved that an *ad hoc* approach would not do. Likewise, it was easier for Justice Blackmun to rationalize the result in *Garcia* by pointing to the Court's difficulties in post-*National League of Cities* decisions such as *EEOC v. Wyoming* and *FERC v. Mississippi.*

Still, one can hope that eventually a majority of the justices will come to realize the mistake made in *Garcia.* Because federalism is an intrinsic component of the constitutional system—indeed, bolsters other constitutional values—safeguarding that process cannot be left to the unrestrained discretion of the political branches. It may be that the authority pronounced in *National League of Cities* (and renounced in *Garcia*) ought to be sparingly used. But it is salutary that the political branches know that the Court has power to step in when the facts point to intervention.

It is no less legitimate and proper for the Supreme Court to concern itself with assuring the health of federalism as it is for the Court to uphold individual liberties as such. In neither case is abdication of the Court's proper role consistent with the principles inhering in the Constitution.

17. FEDERAL PROGRAMS AND CITY POLITICS

Jeffrey L. Pressman

. . . If actors and organizations have conflicting policy preferences, then the technical methods of communication, planning, and coordination are unlikely to resolve the differences between them. More discussion and gathering of information might only result in pointing up differences between the organizations. As for coordination, this much-used term is often proposed as a cure for fragmentation, but it does not offer much guidance to one who wishes to make or to understand policy.[1] If organizations disagree about objectives, then coordination may mean that one wins and the other loses. Alternatively, bargaining between them may result in a solution which is somewhere between the opposing preferences. In fortunate circumstances, an integrative solution can make both parties better off than they were. But in no case is coordination among conflicting parties a bloodless and technical process. Certainly, the creation of multiple coordinators and coordinating boards has not eliminated conflict between federal and local agencies.

The differences in perspective between federal and local bodies are due in part to their differing roles as donor and recipient in the grant-in-aid programs. As in foreign aid, a donor's perspective includes a preference for long-term plans, short-term funding, and a number of guidelines regulating how the money may be spent. The recipient's perspective, on the other hand, includes a preference for short-term plans, long-term funding, and relatively few guidelines on spending.

When the problem of conflict has been addressed by designers of intergovernmental structures, it has been treated as a matter of disagreement over goals—to be remedied by collaborative discussion of those goals. Thus, the emphasis has been placed on molding agreement during the formulation of policy, with implementation presumably

From Jeffrey L. Pressman, *Federal Programs and City Politics* (Berkeley and Los Angeles: University of California Press), pp. 10-16. Copyright © 1975 The Regents of the University of California, reprinted by permission of the University of California Press.

following in the wake of that initial agreement. This strategy is a perilous one, for, as some recent studies[2] have shown, there are many ways in which initial policy agreement can dissipate during the process of implementation.

If federal-city relations are not characterized by pure cooperation (or by temporary lack of communication between the parties that can be solved by more talking and planning), neither are those relations marked by pure conflict. For the organizations involved have many common interests in operating successful programs and in improving the social and economic health of cities. Thus, federal and city agencies may be seen as engaging in what Schelling calls "mixed motive games," which are combinations of cooperation and conflict.[3] For Schelling, such conflict situations

> are essentially *bargaining* situations. They are situations in which the ability of one participant to gain his ends is dependent to an important degree on the choices or decisions that the other participant will make. The bargaining may be explicit, as when one offers a concession; or it may be by tacit maneuver, as when one occupies or evacuates strategic territory. It may, as in the ordinary haggling of the market-place, take the *status quo* as its zero point and seek arrangements that yield positive gains to both sides; or it may involve threats of damage, including mutual damage, as in a strike, boycott, or price war, or in extortion.[4]

Viewing intergovernmental relations as a bargaining process is useful in keeping us from over-emphasizing either the cooperative or conflictual elements of that behavior. Such a perspective helps us to understand strategic moves made by various players and to suggest policy changes which take into account both shared and divergent values.

Power Asymmetry

A further cause of friction between federal and local agencies is the power asymmetry in the relationship between them. The federal government supplies most of the money for grant-in-aid programs, and it generally insists on a range of guidelines and controls to accompany the financial commitment. A city which desperately needs additional funding is in a poor position to argue about the conditions of a grant. "Cooperative federalism" between relatively wealthy and powerful federal agencies and relatively poor and powerless local agencies is an illusion.

Power asymmetry exacerbates the friction generated by differences in goals and policy preferences. This is not to say that weakness is necessarily a disadvantage in a mixed-motive game. As Schelling notes: "The government that cannot control its balance of payments, or collect taxes, or muster the political unity to defend itself, may enjoy assistance that would be denied it if it could control its own resources." [5] Still, there is no question that city leaders resent their dependence on the federal government and the consequent ability of that government to control so many of their actions.

Mutual Dependence

The federal government's comparative strength does not mean that it can achieve its goals merely by imposing its will on local government agencies. If we follow Dahl's definition of power ("[A] has power over [B] to the extent that he can get [B] to do something that [B] would not otherwise do" [6]), then we can see that federal and city government agencies have power over each other. For just as cities depend on the federal government for money, so the federal government depends on city agencies to build support for and implement a range of urban programs. Because federal and city governments depend on each other, they can each get the other party to do things that that party would not otherwise do.

John C. Harsanyi has written that, in cases in which A has power over B,

> it very often happens that not only can A exert pressure on B in order to get him to adopt certain specific policies, but B can do the same to A. In particular, B may be able to press A for increased rewards and/or decreased penalties, and for relaxing the standards of compliance required from him and used in administering rewards and penalties to him. Situations of this type we shall call bilateral or reciprocal power situations. [7]

In such situations, both the extent of B's compliant behavior and the incentives that A can provide for B will become matters of bargaining between the two parties. B can exert pressure on A by withholding his compliance, even though compliance might be more profitable to both parties than noncompliance. B can also exert pressure on A by making the costs of a conflict—including the costs of punishing B for noncompliance—very high.

Even given the supremacy of federal law and the cities' dependence on federal resources, local agencies have a number of bargaining counters. For example, they can threaten to opt out of a federal program; they can threaten a conflict which would be costly for both sides; or they can demonstrate such weakness that emergency federal assistance is made even more likely. Thus, the power imbalance between federal and city governments is not complete; mutual dependence leads to a reciprocal power situation in which bargaining must take place.

The Problem of a Bargaining Arena

For bargaining to take place, the various parties must have some way of transmitting their intentions to each other. As Schelling says, parties to bargaining "must find ways of regulating their behavior, communicating their intentions, letting themselves be led to some meeting of minds, tacit or explicit, to avoid mutual destruction of potential gains."[8] Federal and local officials, with their differing perspectives, career patterns, and associational experiences, sometimes find it difficult to understand each others' policy moves. It has not been easy, therefore, to find effective arenas in which bargaining can proceed. (I will define "arena" as a site at which the exchange of political resources takes place. A list of such resources would include money, authority, information, and physical force, among others.)

Warren Ilchman and Norman Uphoff, whose "political economy" model focuses on exchanges of political resources, speak of such bargaining arenas as "political and administrative infrastructure."[9] They explain that:

> infrastructure economizes on the use of political resources by increasing *predictability* or *mobility*. The establishment of certain exchange relationships, whether mutually beneficial, legitimated, or coerced, provides for predictability in the amount and kind of resources available to maintain other relationships. When benefits, sanctions, norms, or simply expectations are established with respect to a given pattern of political competition or exercise of authority, compliance may be achieved with the expenditure of fewer resources because political activities and attitudes can be more reliably predicted. Infrastructure contributes to the increased mobility of resources in much the same way that transport systems contribute to greater efficiency of economic production. . . . Infrastructure is used to gain support, enforce authoritative decisions, gather information, deploy coercion, and confer status at less cost than would be the case if established patterns did not exist.[10]

Examples of infrastructure are political parties, interest groups, bureaucracies, and educational systems. Each of these institutions may be seen as an arena which facilitates the exchange of political resources by increasing predictability and mobility in bargaining relationships.

It would be a mistake to assume that the mere creation of an institution for bargaining means that resource exchanges will be more predictable or mobile, or indeed that any bargaining will take place in that institution. We ought to distinguish between *effective* arenas, in which bargains that take place will have some impact on the distribution of resources (such as money, authority, information) among the relevant participants, and *ineffective* or *pseudo-arenas*, in which no real exchanges of resources take place. Bargaining in effective arenas has consequences for outside actors and organizations with whom arena participants may deal; bargaining in pseudo-arenas involves no meaningful changes for the participants and does not have an impact on the outside world.

Although it is true that numerous intergovernmental relations offices, federal-city liaisons, Federal Executive Boards, and interagency regional teams have been created to facilitate "communication" between federal and city officials, they have not served as effective arenas because decisions made in those bodies have not been binding on governmental policy. Without the authority to approve projects and commit funds, such institutions have served as good examples of pseudo-arenas in which agreements that are made do not necessarily have any consequences for the political world outside. Schelling distinguished between "talk" and "moves," saying that "talk is not a substitute for moves. Moves can in some way alter the game, by incurring manifest costs, risks, or a reduced range of subsequent choice; they have an information content, or *evidence* content, or a different character from that of speech." [11] Federal-local communications channels have often stimulated talk, but they have proved frustrating to local leaders who are more interested in moves (decisions as to which group will receive federal money; approval or disapproval of projects; appropriation and delivery of funds). The difficulty in creating effective arenas in which such moves can be made with more reliability and speed has been a continuing problem of intergovernmental relations. Even if the goals are agreed upon, projects approved, and funds committed, the need for a bargaining arena does not disappear. For the process of implementation—the carrying out of a policy—requires continuing negotiations and exchanges between relevant governmental actors.

Notes

1. Naomi Caiden and Aaron Wildavsky point out that coordination may have various contradictory meanings: efficiency, reliability, coercion, and consent. As a guide for action, they point out, the injunction to "coordinate" is useless. See *Planning and Budgeting in Poor Countries* (New York: John Wiley, 1974), pp. 277-279.

2. See Martha Derthick, *New Towns In-Town: Why a Federal Program Failed* (Washington, D.C.: The Urban Institute, 1972); and Jeffrey L. Pressman and Aaron Wildavsky, *Implementation: How Great Expectations in Washington Are Dashed in Oakland; Or, Why It's Amazing that Federal Programs Work at All, This Being a Saga of the Economic Development Administration as Told by Two Sympathetic Observers Who Seek to Build Morals on a Foundation of Ruined Hopes* (Berkeley and Los Angeles: University of California Press, 1973).
3. Thomas C. Schelling, *The Strategy of Conflict* (New York: Oxford University Press, 1960), p. 89.
4. *Ibid.*, p. 5.
5. *Ibid.*, pp. 22ff.
6. Robert A. Dahl, "The Concept of Power," *Behavioral Science* 2 (June, 1957), pp. 202-203.
7. John C. Harsanyi, "Measurement of Social Power, Opportunity Costs, and the Theory of Two-Person Bargaining Games," *Behavioral Science* 7 (January, 1962), p. 74.
8. Schelling, *Strategy of Conflict*, p. 106.
9. Warren F. Ilchman and Norman Thomas Uphoff, *The Political Economy of Change* (Berkeley and Los Angeles: University of California Press, 1969), pp. 35-37, 208-255.
10. *Ibid.*, p. 211.
11. Schelling, *Strategy of Conflict*, p. 117.

18. WAYS OF ACHIEVING FEDERAL OBJECTIVES

Martha Derthick

The Federal Government in State Politics

In giving grants and attaching conditions to them, the federal government becomes an actor in the state political system. It is a peripheral actor rather than an integral one, for it has no legitimate role within that system—no formal right to make decisions and no recognized informal right to function as a lobby. Nonetheless, it alters the environment within which the integral actors function, alters the distribution of influence among them, and thus itself becomes an actor in state politics.

The selection of subjects for the public agenda—of "issues" for consideration—is the first step in determining the content of public policy, and it is at this point in the process of state politics that federal influence begins to be felt. By offering grants for specified activities, the federal government places an item on the political agenda: should the aided activity be undertaken or not? The setting of conditions works in parallel fashion. By saying to the state that it will not give money unless a certain rule is adopted (or, if the grant program is already under way, by saying that money will cease to be given), the federal government causes the state to consider whether the required action should be taken. An issue is raised that might not have been raised in the absence of federal action. Strictly speaking, of course, the federal government does not itself place the question on the agenda of state politics. What it does is to stimulate proposals by actors integral to the state political system, such as elected executive or legislative officials, party officials, appointed administrators, or executives of pressure groups. For state political actors who independently share some or all of the federal goals, federal action creates opportunities ("excuses") for the making of proposals.

For these elected officials and for appointed administrators—who together are ultimately the objects of federal influence because they are

Reprinted by permission of the author and the publishers from *The Influence of Federal Grants: Public Assistance in Massachusetts* by Martha Derthick, Cambridge, Mass.: Harvard University Press, Copyright © 1970 by the President and Fellows of Harvard College, 201-214.

possessors of authority to act within the state government—federal sponsorship reduces the cost of making a proposal and taking the subsequent action. Not only are monetary costs transferred to the federal level; if opposition arises, state officials may be able to transfer political costs as well, by imputing responsibility to the federal government. Moreover, federal action increases the cost of inaction— that is, the cost of *not* proposing or taking the actions the federal government seeks to stimulate. Officials who do not respond to federal stimuli become vulnerable to criticism for failing to act—for "failing to take advantage of federal funds" or "failing to meet federal standards."

Federal influence continues to operate as consideration of the federally stimulated proposal proceeds. The terms of the federal offer or requirement affect the content of proposals and discussion within the state. The proponents or action takers have as one important resource of influence, perhaps their principal resource, the claim that action is desirable or necessary because it will secure federal funds. The "normal" distribution of influence among political actors in the state— that is, the distribution that would prevail in the absence of federal action—thus is altered to the advantage of those with whom the federal government is allied.

In summary, the federal government exercises influence in large part by stimulating demands from groups within the state and by placing "extra" resources of influence at their disposal. It works through allies.

The State Agency as Federal Ally

Temporary allies—that is, more or less accidental allies, intermittently active for limited purposes—may contribute substantially to the attainment of federal objectives. In Massachusetts the federal public assistance administration has at various times and for limited purposes been allied with the old-age lobby (the two have also been at odds) and with professional and good-government groups such as the National Association of Social Workers and the League of Women Voters. But the dependence of the federal government on support within the state is such that it needs a permanent ally, one always organized and prepared to take action, always receptive to federal communications, and having interests thoroughly consistent with those of the federal administration. From the perspective of the federal administrative agency, this is ideally the role of its state counterpart. As the formal recipient of federal funds, the formal channel for federal communication with the state, and a possessor of authority within the state government, the state agency has a combination of obligations to the federal administration and assets of influence at the state level that make it by far the most suitable and efficacious of potential federal allies. Much federal activity—some of it designed for that purpose and some not—contributes to making the state agency into an ally, an organization not simply accountable to the federal agency (responsible for the state's conduct and capable of reporting on it), but also *responsive* to it (disposed to make state conduct conform to federal preferences). Such activity is one of the major techniques of federal influence.

The first step in creating a state-agency ally is often to call an agency into existence. Many state and local administrative agencies, especially those in urban renewal, public housing, and antipoverty programs, have been created for the purpose of receiving and administering federal grants. The next step (likely to be more difficult with an established agency than a new one) is to shape its values and conceptions of purpose so that they are consistent with federal objectives, and to enhance its power and autonomy at the state level. To the extent that the state agency shares federal goals, is willing to commit its power to attaining them, and has power so to commit, the probability that federal goals will be achieved is greatly enhanced.

Federal patron agencies and their state counterparts might be expected to have shared values and goals without the federal agency's taking steps to assure this, if only because they share programmatic functions. The sharing of functions, however, is not necessarily sufficient to assure the congruence of a wide range of values among a high proportion of administrators in numerous governments, the governments themselves being representative of diverse value systems and regional subcultures. If federal preferences are to prevail, then, the core of shared values and goals that federal and state administrators derive from the sharing of a function must be elaborated and perfected, in ways of federal choosing, until a high degree of congruence has been achieved. The professionalization of personnel, through which a common body of values and doctrines is disseminated, has been the principal means of doing this.

To the extent that the federal effort to bring about a sharing of values between governments is successful, difficulties of obtaining conformance are much reduced. The state agency becomes highly responsive to federal preferences, and responsive for what federal administrators can only regard as the right reasons. That is, it responds not just because it seeks to maximize the receipt of federal funds (and thus is willing to act as if it shared federal goals); rather, it responds because it does in fact share them. Indoctrination of the state agency is the federal administrators' only defense against the persistent and pervasive problem that arises from the tendency of state governments to agree to federally stipulated actions because doing so will enlarge the flow of federal money. At most, the spread of professionalism at the state level may altogether eliminate the problem of nonconformance. If state agencies come to share federal values and have power to embody them in state policy, they become something more than responsive partners of the federal agency. They also undertake to pursue shared goals independently. The values expressed through public action at the state level then become identical to those that prevail within the federal administration. The result is the elimination of federal-state conflict and hence the elimination of the necessity for the exercises of federal influence. The federal effort to professionalize and to render autonomous the state agency is thus in a way the ultimate adaptation to limits on that influence.

Federal action contributes to state-agency power and autonomy in various ways, of which the most obvious, in the public assistance program, has been the "single state agency" requirement. On the basis of this statutory provision, federal administrators have insisted that the agency possess enough authority to assure that federal conditions are met. Very early in the federal grant program, this resulted in amendments to Massachusetts law that much increased the rule-making powers of the state welfare department.

In the case of the "single state agency" requirement, enhancing the counterpart's power is the primary end of federal action. Although most federal actions obviously do not have this as their major goal, virtually all federal-state interaction through the grant system incidentally yields that result.

As the recipient of federal grants, the counterpart is endowed with resources that would not otherwise be available to it and that come to it more or less independently of action by the governor or legislature, upon whom it would otherwise be altogether dependent for monetary support. How much power the agency thereby gains depends on how much discretion it has in the use of federal money. This use may be closely circumscribed by federal action or by the action of the state legislature. In the Massachusetts public assistance program, the state welfare department was more a passive channel for the routinized flow of federal funds to local agencies (and ultimately to assistance recipients) than an independent allocator of the funds, the crucial decisions about allocation having been made by the legislature (once the cost-of-living formula was passed, at least). Nevertheless, the result of federal grants was to increase, in a subtle way and to an unspecifiable degree, that state agency's power vis-à-vis local agencies. The agency gained leverage in its role as rule maker and supervisor of administration, since its right to function in this role depended both on grants of authority from the state legislature and on the state's sharing of assistance costs.

And the "state" share of costs, from the perspective of local agencies, was the equivalent of the state *and* federal shares combined, for the state welfare department disbursed federal grants to local agencies and had authority to supervise their spending. "Federal" money, having been so channeled, from the local perspective acquired the character of "state" money.

The stipulation of federal conditions or rules to accompany grants had the same effect. Given the nature of a federal system, federal rules can be effective within the state only after being reincarnated as state rules. Therefore the making of federal rules for the grant program stimulates the making of state rules; it stimulates the usage of the counterpart agency's authority. Again, whether the result of this process is to increase state-agency "power" depends on the particular circumstances of the rule making and the particular relationship of power. When the state rule simply repeats verbatim a federal rule and does not entail the use of state discretion, state-agency power in relation to the federal administration is decreased. On the other hand, whether the state agency exercises discretion itself (typically the case) or merely repeats what the federal administration has stipulated (less often the case), its rule-making authority within the state political system has been enhanced by usage. In Massachusetts, for the perspective of the local agencies to which public assistance rules were addressed until 1968, all rules were state rules no matter what the origin of their content. All were experienced and interpreted as manifestations of state authority. All therefore tended to enhance state power as it was exercised in relation to local agencies.[1]

An alliance between federal and state administrative agencies, formed and perfected through the working of the grant system, can become a powerful force in state politics, perhaps the dominant force in the making of policy for the program in question. When federal and state agencies work together, each reinforces the influence of the other, the state agency gaining as a result of the federal partnership, the federal agency being compensated for deficiencies in its ability to exercise influence directly in state affairs. The result is that a relationship of mutual dependence develops such that each accommodates itself, perhaps unconsciously, to the interests of the other. What the federal agency undertakes depends in part on what its state counterpart desires or can be expected to concur in, for the state agency's cooperation is essential to the realization of any federal goal. Similarly, a state agency learns to accommodate its goals to federal ones. Where, as in Massachusetts before 1968, a state agency has little independent strength within the state political system, its dependence on federal patronage becomes very great. It must rely on federal action to create opportunities for action and on the justification of "federal requirements" or the "availability of federal funds" to rationalize and legitimize all that it does. Whatever power and autonomy the Massachusetts welfare department possesses derive very largely from the relationship with its federal patron.

Federal influence, in summary, operates mainly through the agency that receives grants, and with the agency's self-serving cooperation. It operates by enhancing the role that the agency plays in the state political system and by shaping the agency's values, goals, interests, and actions. It operates primarily on the structures and processes of policymaking and administration rather than directly on the substance of policy. This may be a critical limitation, but if the influence on structures and processes is extensive and enduring enough, the result must be to influence policy outcomes as well—*all* policy outcomes, not just those in which the federal government is actively interested. If the federal government can influence the locus of policymaking authority in the state government, how the policymakers perceive opportunities for action, what values prevail among the policymakers, and what resources of influence are at their disposal, it has gone far in influencing the content of policy. It has, in any case, increased the disposition of the state to respond to federal action and to undertake, independently, actions consistent with federal preferences.

The Withholding of Funds

The ultimate resource of federal influence is the withholding of the grant, but this is almost impossible to use, for withholding serves no one's interests. Objections are bound to come from Congress.[2] Although Congress agrees with the administration on certain general statements of federal conditions when the effects on particular constituencies are impossible to foresee, withholding is a specific act, threatening to a particular constituency; this automatically brings a response from that constituency's representatives in Congress and evokes the sympathetic concern of other congressmen, who are made aware of a potential threat to their own constituencies. Even apart from the possible difficulties with Congress, administrators are reluctant to withhold funds because of the damage it might do to program goals and to relations with state governments. Given the limits on its influence, the federal administration is—or at least perceives itself to be—heavily dependent upon maintaining their good will and disposition to cooperate. Partly for this reason, it seeks to avoid direct, hostile confrontations with state governments such as the withholding of funds entails. Above all, it wishes to avoid public sanctions against the state agency (which, at least *pro forma,* must be the object of withholding), for one way of maintaining the state-agency alliance is to avoid embarrassing the agency in public.[3]

These objections to the manipulation of funds as an enforcement technique apply to the withholding of the entire grant, which in principle is the penalty for nonconforming policies or recurrently nonconforming administrative practices, more than to the taking of audit exceptions, which in principle is the penalty for specific nonconforming acts of expenditure. Because they are more feasible to use than withholding, the federal administration is sometimes tempted to use audit exceptions on a large scale as a substitute for withholding; that is, audit exceptions may be applied to a whole class of expenditures in an effort to bring about change in a nonconforming policy or practice, as when the regional representative decided to apply them in Massachusetts in the later 1940s to the salaries of elected board members who were engaged in administration. However, using audit exceptions in this way is subject in some degree to most of the same objections, and to others besides. An audit exception is inconvenient to administer, and as a *post hoc* action that applies only to particular acts of expenditure (selected acts, in the normal case, for not all expenditures are audited) its range of effectiveness is limited. It is particularly difficult to apply to acts of omission. The difficulties of withholding or of taking audit exceptions on a large scale help to explain why the whole aim of federal enforcement activity is to bring about compliance in advance and thus to avoid confrontations in which financial penalties will have to be invoked. Federal administrators consider that they have done their jobs well when the volume of audit exceptions is low.

It would be wrong, however, to infer that the federal ability to withhold funds is of no effect. It is in fact one of the major resources of federal influence—but it is of use mainly as a potential resource. It lies at the foundation, as a weapon in reserve, of all federal enforcement activity, and the nature of that activity is such as to make the best possible use of it.

Federal enforcement is a diplomatic process. It is as if the terms of a treaty, an agreement of mutual interest to the two governmental parties, were more or less continuously being negotiated. In these negotiations, numerous diplomatic forms and manners are observed, especially by the federal negotiators. Typically they are in the position of having made a démarche. Negotiations become active when a new federal condition is promulgated or an old one is reinterpreted, or when a federal administrative review has revealed a defect in the state's administration. Negotiations are carried on privately. The federal negotiators refrain from making statements in public, for they want to avoid the appearance of meddling in the internal affairs of the states.

They refrain from making overt threats. They are patient. Negotiations over a single issue may go on steadily for several years and intermittently for decades. They are polite. In addressing state officials, they are usually elaborately courteous. They make small gestures of deference to the host government, as by offering to meet at times and at places of its choosing.

The objective of the negotiating process is to obtain as much conformance as can be had without the actual withholding of funds. Because federal requirements are typically stated in general terms, administrators have a high degree of flexibility in negotiating terms of conformance. Within the broad guidelines they have laid down, they have been able to adapt to the political and administrative circumstances of each state. If the constraints of the situation so require it, federal administrators may consider conformance to have been achieved even if state action falls considerably short of the federal ideal. As long as federal requirements are vague and general, conformance, though difficult to prove, is equally impossible to disprove. The federal administration may therefore avoid outright defeat no matter what concessions it makes to state political and administrative realities. (The situation changes, of course, if federal requirements are highly specific. Federal administrators then may feel compelled to accept merely formal proofs of conformance that falsify reality and that they *know* to falsify reality, as with caseload standards in Massachusetts.)

The function of intergovernmental diplomacy in a federal system, like that of international diplomacy, is to facilitate communication and amicable relations between governments that are pretending to be equals by obscuring the question of whether one is more equal than the other. In the case of federal-state relations in the United States, that question is obscure in any event, and the function of diplomatic processes may merely be to keep it that way or to obscure, and thereby facilitate, changes in power relations. That this be done is important primarily to the federal government, for it is the aggressive, the states the defensive, actor in intergovernmental relations. It has the greater interest in seeing that change is facilitated. But perhaps the principal advantage of a diplomatic style to federal administrators (and the choice of that style is essentially their choice), is that this mode of behavior makes the best possible use of the technique of withholding funds. It enables federal officials to exploit, without actually using, this basic resource. In cases of federal-state conflict, federal negotiators keep open the possibility of withholding during the process of negotiation, referring to it in oblique and subtle terms. They seek to obscure the low probability that they will actually use it. By not making overt threats to withhold, federal administrators protect their credibility; the state is kept guessing. Diplomatic behavior is thus an adaptation to the impracticability of withholding, as well as to other constraints on federal influence, especially the widespread belief that the federal government ought not to interfere in state and local affairs. By relying so heavily on private negotiations, federal officials avoid "meddling" in public. At the same time, they avoid exposing the state agency to public embarrassment or more tangible federal penalties so that the agency's disposition to cooperate is not discouraged.

It might seem that, as time passes, the federal administration's failure to withhold funds would undermine its credibility and render withholding useless even as a negotiation weapon. In fact, the federal willingness to withhold funds itself diminishes with time. It is much easier to withhold (or delay the granting of) funds at the outset of a grant program, when the volume of the grant is low and the program not yet routinized. In the first five years of the public assistance program, the federal administration did make several attempts to withhold funds, and it was not altogether implausible, when a dispute with Massachusetts arose in 1939-40 over the merit-system requirement, that it would try to do so again. The welfare commissioner, apparently believing that it would, gave in to the Social Security Board very quickly. Ten years later, when the issue over board member-administrators arose, it was much less plausible that withholding should be tried, and by 1964-65, when the dispute over the educational requirement developed, withholding was altogether implausible. But not everyone knew this (many state legislators did not), and some people who did know it, especially the welfare commissioner, preferred to pretend that they did not. Withholding would probably not remain effective as a resource of influence were it not for the federal alliance with the state agency; when the two cooperate in pursuit of a shared goal, the state agency exploits the possibility of federal holding and vouches for the credibility of it.

The fact that the state agency is the sole official recipient of federal communications and the official interpreter of them within the state gives it an important advantage. It can make decisions about dissemination and interpretation in such a way as to facilitate attainment of its own ends. This is likely to mean, as in the dispute over the educational requirement, that the state agency will encourage the belief that a serious threat of federal withholding exists. The federal administration, which alone might provide an accurate inter-pretation of its own intent, refrains from doing so as a tactical necessity. Attempts to elicit clear statements of intent are unavailing, whether they come from the state agency or other sources. But whereas the federal agency refrains from issuing threats of withholding itself, it does nothing to dispel threats that others issue in its name. Its interests will best be served if those statements are believed. In these circumstances, federal intentions may be difficult for anyone to evaluate, even those who, like state administrative officials, have direct access to the federal agency and experience in the administration of grant programs. For others, such as state legislators, who have no such access and no such experience, federal intentions are virtually impossible to evaluate. In any case, it is always impossible for the opponents of federally sponsored action to demonstrate that the federal administration will *not* withhold funds.

The limited capacity of state legislators to appraise federal intentions with respect to withholding is one advantage the state agency has whenever it undertakes an action with federal sponsorship. It might be supposed, however, that opponents of federally sponsored action would get help from Congress, which is thought to be responsive to the appeals of parochial interests and skilled at overturning the acts of federal administrators. Judging from the Massachusetts experience, however, appeals to Congress appear to bring few results to those who make them. When federal and state agencies act cooperatively, they have much protection, individually or together, against unwanted intervention from legislatures at either or both levels of the federal system.

They have, of course, the usual assets of administrators confronting legislators: they are the full-time specialists in their function, while legislators have only a part-time interest in that function. For a congressman to intervene successfully once the federal administration has committed itself to a particular action in a particular state requires an intense and sustained interest in the matter and a great mastery of administrative detail. The Massachusetts case suggests that these conditions will rarely be met. Although congressmen, in response to constituents' requests, at critical times inquired of the federal administration about its intentions in Massachusetts, these inquiries almost without exception were routine and perfunctory. The letter from the constituent was forwarded to the administration with a form letter from the congressman requesting a response. A response— couched in oblique, noncommittal language that tended to minimize the degree of disruption being experienced within the state and the degree of the federal administration's responsibility for it—then went to the congressman, who presumably relayed it to the inquiring constituent as proof that he had acted on the constituent's request. Typically, these congressional inquiries revealed little knowledge or specialized interest in the case on the part of the congressman, and the replies from the administration were designed to avoid increasing either.

The only important exception to this pattern was the activity of Congressman [John] McCormack with respect to the directive on educational requirements. If ever there was a situation in which congressional intervention might be effective, this seemed to be it. Here was a congressman—the Speaker of the House, no less—who was opposed to an important action of the administration, an action profoundly damaging to the career prospects of perhaps eight hundred local government employees in his state. His objection was largely spontaneous and strongly enough felt to produce protests to the secretary and the undersecretary of health, education, and welfare. But in the end it had very little effect on the administration's action. None of this means that federal public assistance administrators are not subject in profoundly important ways to congressional controls. What the administrators undertake to do depends heavily on what Congress has authorized and on the administrators' guess of what Congress will tolerate. Contrary to what is perhaps the usual impression of Congress' performance, the evidence from public assistance suggests that Congress is more effective in making broad policy than in doing "casework" for particular individuals or groups of aggrieved constituents.

In addition to the defenses that administrators normally have against legislators, the grant system offers special ones, a result of the diffusion of responsibility it entails. When called to account for controversial actions, administrative agencies at both federal and state levels can escape responsibility vis-à-vis their own legislatures by attributing responsibility to a counterpart at the other level. In parallel fashion, each legislature can escape responsibility vis-à-vis its own constituents. The ability of all major official actors to deny responsibility very much reduces the chances of successful opposition.

Notes

1. From the perspective of the state agency, federal efforts to enhance the agency's authority and to stimulate exercise of that authority are not unambiguously beneficial. How welcome they are depends on how highly the state agency values the ends prescribed by the federal administration; on the amount of resistance that pursuit of them is likely to provoke within the state; and on the federal ability to endow the agency with resources of influence to overcome the resistance. The danger is that federal action will force the state agency into situations of conflict without sufficiently compensating it.

2. See U.S. Senate, *Proposed Cutoff of Welfare Funds to the State of Alabama,* Hearings before the Committee on Finance, 90th Cong., 1st sess. (1967), for a recent example.
3. In doing research for this book, I found that the one restriction on the cooperation of federal regional officials was a concern that their relations with state officials might be damaged. I was given access to federal files with the understanding that I would not use them to attack or gratuitously embarrass the state agency. I was asked to use the material "objectively," a condition that I was of course happy to accept. When the completed manuscript was made available for comment, the federal office did not ask for any deletions.

Part II

REVIEW QUESTIONS

1. What would be a plausible explanation for the racial differences in public opinion about intergovernmental matters, as found in the ACIR survey? What is the significance of this split? In your answer, draw not only from the readings in this section but also from Riker's analysis in Part I. If Riker is correct in saying that the civil-rights era has successfully removed the race-based significance of federalism, do you expect the observed difference in public opinion to decline over time? Are there any policy implications that can be drawn for the 1990s, a period in which the states seem to be especially active?

2. What intergovernmental policy implications follow from the fact that American government structures are bewilderingly diverse? Are rational action and reform possible in such an intergovernmental system? In your answer, consider Reischauer's discussion of the negative consequences of this diversity; can you suggest any positive ones?

3. What political and structural impediments stand in the way of efforts to attempt equalization of governments' resources through the grant system, even if budgets were not as tight as they have been in recent years?

4. What are the sources of potential strength and weakness for the PIGs?

5. Describe the shifts in position and tensions felt by the main PIGs during the 1990s. What conclusions drawn by Haider might be challenged by the evidence presented in Walters's essay? What political behavior would one expect to see on the part of the PIGs if a president were to propose a wholesale shift of funding from categoricals to block grants and a further cutback in total assistance? Why would the PIGs react as you predict?

6. Why do opponents of intergovernmental change have a strategic advantage in intergovernmental politics?

7. Interpret the models of the intergovernmental system, presented by Wright in Part I, in light of the evidence presented by Beyle on the governors' activism on education policy and other matters. If the states are not now largely reactive, or passive, in the complex network, which model most satisfactorily interprets current activity? Is a new model needed?

8. In a portion of his argument not excerpted in this volume, Anton predicts "permanent instability" in the dynamics of an intergovernmental political system such as he has described. Can you explain why this prediction might seem to follow? Can you identify any evidence on this point?

9. Explain the link between the increasing use of formula entitlements by the federal government and the growth in grant litigation in recent years.

10. Does Pressman's bargaining framework and analysis of the donor-recipient relationship conflict with Elazar's interpretation of intergovernmental relations in the nineteenth century? If so, explain the divergence.

11. Your friend is very concerned with the apparently overpowering role of the federal government in intergovernmental relations during the 1960s and 1970s. On the basis of the analyses presented by Pressman and Derthick, how would you explain to your friend the sources of strength and weakness in both the national government's role and the states' role? Can you explain the shifts since the late 1970s via these perspectives? Does Howard's discussion of the Supreme Court's role in the *Garcia* case cause you to modify the analyses by Pressman and Derthick?

12. Can you make a case in favor of letting *politics* determine the respective spheres of national and state authority—that is, can you argue that Howard's critique of the *Garcia* decision is exaggerated, or off the mark? On the other hand, can you defend the idea that the Court should be responsible for protecting a clear state role? Are there dangers in letting "merely" politics decide?

13. Derthick claims that the federal government hardly ever cuts off funding for a grant program, despite the fact that, frequently, states

and locals fail to meet federal requirements. Why not? Does this mean that the threat to eliminate funding is empty?

14. Derthick says, "The function of intergovernmental diplomacy in a federal system, like that of international diplomacy, is to facilitate communication and amicable relations between governments that are pretending to be equals by obscuring the question of whether one is more equal than the other." Is this analogy to diplomacy reasonable? Why or why not?

15. Compare Derthick's analysis of the troubling implications of the pattern of influence in intergovernmental politics to Grodzins's more sanguine assessment. Be sure to analyze the topics of diffusion of responsibility and bureaucratic barriers to outside influence. Does Anton's coverage of the complex coalitions of intergovernmental politics help to render Derthick's case description more understandable? Or does Anton's analysis suggest that the politics of many intergovernmental programs are likely to be even *more* complicated than public assistance in Massachusetts?

Part III

FISCAL ASPECTS OF
INTERGOVERNMENTAL RELATIONS

Money may or may not make the world go 'round, but there may
be no better way of seeing the interdependence and complexity of
today's intergovernmental system than by "following the money trail,"
or examining the fiscal aspects of the network. Power and control, after
all, follow money. And nowadays, financial instruments—especially the
grant-in-aid—are one of the most important ways by which American
governments at all levels are tied together in a bewilderingly intricate
and dense set of obligations, opportunities, and dependencies.

As of 1988, for instance, and despite the cutbacks in aid under
Reagan, federal dollars constituted 18 percent of state and local
budgets. Estimated 1992 intergovernmental aid from Washington
totaled $149.4 billion, while in 1988 such aid from the states to local
units itself amounted to $149 billion.[1] Clearly, then, these indicators
suggest considerable financial interdependence and complexity.

The readings in Part III document some of the fiscal developments in the system during recent years, explain the significance and
purposes of intergovernmental fiscal instruments, and analyze some of
the donor and recipient behaviors generated by intergovernmental
fiscal activity. Once again, however, it will prove impossible to cover
these aspects of the American system without paying considerable
attention to other features, especially the *political* significance of fiscal
mechanisms. Thus, a lesson in this section, as in the preceding one, is
that the various dimensions of the intergovernmental pattern are
inextricably related.

Even with the wide range of issues and topics addressed in the
readings that follow, some important fiscal issues receive little or no
attention. Most of the block grants from the federal government, for
instance, are not treated individually here, nor is the contentious topic
of urban-suburban fiscal disparities. The impact of the Reagan
cutbacks is addressed, but not in exhaustive detail. The repercussions of
this period are, however, dealt with again in later parts of the book.

The introductory chapter of this volume identifies some of the
most important fiscal instruments. Various forms of grants have been

significant in the development of the fiscal aspects of the intergovernmental system. Several readings in this part address the economic and
political purposes of these tools.

Part III begins with George Break's classification of fiscal
mechanisms according to their expected economic effects (no. 19). His
discussion is especially helpful because it treats not only fiscal mechanisms employed by the national government but also the economic
impact of state aid to local governments. Break's analysis is grounded in
economic theory. But one can also examine empirically the actual
operations of the fiscal instrumentalities and assess the overall state of
affairs of the fiscally interdependent system. The next reading (no. 20),
by Phillip Monypenny, does so by comparing the conventional justifications for aid with the aid's practical impact.

In Monypenny's frequently quoted essay, the effects of the
intergovernmental grant system are analyzed in toto. Writing during an
earlier debate about the intergovernmental network and its future,
Monypenny finds that the oft-cited economic and fiscal ends attributed
to the grant system are not supported by the data. In other words, most
of these justifications for the system are unfounded. He then argues that
this system of fiscal instruments actually serves some political functions.
His logic supports the view, advanced in the introductory chapter of
this book, that American intergovernmental relations constitute an
amalgamated pluralism and that indisputable links exist between fiscal
and political aspects of the system.

The form of the specific instruments of fiscal assistance, however,
does matter. Three readings in this part (nos. 21-23) focus on various
types of mechanisms to elucidate their impacts.

Increasingly popular in recent years have been assistance programs based on formulas rather than on project grants. Because of the
absence of overt unit-versus-unit competition, formula grants may seem
a more "objective," less partisan method of channeling intergovernmental aid. However, this is an oversimplified view. Richard Nathan
demonstrates this point in an essay (no. 21) on the "politics of
printouts" that now accompany any effort to establish a formula grant.
He concentrates on issues surrounding the revenue-sharing program,
prior to its demise, and the Community Development Block Grant
program—an initiative still in place. As his analysis makes evident, the
process of establishing formula-based aid involves a complex interplay
of technical and political considerations. This essay may also help to
explain the finding, reported by Monypenny, that the system does not
accomplish much financial equalization across jurisdictions; Nathan
shows that values like "equalization" may be complicated blends of
competing considerations.

The choice between formula and project grants clearly involves multiple trade-offs. The same is true when one considers the options of categorical versus broader forms of assistance like block grants. As the federal treasury has become overburdened, Congress (and interest groups supportive of specific forms of activism) has found itself tempted toward narrowing some of the discretion earlier provided to the states and local governments via block grants. One method increasingly attempted is to "earmark," or set aside, part of a large and broad grant program for more specific purposes. As novel policy issues seem to demand attention but too few funds are available from Washington for a concerted effort with a new program, earmarking can seem attractive to those at the center. However, nonnational governments often bristle at such constraints, seeing in them increasing demands from the national level and an overly standardized view of what the priorities must be across highly diverse communities and regions. Cheryl Arvidson (no. 22) provides a view of this struggle as it plays itself out in today's intergovernmental arena.

Regardless of the fate of the major block grants, however, and despite the variety of fiscal instruments available, *categorical* aid still dominates the system and is likely to do so for the foreseeable future. Why? Part of the reason is found in the excerpt from a study of categorical grants conducted by the Advisory Commission on Intergovernmental Relations (no. 23). This analysis examines economic and political inducements to adopt this form of financial assistance.

The final three essays (nos. 24-26) in this part of the volume document different ways in which the interdependence of the system affects various actors and perspectives.

Margaret Wrightson (no. 24) analyzes another important Supreme Court case of recent vintage, *South Carolina* v. *Baker,* the results of which seem to challenge state and local claims to immunity from federal taxation—in this instance, regarding municipal bonds. (Municipal bonds are used by municipalities to finance debt. The holders of such bonds have been exempt from federal taxation on the proceeds, and this feature has allowed these local governments to borrow at substantially lower costs than would otherwise be the case.) Wrightson's study of the details of decision-making on this issue vividly demonstrates interdependence in the system: not only fiscal interdependence of the governments themselves, but also complex links among courts, constitutional principles, and the nitty-gritty budget-balancing needs of the nation's cities. Many other demonstrations of fiscal interdependence among American governments could be offered—for instance, national reform of the federal income tax law in 1986 had profound effects on taxes and receipts of many states as well, since the minutiae of income tax law and regulation of different levels of government have become woven together over the years. But Wrightson's coverage of the municipal-bond matter demonstrates the broader point impressively.

Cities all over the country, of course, have had to respond more immediately to the intergovernmental aid cutbacks of recent years. David Morgan and William Pammer (no. 25) investigate just how a sample of cities have responded to this crunch. Their findings indicate that cities and their managers have resorted to many approaches during this period, but that it is exceedingly difficult to predict just which types of responses a city is likely to exhibit. This "garbage can" reaction—a nearly random reply to the unpleasant reality of diminished federal funding—seems consistent with other studies of government decision making under conditions of cutbacks.

In the final reading of this section James Skok (no. 26) discusses a different sort of impact of the detailed fiscal ties among governments. State legislatures, like the national one, jealously guard their authority over the public treasury; yet, as was clear in Derthick's essay, intricate financial agreements and transfers between governments may make this control especially difficult to retain. Skok discusses state legislatures' recent efforts to gain more control over fiscal aspects of intergovernmental relations, specifically during a reform of state financial procedures in Pennsylvania. His analysis documents an irony: interdependence and complexity have stimulated some actors (like state legislatures) to become more involved in and acquire more control over intergovernmental processes; the results may be even more complexity and expanded patterns of interdependence.

Note

1. U.S. Advisory Commission on Intergovernmental Relations, *Revenues and Expenditures*, vol. 2 of *Significant Features of Fiscal Federalism 1990* (Washington, D.C.: ACIR, August 1990), 42, 48.

19. THE ECONOMICS OF INTERGOVERNMENTAL GRANTS

George F. Break

. . . Grants-in-aid may be classified in numerous ways.[1] The classification in Table 2 highlights both the flexibility of grants as a fiscal instrument and the diversity that complicates the assessment of the effects of different grant programs. Four basic types of grant are widely used.

Categorical grants of the open-ended matching variety (3e) have the economic effect of stimulating state and local expenditure in designated functional areas (1d) by lowering the price at which grantees can acquire the program benefits; grantees are free to buy as much as they like at that lower price. The grants are allocated by formula with administrative checks on their use (2c). Federal grants for public assistance and medicaid, which accounted for about 18 percent of total federal grant expenditures in fiscal 1978, fall in this category. State matching grants of any kind are rare.

Unconditional general grants allocated by formula fall at the opposite end of the economic spectrum. Their effect is to increase the money income of recipient governments but not to change the prices at which they can purchase goods and services for their citizens. Though there are no examples of a completely unrestricted federal general grant (1a, 2a, 3a) in the United States, general revenue sharing (1b, 2b, 3b) comes close.[2] About 10 percent of state grant funds goes for general support of local government.

Fixed-amount grants for specified purposes are the most popular type of grant in the United States, accounting for 88 percent of federal grant expenditures in fiscal 1978 and over 85 percent of state grant expenditures in fiscal 1972. This category includes the traditional federal categorical matching closed-end grant (1d, 2c, 3cd), federal block grants (1c, 2bc, 3b), and most state grants for education and highways.[3] Though messy in the eyes of many economists because they combine income and price effects in ways that are difficult to

From George F. Break, *Financing Government in a Federal System* (Washington, D.C.: Brookings, 1980), 73-76.

Table 2   The Many Dimensions of Intergovernmental Grants

1. **How funds are used by recipient**
   a. Unrestricted
   b. General, with limited restrictions
   c. Block, within broad program areas
   d. Categorical or functional, within narrow program areas

2. **How funds are allocated to recipient**
   a. Formula, unrestricted
   b. Formula, subject to limited restrictions
   c. Formula, with administrative checks
   d. Competitive applications by grantees (project grants)

3. **Degree of participation by grantor**
   a. None (beyond provision of grant funds)
   b. Administrative oversight
   c. Technical services; cooperative management
   d. Grantee matching requirements up to the limit of grantor funds (closed-end matching grants)
   e. Grantee matching requirements with unlimited grantor funds (open-ended matching grants)

disentangle, these fixed-sum special-purpose grants have numerous attractions. Not the least of these may be their ability to conciliate appearance and reality, seeming to support some function close to the heart of the grantor while in reality allowing the grantee to use the funds for any local purpose desired. Closed-end grants have the further advantage of greatly simplifying the budgetary and administrative problems of the grantor. Open-ended grants, in contrast, create budgetary uncertainties by committing the grantor to the provision of whatever funds grantees choose to match. And if the aided activities are not tightly defined, recipients may exert explosive pressures on spending levels by diverting open-ended grant funds to programs the grantor had neither intended nor wished to support.[4]

Project grants are distinguished by the requirement that donees compete for the available funds by submitting detailed plans concerning their use (2d). Some potential recipients may choose not to compete, either because they lack the technical expertise needed to prepare the required plans or because they regard the risks of failure as too high to justify the costs of applying. For the grantor, on the other hand, project grants provide welcome opportunities to reject low-priority proposals and to adjust the terms of support for others so as to maximize the public benefits to be obtained from the funds expended. In fiscal 1972, project grants accounted for 21 percent of federal grant expenditures but less than 2 percent of state grant spending.

The greater importance of project grants in the federal grant system suggests that the relationship between the two parties to a transaction may have a significant impact on grant design. The degree and type of controls exercised by grantors might well be different on grants between two independent powers than on grants between superior and subordinate powers or grants involving a mixture of independent and subordinate powers.

Notes

1. See, for example, Jesse Burkhead and Jerry Miner, *Public Expenditure* (Aldine, 1971), p. 285; ACIR, *Federal Grants, Their Effects on State-Local Expenditures, Employment Levels, Wage Rates: The Intergovernmental Grant System: An Assessment and Proposed Policies*, Report A-61 (GPO, 1977), pp. 25-29.
2. In Canada, federal-provincial tax equalization grants fall in the completely unrestricted category. Australia also uses unconditional financial assistance grants. See ACIR, *In Search of Balance: Canada's Intergovernmental Experience* (GPO, 1971); David B. Perry, "Federal-Provincial Fiscal Relations: The Last Six Years and the Next Five," *Canadian Tax Journal*, vol. 20 (July-August 1972), pp. 349-60; James A. Maxwell, "Revenue-Sharing in Canada and Australia: Some Implications for the United States," *National Tax Journal*, vol. 24 (June 1971), pp. 251-65.
3. In states with separate school districts, education grants looked at from the point of view of the state government are grants restricted to one function; but from the point of view of the school district, they are general-purpose grants unless their use is restricted to particular education programs.
4. Martha Derthick, *Uncontrollable Spending for Social Services Grants* (Brookings Institution, 1975).

20. FEDERAL GRANTS-IN-AID TO STATE GOVERNMENTS: A POLITICAL ANALYSIS

Phillip Monypenny

The federal system is always in danger and it is always rising anew from the ashes of its earlier existence. The current concern about the federal system, which has an obvious base in the party battle, is indicated by the number of reports and studies, non-partisan, if not non-political in character, which are concerned with it. Though these contribute a great deal of information about the current state of federal-state relations, it cannot be said that they settle any of the questions currently in dispute, in particular the question of whether the position and significance of the states as policy making centers has been significantly changed by the changing scope of the activity of the national government. . . . It is to the scope and character of the grants system, and to its political conditions, that this paper is directed. Incident to this discussion there may be an opinion, if not a conclusion, as to the effect of the grant system on the policy making freedom of state government.

[The author analyzes developments in the grant system, documents the patterns of grants-in-aid, and then compares the results with some of the most frequently cited justifications for the American system of fiscal interdependence.—Ed.]

. . . The picture presented, both in terms of the distribution of aid among the states, and the apparently arbitrary selection of purposes for which aid is extended do not square very well with the textbook justifications for a grant-in-aid system. The classic case for the extension of financial assistance by one government to another is that it provides money for local units which need it in order to support essential activities at a minimum level. This implies a larger measure of support for some units than for others, depending on the relative ability of units to finance the programs supported. No *major* federal grant is based primarily on an equalization factor, and those which include such a factor do not begin to produce a uniform level of service. . . . Perhaps

From *National Tax Journal* 13 (March 1960): 1, 11-16. Reprinted by permission of the National Tax Association.

the most comprehensive justification of the federal grant system would be that it provides a measure of service which national interest requires without complete federal assumption of the function. ... Every grant, from the construction of wildlife refuges to the piddling expenditures for civil defense, serves some purpose which its defenders regard as properly national. The only difficulty is that the attributes of matters of national concern are by no means obvious. ...

The stimulation of state and local activity in fields of national interest is often cited as a proper basis of federal aid. Apart from civil defense, in which the national expenditure is minute, there are no grant fields which had not developed prior to the grants as activities of state governments under their inherent powers. This is true of higher education, of the agricultural and home economics extension service, of orthopedic care for crippled children, of state financing of highway construction, of unemployment compensation, or whatever. It is true that federal aid may have been a factor in persuading the less-ready states to undertake what had already been undertaken elsewhere. It is hard to make a case for federal aid as a pioneering measure.

Finally, the difficulties which state and local governments face in raising revenue are often urged as a basis for increased federal assistance. The enormously wide variations in the ratio of resources to populations among the states make this absurd if it requires aid to all states on a uniform basis. Admitting the greater difficulty of tapping wealth in a smaller area than a large one, in dealing with a national system of production and distribution, most of the difficulties of the states in raising revenue are self-imposed. The states increased revenue drastically in the middle of the depression, at a time when it would seem to have been economic folly to raise taxes, and expanded their own scale of operations equally drastically. If a tax on real estate remains the prime resource of local governments to support their ever more expensive functions, this is the doing of the states, not the federal government. Those cities whose fiscal difficulties are most prominently displayed house the greatest concentrations of wealth.

The claim of greater administrative competence on the part of federal authorities may be viewed with some skepticism. Wisconsin supplied key members of the federal staff in the early days of employment security, and the states have contributed a considerable contingent of public health officers to the U.S. Public Health Service. It is true that the federal service escapes some of the impediments which hamper administrators of state programs. They are freer of the fear of political reprisals from minor political figures, and they are able to handle the recruitment and assignment of personnel with far less concern about the patronage obligations of executive and legislative leaders. On the other hand, the introduction of federal aid administration imposes another administrative and legislative layer, and to that extent dilutes responsibility, slows action, and increases the necessity of documentation. A great many states could probably build highways just as well without the oversight of the [federal bureaucracy], and administer unemployment compensation and the public employment services without the watchful eye of the [national agency responsible].

Nevertheless, federal aid is here to stay and it is not likely to become any more consistent from one program to another. The balance of federal to state authority, which varies from one program to another, is not likely to shift very much.

The standard explanation of taxpayers' organizations for the federal aid programs is that they represent the triumph of expenditure without responsibility. There is an element of truth in that, but it is not the whole story. It is obvious that many states choose to spend less than others in the very fields in which federal aid pays the highest bonuses for state expenditure. A dollar raised from taxes is still a dollar, whether it brings additional money in federal grants or not. The pressure against the tax is just as heavy by those who have no interest in the expenditure. Obviously, too, Congress has not escaped the need to tax to support these programs, and what its members stand to gain by satisfying demands for larger grants, they lose by imposing taxes. The increase in state tax revenues has been dramatic, and it has been incurred to meet increasing state responsibilities in the very fields in which federal aid has been least available—public education, mental hospitals, and, in the wealthier states, general assistance.

Nor is there much evidence that federal aid causes costs to be incurred for certain purposes despite a lack of interest in them by people in the state. In many of the fields where state expenditure is relatively low, . . . federal grants have been unsuccessful in luring increased expenditure. Where there is local support for the activity as in highways and vocational education, expenditures in many states are far larger than the minimum that would be required just to match federal allotments. On the other hand, in the fields in which excessive expenditure is alleged to be created by federal aid, public assistance, especially for the aged, there is the strongest local support for large expenditure, and the state programs long preceded federal grants.

It is unlikely therefore that the prospect of free expenditure by the states, without the assumption of concomitant tax obligation is the chief root of the grants system. What is then the root of this apparently contradictory phenomenon of patchwork assistance to states in which each field of activity has its own basis for granting money and its own set of administrative requirements, varying from very stringent, to very undemanding? It must be sought in the political system of the United States itself, which refuses to conform to the nice legal distinctions of a federal system, or to the logical consistencies of the advocates of executive responsibility and responsible party government.

That system has been adequately sketched in other places and by more skillful hands than those which shape these paragraphs. The population of the United States is divided by loyalties to a thousand different causes. People look to the complex fabric of government for means to pursue these causes, acting at points which are responsive, whatever the formal jurisdiction of the officials who respond. Groups within the population use their influence in one part of the fabric to negate the influence of their opponents at other points, to impose controls, or to escape them. The population acts through political parties and outside of them; it divides in elections for office, and recombines in pursuit of more particular goals. It uses the weapons of numbers, or of status, of publicity, or of intensity of organization, of money, or of familial and personal connection, as they are appropriate.

For such a population the federal grant-in-aid is a made-to-order device for securing unity of action without sacrificing the cohesiveness which is necessary for political success. The great obstacle to effective political action in a country such as the United States is the particularity of the ends of a great part of the politically active public. There are political organizations which will gladly lose national elections if they can keep their hold on local office, and followers of a national leader who are indifferent to the local office base of the party leadership whom they wish to enlist in their campaign. There are local labor organizations which will sacrifice any doctrinal commitment which their parent organizations may have if they can maintain their jurisdiction over jobs which members hold in public employment or in the work under government contract. There are wheat farmers who see farm programs in terms of wheat, and growers of perishable commodities who are more interested in the financing of production and distribution and in cooperative marketing than they are in price supports. Specificity of aim limits the possibility of getting sufficient support to outweigh opposition. Commitment to a political party as a means of political action is not binding enough to make parties a means of achieving unity of program.

Action through a single government, whether it be state, nation, or local unit, obviously requires some specificity of aim. Legislation must be drafted so as to embody with some precision the aims of those who promote it. Once drafted, it is apt to estrange some of those who were linked in the coalition when it had only partially defined aims. Once drafted, the legislation also defines the opposition, which before lacked a firm base of coalition. The course of legislation may unite persons of very different views because of what they dislike.

The situation changes at once when it is proposed to act through grants to another governmental unit rather than by direct action. By state grants to local units, as in the field of education, a minimum state program is assured, but wide room may be left for differences of local emphasis. The obstacle to the realization of educational goals which lies in local tax limits is the common problem of persons with very divergent educational goals. They can unite to escape this common problem without reconciling their divergences on program.

If this is so in the states, where there is an extensive legal power of regulating the policy, as well as the structure and finance of local units, it is the more so in the federal government. The fiscal power of the federal government can be invoked without bringing to play its policy-making powers, except for that minimum on which those desiring the fiscal assistance can agree. This does not imply that those who support federal financial assistance escape the problem of levying taxes to support the expenditure they sponsor. At the federal level, however, they can both spend and tax; at the state level claims on fiscal resources are less successful. It is possible to get unemployment compensation on a virtually national basis without battling to the wall every combination of employers determined to pay for no more than a minimum program, and yet get a more extensive program in those states where there is support for it. It is possible to get the semblance of a national highway program while still enabling each state to decide whether it will support a more extensive or an intensive program of highway construction; to have many miles of roads to a less high standard, or fewer to a higher. It is notable that in approving the interstate system, which is built with 90 percent federal money, and very extensive federal controls over routes and design, Congress attempted to box in the [federal agency charged with execution] with requirements of Congressional approval of specific administrative decisions not present in earlier highway legislation.

It can be asserted therefore that politically speaking, federal aid programs are an outcome of a loose coalition which resorts to a mixed federal-state program because it is not strong enough in individual states to secure its program, and because it is not united enough to be able to achieve a wholly federal program against the opposition which a specific program would engender. In this connection the uneven responsiveness of governmental units to various population segments undoubtedly plays a part in the resort to federal or to state action, or to a combination of both. Mayors expect Congress to support housing programs which do not get sympathetic attention in state legislatures.

Water, wildlife, forest, and soil conservationists generally look to Washington rather than to the states. Characteristically taxpayers' federations concentrate their attention on state governments, and resist the transfer of questions from that arena to another in which they have less confidence.

Viewed in this light, the grant-in-aid programs make sense. Each is the product of a specific coalition, and the terms of that coalition are evident in the statute and in the administrative practices which result from it. . . .

. . . The grant-in-aid system is by no means an undermining of federalism, but rather a refinement of it. It corresponds to a pragmatic pluralism, which has long been remarked as a characteristic of politics in the United States. It has built into it the characteristically different policy tendencies of states and of the national government. It is scarcely a means of enforcing similarity between them. Although direct administration by either government would have the advantage of political and administrative clarity and consistency, the choice of federal aid schemes as an alternative to either is sufficient evidence that these simpler measures were not a practical means for the attainment of political objectives whose achievement was only possible if they were not too minutely specified.

21. THE POLITICS OF PRINTOUTS: THE USE OF OFFICIAL NUMBERS TO ALLOCATE FEDERAL GRANTS-IN-AID

Richard P. Nathan

Federal grants-in-aid to state and local governments, expressed as a percentage of the general revenue raised by state and local governments, tripled from 10 percent in the mid-1950s to 30 percent in the mid-1980s. This growth substantially outpaced inflation. Based on federal budget data, federal grants to states and localities rose from $10 billion in 1964 to nearly $100 billion in 1984. In the process, not surprisingly, the form of federal aid also changed. In the 1970s, there was a shift to larger, more flexible, and more automatic programs as expressed in "the revenue-sharing idea." These new forms of intergovernmental fiscal subvention are the focus of this chapter. Large amounts of federal funds under these programs (both revenue sharing and block grants) have been distributed to state and local governmental jurisdictions on the basis of formulas that use official data from the U.S. Bureau of the Census. This shift to broader grants has had an important behavioral impact that can be described as a movement from pork barrel politics to printout politics.

The growth of broad formula grants and the emergence of printout politics in domestic policymaking have three main causes. One is a function of the sheer size of federal grants. As this aid stream grew, logistics alone required larger and more easily managed grants. The role of federal grants as a major revenue source in domestic public finances simply outgrew the capacity of federal agency officials to make project-by-project awards and then oversee these projects individually.

Technology also played a role in this shift to broader, less conditional, and more automatic federal aid flows. Computers came of age and allowed policymakers to develop more elaborate formulas and then modify and test them quickly in the political cauldron.

Politics, too, had a role in the rise of these newer grant forms. Nixon's New Federalism program featuring revenue sharing and block

Reprinted from William Alonso and Paul Starr, editors, *The Politics of Numbers*, 331-342. Copyright © 1987 the Russell Sage Foundation. Used with the permission of the Russell Sage Foundation.

grants grew out of the frustrations of the 1960s with the "proliferation" of federal grants. . . .

The complexities of categorical grant programs stimulated support for automatic federal aid that would give states and localities greater discretion. . . .

The remainder of this chapter explores the way in which data collected by the Bureau of the Census are used in decisions about the allocation of federal grants-in-aid to state and local governments under revenue sharing and the community development block grant (CDBG). The revenue-sharing program ended in 1986; the CDBG program continues in existence. The two programs are important for understanding the major changes that occurred in federal grant-making in the 1970s.

Both of these programs provide aid from the federal government *directly* to local governments (cities, counties, townships). As a class, direct federal-local grants are relatively new; they began in the post-World War II period. Previously almost all federal funds were paid to the states. However, computers facilitated direct federal-local grants, which for tactical and political reasons as well, grew substantially in the Republican years of the 1970s. The revenue-sharing program enacted under Nixon provided 70 percent of its funds directly to local units when initiated in 1972. Under President Carter, state governments were removed from revenue sharing, and all funds ($4.5 billion in fiscal year 1984) were provided directly from Washington to localities. Three-quarters of the funds distributed under the community development block grant ($3.5 billion in fiscal 1984) went to local governments.

The federal-local link creates extraordinary problems. Although federal funds under both programs flow directly to local subdivisions, the boundaries, functions, and finances of these units are not centrally determined. In 1977 there were 38,726 general-purpose units of local government in the United States, according to the Census Bureau's quinquennial canvass, which is the ultimate authority for the political geography on which federal allocations are based. Moreover, these multitudinous local subdivisions do different things and have highly varied fiscal systems.

Another major characteristic of modern American federalism poses a formidable challenge. Local governments overlap, and they overlap in different ways. Sometimes there are as many as four layers (town, city, county, and school and special districts) in a community. In other, less frequent cases, there are no overlying local governments. New York City has only two overlying special-district governments; by contrast, the 1977 Census of Governments shows 520 local governments serving the people who live in the city of Chicago.

The role of policymakers in writing formulas involves more than overcoming these technical challenges. The formulas express values—beliefs about a just distribution—through special factors that differentiate among types of local governments. Some local governments get *more* on a per capita basis than others. Some are awarded larger per capita funds because they do more; some because they exert greater effort; and some because they have greater need. Measuring need involves "equalization," or what is often called "targeting," that is, targeting federal resources on the most needy individuals and communities.

We now turn to the two programs—general revenue sharing and CDBG—before addressing more basic political issues. Much of the discussion is based on personal experience working on these programs in and out of government.

Revenue Sharing

When the U.S. House Ways and Means Committee reported its version of the revenue-sharing bill that was eventually enacted in 1972, one dissatisfied member, after describing the committee's effort to develop an acceptable allocation formula, concluded: "We finally quit, not because we hit on a rational formula, but because we were exhausted. And finally we got one that almost none of us could understand at the moment." [1]

Two decisions made by Nixon and others were responsible for the difficulty in devising a formula: First, all local governments were to be aided, and second, the formula was to include a needs, or targeting, factor. It would have been possible to take the opposite position on both issues. The original revenue-sharing proposal made to President Johnson by Walter Heller and Joseph Pechman, director of economic studies at the Brookings Institution, called for allocations exclusively to the states. The states, in turn, were to decide how to apportion these funds within their borders. This was the view of many experts on American federalism, who cited "Dillon's rule" . . . that local governments are creatures of the states and that the federal government therefore should not enter into direct relations with them.

The argument to include localities was both technical and political. It was technical in the sense that the newly available data-processing technology made it easier to do. It was political in the sense that including the localities made the legislation easier to pass. Nixon faced a Democratic Congress that was, to say the least, highly receptive to the arguments of the mayors for including the cities in revenue sharing. Revenue sharing thereby became the first grant program that covers all local governments in the nation. Previous grant programs tended to provide aid to localities on a project (as opposed to a formula) basis, and then only for some special purpose, such as public housing, airports, urban renewal, or model cities.

The second major decision—to include equalization features in the formula—could also have gone the other way. Shared revenue might have been allocated on a straight per capita basis.[2] However, Nixon, his advisers, and other participants in the decision process believed it necessary to incorporate measures of need and tax effort. Not everyone agreed. Caspar Weinberger, then deputy director of the Office of Management and Budget (OMB), objected to the tax-effort factor on the grounds that jurisdictions ought not to be rewarded for their high taxes. Weinberger's argument did not prevail, and from quite another vantage point, it was a good thing it did not. The tax-effort factor prevents areas with many overlying governments from getting a disproportionately large share of aid compared to areas where local governments are not "layered."

When the dust settled, there were over 38,000 jurisdictions— states, counties, cities, and Indian tribes—eligible to receive federal shared revenue. Some of the units to be aided were so small that the only statistic that could be used with confidence was their decennial population.[3]

Revenue-Sharing Data Needs

Three main types of official numbers are needed to operate the revenue-sharing formula: population, income, and revenue. The latter requires that taxes, intergovernmental revenue, and public school expenditures be known for each locality to arrive at the figure the formula requires—"own-raised nonschool" revenue. Although one special canvass was conducted in 1972, the basic data came from U.S. Census of Governments. These numbers were not collected to serve the revenue-sharing program.

Revenue sharing began in 1972. Population and income figures from the 1970 decennial census were still fresh and could be used with reasonable confidence. In later years, the Census Bureau updated these figures by estimates from birth, death, and other local records. These updated estimates posed problems. The data demands of the revenue-sharing formula and the tight time schedule for its implementation placed a strain on the Census Bureau's system for collecting information about local governments. Revenue sharing also increased the need for accuracy. Figures collected by the federal government for descriptive purposes—mainly by mail questionnaires and on a voluntary basis from officials of thousands of local governments—were now being called upon in the allocation of large amounts of money.

To make matters more complicated, the allocation formula was in flux throughout the original legislative deliberations. The Senate and House passed different formulas for allocating shared revenue to state areas. The Senate adopted a three-factor formula that favored rural and smaller states; the House, a five-factor formula more favorable to urban states. The Solomon-like compromise struck at the last minute consisted of having each state receive its allocation under whatever formula was more favorable to that state, with total allocations prorated down to fit the total amount of money authorized. The original act provided funds for five years; however, revenue sharing was extended in 1976, 1980, and 1983 without modifications in the allocation formula.[4]

"An Old Formula Is a Good Formula"

The problems and anomalies of the distribution formula—for example, defects in the measurement of fiscal capacity and tax effort and in the treatment of county governments—received close scrutiny from experts. But despite the consensus among experts that serious (though not overwhelming) problems needed attention, the formula *status quo* was maintained. This point merits comment.

Although technicians persuaded the interested political officials in the executive branch and on Capitol Hill that there were problems of some consequence with the formula, the problems were not seen as serious enough. The political system had labored and produced a workable, widely accepted allocation formula; Congress was not willing to reopen the debate. The defects were never repaired.

It is interesting that the most serious challenges to the revenue-sharing allocation system arose in the courts when population data from the 1980 decennial census were introduced into the system. Complaints came from big-city governments about the undercount of their residents, particularly members of minority groups. Highly exaggerated (in fact, inaccurate) claims were made of losses of as much as $200 per uncounted citizen. A number of court cases ensued, but no adjustment was made for the census undercount.[5]

The Community Development Block Grant

Enacted in 1974, CDBG, like revenue sharing, was a Nixon New Federalism initiative proposed as means of furthering decentralization.[6] The act consolidated into one block grant several programs administered by the U.S. Department of Housing and Urban Development (HUD) and provided discretionary grant funds for smaller communities. The programs consolidated into CDBG were urban renewal, the neighborhood development program (successor to urban renewal), model cities, water and sewer grants, neighborhood facilities, open spaces, and loans for public facilities.

This block grant legislation authorized $2.5 billion in the first year and $3 billion in the second and third years for a wide variety of eligible community development activities. It emphasized physical development projects, although public service spending was also permitted. The program was extended in 1977, 1980, and 1983, each time for an additional three years. In 1981 funding for the CDBG program was reduced under President Reagan by 13 percent, and the funds for small cities were allocated to state governments for distribution, rather than having them distributed by the secretary of HUD.[7]

Understanding the CDBG allocation system requires a knowledge of some formula-writing jargon. One term is *hold harmless*, which refers to the idea that a jurisdiction should not lose when a new grant allocation system comes into effect. A second concept is *folded-in* programs—those consolidated into a block grant. A third is the *lumpiness* of grants. Capital grants are "lumpy" in the sense that they are received by jurisdictions in spurts rather than in an even flow. Now, we can put all of our jargon together in one statement: The conclusion of many participants in the CDBG policymaking process was that, because of the *lumpiness* of many of the categorical grants *folded into* the new CDBG program, it was decided that recipient jurisdictions should be *held harmless* for a time—but not indefinitely.

Based on this analysis, formula writers involved in the CDBG decision process in 1974 devised what they called a "declining hold-harmless provision" for the CDBG formula. Recipient governments in the first three years of the CDBG program would receive either an amount set in the new formula or the average of the amounts received under the grants folded into the new block grant over the five-year period, 1968 to 1972, whichever was higher.[8] The hold-harmless provision was to be phased out, beginning in the fourth year of the CDBG program, by one-third each year. The goal was that, by the sixth year, the program would be operating fully under the new allocation system established in the original 1974 law. Communities receiving hold-harmless grants, but without formula entitlements, would then shift over to the discretionary part of the CDBG fund to compete with other small communities for block grant money.

Steps in the Allocation Process

The new CDBG formula allocation system when fully effective is best understood as a series of steps. The first step is the division of funds between metropolitan and nonmetropolitan areas. The second step is the allocation of funds for each type of jurisdiction (cities and urban counties), after setting aside some funds to be distributed by the secretary of HUD on a discretionary basis. A crucial point in the operation of the original system is that, as the hold-harmless provision was phased out, a large part of that money was designated to go into the discretionary fund for distribution to small communities in metropolitan areas.

For the central cities of standard metropolitan statistical areas, all of which are entitled to aid under CDBG, the formula in the 1974 act used three main factors: population, overcrowded housing, and poverty (double weighted). The housing and poverty data also came from the 1970 census, but annual updating based on estimates was subsequently employed.

As in revenue sharing, the formula was built on the existing official numbers and political geography. In particular, the concept of a "central city" (clearly an artifact) now came to be a matter of big money. This increased the importance after 1974 of OMB's designation of standard metropolitan statistical areas. However, no new numbers or census geography came into being for the CDBG program. An "urban county" eligible for aid is simply a large county, that is, one over 200,000 in population. The inclusion of urban counties was a victory for the National Association of Counties, which also made sure that county governments—all 3,042 of them—received revenue-sharing payments.

The Impact of the Formula

On close examination, the new CDBG formula was found to have a decidedly different allocational pattern from that implied in the speeches and commentaries of the people involved in its adoption. The situation was unusual. Because of the declining hold-harmless arrangement, the new act expired before the new formula took effect fully in the sixth year of the program. Moreover, there were indications that the framers of the act felt that the formula "was not quite right" but that there would be an opportunity to fix it later on. The original law specifically directed HUD to study the formula to determine how well it distributed the money relative to community development needs (Sec. 106[1]).

It was in this setting that the Brookings Institution entered into a contract with HUD to undertake an evaluation of the CDBG program, which included a study of the allocation system. We concluded that when fully in effect the formula would lack what we referred to as "urban focus." The formula shifted funds from large cities and distressed cities to smaller and better-off jurisdictions, many of which had received very little or no aid under the folded-in programs. By law, the share of funds to metropolitan areas (SMSAs) declined immediately from 87.4 percent in the hold-harmless base to 80 percent, with the other 20 percent being earmarked for nonmetropolitan areas.[9] The share received by central cities declined from 71.8 percent in the hold-harmless base to 42.2 percent under full formula funding.[10] We stressed that the standard used—"urban focus"—was derived from what many of the authors of the law had said about its goals when it was debated.

Previously, we had experimented with various statistical index techniques designed to show the relative socioeconomic condition of cities. We used these techniques to analyze the CDBG formula and concluded that the original formula did not reflect the physical development needs of old industrial cities, which have problems associated with aging infrastructure and industries not easily captured in census data. To deal with this problem, we suggested the use of an available census statistic—age of housing—as a proxy for the age of cities and the conditions of their infrastructure. Our judgment was that the results generated by using age-of-housing data as a proxy indicator was a feasible one for taking into account this widely perceived physical dimension of "urban focus." After reviewing a number of possible formulas, we recommended one alternative, a "dual formula" that seemed to us to correct the lack of "urban focus."

The Dual Formula

The dual approach that we suggested in our report retained the original formula for all jurisdictions that would be better off under that formula. These tend to be growing cities, particularly in the South, many with high levels of poverty. At the same time, we suggested a second formula, including the number of pre-1940 housing units, that would more strongly reflect physical development needs. Jurisdictions would receive their CDBG allocation on the basis of the second formula if it was more favorable to them. To prevent any jurisdiction from losing as a result, it was necessary to provide additional money—in effect, to "buy" the new formula. We suggested that most of the additional money be taken from the metropolitan discretionary fund.

Although skepticism initially greeted the idea of a dual formula, the Ford administration endorsed it in 1977. We expected (as did others) that President Ford's defeat in the 1976 election would doom this proposal, but the Carter administration made minor changes and claimed the idea, with the modest revisions, as its own. Despite strong protests by members of Congress from newer cities that the existence of old (for example, "Georgetown") housing was a bad test of urban need, the dual formula remains in effect.

The CDBG case was unusual. While it violates the earlier maxim that "an old formula is a good formula," the changes made in this instance reflected the seriousness of the problems. The purposes of the original legislation were not being served by the original formula. The system was modified, but in a manner that drew on the available supply of official numbers, and new money was provided to prevent any losses to existing recipients.

The two major cases studied here are significantly different, but their implications for domestic policy are similar; I turn now to this final subject.

Conclusion

A new form of political discourse and action emerged in domestic policymaking in the 1970s—the politics of printouts. No member of Congress today would vote on an important grant-in-aid formula without a printout to see who wins and who loses. But it was speeded up (in a sense, made more productive) by the new information-processing technology—a technology ideally suited to formula writing under conditions where the stakes involved warrant the costs of high-speed data.

What has been the result of printout politics? The technology may have made the outcomes more "distributive," to use Theodore Lowi's term;[11] that is, it may have reduced the targeting effect, since legislators now have better information about how to spread benefits to their districts. But one needs to be cautious on this point. Federal aid payments have never been highly targeted. Moreover, the rapid growth of Sunbelt cities and suburban jurisdictions undoubtedly was a strong underlying reason for the allocation patterns that occurred under the new grant programs of the 1970s.

To summarize, the technology may have facilitated the use of direct federal-local formula grants, and it may have influenced the outcome in the direction of being more broadly distributed than would otherwise have been the case. But we are not in a position to know the counterfactual, that is, what would have happened if computers had not been invented and large and direct federal formula grants to localities had not emerged.

Did policy and institutional changes affect the form and format of official numbers? In this case, the underlying data—the official numbers—were not changed because of the establishment of direct federal-local formula grant programs and the politics of printouts. Old numbers were simply used for new jobs. There was a modest amount of updating, but no basic revision of the Census of Governments or, as far as I know, of any other Census Bureau concepts and data series. The use of the age-of-housing data as a proxy for city age in the CDBG formula illustrates this point. These data were used for lack of better numbers and tested in the cauldron of printout politics. Once their use had been legitimized, it was not easy—or apparently desirable—to change this element of the formula. New data are rarely needed because so many ways are available to work out formulas with existing data that do what policymakers want to do. Moreover, the decision process moves rapidly once serious formula writing gets underway. It is not easy to stop this train and lay new tracks once it has left the station.

But there is no question that the use of statistical formulas for distributing revenue put statistical policy under a political spotlight. The legal challenges to the 1980 census reflected the increased fiscal importance of the data. The official designation of standard metropolitan statistical areas became a point of political conflict because money began to ride on the designations. The politics of printouts did not generate new data, but it did generate a new politics of statistics and statistical geography.

Notes

1. Rep. James C. Corman (D.-Calif.), cited in *Monitoring Revenue Sharing* by Richard P. Nathan, Allen D. Manvel, Susannah E. Calkins, and Associates (Washington, D.C.: Brookings Institution, 1975), p. 135. Much of the analysis in this chapter is based on this book, which contains detailed information on the history and operation of the formula for allocating revenue-sharing funds. I am indebted to Allen D. Manvel, my colleague at the Brookings Institution, who played the lead role in this part of our analysis and who provided helpful comments on an earlier draft of this chapter.
2. Strictly speaking, this, too, is an equalization approach, that is, in relation to the sources of revenue raised.
3. All governments eligible for more than $200 in revenue-sharing payments per annum were given funds. In the final analysis, Congress decided that, for small governments, the secretary of the treasury should have authority to use income and financial data of the overlying county on a per capita basis as a proxy for local statistics.
4. As noted earlier, the revenue-sharing program expired in 1986.
5. Such undercount adjustments had been computed, but not used, in the recent census. Some experts tried to show that an adjustment in 1980 would not have had the effects claimed. In fact, in some protesting cities, it would have resulted in less federal aid. See Arthur V. Maurice and

Richard P. Nathan, "The Census Undercount: Effects on Federal Aid to Cities," *Urban Affairs Quarterly* 17 (March 1982): 251-284.

The only time the decennial population census has been adjusted was in 1870 after the Civil War because the figures seemed out of line and it was argued that the impact of the Civil War had affected the completeness of the count. . . .

6. I am indebted to my former Brookings colleague, Paul R. Dommel, for his substantial assistance on this section. For more information on this program, see Paul R. Dommel and Associates, *Decentralizing Urban Policy: Case Studies in Community Development* (Washington, D.C.: Brookings Institution, 1982).

7. See John William Ellwood, ed., *Reductions in U.S. Domestic Spending: How They Affect State and Local Governments* (New Brunswick, N.J.: Transaction Books, 1982), p. 168. Further cuts [were] proposed by Reagan [after] 1981; a 10 percent reduction was proposed for fiscal year 1986.

8. For a full explanation of the operation of the formula, see Richard P. Nathan, Paul R. Dommel, Sarah F. Liebschutz, Milton D. Morris, and Associates, *Block Grants for Community Development* (Washington, D.C.: U.S. Department of Housing and Urban Development, 1977).

9. Nathan, et al., *Block Grants for Community Development*, p. 179.

10. Ibid., p. 180.

11. Theodore J. Lowi, *The End of Liberalism* (New York: Norton, 1969), part III.

22. AS THE REAGAN ERA FADES, IT'S DISCRETION VS. EARMARKING IN THE STRUGGLE OVER FUNDS

Cheryl Arvidson

It's a question of priorities. The states say they should be allowed to set their own, even when federal funds are involved, because they are closer to the problems. Congress says when it gives money to the states, it has the right, with its nationwide responsibilities, to some control over how it is used. These are the battle lines in a renewed struggle over Washington's propensity for attaching strings to grant money.

A good example of the conflict involves the funding of programs to combat drug abuse. In states with large urban populations, intravenous drug users have become such a significant problem that they cannot be ignored, particularly in the face of an AIDS epidemic fueled by the sharing of hypodermic needles. In less urbanized states, however, IV [intravenous] drug users can be a much lower priority for taxpayer-funded services, especially if other groups, such as adolescents or alcohol abusers, pose a bigger problem, to say nothing of being more socially acceptable beneficiaries of taxpayer dollars.

State and local officials welcome federal aid to help fight the drug battle, but they want to put that assistance where they see the greatest need or the greatest potential payoff. Congress, on the other hand, watches with alarm as the AIDS virus spreads and wants intravenous drug users to be a top priority everywhere, first in line for the federal buck.

During the past 18 months, as Congress has reviewed a number of giant grant programs designed to address the nation's ills and needs, quandaries such as this one have become a significant component of the legislative debate. Increasingly, federal lawmakers have sought to address their own special concerns by carving out a percentage of the funds provided in a federal grant and specifying what it must be spent on.

These set-asides for specific uses within a broader grant of federal funds represent congressional value judgments. Their practical effect is to put strings back on some federal "block grants" that were created a

From *Governing* 3 (March 1990): 21-27. Copyright © 1990 *Governing* magazine. Reprinted with permission.

decade ago precisely to make those monies string-free. In a broader historical sense, the recent proliferation of set-asides may signal the end of the philosophy of giving greater discretion to state governments that was a hallmark of the Reagan years. It is a move back from the block grant concept toward "categorical grants," which restrict the use of federal funds to narrow, precisely defined purposes.

"It's frustrating for the people back home" who have to run the programs, says Ann Sullivan, director of Connecticut's Washington, D.C., office. "When they receive the funds, the first thing they have to do, instead of saying where is the most need, is sit down and say we need 5 percent here, and 10 percent there, and let's be sure we have a population eligible."

State officials, in particular, have argued for years that tying their hands with categorical grants is a mistake. They maintain that letting governments closer to the people determine spending priorities is the best way to solve problems and letting them run the programs without federal red tape is the most cost-efficient. Small wonder that they embraced President Reagan's plan to "get the government off the backs of the people"—and cheered when Congress went along, consolidating 54 categorical programs into nine block grants in the areas of social services, low-income energy assistance, substance abuse and mental health. But it was not without cost. In exchange for greater discretion in allocating funds, the states settled for some 30 percent less money than under the categorical grant programs.

All too soon came the Reagan administration's skyrocketing budget deficits, and the days of new federal programs to address new and growing needs were but a memory. Disappearing right along with them was the ability of members of Congress to take credit for bringing the home folks what they wanted. Now, as the Reagan-era block grants begin to come up for congressional review and new funding, legislators are anxious to take some of the discretion away and channel money into their own priorities. Their goals do not yet demand a total return to categorical grants; for now, at least, set-asides are filling the bill.

"It's a way where Congress can, in effect, bring the bacon home," says a northeastern state lobbyist.

"What's happening is Congress is saying 'We've got some priorities here, there are fewer federal dollars and a lot of new federal money isn't coming. If they are federal dollars, we're going to make sure that federal dollars are being spent to meet federal priorities,'" adds Michael Werner, senior legislative analyst in Maryland's Washington, D.C., office.

One of the first instances in which Congress added strings to a block grant came in 1988 when the giant alcohol, drug abuse and mental health grant program came up for renewal. Led by Representative Henry A. Waxman, a California Democrat and one of the leading congressional voices on health and environmental issues, Congress stipulated that half the drug money doled out to states must be used for services to IV drug users.

Waxman believed—and his colleagues agreed—that control of the spread of the AIDS virus was a national priority, and if the states weren't paying enough attention to the IV drug user, it was up to Congress to see that they did.

Diane Canova, director of public policy for the National Association of State Alcohol and Drug Abuse Directors, objects to the 50 percent set-aside.

"The AIDS crisis is of epidemic proportions, but it's not uniformly spread around the country," she says. "New York, Florida, California, and New Jersey may need to spend the money that way, but Montana and Wyoming don't need to spend the same proportion. It's difficult for the states to meet the mandate at the federal level while at the same time meeting the needs as they see them."

A congressional staff aide counters Canova's argument. "Obviously, North Dakota and Montana have fewer IV drug users than New York City, but they're only serving 20 percent of what they've got. They want to put [the federal aid] in alcohol abuse because that's more of a problem for them. The federal government is saying maybe that's so, but drug addicts who share needles are a problem for the country."

Paul Behnke, deputy director of the Arkansas Division of Alcohol and Drug Abuse Prevention, was able to get a partial waiver of the 50 percent set-aside, but he still fumes when he talks about Congress's substituting its priorities for the states'.

"We would have had to go out and recruit IV drug users," he says, adding that alcohol is far and away the biggest substance-abuse problem in Arkansas. "Washington seems to ignore the fact that there's an alcohol problem in this country. What they tried to do is use the alcohol and drug portion of the block grant to fight AIDS rather than to fight drug abuse."

A different sort of motivation for a restriction on the uses of federal money can be found in another part of the renewed alcohol, mental health and drug abuse grant program, this one also pushed by Waxman. It requires that 55 percent of the federal dollars sent to each state to fund mental health programs must be used to support new or expanded mental health services rather than ongoing programs. The reason: Waxman, fearful that innovation is lagging in the mental health field, wants to see federal funds used as seed money for new approaches. For state officials, however, the set-aside means they will have to find other courses for nearly half the money they need just to continue funding ongoing mental health programs.

Education is another area where a desire to ensure that specific national needs are addressed may lead Congress to dictate exactly what states must do with a federal grant.

When the Senate takes up the funding for vocational education this year, it will be considering a proposal to require that states spend from 65 to 75 percent of their block grant money on high school vocational education programs. Current law permits the states to decide for themselves how to divide the money between high school and post-secondary voc ed programs.

But Senator Claiborne Pell, the Rhode Island Democrat, has persuaded a bipartisan majority of the Senate Labor and Human Resources Committee that Congress must pay more attention to the "forgotten half" of the nation's young people: 17-, 18-, and 19-year-olds from working-class or middle-class families who received no benefit from federal aid in their elementary school years because they didn't live in poverty areas and who won't receive federal higher education money, since they won't be heading to college.

The plan has drawn the ire of states like Minnesota and New Mexico, which now spend nearly all their voc ed grant money for post-secondary vocational education at community colleges, technical schools and the like.

"We're saying, 'Wait a minute, guys. Cut us some slack here,'" says Tom Lehman, associate director of Minnesota's state office in Washington. "Minnesota spends about 91 percent of our federal vocational education dollars on post-secondary education. We have the lowest [high school] dropout rate in America. If that's a problem in some other state, they should spend the money on high school, but it's not a problem in Minnesota. Why should we be forced to spend all our federal dollars on a problem that doesn't exist?"

Susan Greene, the National Governors' Association's education specialist, is not sure the NGA will fight the voc ed restrictions on the Senate floor, however, partly because she's hopeful the House will eliminate them in the conference committee. Even more important, the pending legislation does something the states want badly, eliminating a half-dozen set-asides enacted earlier that required chunks of the voc ed money to be spent on special population groups, ranging from displaced homemakers to prison inmates. In this case, Congress was responsive to arguments that such set-asides weren't meeting the needs and that too much money was either not being spent or was being wasted.

A test of how deep the sentiment runs to move even further toward strict categorical funding will come this year as Congress works on legislation allocating an additional $415 million to the nation's anti-drug effort.

The Senate version of the bill is a pure block grant—no strings. But the House version would create four new categorical programs and specify exactly how 60 percent of the money, $250 million, must be allocated among them: for rural residents; for pregnant women and infants; for low-income individuals; and to reduce waiting time at existing drug treatment facilities. What's more, under the House bill, the money in the new categorical programs would be distributed on a competitive basis, meaning that applicants for the funds would submit proposals showing what they wanted to do with the money, and those judged best by the federal administrators would get funded. Local governments and private non-profit groups, as well as states, could apply.

Canova, for one, worries that the places with the most sophisticated grant-writers, rather than the places with the greatest need, would wind up with all the money. "There's no guarantee on how the funds will be distributed," she says. "It's possible California and New York could get them all." Even though the House bill allocates $100 million, nearly one-fourth of the money, to rural areas, Behnke, the Arkansas drug abuse director, considers it "a disaster. All of the competitive funds are going to the two coasts where they can demonstrate [big] numbers. Mid-America and the rural states will come out on the short end."

Yet the earmarking of the funds for drug abuse programs in rural areas illustrates one of the reasons why members of Congress like categorical grants and press hard to get them. During the debate, Democrat Mike Synar of Oklahoma, co-chairman of the rural health caucus, complained that repeated efforts by lawmakers to stress the need for getting federal funds out into rural areas have fallen on deaf ears in state capitols. "You can lead a horse to water, but you can't make it drink," he said.

Similar pressure to use set-asides has traditionally come from representatives of the cities, who have the same quarrel with state governments. In this post-Reagan era, representatives of and for the cities are stepping up their efforts to obtain direct funding, bypassing state legislatures and administrators, but the population shifts that are so weakening the voice of the cities in Congress leave the outcome in doubt.

Interestingly, despite the fact that President Bush's chief of staff, John H. Sununu, is a former New Hampshire governor who has made eloquent statements on the dangers of federal micro-management, the Bush budget for next year makes a number of proposals for what look remarkably like categorical grants. In the education area alone, there are at least four that target precise amounts of money for precisely stated objectives. Example: Bush would give $25 million to the states to improve the training of future school principals and specifies that this would be done by providing "a short period of residential training and a year working with a successful 'exemplar' principal." Other aspects of the Bush budget would eliminate at least a few strings, however. For example, he suggests repeal of the federal ban on funding toll roads with federal highway aid money.

As Washington generally moves away from pure block grants, it is an interesting historical footnote that the Reagan administration, which successfully achieved greater state discretion over federal dollars, also planted the seeds for its destruction.

When the Reagan block grant programs passed in 1981, the deal was greater flexibility in exchange for less money. At the same time, the number of record-keeping and reporting requirements imposed on the fund recipients was reduced. And there seemed to be no interest in requiring uniformity of records.

Some states continued to collect detailed data on how their grants were being spent, and some collected virtually nothing. But in the end, the reports were all different, so there was no way to illustrate the bang from the federal buck or how one state compared with others in its region or the nation as a whole.

Consequently, if members of Congress decide today that the states aren't adequately addressing a certain need that they consider a priority, it's difficult to prove them wrong. Thus, when the maternal and child health block grant program was being considered, both Waxman and Senator Lloyd Bentsen, the Texas Democrat who chairs the Senate Finance Committee, were determined not only to impose set-asides for two priority areas—preventive and primary care services for young children and services for disabled or chronically ill children—but to impose uniform reporting requirements as well. In exchange, Congress did increase the overall size of the block grant.

A state maternal and child health official says that while the states were pleased with moves to improve accountability, it "remains to be seen" whether the new set-asides will be a problem. "We had some concerns that it could have a detrimental impact in some states, but it's not something we can tell for sure until the states have an opportunity to work with it," she says. And why can't the state directors tell for sure?

"There are not good numbers on that. No one has a good grasp on how states are allocating their money."

While set-aside opponents can usually find someone to champion their cause, the congressional sponsors of the restrictions usually have tried to minimize the arguments that can be made against their decisions. Often, the set-asides that are proposed come close to the actual spending patterns of the majority of states, as near as anyone can determine, so it's hard to find more than a handful of states that are sufficiently upset to pressure their senators or representatives to mount a real battle.

"A lot of states are in those ranges, so it's hard to argue that they're absurd," says Greene of the NGA. "So our defense is discretion. States are willing to accept the accountability, but we need discretion and flexibility."

In an effort to gather the hard facts needed to oppose the movement to more strings, the NGA and other associations of state officials are stepping up their efforts to get better data that will convince Congress that the states are addressing federal priorities and doing a good job in serving specific population groups.

Greene says the NGA, for example, is surveying states to determine whether the proposed restrictions in the vocational education grant are of sufficient concern to warrant a full-fledged Senate fight. Canova, the chief lobbyist for state alcohol and drug abuse directors, is taking it a step further, asking state substance abuse officials to break down current spending and project information by congressional district.

Canova says she is convinced that the states have the data. "It's just a question of getting it. Some data needs to be improved and perhaps refined to get at the answers," she says. But reconstructing the data by congressional district is important, she adds, because "it's hard for members [of the House] to take credit for or to realize that the funds out of the block are going to their particular district. It's easier with a water project or a bridge to show a constituent how funds are going to benefit a local community. Block grants are a little different."

The recent history of set-asides confirms that point. While the strings put on the vocational education grants in the Senate committee are an exception, in general the Senate has been less restrictive. For example, a bill passed by the House for maternal and child health programs would have given states discretion over only 10 percent of the total grant money and would have specified the areas of spending for the remaining 90 percent. The Senate balked, and the program that ultimately was agreed upon gave the states discretion over 40 percent of the money.

The House has always been more supportive of efforts to put strings on federal dollars because congressmen answer only to a single district, and their constituents can see a clearer benefit from narrowly defined funding. Senators, on the other hand, represent an entire state and are more likely to side with the governors who see different needs in different parts of their states and want the discretion to fund them.

"It mostly comes from the House," says Jim Martin, chief lobbyist for the National Governors' Association. "The House has a jurisdictional view, and it's natural. I wouldn't expect a congressman to think of a state view because he has a district view. If there are only a couple of dollars to go around, he naturally wants those couple of dollars in his county or town. That's probably what he should be doing."

23. WHY CATEGORICAL GRANTS?

U.S. Advisory Commission on Intergovernmental Relations

The development of American federalism since the Civil War, which settled the most fundamental issues, is in large part the story of an expanding system of categorical aids. . . .

Cumulatively the events over this period of a century established an intergovernmental system in which, by 1976:[1]

- 24.7% of state and local expenditures were supported by federal assistance;
- 21.7% of federal domestic outlays were made through state and local governments by means of grant programs;
- the federal government had some financial involvement in almost every major field of state and local activity; and
- more than 448 separate programs of federal assistance to state and local governments existed, almost all of which were conditional grants for narrowly defined services and activities.

These features of American federalism were not, in any clear sense, preordained. Other advanced democracies having a federal constitution have followed different developmental patterns.[2] Among the most obvious historical alternatives that might have been, but were not, adopted are: a pattern of financial self-sufficiency on the part of state and local governments; direct performance by the national government of all its domestic functions; a clear distinction between national and subnational services and responsibilities; and the use of broad-gauged general support and functional (or block) grants for the equalization of fiscal capacities and service levels among the states. In the light of such alternatives, the question to be considered is: Why was the development of the American federal system characterized by the extensive use of categorical assistance programs rather than by the alternative federal-state-local relationships?

From U.S. Advisory Commission on Intergovernmental Relations, *Categorical Grants: Their Role and Design* (Washington, D.C.: ACIR, 1977), 49, 51, 53-57. Reprinted by permission.

Possible answers to this query ... suggest the importance of at least three factors: (1) economic and fiscal considerations; (2) the constitutional and philosophical traditions of the United States; and (3) features of the decision-making process in the American political system. ...

Economic and Fiscal Factors

[Most of the economic and fiscal factors covered by the author, including the tax structure at various levels of government in the United States, the depression, and the economic diversity of the country, were summarized in the introductory chapter to this volume. This excerpt resumes with a discussion of one economic-fiscal factor not explicitly covered thus far in this book.—Ed.]

Some economists have suggested another conceptual framework for the growth of categorical aids. This explanation involves recognition of the "spillovers" or "externalities" that occur in the provision of many state and local government services. The benefits flowing from public programs are not necessarily restricted to residents of the jurisdiction that provides and finances them through its taxes. Some spill over to the residents of nearby areas or to the general public. Wastewater treatment is one clear case; the beneficiaries of cleaner water often are those who live downstream from a source of pollution, not those whose effluent is treated. Highways that carry a large volume of interstate traffic are another obvious example of a state service that benefits nonresidents. Higher education, because of the frequency with which college graduates migrate to other states, might be a third instance.

The danger in these situations is that the amount of public services provided will be inadequate, because local voters and taxpayers have no incentive to pay for activities that benefit others. One solution is to have a share of the costs proportional to the actual distribution of benefits borne by a higher level of government, which can be accomplished by a properly designed grant-in-aid. In 1967 George F. Break concluded that:

> ... external benefits, which will probably continue to grow in importance, are already pervasive enough to support a strong prima facie case for federal and state functional grants to lower levels of government.[3]

Grants aimed at correcting these spillovers usually are categorical and would be necessary even if a state or locality possessed a strong fiscal base.

This theory, although accepted by many experts in public finance, is subject to certain criticisms. First, it is based upon the somewhat tenuous assumption that state and local governments know the needs or preferences of their citizenry and act to maximize their residents' economic welfare.[4] Other economists, although accepting the basic argument in certain instances, suggest that many existing grants are not actually based upon the externality principle. Concerning this interpretation, Charles L. Schultze concludes that externality

> . . . is not very useful for analyzing most of the existing social grants. Rather, many of these grants are a means by which the federal government uses state and local governments . . . as agents or subcontractors to produce centrally determined amounts and kinds of collective goods, since, for a number of reasons, principally historical and political, the federal government itself virtually never delivers collective goods or services at the local level.[5]

. . . One set of estimates of the importance of the externalities involved in various functional fields [indicates that] the federal government makes financial contributions to some fields in which externalities are slight (police protection, libraries), while the states and localities retain substantial fiscal burdens in activities that involve the largest externalities (education, welfare). Moreover, as Schultze adds, most federal grants do not have the specific characteristics that the externality theory suggests are desirable. . . .

[Constitutional and historical factors, which are discussed next, have been summarized in the introductory chapter.—Ed.]

Political Factors

The categorical grant program also appears to many analysts to be an expression of basic American political patterns and institutions. Important influences may be found in the operations of interest groups, the attitudes of federal officials, the structure and procedures of Congress, and the social and political diversity of the population.

Interest Group Influences

A political interpretation of grants-in-aid, based on observations about interest group activities, was offered several years ago in an article by Phillip Monypenny. Monypenny found that the growing grant system largely failed to satisfy the standard textbook justifications for federal aid. It did not provide for substantial fiscal equalization among the states, for example, and the programs did not appear to fall into areas of special national interest or concern by any consistent definition.

Monypenny believed that the actual source of the grant programs lay in features of the political system. A sharing of program responsibility, using federal fiscal resources but offering some discretion through administration by the states, was produced when an interest group lacked sufficient strength to gain all of its objectives in either the state capitals or Congress. . . .

Federal Distrust

The use of categorical aid programs also has been encouraged by a set of attitudes shared by many officials in the national legislative and executive branches. In its most moderate form, this attitude appears in the view that the government that raises money via taxation should also control the expenditure of that money. A preference for categorical aid reflects the judgment that this instrument maximizes accountability in the use of federal funds. Not infrequently, however, a more extreme position is taken, based upon a deeply felt distrust regarding the intentions, performance, and general competence and representativeness of state, municipal, and county governments.

The 1955 report of the Kestnbaum Commission highlighted the need for accountability through categorization, concluding that:

> . . . when federal aid is directed toward specific activities, it is possible to observe the effects of each grant, to evaluate the progress of aided activities, and to relate the amount of financial assistance to needs. There is more assurance that federal funds will be used to promote the nation's primary interests.[6]

More recently, a congressional committee professional staff member, Dr. Delphis C. Goldberg, has described this position from the legislative perspective, contrasting categorical programs with broader-purpose grants:

> There are practical disadvantages to assistance mechanisms that carry few or no conditions. The federal government may become locked into supporting ineffective and inefficient activities, and the information needed to evaluate programs becomes difficult or impossible to obtain. In discharging its responsibilities, Congress generally desires more than assurance of fiscal probity; it wants to know how well the money is spent and who benefits.[7]

Distrust or actual hostility toward subnational governments was indicated in the views expressed by Wilbur J. Cohen, a former secretary of the Department of Health, Education and Welfare, in an interview in 1972. Secretary Cohen described his comments on the revenue-sharing proposal to a group of Democratic mayors.

> I told them, I found it hard to argue—in fact I am very unsympathetic with all you fellows asking for this federal revenue

sharing when most of you run political machines that don't allow competent people to administer programs and you're shackled to a lot of political hacks.[8]

Only the federal government, in Secretary Cohen's view, could guarantee rapid action on pressing social problems.

> . . . I think in the nature of problems we face in our society, there's no question in my mind that we wouldn't be where we are today if there were no federal people pushing civil rights, desegregation or equal treatment for women. Take big, social-economic-ideological problems, and if left to just disorganized state and local action, or citizen action, I'm not saying that they might never get done, but they might take 100, 200 years. Whereas, the federal government action in the problems, whether it's against mental retardation, old-age assistance or whether it's building libraries—take any of the categories—I think have resulted in faster, more effective meeting of the nation's social problems.[9]

Historically these criticisms have had both administrative and political dimensions. In the 1920s and 1930s, the former was paramount, and federal aid was widely credited with improving the administrative practices of the states.[10] Many grant requirements were directed specifically toward this end. The Kestnbaum Commission, along with many other students of government, concluded that, "When used effectively, the (categorical) grant not only has increased the volume of state and local services, but also has promoted higher standards both in service and administration. . . ."[11]

In the 1960s and 1970s certain political issues received greater stress. States were regarded as unrepresentative and unresponsive to urban needs, encouraging the development of direct federal-local project grant programs.[12] Yet many policymakers believed that cities also neglected the interests of their least fortunate citizens. As noted by Edward R. Fried and his associates in the 1972 Brookings Institution report, *Setting National Priorities:*

> . . . states and localities may fail to meet the needs of some groups of citizens, especially those with little power and status in the community. Although a few states and localities have at times been more progressive than the national government, most have been relatively unresponsive to the needs of the poor minorities. Disadvantaged groups (for example, labor unions in the 1930s and the blacks and the poor in the 1960s) have often turned to the federal government for help after failing to arouse state and local governments to awareness of their plight. The goal of providing more nearly equal opportunities for the disadvantaged—which was a growing national concern in the 1960s—cannot be met by relying

on the highly unequal resources of state and local governments or on their willingness to provide the services that the disadvantaged require.[13]

One expression of this critical view under the Great Society was the provision of federally funded services through limited-purpose governments and private nonprofit organizations, thus bypassing the traditional state-local system entirely.

The federal government, however, has sometimes stepped into fields in which states actually have served as innovators, as well as those in which they seem to have lagged. Morton Grodzins has pointed to instances in the historical record (such as unemployment compensation, aid to the aged and blind, and road construction) in which the federal government has acted as an emulator of state programs by making national programs of their successes. Thus, he notes, "the states can lose power both ways." [14]

Congressional Influence

Certain features of the structure and milieu of the national legislature also encourage the heavy use of categorical grants. Students of the legislative process indicate that specialization is a dominant feature of the modern Congress, particularly the House of Representatives. Power is concentrated at the committee and subcommittee level, while the central organs of leadership have limited control over activities in either chamber. Individual congressmen are expected by their peers to become expert in some narrow, particular field of public policy, normally a field related to their committee or subcommittee assignments. In this manner Congress as a whole gains the expertise necessary to deal with complex social and economic issues.

This norm of legislative specialization is accompanied by another—that of deference. Next to their own personal judgment, congressmen rely most heavily in determining their issue positions on the opinions of their colleagues. Those thought to be most expert in a field, quite naturally, are usually the members who sit on that particular area's committee or subcommittee, and their views are respected.[15] Deference goes beyond this respect for one's colleagues, however. At least in the past, freshman legislators were expected to refrain from even speaking out on matters outside their committee work unless their home district was affected directly.[16]

Specialization also is tied to the practice of decisionmaking by "logrolling." Individual congressmen generally seek committee assignments that relate to the interests of their constituents and, therefore, their own reelection prospects. For this reason they often have a direct stake in the promotion of new and beneficial programs. Other congressmen hesitate to undercut the electoral base of their colleagues and expect this favor to be returned.

A consequence of these practices is that in many fields, the basic decisions are made at the committee or subcommittee level and are seldom challenged on the floor. This situation appears to have had a direct impact on the development of the grants system. The fragmentation of responsibility in Congress inclines it toward the creation of a large number of specialized grants, which may provide duplicative or even conflicting services. Harold Seidman stated:

> It's no accident that we have four different water and sewer [grant] programs, because these come out of four separate committees of Congress. These are very important programs for a Congressman's constituency, and a Congressman wants to be sure that it will remain in an agency under the jurisdiction of his committee.[17]

Similarly, the weakness of central legislative organs means that each committee is largely free to follow its own inclinations regarding procedural matters, such as planning requirements, recipient administrative organization, matching and allocation formulas, and so forth. As a consequence grant programs vary greatly in these administrative particulars.

Although some specialization is certainly necessary in dealing with complex legislative problems, the fragmentation of Congress fails to provide for an equally urgent requirement—the task of integrating the manifold activities of government. As Samuel P. Huntington has stressed, the complex modern environment requires both a high degree of specialization and a high degree of centralized coordinative authority. Congress has adjusted only half-way by accommodating the former but not the latter function.[18]

Although establishing a direct cause-and-effect relationship would be difficult, the dispersion of authority in Congress has increased over the course of this century along with the expansion of the intergovernmental grant system. The increased development of categorical aid during the World War I era followed a revolt in 1910-11 against Rep. Joseph G. "Boss" Cannon, who as Speaker of the House had acquired extensive control over the House of Representatives. The effect of this revolt was to strengthen the position of committee chairmen.[19] The post-World War II growth of assistance occurred after another set of reforms embodied in the *Legislative Reorganization Act of 1946*. That act, which reduced the number of congressional committees and was intended to strengthen them, had what was in many respects the contrary result, because it led to a proliferation of subcommittees and actually intensified the dispersion of power. At the same time congressional committees acquired their first permanent professional staff positions.[20]

The number of subcommittees grew steadily in the 1950s and their autonomy increased. Earlier struggles for control between committees and the central legislative leadership were replayed between the subcommittees and committee chairmen. As in 1910 the forces for dispersion proved the more powerful. By 1962—just before the period of the most rapid increase in categorical programs—it could be said that, "given an active subcommittee chairman working in a specialized field with a staff of his own, the parent committee can do no more than change the grammar of a subcommittee report." [21]

This trend has continued. In the 94th Congress (1975-76), 144 subcommittees were in existence, a significant increase from the 83 functioning 20 years ago. Moreover each subcommittee now possesses some staff. Most authorization hearings in recent years have been held at the subcommittee level, rather than by the full committee, as had been the practice in the past.[22] According to a recent observer, the problem of overlapping jurisdictions has increased. Duplication in hearings and frequent legislative delays occur, and a situation has arisen in which legislation is drafted in isolated environments that may not reflect the views of the membership at large.[23]

The growth of the modern executive bureaucracy has paralleled the structure of congressional subcommittees established since 1946.[24] The administrative agencies, in turn, reinforce the pattern of congressional organization. Bureaus and subcommittees closely work together and with the interest groups concerned with their specific policy areas. These "subgovernments," as they have been termed, are the spawning ground of many new aid programs. They form "iron triangles," which have often been criticized for operating beyond the control of the congressional leadership, the presidency, and the public-at-large.[25]

Social Pluralism

The great social diversity of the United States also has had an impact upon the nature of its public policy. The nation is composed of a very large number of cultural and economic groups, each possessing different political objectives and concerns. As a consequence the existence of a large national majority actively committed to any specific major social policy change would be unusual. This fact is reflected in Congress, where modest, incremental programmatic steps, typified by the smaller categorical grant programs, are most readily accepted. Gary Orfield, an analyst of Congress, indicates:

For a number of readily understandable reasons, Congress is far more responsive to the need for new (categorical) programs than to basic fiscal or social rearrangements. Redressing general social or economic imbalances always means helping some while denying to others a portion of their goods or of their social objectives. . . . Most new grant programs, on the other hand, give additional benefits to some groups while seldom disturbing the others. When a Senator fights for more housing or better health care for old people, or for better education benefits for veterans, he usually gains strength from a segment of his constituency without deeply offending anybody else.[26]

Education provides an example. This field was the first area of federal assistance, and it is one in which programs have been particularly numerous. The current variety of categorical education programs reflects the inability in past decades of the supporters of federal aid to education to agree upon a system of general education support. Legislation to create a program of general assistance for education was considered repeatedly by Congress after 1870, with bills introduced into the House or Senate during most sessions over this period of nearly a century.[27] However division among the advocates of aid—especially those within the Democratic party—made passage impossible, with religion and race the most divisive issues.[28] The result was that consensus could be reached on the desirability of programs for specific education purposes but not for general aid. Jesse Burkhead has commented:

Specific grants for special purposes can be devised which avoid the problems that block the approval of [general] federal aid [to education]. The past experience has been that pressures for federal aid have most frequently found expression in the passage of just such specialized programs. The agitation of the 1870s and 1880s was capped by the enactment of a vocational education law. The struggles of 1948 and 1949 brought educational legislation for impacted areas. And the 1956-57 House battles culminated not in a construction bill, but in the [National Defense Education Act].[29]

Similarly in the early 1960s, attention was initially focused on assistance for higher education, which generated less opposition than aid to elementary and secondary schools.[30]

Social pluralism and divergent interests also abet the enactment of comprehensive bills, including a number of distinct programs. Title after title is added in the process of building a supportive coalition. The 1965 *Elementary and Secondary Education Act* (ESEA) provides an example. In five titles ESEA provided aid to the educationally disadvantaged, authorized funds for school textbooks and libraries, established supplementary education centers for adults and children, developed a national network of regional educational laboratories, and assisted the strengthening of state departments of education. U.S. Commissioner of Education Francis Keppel, who served as a "broker" among various interests in developing the legislation, developed a coalition that fit together as intricately as a "Chinese puzzle." [31]

Notes

1. Office of Management and Budget, *Special Analyses, Budget of the United States Government, 1978,* Washington, D.C., U.S. Government Printing Office, 1977, p. 273.
2. See R. J. May, *Federalism and Fiscal Adjustment,* London, Eng., Oxford University Press, 1969.
3. George F. Break, *Intergovernmental Fiscal Relations in the United States,* Washington, D.C., The Brookings Institution, 1967, p. 63. Break's text provides a full discussion of the externality rationale for categorical grants. See especially pp. 63-68.
4. Wallace E. Oates, *Fiscal Federalism,* New York, N.Y., Harcourt Brace Jovanovich, Inc., p. 73. Oates comments that although these weaknesses are such that some might believe that the Pigovian prescriptions for intergovernmental grants to correct spillovers should be rejected entirely, his own view is that a case for such grants does remain in many instances.
5. Charles L. Schultze, "Sorting Out the Social Grant Programs: An Economist's Criteria," *American Economic Review,* 64, May 1974, pp. 182-83. He defines "collective goods" as "those goods actually produced and distributed free (or at highly subsidized prices) by governmental organizations."
6. *Commission on Intergovernmental Relations,* U.S. House of Representatives, 84th Cong., 1st Sess., June 28, 1955, p. 122.
7. Delphis C. Goldberg, "Intergovernmental Relations: From the Legislative Perspective," *Annals of the American Academy of Political and Social Science,* 416, November 1974, p. 63.
8. "Wilbur J. Cohen: A Defender of Categorical Grants," *National Journal,* Dec. 16, 1972, p. 1912.
9. *Ibid.*
10. For example, see V. O. Key, Jr., *The Administration of Federal Grants to States,* Chicago, Ill., Public Administration Service, 1937, pp. xiv, 368.
11. *Commission on Intergovernmental Relations, op. cit.,* p. 126.
12. For a summary of this view, see Roscoe C. Martin, *The Cities and the Federal System,* New York, N.Y., Atherton Press, 1965, especially *Chapter 3.*
13. Edward R. Fried, et al., *Setting National Priorities: The 1974 Budget,* Washington, D.C., The Brookings Institution, 1973, p. 173.

14. Morton Grodzins, *The American System: A New View of Government in the United States*, Chicago, Ill., Rand McNally & Co., 1966, p. 317-18.
15. Charles L. Clapp, *The Congressman: His Work as He Sees It*, Washington, D.C., The Brookings Institution, 1963, p. 149.
16. *Ibid.*, pp. 20-24.
17. Seidman's remarks are contained in Douglas M. Fox, "A Mini-Symposium: President Nixon's Proposals for Executive Reorganization," *Public Administration Review*, 34, September/October 1974, p. 489.
18. Samuel P. Huntington, "Congressional Responses to the Twentieth Century," *The Congress and America's Future*, David B. Truman (ed.), 2nd Ed., Englewood Cliffs, N.J., Prentice-Hall, Inc., 1973, p. 22.
19. Gary Orfield, *Congressional Power: Congress and Social Change*, New York, N.Y., Harcourt Brace Jovanovich, Inc., 1975, p. 16.
20. Michael J. Malbin, "Congressional Staffs—Growing Fast, But in Different Directions," *National Journal*, July 10, 1976, p. 958.
21. George Gordon, Jr., "Subcommittees: The Miniature Legislatures of Congress," *American Political Science Review*, 56, September 1962, p. 596.
22. Bruce I. Oppenheimer, "Subcommittee Government and Congressional Reform," *DEA News Supplement*, Summer 1976, p. S-8.
23. *Ibid.*, p. S-11.
24. Richard E. Neustadt, "Politicians and Bureaucrats," *The Congress and America's Future, op. cit.*, p. 120.
25. The "subgovernment" system is discussed in *Chapter I* of another Commission report in this series: Advisory Commission on Intergovernmental Relations, *Improving Federal Grants Management* (A-53), Washington, D.C., U.S. Government Printing Office, February 1977.
26. Orfield, *op. cit.*, p. 262.
27. Jesse Burkhead, *Public School Finance: Economics and Politics*, Syracuse, N.Y., Syracuse University Press, 1964, pp. 237-38.
28. Orfield, *op. cit.*, pp. 126-27.
29. Burkhead, *op. cit.*, p. 265.
30. *Ibid.*
31. Jerome T. Murphy, "The Education Bureaucracies Implement Novel Policy: The Politics of Title I of ESEA, 1965-72," *Policy and Politics in America: Six Case Studies*, Allan P. Sindler (ed.), Boston, Mass., Little, Brown and Co., 1973, pp. 162-65.

24. THE ROAD TO *SOUTH CAROLINA:* INTERGOVERNMENTAL TAX IMMUNITY AND THE CONSTITUTIONAL STATUS OF FEDERALISM

Margaret T. Wrightson

In deciding *South Carolina* v. *Baker,* the Supreme Court struck a powerful blow at constitutional federalism.[1] Because the Court has the final say on the meaning, if any, of the Tenth Amendment to the U.S. Constitution, which reserves to the states, or to the people, those powers not delegated to the national government or constitutionally denied the states, the Court is in the key position to determine the degree of constitutional protection to be afforded the states in the federal system.

In 1803 Justice John Marshall stated, "It is emphatically the province and duty of the judicial department to say what the law is." [2] In *South Carolina* the Supreme Court in effect said what it is not. Following the precedent set in *Garcia* v. *San Antonio Metropolitan Transit Authority* (1985), the Court restated unequivocally that the Constitution contains no substantive protections against national regulatory powers vis-à-vis state and local governments. Instead, national intervention may be limited only when the political structure that authorized it is proven defective in representing these governments.[3]

As has often been true, the litigation that produced this important event did not itself appear very historic. The dispute involved the question of whether the Congress could condition federal tax exemption of municipal bond interest on a requirement that state and local governments issue their securities in "registered" rather than "bearer" bond form.[4] Specifically, South Carolina and the National Governors' Association (NGA), which intervened in the case, contended that section 310(b)(1) of the Tax Equity and Fiscal Responsibility Act of 1982 (TEFRA) violated: (a) the Tenth Amendment and (b) the doctrine of reciprocal tax immunity.

Invoking the Supreme Court's original jurisdiction, South Carolina filed suit in 1983. The case was decided on 20 April 1988. Not only did the Court reiterate *Garcia*, but it also rejected the claim that *Pollock* v. *Farmers' Loan and Trust Company*, a 93-year-old Supreme Court decision, provided the legal precedent for municipal bond tax

Reprinted with permission from *Publius: The Journal of Federalism* 19 (Summer 1989): 39-55.

exemption. In the process, the majority opinion cast doubt on the very existence of state and local tax immunity, even in regard to the most direct forms of taxation.

The Road to *South Carolina*

One way to view the *South Carolina* decision is as an ending, not for one, but for two stories. By reemphasizing *Garcia*, the Court concluded for the time being the debate over the constitutional division of powers between national and state governments, and it also ended the legal controversy surrounding federal tax treatment of municipal bonds, fiscal instruments which historically have been the major source of financing for traditional and more recently nontraditional state and local capital projects. . . .

[The author then discusses the *Garcia* decision and its significance. This excerpt resumes with the analysis of the tax issue.—Ed.]

Reciprocal Immunity: Tax Tradition Meets the Tenth Amendment

As every student of American federalism knows, *McCulloch* v. *Maryland* (1819)—which established the judicial doctrines of national supremacy and implied powers, as well as the idea that the "power to tax is the power to destroy"—begins the history of intergovernmental tax comity.[5] In *McCulloch,* Chief Justice Marshall declared that by placing a tax on the operations of a nationally incorporated bank, Maryland had put an undue burden on the national government and threatened its sovereignty. The unconstitutionality of state taxation of federal instrumentalities was thereby established.[6]

However, because the federal government had no income tax prior to the Civil War, the questions of whether tax immunity was reciprocal and the range of areas which would be covered by such a principle were not explicitly addressed until 1861 when the Court declared, in *Collector* v. *Day,* that federal taxes could not be imposed on income received pursuant to a state government contract because such a tax was equivalent to a tax on the government itself.[7] Owing to the abandonment of the federal income tax in the postwar period, the matter of state tax immunity lay dormant for some thirty years thereafter.

In 1894, a federal income tax was reenacted and judged unconstitutional a short year later in *Pollock* v. *Farmers' Loan and Trust Company.* In the process, the Court also affirmed the broadest possible interpretation of reciprocal immunity, stating that the tax in question is a tax on the power of the states and their instrumentalities to borrow money, and consequently repugnant to the Constitution.

Ratification of the Sixteenth Amendment in 1913 established the authority of the federal government to levy an income tax, but it produced very little discussion of municipal bond (or any other) reciprocal tax immunity. Many state and local officials maintain that congressional and state legislative quiescence during the ratification debates signaled tax immunity inviolability, as was consistent with jurisprudence at the time of the amendment's passage.[8] Critics of municipal bonds strongly disagree, and they cite as support for their view the plain language of the amendment ("The Congress shall have the power to lay and collect taxes on incomes, *from whatever source derived*") and the long history of executive branch efforts to abolish the exemption, beginning with Treasury Secretary Andrew Mellon in 1921.

Regardless of the validity of these claims, the Congress (beginning in 1968) and the federal courts (beginning in 1939) have taken steps to reduce the scope of reciprocal tax immunity, including actions directly affecting municipal bonds.[9]

Congressional Activity Prior to Tax Reform. Although many analysts have long argued that municipal bonds violate cardinal principles of taxpayer equity and economic efficiency, as long as these public finance instruments continued to be used predominantly for traditional governmental purposes (e.g., road and public school construction), the exemption retained strong congressional support.[10] So much so that, from the creation of the income tax in 1913, for over fifty years municipal bonds remained entirely unregulated by the national government.

Then, in 1968, the Revenue and Expenditures Control Act established the first tests to distinguish between tax exempt and taxable bonds. Since that time, restrictive congressional action has steadily escalated in response to the growth of private-activity bonds through which states and localities issue securities for governmental as well as nongovernmental purposes.

Each new round of restrictions has been uniformly opposed by state and local governments as a transgression on their sovereign taxing powers. Yet, while mayors and governors view such bonds as a way to foster public-private partnerships, a majority of public finance economists and national government tax experts regard them as federally subsidized pork barrels. As George Peterson described the problem from the latter perspective:

> States and localities have stretched their imaginations to find new ways to use tax-exempt bonds. They have defined for themselves a "social banker" function, in which they borrow large sums of

money at tax-exempt interest rates, then relend the funds at below-market rates for politically popular purposes.[11]

Especially in the 1980s the seeds of long-standing objections by academic economists, Treasury Department officials, and congressional staff of the Joint Tax Committee (JTC) began to bear fruit. In this period, the blossoming of the private-activity bonds seemed to validate the worst criticisms of these experts. Thus, the mortgage revenue bond (MRB) program came under attack for benefiting high-income homebuyers, and stories of arbitrage schemes and bond-financed race tracks, K-Mart stores, and McDonald's restaurants circulated widely. As a result, members of Congress became increasingly willing to attack perceived abuses. Moreover, as the federal budget deficit mounted, laissez-faire attitudes toward tax expenditures became less acceptable overall, and per capita bond volume caps gained new admirers on Capitol Hill.

The Mortgage Subsidy Bond Tax Act (MSBTA) of 1980, the Tax Equity and Fiscal Responsibility Act (TEFRA) of 1982, and the Deficit Reduction Act (DEFRA) of 1984 reflected these changing attitudes by, among other things, removing the tax exemption from some kinds of industrial development bonds (IDBs), by marking others for increased targeting and/or extinction, and by excluding some forms of public transportation from the category of governmental bonds.

While this succession of restrictions and exceptions eliminated some abuses, in terms of mitigating federal tax losses, the reforms proved no substitute for stringent, unified volume caps. Indeed, the nation's municipal bond volume, which stood at $49.1 billion in 1978, climbed to $114.3 billion by 1984—much of this growth attributed to private-activity bonds. Thus, despite constant tinkering between 1980 and 1984, federal restrictions did little more than temporarily halt the rapid rise of private-activity bonds. Swings in volume suggested a cat-and-mouse game in which Congress devised clever means to catch abuse, while bond issuers found ways to circumvent many of these congressionally set traps. To many observers, it seemed that traditional government obligation bonds and especially the many legitimate uses of revenue bonds became increasingly tainted by association with excesses.

Congressional Action during Tax Reform. Arguably, the Congress has always had the means to eliminate various uses and reduce the volume of tax-exempt bonds. What had been missing prior to tax reform was political motivation. That the tax-writing committees did not adopt tougher measures prior to 1986 may, in small part, be attributed to state and local tenacity. In much larger part, however, it is simply a reflection of the broader pattern of tax politics prevailing at the time.

As all contemporary analyses of tax policy have concluded, the "distributive" character of tax-writing prior to the Tax Reform Act of 1986 (TRA) had produced a tax code strongly favoring smaller, organized interests (including states and localities) at the expense of the broader tax-paying public.[12] Moreover, because of the "incremental" nature of tax-writing, changes occurred only gradually, in the form of modest expansions or reductions in tax benefits. This fact accorded interest groups plenty of time to redress grievances and press advantages.

In the case of municipal bond tax-writing, state and local government advocates undoubtedly benefited from collateral political pressure exerted by a much broader coalition of interests also concerned with the fate of these securities. Indeed, PAC [Political Action Committee] and professional organizations representing bond lawyers, charitable organizations, private universities, and the real estate, hospital, and investment banking industries all strongly supported the status quo. Prospects for favorable treatment by the tax-writing committees were also improved by the fact that many housing, health-care, and economic development projects subsidized by bonds were the kind that members could take credit for back home.

Overall, prior to tax reform, congressional politics and federalism interests seemed to go hand in hand. Until tax reform altered these familiar alliances and incentives, Congress had no compelling reason to substantially restrict tax-exempt bonds and every reason to tolerate or even improve their treatment. In this way, states and local governments benefited from a pattern of politics in which they were never among the most influential participants.

By late 1985 and early 1986, however, tax reform's new political imperatives—including partisan and institutional competition, the glare of publicity, blame avoidance, and the role of powerful, popular symbols—had led members of Congress to abandon all pretense of concern over the impact of national tax policy on state and local finance. Most significant for state and local governments during the process was the stricture of revenue-neutrality, which—by virtue of pinning vastly lower tax rates onto comparable tax savings—placed nearly every credit, exemption, and deduction on tax reform's chopping block. This kind of discipline was an incredible turnaround from existing tax-writing conventions. It temporarily swept out the old rules and relationships that had previously sheltered state and local interests and elevated to unprecedented levels of influence norms favoring wholesale purification of the federal tax code.

Other Actions. Looking beyond tax reform, there were other, less well publicized events unfolding in 1986 which also threatened state and local financial interests. Understandably, the politics of tax reform consumed nearly all of the resources of the state and local finance community. Few participants were able to track carefully the progress of *South Carolina,* and nearly everyone failed to appreciate the potential judicial disaster. Yet, throughout tax reform, a Special Master appointed by the Supreme Court was building a case to reject the contention that TEFRA registration provisions violated the Tenth Amendment and the doctrine of reciprocal tax immunity.

Court Restrictive Action. Judging from some of the reactions to it, the Court's decision in *South Carolina* not to accord tax immunity to municipal bonds might seem without precedent. This was not the case. Rightly or wrongly, Justice Brennan chose to define this particular tax exemption as the single surviving application of a long-repudiated Court precedent, one which once shielded earnings derived from all state and local government contracts. In so doing, he was able to cite substantial precedent for formally overruling *Pollock.*

[Although] for twenty-five years after the enactment of a federal income tax, income derived from employment contracts, vendor earnings, and even from lands leased from states was exempted from federal taxation, in 1939 the Court began to restrict the scope of tax immunity for both state and national governments.[13] That year, in *Graves* v. *New York ex rel. O'Keefe,* the Court required state government employees to pay federal income taxes for the first time. Significantly, the Court justified the change on the grounds that "The theory . . . that a tax on income is legally or economically a tax on its source, is no longer tenable." [14] Although the Court offered little in the way of explanation, there is substantial evidence that by 1939 government efforts to tax such income ran both ways in the federal system, with the states making numerous attempts to tax federally derived income and vice versa. Moreover, as the income tax grew in significance to taxpayers overall, equity questions were increasingly raised about the immunity "loophole."

As a result of this and subsequent decisions, by the time of *South Carolina,* Justice Brennan was able to say that, "The only pre-modern tax immunity for parties to government contracts that has so far avoided being explicitly overruled is the immunity for recipients of governmental bond interest." [15]

One Ending for Two Stories

Looking back to the beginning of 1988, tax exemptions for municipal bonds were viewed with great skepticism and considerable disdain on Capitol Hill. Further, exemptions were regarded as a subsidy regulable by Congress, not a right accorded to sovereign governments. This assumption was explicitly validated by the Court in the Spring of 1988. . . .

Politics In, Pollock Out

[The author then covers some of the details of the *South Carolina* case and the reasoning used by the Court in its decision. This excerpt resumes with the concluding portion of this subsection.—Ed.]

In summary, it seems clear that *South Carolina* established a new doctrine of reciprocal tax immunity, one which is wholly consistent with a philosophy of a supremely powerful national government and semi-sovereign states. Whereas the old doctrine implied a measure of equal treatment, the Court's interpretation makes it official—national tax sovereignty is always greater. As Brennan declared:

> Many of this Court's opinions have suggested that the Constitution should be interpreted to confer a greater tax immunity on the Federal Government than on States because all the people of the States are represented in the Federal Government whereas all the people of the Federal Government are not represented in individual States. . . . To some, *Garcia* v. *San Antonio Metropolitan Transit Authority* may suggest further limitation.[16]

The new doctrine states:

> Under current intergovernmental tax immunity doctrine the States can never tax the United States directly but can tax any private parties with whom it does business, even though the financial burden falls on the United States, as long as the tax does not discriminate against the United States or those with whom it deals. . . . The rule with respect to state tax immunity is essentially the same . . . *except that at least some nondiscriminatory federal taxes can be collected directly from States even though a parallel state tax could not be collected directly from the Federal government*. We thus confirm that subsequent caselaw has overruled the holding in *Pollock*.[17]

Given the clear language of *South Carolina's* affirmation of *Garcia* and the Court's implicit threat that even direct taxation of states might be upheld under it, two conclusions are obvious. First, the question of whether issuing tax-exempt bonds is a sovereign right of the states or a privilege they are accorded by the Congress has been settled. Immunity is not a right under the Tenth Amendment. The doctrine of intergovernmental tax immunity has been officially replaced by principles of taxation that accord superior powers to the national government.

Second, a majority of justices intended *South Carolina* to cast serious doubt on the reciprocity of immunity from direct taxation as a constitutional principle.[18]

The implications of these conclusions are multifold. Not only is the future course of intergovernmental fiscal policy certain to be changed, but the basic character of the political partnership will in all likelihood be affected as well.

Policy and Political Implications

The most obvious lesson of *South Carolina* is a general one: American federalism has been construed by the Court as a political and administrative relationship rather than a constitutional one. Thus, whether state and local governments will be able to enhance their fiscal and programmatic prerogatives as a quid pro quo for increased domestic responsibilities, indeed whether they will even be able to retain those they now have, will be resolved in the political arena, not the judicial one.

Current evidence of state and local government renaissance notwithstanding, the overwhelming superiority of the national government—which has long been judicially sanctioned with respect to regulatory and spending powers—has now been validated by the Court with respect to taxing powers as well. Together, these constitute a powerful triad. Against it, states have only their political powers. Yet, many political scientists discount the protective value of formal political powers, such as the electoral college and state representation in the Senate, items specifically cited by the Court as structural protections.[19]

The second lesson of *South Carolina* is for public finance in particular. Congressional leaders of the tax-writing committees were quick to gloss over the implications of *South Carolina*. On 20 April 1988, Senate Financial Committee Chairman Lloyd Bentsen (D-Texas) soothed troubled bond markets by reminding them that during tax reform Congress had resisted Reagan administration efforts to remove the exemption for all but the most narrowly defined category of government bonds.[20] He further asserted, "The fact is, the tax exemption for general obligation bonds is extremely popular in the Congress. There is a strong feeling the federal government should not interfere with those bonds." [21] Ways and Means Committee Chairman Dan Rostenkowski also discounted prospects for immediate action, stating that "The decision merely reiterates a doctrine that in fact has been the presumption in the Congress for the past twenty years. That is that the federal tax treatment of state and local government bonds is a matter of statutory law, not constitutional principle." [22]

Should states and localities believe these promises? Is the prospect of *South Carolina* opening the floodgates an irrational fear? Recent reform politics, the standoff between the president and the Congress over new taxes, and the continuing pressure on the tax-writing committees to contribute their required share to meet Gramm-Rudman deficit-reduction targets and to fund recent increases in domestic programs suggest otherwise.

In particular, congressional leaders have been careful not to make promises about the status of private-activity bonds, which, in the 1980s, have been redefined by Congress to capture a greater and greater share of non-traditional, but arguably public-purpose activities. In bonding authority, as in general, Justice O'Connor is probably correct when (quoting Laurence Tribe) she asserted, "If there is any danger, it lies in the tyranny of small decisions—in the prospect that Congress will nibble away at state sovereignty, bit by bit, until someday essentially nothing is left but a gutted shell." [23]

Likely to be more instructive than member commentary are recent professional proposals. Historically, JTC and committee staff professionals, not members of Congress, have had the greatest hand in shaping federal municipal bond policy. Key experts and professional staff—including those most responsible for drafting the TRA provisions on bonds—regard these provisions as administratively complex, internally inconsistent, and ineffective in important respects. Although the ink is barely dry on the most sweeping reform of the federal income tax in over fifty years, there is near universal agreement that this area of present law needs an overhaul. Professionals also agree that extra care must be taken in rewriting bond provisions because permissiveness and lack of specificity increase what they regard as economic inefficiency and taxpayer inequity. According to economic reasoning, this is largely due to perverse incentives. As Bruce Davie and Dennis Zimmerman argue:

> Without [volume and use] limits state and local officials and the private sector have incentives to utilize conduit financing until the taxable debt market is subsumed by the tax-exempt debt market, and state and local taxpayers have incentives to broaden continuously the definition of local responsibilities in what might be called creeping "municipal socialism." [24]

Proposals may not receive congressional consideration for some time to come, but the broad outlines of recommendations are in view:

> A new approach to limiting tax-exempt bonds based on some combination of local fiscal responsibility, a list of acceptable uses, and volume limits could be developed. This policy might focus on

defining good or acceptable uses of the bonds rather than defining bad uses and allowing exceptions.[25]

Prescribing valid uses of bonds rather than proscribing abuses would be an effective way of controlling activity from the national perspective. From the point of view of state sovereignty and local self-governance, however, such a strategy risks turning all but the most old-fashioned uses of this form of financing into a capped, categorical grant.

If this were to happen—and there is nothing in the present politics or makeup of the tax-writing committees to suggest it would not—the strategy would be consistent with other intergovernmental fiscal trends in the 1980s. There would be less state and local aid available and more regulation to accompany the remaining subsidy. This would be consistent with a more general trend identified by a number of recent scholars, including Martha Derthick, who warned:

> [T]here is a danger that Congress, in striving to close the gap between its desire to define large goals and its unwillingness to provide the administrative means to achieve them, will try to conscript the states. That is, it will give orders to them as if they were administrative agents of the national government, while expecting state officials and electors to bear whatever costs ensue.[26]

If the Past Is Prologue

Some thirty state and local interest groups led by the GFOA—including the NLC, NGA, National Association of Counties (NaCo), the National Conference of State Legislatures (NCSL), and the National Association of State Budget Officers (NASBO)—have now geared up as a formal coalition to meet new challenges to state and local taxing authority. For instance, this group has sponsored a large number of regional symposiums to educate state and local officials and build support. There is little doubt that such coalitional activity demonstrates an increase in state and local appreciation for the importance of grass-roots and constituency support when it comes to cultivating the tax-writing committees.[27] However, while in the post-TRA period tax policymaking is likely again to be incremental, it is highly unlikely to return to its former distributive character. Nor should anyone expect the Court to resurrect the Tenth Amendment as a protection against indirect taxation. In *South Carolina,* even though some justices stopped short of joining the reasoning which hinted that direct taxation might be constitutional, in the matter of Tenth Amendment (or any doctrinal) protections against indirect taxation, the decision was 7-1 against.

Future intergovernmental relations, therefore, will present a formidable challenge to federalism as a pillar of the American system of governance. This challenge also carries a simple warning to policymakers in whose hands the relationship lies: as state and local governments prepare for the worst in their policy dealings with the national government, while doing their political best to improve the odds. Looking ahead—if the past is prologue—this guidance may be the ultimate lesson of *South Carolina.*

Notes

1. *South Carolina v. Baker, Treasury Secretary of the United States,* 485 U.S. [505], 99 L.Ed.2d 592, 108 S.Ct. [1355].
2. 1 Cranch 137 (1803).
3. *Garcia v. San Antonio Metropolitan Transit Authority,* 105 S.Ct. 1005 (1985).
4. The difference between registered and bearer bonds is the mechanism used for transferring ownership and making payments. As the Court noted in *South Carolina* (at 600), "Ownership of a registered bond is recorded on a central list, and a transfer of record ownership requires entering the changes on that list. The record owner automatically receives interest payments by check or electronic transfer of funds from the issuer's paying agent. Ownership of bearer bonds, by contrast, is presumed from possession and is transferred by physically handing over the bond. The bondowner obtains interest payments by presenting bond coupons to a bank that in turn presents the coupons to the issuer's paying agent."
5. 4 Wheaton 316 (1819).
6. Later cases confirmed this precedent. See, *Weston v. City Council of Charleston,* 2 Pet. 449 (1829), finding that federal bond interest was immune from state taxation; *Dobbins v. Commissioners of Erie County,* 16 Pet. 435 (1842), finding that federal employees were immune from state tax on salaries; *Gillespie v. Oklahoma,* 257 U.S. 501 (1922), finding that income derived from federal leases was immune from state tax; and *Panhandle Oil Co. v. Knox,* 277 U.S. 218 (1928), finding that vendors were immune from sales tax on vendors' proceeds from sale to the United States.
7. *Collector v. Day,* 11 Wall. 113 (1871). For a short history of Court precedent on these points see Bruce F. Davie and Dennis Zimmerman, "Tax-Exempt Bonds After the *South Carolina* Decision," *Tax Notes,* 27 June 1988, pp. 1573-1580.
8. See, for example, John Keohane, "The Federal Government and State/Local Government Securities: A Short History of Reciprocal Immunity," *Government Finance Review* 4 (June 1988): 7-11; "Griffin Bell on GFOA's Case Against the Tax Act," *Government Finance Review* 3 (December 1987): 30-31; Government Finance Officers' Association, *Brief of the Government Finance Officers' Association as Amicus*

Curiae in Support of Plaintiffs [South Carolina and NGA] (Washington, D.C.: GFOA, 1987).

9. For an account of congressional efforts, see Dennis Zimmerman, "The Intergovernmental Struggle Over Tax-Exempt Bond Reform," *Research in Urban Economics: State and Local Finance in an Era of New Federalism,* ed. Michael Bell (Greenwich, Conn.: JAI Press, 1988), pp. 101-123.

10. See, for example, James A. Maxwell, *The Fiscal Impact of Federalism in the United States* (Cambridge, Mass.: Harvard University Press, 1946), p. 374.

11. George Peterson, "Federalism and the States," in *The Reagan Record,* ed. John L. Palmer and Isabel V. Sawhill (Washington, D.C.: The Urban Institute, 1984), p. 233.

12. See, for example, John F. Witte, *The Politics and History of the Federal Income Tax* (Madison: University of Wisconsin Press, 1985); Jeffrey Birnbaum and Alan Murray, *Showdown at Gucci Gulch: Lobbyists, Lawmakers, and the Unlikely Triumph of Tax Reform* (New York: Random House, 1987); Timothy J. Conlan, Margaret T. Wrightson, and David R. Beam, *Taxing Choices: The Politics of Tax Reform* (Washington, D.C.: Congressional Quarterly Press, 1989).

13. On the latter, see, for example, *Burnet* v. *Coronado Oil,* 285 U.S. 393 (1932).

14. *Graves* v. *New York ex rel. O'Keefe,* 306 U.S. 466 (1939) at 480. Prior to this case the Court had already confined *Collector* v. *Day* to its facts in *Helvering* v. *Gerhardt,* 304 U.S. 405 (1938), which upheld the constitutionality of a federal tax on the salaries of state employees involved in state construction projects.

15. *South Carolina* at 609.

16. at 607, n. 10.

17. at 610 (emphasis added).

18. As a direct result of the Court's language, for example, GFOA and NLC dropped their case against the U.S. Treasury Department under which they had objected to the inclusion of governmental bond interest as a preference item in the corporate and individual alternative minimum taxes and to the arbitrage rebate requirement on governmental bonds as a violation of the Tenth Amendment and the doctrine of reciprocal tax immunity.

19. See Timothy Conlan, *New Federalism: Intergovernmental Reform from Nixon to Reagan* (Washington, D.C.: Brookings, 1988), ch. 11, and U.S. Advisory Commission on Intergovernmental Relations, *The Transformation in American Politics: Implications for Federalism,* A-106 (Washington, D.C.: U.S. Government Printing Office), pp. 81-91, 111-122.

20. In this regard, the Treasury I plan proposed that all bonds in which more than 1 percent of the proceeds benefited directly or indirectly a private party would be taxed. If adopted, the proposal would have reduced total bond volume by an estimated 80 percent.

21. Senator Lloyd Bentsen, cited in *Tax Notes,* 25 April 1988, p. 438.
22. Congressman Dan Rostenkowski, 20 April 1988, as cited in *Tax Notes,* 25 April 1988, p. 438.
23. Justice Sandra Day O'Connor dissenting in *South Carolina* at 616. See also Laurence H. Tribe, *American Constitutional Law* (Mineola, N.Y.: Foundation Press, 1978), p. 302.
24. Davie and Zimmerman, "Tax-Exempt Bonds," 1575.
25. Ibid., 1580.
26. Martha Derthick, "Preserving Federalism: Congress, the States, and the Supreme Court," *Brookings Review* 4 (Winter-Spring 1986): 32.
27. For a discussion of the formation and activities of this group see Frank Shafroth, "Thirty Public Interest Groups Meet on Local Bonds Issues," *Nation's Cities Weekly,* 19 September 1988, p. 8.

25. COPING WITH FISCAL STRESS: PREDICTING THE USE OF FINANCIAL MANAGEMENT PRACTICES AMONG U.S. CITIES

David R. Morgan and William J. Pammer, Jr.

The urban fiscal crisis is not over yet. With the elimination of general revenue sharing in late 1986, a number of municipalities are scrambling to make ends meet. According to a recent survey of the National League of Cities, close to one-third of the nation's cities and towns will see an actual reduction in revenue during the late 1980s unless new sources of income can be found (*Nation's Cities Weekly*, June 29, 1987). The survey of 545 communities shows that for 1987, 52% reduced capital spending, 26% cut employees or had hiring freezes, and 58% hiked user fees or other nontax revenue. As Glassberg (1981) put it several years ago: The urban fiscal crisis has become routine. The real question now is what gets cut and how. What other courses of action are open to cities under stress? Are certain cities more likely than others to pursue certain options? How much, in fact, do we know about how cities of all sizes across the country react to the increasing frequency with which retrenchment actions must be taken?

Case studies, checklists, and theoretical considerations abound, and a growing body of more systematic comparisons of retrenchment actions are beginning to appear (Clark and Ferguson, 1983; Walzer, 1985; . . .). Yet we still do not have definitive answers to all the pertinent questions. The purpose here is to provide a few more insights into the process by which cities react to mounting fiscal pressures. . . .

. . . [T]he two basic propositions guiding this research are as follows: (1) the retrenchment decision-making process is confused and unstructured, making it difficult to predict just what financial management strategies cities will pursue, and (2) the chief executive will be the dominant figure in the process, so that whatever action is taken will reflect that person's perceptions of what the situation demands. . . .

. . . To determine the type of austerity strategies used by large cities, survey data were collected from municipal officials in large U.S.

From *Urban Affairs Quarterly* 24 (September 1988): 69-86. Copyright © 1988 by Sage Publications, Inc. Reprinted by permission.

cities as part of a nationwide effort to study fiscal austerity. Questionnaires were sent to each mayor, a senior council member knowledgeable about financial affairs, and a city administrator in all cities of 25,000 and over in 35 states.... City administrators include city managers (or assistants) or chief administrators or finance officers in nonmanager cities.

City administrators were asked (1) to indicate from least to most important their city's use of 32 revenue and expenditure strategies; (2) to estimate their perception of the severity of 11 financial problems confronting their city; and (3) to describe the extent to which their city was using six different financial planning and management tools (for example, performance measurement, revenue forecasting, and accounting and financial reporting). In addition to the survey information, data on a variety of social, economic, and fiscal characteristics of the cities are available from published census sources, along with certain information on government structure taken from the 1983 *Municipal Year Book*.

The fiscal austerity strategies, which represent the dependent variables, are based on the administrators' assessment of the importance of the various revenue and expenditure measures. Because the number of possible retrenchment actions is so large, grouping them in some appropriate way becomes essential. Most research recognizes that when financial troubles hit, cities can respond in three ways: (1) raise revenue, (2) cut spending, or (3) improve productivity. Following Clark et al. (1984), the 32 cutback strategies have been grouped into three basic categories: revenue raising (for example, increasing taxes, user fees), productivity improvements (for example, improving efficiency in management), and attempting to reduce expenditures, ranging from making across-the-board cuts to programmatic reductions. The differentiation between improving productivity and cutting expenditures is a crude attempt to capture the idea expressed by Levine et al. (1981) that cities in financial trouble stretch resources before resorting to more severe budgetary reductions.... The three composite measures used here are weighted averages based on administrators' perceptions of the "importance, in dollars, of each strategy," from 0 (not used) to 4 (most important).

...Four of the seven predictor variables are composite indices based on questionnaire responses—group spending pressure, mayors' and councils' spending preferences, administrative sophistication, and administrators' perceptions of financial problems. Each of these measures was constructed by summing a series of weighted items (normally 1 to 4) so that higher scores indicate more intensity or higher preference....

Predicting the Use of Retrenchment Strategies

Here it seems appropriate not only to investigate the extent to which the various financial management tools are actually being used by this large group of cities, but also to examine administrators' views about how important they think the strategies are for relieving financial problems.

Table [3] shows the 32 strategies grouped by the three categories discussed earlier. Looking first at the revenue enhancement items, increasing user fees is ranked as the most important among city administrators (mean score = 2.4). Moreover, an overwhelming proportion of cities (87.3%) raised or added user fees, and a considerable number (76.5%) also sought new local revenue sources in general. Seeking new revenue sources, however, was considered slightly less important than raising user fees. Despite potential taxpayers' resistance, administrators ranked increasing taxes the third most important strategy along with making efforts to draw down surpluses. Finally, it should be noted that acquiring more intergovernmental aid does not rank high among administrators—it is fourth among the revenue strategies. Some researchers have identified this as an early response, a step cities take before tapping local resources. The low rating is perhaps attributable to the reductions in federal aid to cities that began as early as 1978 and were accelerated under the Reagan administration.

Among the productivity reorganization actions, the effort to "improve productivity by better management" was perceived as the most important way to stretch resources (mean score = 2.1). City administrators also considered labor-saving techniques as another valuable method to increase productivity, followed by contracting services to the private sector. A variety of reductions was pursued by a number of communities (shown in the last category of Table [3]), with attrition (1.8), reduction in expenditures for supplies (1.5), and capital expenditures (1.5) being the most important. Clearly most of these cutting actions are not drastic. For example, the top of the list is dominated by efforts to reduce resources either over a period of time or to avoid reducing personnel and service levels. In all, a clear preference appears for those cutting strategies that are the least controversial and least likely to stimulate negative political reactions.

One other observation should be made concerning the list of strategies shown in Table [3]. With the exception of most revenue items, those actions ranked as most important can be implemented directly by the chief executive without direct action from the city council or the electorate. The city administrator can indeed play a

Table 3   Retrenchment Strategies Employed by a Group of U.S.
Cities of 25,000 and Over Population 1980-1983 (n = 408)

	Mean Score[a]	Percent of Cities Using
Revenue Strategies		
1. Increase user fees	2.4	87.3
2. Seek new local revenue sources	2.1	76.5
3. Draw down surpluses	1.7	66.9
4. Increase taxes	1.7	60.8
5. Obtain additional IGR	1.2	53.7
6. Increase long-term borrowing	0.7	36.3
7. Sell assets	0.6	40.4
8. Defer some payments	0.6	36.3
9. Increase short-term borrowing	0.6	35.3
Productivity Improvement/Reorganization Strategies		
1. Improve productivity by better management	2.1	75.2
2. Improve productivity by adopting labor-saving techniques	1.7	63.7
3. Contract out services with private sector	1.0	45.6
4. Joint purchasing agreements	0.9	45.6
5. Shift responsibilities to other units of government	0.5	29.7
6. Contract out services with other units of government	0.5	27.7
Cutting Strategies		
1. Attrition	1.8	71.6
2. Reduce expenditures for supplies/travel	1.5	70.1
3. Reduce capital expenditures	1.5	60.3
4. Impose hiring freeze	1.4	60.3
5. Impose across-the-board cuts	1.4	57.1
6. Reduce overtime	1.2	55.9
7. Reduce administrative expenditures	1.2	53.2
8. Keep expenditure increases below inflation	1.2	49.3
9. Eliminate programs	1.0	48.3
10. Lay off personnel	1.0	44.4
11. Cut least efficient departments	0.9	37.3
12. Reduce services funded by own revenue	0.8	39.5
13. Deferred maintenance of capital stock	0.7	38.2
14. Reduce services funded by IGR	0.7	36.3
15. Institute wage freeze	0.7	32.8
16. Early retirement	0.4	27.0
17. Reduce employee compensation levels	0.4	24.8

[a] The mean score is based on a range of 1 (least important) to 4 (one of the most important). Missing data are coded as 0, or no usage.

critical role in determining the municipality's response to fiscal stress. As a result, administrative variables . . . should be a powerful factor in determining how cities will respond to a decline in resources.

We now turn to the multivariate analysis. . . . [The authors offer evidence regarding possible explanations of why cities chose the various approaches. General summary findings are presented here.— Ed.] The measures taken together can account for a very small proportion of the variation in the strategies. This finding obviously supports the notion that the retrenchment process is unstructured, making it difficult to predict just what financial management tools cities will adopt. . . .

Since the chief executive is hypothesized to play a dominant role in the retrenchment process, it might be appropriate to begin by examining the effects of the administrative variables. As expected, the administrative measures generally are the best predictors of retrenchment strategies. In particular, administrators' perceptions of financial difficulties create a powerful stimulus to search for ways to increase revenues . . . and cut resources. . . . The degree of administrative sophistication is also a strong predictor of productivity improvement measures. . . . Note the negative sign. This suggests that the use of various techniques to improve financial planning and management may serve as a substitute for the specific productivity/reorganization strategies shown in Table [3]. Apparently, an increase in management's ability to control and direct resources lessens the need to implement various productivity programs that, in some cases, are designed for the same purpose.

Although not as powerful as the administrative variables, the environmental factor is of some consequence. For example, the equation suggests that socioeconomic decline generates pressures to increase productivity. The fiscal stress indicator, on the other hand, appears as a notable predictor for only one group of strategies—productivity improvement. Unexpectedly, however, the [evidence] suggests that communities are less willing to implement ways to increase productivity when their relative financial burden increases. Perhaps fiscal strain acts as a barrier to productivity improvement. Attempts to enhance productivity may require a considerable monetary investment with no guarantee that such efforts will reduce costs and thereby relieve the pressure from limited resources. As Elmore and McLaughlin (1981: 114) point out, during periods of fiscal retrenchment a change in policy that backfires may pose an unacceptable political risk for the bureaucracy. Hence administrative logic dictates that, where possible, policies continue the known and predictable.

The most striking feature of these results is the poor performance of the political variables (group spending pressure and mayor and council spending preferences). None of these measures achieves statistical significance, and their ability to affect austerity actions is relatively small compared to the other predictors. Perhaps this finding is attributable to the nature of the strategies derived in this analysis. As indicated above, many of these approaches are subject more to administrative approval than the direct consent of the council and, for the most part, are insulated from political pressure.

Overall, [the evidence] reveals quite clearly that the retrenchment process is a difficult phenomenon to explain. Nevertheless, it highlights the importance of the city administrator in the decision-making process. Specifically, administrators' perceptions of financial problems play an important role in the application of strategies that raise revenues and reduce spending. The effect of administrative sophistication, on the other hand, is limited to the productivity improvement/reorganization measures.

Administrators Dominate in Choice of Retrenchment Strategies

This analysis underscores above all the pivotal role of the city administrator in the choice of fiscal austerity strategies. Since administrative measures are much stronger predictors of strategies than both the environmental-decline factor and the fiscal-strain indicator, regardless of the socioeconomic condition of cities, actions will not be forthcoming until administrators are convinced that a problem exists. Despite the significance of this finding, the model offered here leaves unexplained a considerable amount of variation in the use of strategies.

Ordinarily, an inability to provide greater explained variance would be a source of considerable concern. Some might submit that such indeed is the case here. Nevertheless, as articulated early on, we suspect that the urban fiscal retrenchment process may be an almost textbook case of the garbage-can model of decision making set forth by Cohen et al. (1972). Perhaps the lack of explained variance by itself does not constitute an adequate test of this model. Yet, the results reported here certainly seem consistent with that explanation. To the extent cutback decisions occur in a setting characterized by lack of good accounting data (see Martin, 1982), without established precedents, and with high levels of uncertainty about the ultimate consequences of certain actions, it seems likely that the coping strategies employed by city officials will lack coherence and consistency. This is precisely the outcome predicted by the theory of nondecision making.

It is always possible, of course, that part of the problem may be attributable to weaknesses in measuring the predictor variables, especially the political items. Yet we are not alone in our inability to account for the actions cities take when confronting fiscal decline. Clark et al. (1984) capture less than 14% of the variance in three basic retrenchment strategies using a 12-variable regression model. In another, related, study, Clark and Walter (1984) fail to establish a linkage between certain austerity strategies and socioeconomic characteristics and administrative behavior. This finding led them to conclude that perhaps the retrenchment process is unstructured. Finally, Levine et al. (1981) were not very successful in predicting responses to fiscal stress in their four cities. As a result, they speculated that retrenchment proceeds by default rather than by direction. Based on these studies, the findings presented here are not unusual.

Finally, we should acknowledge that the absence of significant relationships between municipal characteristics and retrenchment actions may indicate that financial problems are not severe enough in most cities to produce any systematic response. Even if that were so, the logic of the nondecision-making model suggests that the more serious the plight, the more erratic and unstructured the response by city authorities. In either case, severe pressure or not, policies to head off the adverse effects of revenue shortfalls appear to be the result of more random forces than might have been expected originally.

References

Clark, C., and B. O. Walter (1984). "The role of administrative sophistication in determining city fiscal retrenchment strategies." Presented at the Annual Meeting of the American Political Science Association, Washington, D.C., August 30-September 2.

Clark, T. N., and L. C. Ferguson (1983). *City Money: Political Processes, Fiscal Strain, and Retrenchment.* New York: Columbia University Press.

Clark, T. N., M. Burg, and M. DeLanda (1984). "Urban political cultures and fiscal austerity strategies." Presented at the Annual Meeting of the American Political Science Association, Washington, D.C., August 30-September 2.

Cohen, M., J. March, and J. Olsen (1972). "A garbage can model of organizational choice." *Admin. Sci. Q.* 17 (March): 1-25.

Elmore, R., and M. McLaughlin (1981). *Reform and Retrenchment: The Politics of California School Finance Reform.* Santa Monica, Calif.: Rand.

Glassberg, A. (1981). "The urban fiscal crisis becomes routine." *Public Admin. Rev.* 41 (January) 165-172.

Levine, C. H., I. Rubin, and G. Wolohojian (1981). *The Politics of Retrench-ment.* Newbury Park, Calif.: Sage.

Martin, J. K. (1982). *Urban Financial Stress: Why Cities Go Broke.* Boston: Auburn House.

Walzer, N. (1985). "Fiscal austerity in mid-size cities: preliminary findings," pp. 161-173 in *Research in Urban Policy*, vol. 1., ed. T. N. Clark. Greenwich, Conn.: JAI.

26. FEDERAL FUNDS AND STATE LEGISLATURES: EXECUTIVE-LEGISLATIVE CONFLICT IN STATE GOVERNMENT

James E. Skok

As problem-solving institutions in modern American society, state legislatures hold great potential for developing solutions to the vast array of public policy problems facing our nation. In the public's perception, however, the performance of the 50 legislative bodies has not been impressive. The Citizens Conference on State Legislatures observed in 1971 that "State legislatures would undoubtedly rank low on most Americans' lists of governmental institutions that make a difference in dealing with the issues and problems that bother us." [1] With the momentum given to legislative reform by the reapportionment decisions of the 1960s, various groups such as the National Conference of State Legislatures (NCSL) and the Advisory Commission on Intergovernmental Relations (ACIR) have called for broad reforms of state legislatures designed to improve their policy-making capabilities.

Focusing upon one problem currently facing many state legislatures—their inability to control the use of federal funds coming into the state—the ACIR has recommended that state legislatures specifically appropriate all federal aid, prohibit spending of federal funds over the amount appropriated, and establish sub-program allocations. [2] This proposal has caused state legislatures across the country to reexamine their procedures for appropriating federal funds and has sparked a debate in state government and academic circles over the proper relationship between the executive and legislative branches in the administration of federal grant programs. Controversy has developed over proposed changes in the traditional relationship with legislators advocating more explicit procedures to improve their policy control and executive officials fearing legislative interference with the governor's constitutional powers over administration. . . .

From *Public Administration Review* 40 (November-December 1980): 561-564, 566-567. Reprinted with permission from the author and *Public Administration Review*. Copyright © 1980 The American Society for Public Administration, 1120 G Street, N.W., Washington, D.C. All rights reserved.

Current State Practices

Methods of administering federal funds vary widely among the states with variations ranging from a "boilerplate" approach (virtually no legislative involvement) to a legislative control-oriented approach. According to recent surveys by the National Association of State Budget Officers (NASBO) and the National Conference of State Legislatures (NCSL), the legislatures in 43 of the 50 states appropriate federal funds in some degree of detail.[3] When examined more closely, however, the NASBO study indicates that this apparent legislative power seems illusory in many cases. In 19 of these states the appropriations of most federal funds were made only in general, open-ended language leaving much discretion over use of federal monies to the state's executive branch. In 27 of the 43 states lump sum appropriations were used for federal funds, a practice which normally allows executive branch officials to authorize transfers among programs covered by the appropriation. Finally, in 24 of these states, unanticipated federal monies which became available in mid-year (after legislative enactment of the budget) were automatically appropriated or made available for expenditure solely by executive branch officials. In only four states were legislative powers extensive in all three of these aspects; that is, the legislatures reported power to appropriate federal funds, including interim funds, in specified amounts by object-class or line-item detail. Getting beyond these formal power arrangements, only seven states in the NCSL survey reported an active legislative review of federal funds, while 22 reported a moderate review and 16 a limited review.

Typical of the limited review or "boilerplate" approach is the set of procedures used in Pennsylvania prior to 1976. Executive branch agencies in preparing annual budget requests would estimate the amounts of federal funds to be received during the forthcoming fiscal year. State funds were appropriated in lump sum amounts; however, the appropriations act did not list specific amounts of federal funds. Rather, each agency was simply authorized to spend whatever federal monies were received during the year. The nature of the federal grant program generally would determine the nature of the agency's state budget presentation and the information presented to the legislature.

For categorical entitlement or formula grant programs (Aid to Families with Dependent Children, for example), the agency would calculate a total amount needed to fund the estimated caseload at a given level of support (a percentage of the state standard family subsistence income). The federal entitlement formula would then determine the state appropriation needed and the expected federal grant level. Both amounts and the calculations used would be shown in the agency's budget request forms. These types of programs caused few problems from the standpoint of legislative control under the "boiler-plate" approach since the agency's discretion was severely limited by federal regulations and the options were clear to all involved. Funds could not be transferred to any other use.

In the case of more open-ended categorical assistance grants (Social Services grants, for example) and block grants, the problems of legislative control become infinitely more complex. To illustrate, Title 20 Social Services Grants may be used for a wide range of projects (day care, homemaker/housekeeping services, counseling, family planning, health diagnosis and help in securing treatment) subject to approval of a Comprehensive Annual Services Plan by the U.S. Department of Health, Education and Welfare [now Health and Human Services]. Traditionally such plans have been developed by the state welfare agency with little or no state legislative involvement. Mid-year amendments to the state plan may be made with HEW approval and frequently additional unallocated federal monies become available during the fiscal year. Under these circumstances, the "boilerplate" procedures are highly unsatisfactory from the standpoint of legislative control. The agency budget submission would show the total amount of social services funds expected, and break the total amount down into specific amounts for the various projects to be funded. The agency, however, had great discretion over the projects in which federal funds should actually be used. Since all federal funds were appropriated in a general, open-ended grant of authority, the agency was free to make shifts from one use to another during the fiscal year with approval of the Governor's Budget Office. Additional federal monies that became available during the year were budgeted and expended without additional legislative approval as long as the 25 percent state matching requirement could be met from existing state appropriations. The problems associated with federal block grants . . . were similar to those of the Title 20 grants.

While the "boilerplate" approach had the advantage of allowing agencies much administrative flexibility to seize opportunities to capture federal funds as soon as an occasion arose, it also produced among legislators a feeling of impotence when trying to control state spending. In 1976, the Pennsylvania General Assembly enacted legislation (over Governor Shapp's veto) forbidding expenditure of federal funds or state matching funds unless both were specifically appropriated by the General Assembly.[4] Since 1976, the annual General Appropriation Act has provided state funds only. Federal funds are now appropriated annually in a separate act by specific amount, department, and grant category. To illustrate, in 1976 the state Justice Department received 17 specific appropriations from state funds and 24 additional specific appropriations from federal funds. Funds now may not be transferred among the specified purposes nor may additional federal funds which become available during mid-year be allocated for expenditure without enactment of new appropriations by the legislature.[5]

The Arguments: Proponents of Executive Power Versus Legislative Partisans

Proponents of increasing state legislative control over the appropriation of federal funds argue that current budgetary practices were established during a time in which federal funds made up only a very small part of total state budgets.[6] Increases in the amounts of federal funds and the development of new federal discretionary grants such as General and Special Revenue Sharing, the proponents argue, have been used by administrators to increase their control over policy at the expense of the state legislatures. The representative character of state government, they continue, is lost if executive agencies, which do not have to face the voting public, can use federal funds to finance activities which their legislatures have refused to fund. Legislatures, this argument continues, lose oversight control if executive agencies feel they alone control the allocation and expenditure of federal funds totaling from 20 percent to 30 percent of the typical state budget. Finally, program administrators at the state and federal levels develop channels of communication and a common professional-agency bias which often ignore the general public interest and exclude the state legislatures from significant areas of policy making.

To illustrate, a state legislator in Pennsylvania has claimed that agencies in his state have: (1) purposely expanded their staffs on "soft" federal money, thus forcing the legislature to provide additional state funds when federal funds expired (Board of Probation Parole); (2) purposely overestimated federal receipts for mental institutions, thus forcing the legislature to appropriate state funds to cover the deficit (Welfare Department); and (3) shifted federal Title 20 funds from day care after the legislature had increased the state day care appropriation above the amount requested by the agency (Welfare Department).[7] In Pennsylvania, as well as other states, many legislators perceive administrators as being deceitful, arrogant, and overbearing in their attempt to exclude legislators from effective participation in the policy-making process.

Countering these arguments, opponents of extending state legislative appropriation powers over federal funds contend that handling these funds at the state level is an administrative function and emphasize that state governors generally have constitutional powers as chief executive.[8] Congress, they argue, has already made the critical policy decisions guiding the use of federal grants; and subsequently, federal executive branch agencies enter virtual contractual relationships with state administrators controlling the use of federal grant funds. Echoing the thoughts of some of the early writers on public administration, these advocates of executive power articulate the following arguments.

Structurally and functionally legislatures are policy-making institutions. They are neither designed nor staffed to perform efficient, non-partisan administration. Many state legislatures meet only a limited number of days each year; are prone to partisan deadlocks; and are characterized by bargaining, logrolling and other types of "nonrational" decision making. State legislatures are subject to the demagogic behavior of vocal minorities advocating racial discrimination or narrow partisan and personnel objectives which would threaten to undermine national objectives established by Congress in federal legislation. State legislatures are unable to act with dispatch when rapid decisions upon federal funds are required. Their participation in the federal funds process presents a threat to the constitutional principle of federal supremacy. Executive branch agencies are structurally and functionally efficient decision-making systems, and to force the governor's guardianship of federal funds to become subject to partisan state legislative control violates the intent of many federal grant programs and reduces the governor's constitutional power as chief executive to, merely, a ministerial function. Finally, allowing state legislatures to control federal funds through the appropriation process creates inefficiency, delays, and excessive red tape; and, ultimately, it raises the possibility that program administration will become politicized.

Evaluating the Arguments:
Executive-Legislative Conflict in Pennsylvania

Interviews with 15 executive and legislative staff officials subsequent to the enactment of Act 117 in Pennsylvania have revealed information useful in evaluating these arguments. All officials interviewed conceded that legislators are within their constitutional powers in requesting greater involvement in the federal funds process. The consensus of those persons interviewed is that the new procedures seem workable but cumbersome—capable of producing massive amounts of detail but at the expense of administrative flexibility. The following range of problems has been experienced by the commonwealth agencies receiving federal funds: minor conflict situations, policy confrontations between the executive branch and the legislature, constitutional confrontations between the state legislature and the federal government, and, finally, the politicization of state administration. . . .

[In his complete essay, Skok provides explanations for and examples of each of these difficulties.—Ed.]

Conclusion

The assertion of state legislative powers over federal funds is a reform national in scope undertaken in good faith throughout the country. It has the support of "good government" groups such as the National Conference of State Legislatures and the Advisory Commission on Intergovernmental Relations. Indeed, ACIR's vocal support of the reforms in Pennsylvania was cited by the court majority in *Shapp* v. *Sloan* as a factor influencing their decision to uphold the constitutionality of Act 117.[9] The political nature of the Pennsylvania case should not be used to discredit the legislative reform movement. Ultimately, each state must consider the facts and circumstances of its particular case. To those states considering adopting procedures similar to the Pennsylvania process, the conclusions drawn from this study might prove informative.

All persons interviewed supported the right of the legislature to improve its policy-making capability in relation to federal funds. Likewise, all interviewees concluded that the Act 117 procedures are being complied with by the bureaucracy and that minor delays and increased paperwork are the most common operational problems. By a large majority, however, the interviewees felt the new procedures are cumbersome, time consuming, and not productive of real improvement in the policy-making process. During periods of legislative recess or deadlock there is an inability to act upon federal funds. While the legislature does receive much more detailed information under the new procedures, there is the danger that legislators, deluged by detail, might actually be diverted from larger policy questions. Adequate legislative staffing to cope with the additional flow of paper is essential. Finally, the potential for politicization of matters that have been considered essentially administrative in character is underscored by the Pennsylvania experience.

Notes

1. *The Sometime Governments* (Kansas City: Citizens Conference on State Legislatures, 1971), p. 2.
2. "State Legislatures and Federal Grants," *Information Bulletin* No. 76-4 (Washington, D.C.: Advisory Commission on Intergovernmental Relations,

November 1976). (Hereinafter cited as *ACIR Information Bulletin.*)
3. The National Association of State Budget Officers, *Federal Funds Budgetary and Appropriations Practices in State Government* (Lexington, Ky.: Council of State Governments, 1978), p. 7 . . . ; *State Legislative Oversight of Federal Funds: Preliminary Report and Suggested Activities* (Denver, Colo.: National Conference of State Legislatures, 1979). (Hereinafter cited as the *NCSL Survey.*)
4. Act No. 117, July 1, 1976; 72 P. S. 4611.
5. Unlike some states, the Pennsylvania law does not designate the Appropriations Committee or some other unit as a joint clearinghouse to act for the entire legislature in approving changes to the federal funds appropriation throughout the fiscal year. A process similar to this is currently used in 12 states although at least three states have constitutional prohibitions to such a procedure. *NCSL Survey,* Appendix A, Table 11.
6. These arguments are abstracted from various sources. See for example, the comments of Michael Hershock of the staff of the Pennsylvania House of Representatives in *ACIR Information Bulletin,* p. 2. See also the testimony of Representative Stanley Steingut of the New York State Assembly in "Role of State Legislatures in Appropriating Federal Funds to States," Hearings before the Subcommittee on Intergovernmental Relations of the Committee on Governmental Affairs. U.S. Senate, 95th Congress, First Session, June 16, 1977, pp. 2-50. (Hereinafter cited as *U.S. Senate Hearings on Role of State Legislatures.*)
7. These situations are summarized from testimony by Representative James P. Ritter of the Pennsylvania General Assembly in the *U.S. Senate Hearings on Role of State Legislatures,* pp. 56-60.
8. These arguments are abstracted from various sources. See, for example, the testimony of John P. Mallan of the American Association of State Colleges and Universities in *U.S. Senate Hearings on Role of State Legislatures,* pp. 114-203. See also the brief for appellants in *Shapp* v. *Sloan* in *U.S. Senate Hearings on Role of State Legislatures,* pp. 134-197. These arguments are primarily those of lawyers and practicing governmental officials rather than academicians or administrative theorists; however, the influence of the early literature of public administration is apparent. For a review of this early literature see: John A. Worthley, "Public Administration and Legislatures: Past Neglect, Present Probes," *Public Administration Review,* Vol. 35 (September-October 1975), 486-490.
9. Pa. 391 A2d. 595, 605. One wonders whether the ACIR would have been so vocal in its support if all the facts had been available to them at the time.

Part III

REVIEW QUESTIONS

1. What are the relative strengths and weaknesses of the different types of intergovernmental aid mechanisms—for instance, formula, project, categorical, and block grants? Be sure to include both economic and political considerations.

2. Analysts of American intergovernmental relations frequently allude to the interdependence of units in the system. How would you document this interdependence using fiscal data? Judicial decisions? Local decision making?

3. George Break says that fixed-amount grants for specified purposes may "conciliate appearance and reality" because they seem to support functions deemed important by the grantor while really allowing grantees to use the funds for any local purpose. Please explain this effect of the fixed-amount grant.

4. What are open- and closed-ended grants? What are their relative advantages and disadvantages?

5. Arvidson documents a squeeze currently being experienced by state and local officials throughout the country: less intergovernmental aid, in relative terms, coupled with more and more conditions attached to that aid. Can you offer an explanation as to why they are being placed in such a position? Is this the worst of all worlds from the standpoint of the nonnational governments? Or does their response suggest that benefits as well as headaches accompany this circumstance?

6. Imagine that a presidential election has just taken place. The winner has campaigned on the issue of reforming the system of intergovernmental aid so that public functions would be sorted out by level of government. "Matters of national concern should be handled at the national level," the president-elect

says, "and matters of more limited concern should be handled by the state and local governments. One of my first priorities is to redirect the system in this fashion." The new national chief executive calls on you, an expert in intergovernmental relations, for advice on how to carry out this program. What do you say? Be sure to consider Monypenny's analysis of the political functions of fiscal assistance, as well as the ACIR's discussion of the attractions of categorical grants and Wrightson's coverage of the federal judiciary's treatment of the municipal bond issue.

7. In an essay in Part II of this volume, Reischauer explains how the diversity among American governmental structures and functions impedes any efforts to design rational fiscal instruments. Monypenny seems to imply that the prevalence of grants is in large measure the *result* of diversity. Are these two claims necessarily inconsistent? Discuss.

8. In today's era of cross-cutting mandates (similar or identical strings, such as nondiscrimination requirements, attached to many different grants offered in divergent policy sectors), does Monypenny's assertion that narrow coalitions are responsible for individual programs still seem valid? In answering this question, consider Anton's analysis of coalitions from Part II of this book. Anton's discussion of *vertical* coalitions is heavily influenced by Monypenny's ideas. Yet do other kinds of coalitions in the modern system complicate the picture? Explain.

9. Some critics of the American system of intergovernmental relations claim that the current pattern of categorical grants constitutes an aberration from the fundamental features of the American political system, like governmental accountability. Is this a valid criticism? In your answer, give some attention to the forces encouraging the establishment and maintenance of categorical programs.

10. Should control over funding formulas and the expenditure of aid be placed in the hands of technical experts so that politics can be eliminated from the design of intergovernmental fiscal instruments? Why or why not? (Note Nathan's analysis, and also consider the evidence presented by Morgan and Pammer about the decision-making patterns of local officials during times of retrenchment.)

11. Suppose a friend compares city officials dealing with state or federal governments to addicts hooked on narcotics (in this case, money): they can't wait to get hold of their "drug"; they try to inject it into their most vital parts; and they become, thereby, dependent on it. Does the study by Morgan and Pammer suggest any flaws in this analogy?

Part IV

ADMINISTRATIVE ASPECTS OF
INTERGOVERNMENTAL RELATIONS

In one policy sector after another, intergovernmental administrative arrangements are responsible for many of the most significant public decisions and the consequences of those decisions. Yet these arrangements are relatively obscured from public view. Even the most prominent bureaucratic units within individual governments, such as the cabinet-level agencies in Washington, can be almost incomprehensible to the citizenry. Their byzantine procedures, obscure jargon, and legions of specialists often make them seem remote and intimidating. Complexity and misunderstanding are magnified when the administration of programs takes place in operations that span two or more government levels.

A survey of some intergovernmental administrative activities may indicate how important, if confusing, this topic is. Many of these activities are aimed at implementing some general policy idea, usually established in broad outline at the national level. Converting this general intention into specific actions while also incorporating state and local objectives may entail a set of formidable tasks. At the national level, administrative actors may be deeply involved in deciding which government units are to receive how much aid—if indeed financial assistance is to be part of the intergovernmental program—as well as in developing program regulations, mediating and negotiating with state and local agencies, reviewing plans and operations of other levels of government, and coordinating intergovernmental programs handled by various federal agencies. At other levels, intergovernmental administration includes such activities as drafting plans (and seeking support for them within the community, the government, and higher levels of administration), negotiating with other governments, managing programs (which can involve designing, staffing, and evaluating complex efforts), dealing with program beneficiaries and their representatives, and attempting to coordinate state and local programs with one another and with other state and local activities.

Not all of these activities, of course, can be investigated through the readings in Part IV. However, the readings do illuminate some of the most important facets of and developments in the administrative sphere of intergovernmental relations. Three general comments can be made about the selections included here. First, of course, the articles illustrate the links among political, fiscal, and administrative aspects of the American intergovernmental pattern. Many administrative problems and opportunities in the system are tied to aid programs, and very often administrative disputes between and among governments reflect political disagreements. Second, these articles (and, in fact, most studies of administrative aspects of intergovernmental relations) understandably focus on negative topics—problems and dilemmas of the system. Still, it is important to recognize that in many policy areas much of the time calm, workable arrangements have developed. The fact that the system often works can be obscured by both political rhetoric and the network's very complexity.[1] Third, much of today's debate about intergovernmental relations tends to lay the blame for the weaknesses in the system, including the costliness of programs and the frequent lack of coordination, on the federal government. However, the readings in this section highlight the oversimplifications underlying this explanation. While the federal government is surely not free of blame for intergovernmental administrative difficulties, neither is it the sole culprit. Solutions to these problems do not lie with a simplistic castigation of the national bureaucracy.

Part IV begins with an article that implies this point. Helen Ingram studied the operations of a small intergovernmental program, water resources planning grants to states authorized by Title III of the Water Resources Planning Act of 1965. Her picture of federal-state administration is a far cry from the image of a hierarchical, command-and-control implementation chain. Indeed, her study is a classic depiction of an intergovernmental program in operation and, as such, frames the other readings in this part of the book. Drawing from her field investigations, as well as the explicit models of intergovernmental politics developed by Jeffrey Pressman and Martha Derthick (excerpted in Part II), she asserts that when federal administrative agencies deal with state units, bargaining is the predominant behavior observed. The federal government does not control the administration of programs; nor, claims Ingram, is there any substantial chance that it *could* do so, even by using stronger threats of sanctions. In this excerpt Ingram develops a set of propositions on the extent and (especially) the limits of federal administrative influence. She implies that administration in intergovernmental relations—even more than administration within a single government—involves more subtle activities than simply giving and receiving orders.

Ingram analyzes the context in which intergovernmental financial assistance is used to reach program goals. Her conclusions are not strictly dependent on the existence of a grant-in-aid. The presence of a financial inducement clearly facilitates, however, the bargaining that is a regular part of administration in the intergovernmental system. What happens, then, when grants cannot be employed to assist the bargaining process? Here one can expect the style of negotiation to be altered, although bargaining itself is likely to remain ubiquitous. This issue is increasingly important in the 1990s, an era of substantial intergovernmental regulation. Whereas governments have long used strings on grants-in-aid to attempt to control other levels of government, the quantity and perceived intrusiveness of intergovernmental regulation have accelerated. A major instrument of influence across levels will continue to be grants, as the analysis in this book has shown. However, the present budget constraints make it likely that as new issues press for consideration on the agendas of American governments, efforts will often be made to address them without making commitments to substantially higher levels of spending. In recent years the federal mandates have increased substantially for state and local governments; while states themselves, pressed to achieve ever more and faced with limitations on new spending from Washington, have expanded their own regulation of local units. Reformers have responded by seeking ways to control the intrusiveness and excesses of these potentially conflictual intergovernmental links. Today this subject of intergovernmental regulation, or mandating, is receiving a great deal of attention from politicians, administrators, and study groups concerned about the intergovernmental system. Accordingly, the remainder of the readings in Part IV concentrate on various aspects of this emerging issue.

The first of these selections is reading no. 28, excerpted from a study by the Advisory Commission on Intergovernmental Relations (ACIR), *Regulatory Federalism,* which focuses on the increased regulatory activity in the intergovernmental system. In this excerpt the commission distinguishes various types of regulatory mechanisms used in intergovernmental administration. Some of these varieties of regulation are associated with grants-in-aid, while others are imposed through federal laws or rules divorced from any aid program. The ACIR report, published in the mid 1980s, documents that much of the regulation has been generated relatively recently. (As some of the other selections in Part IV demonstrate, the pace has not slackened since.)

Following this general introduction are four other selections. The initial pair (nos. 29 and 30) examine the impact of federal regulation at the local level, but they reach markedly different conclusions. The first (no. 29), by then-mayor Edward Koch of New York City, is a vivid critique of the trends in federal regulation. Koch points out how many problems can be caused for localities by well-intended but poorly considered mandates from Washington. (We should note that, in the case of Koch's example of the Section 504 regulations, which covered access to mass-transit facilities for the handicapped, federal rules have been changed since the original publication date to provide more flexibility to local governments.) [2]

Although Koch portrays federal administrators as domineering and unyielding, Frederick Lazin's argument (no. 30) is much different. Lazin studied national-local bargaining on equal opportunity in public housing in Chicago and found that bureaucrats in the Department of Housing and Urban Development were extremely, indeed excessively, deferential toward the local power structure. Whereas Koch points to the strength of the federal presence in intergovernmental administration, Lazin emphasizes local influence. Lazin's essay shows that the frequent portrayal of state and local officials as hard-working, decent, unfairly put-upon public servants harassed by Washington is not universally accurate.

Lazin's article was written during an era of expansive national presence in the intergovernmental system, and Koch's essay was originally written in 1980, after a decade of mandate expansion. However, developments since that time have also become important. The final two articles in this section (nos. 31 and 32) cover some of these additional significant aspects of the mandate theme.

Kathleen Sylvester (in no. 31) examines the expansion of *state* mandates on local governments. She demonstrates that, while this issue is not new, it has become much more important in recent years. Furthermore, in her coverage of recent efforts to control or discourage excessive state-local regulation, Sylvester demonstrates how persistently recalcitrant this channel of intergovernmental influence can be to efforts at control.

In the final reading, David Beam and Timothy Conlan discuss federal efforts to control the growth of regulation during the Reagan era. They too conclude that attempts to retrench were, with some exceptions, largely unsuccessful. Indeed, despite popular perceptions, Reagan presided over an era of further expansion of Washington's regulatory reach. Although the successor Bush administration also affirmed a commitment to trim federal regulations (with Vice President Dan Quayle chairing a high-level national commission on this subject for several years), it too has experienced relatively little success. The study by Beam and Conlan illuminates reasons for the resolute resistance of the intergovernmental system to cutbacks in these mechanisms of administrative interdependence.

Notes

1. Paul Peterson, Barry G. Rabe, and Kenneth K. Wong, *When Federalism Works* (Washington, D.C.: Brookings, 1986).
2. ACIR, *Regulatory Federalism: Policy, Process, Impact, and Reform* (Washington, D.C.: ACIR, February 1984), 229-230.

27. POLICY IMPLEMENTATION THROUGH BARGAINING: THE CASE OF FEDERAL GRANTS-IN-AID

Helen Ingram

. . . The underlying logic of federal grants-in-aid as an implementation technique is that the federal government can hire states with money to run its errands and do its will. A large literature on the impact of grants-in-aid upon the federal system generally agrees with William H. Young, who states that grants have been the "most powerful engine in this century for reshaping national-state relations." [1] Whether federal grants-in-aid can actually achieve policy goals has, however, never been carefully tested. This paper will argue that rather than compelling states to move toward the policies that the federal government has set, federal grants simply provide guides to states which they may set aside as they pursue agendas of their own making. The result is that implementation of federal policies becomes diverted. . . .

The first task of this paper is to establish an alternative conceptual framework that centers on policy rather than institutional structure and views implementation as a process of bargaining rather than federal intervention into state jurisdiction. Once a policy perspective and a bargaining framework are established, it is possible to set forth a series of logically related propositions. These propositions will suggest that certain federal goals are more likely to be accomplished through grants-in-aid than others, and that certain conditions facilitate the realization of federal goals by grants-in-aid. . . .

A Conceptual Framework for Examining Grants-in-Aid

The usual rationale for grants-in-aid to states assumes federal dominance of an essentially hierarchical process of handing downward

Author's note: While the shortcomings of this article are the fault of the author, the helpful review and comments of the following persons should be gratefully acknowledged: Elizabeth Haskell, Aaron Wildavsky, Sheldon Edner, Henry Kenski, Frederick Anderson, Scott Ullery and Geoffrey Wandesforde-Smith.

From *Public Policy* 25 (Fall 1977): 499-526. Copyright © 1977, John Wiley & Sons, Inc., Publishers. Reprinted by permission of John Wiley & Sons, Inc.

both federal goals and the financial resources necessary to accomplish them. States are thought of as either unwilling or unable to perform a task important to national decision makers. Consequently, federal funds are employed to alter state behavior. The promise of available money is expected to lure states into actions they otherwise would not take, while federal financing is intended to upgrade state capability to do what federal policy specifies. Supposedly, grants-in-aid implement federal policies indirectly by steering state agencies toward federal objectives. The reins for this process of implementation are the "strings" or conditions attached to grants which grantees must satisfy in order to qualify for funds.

A bargaining framework fits more accurately than a superior-subordinate model the complex intergovernmental relations involved in grants-in-aid. Instead of a federal master dangling a carrot in front of a state donkey, the more apt image reveals a rich merchant haggling on equal terms with a sly, bargain-hunting consumer. Bargaining is the decision-making mode used when participants share a common interest in coming to a decision but have divergent values and objectives. Both the federal agencies administering grants and the state agencies designated as the receptors of grant monies want the grant transaction to take place. While federal agencies would like the transaction to bind state recipients to federal policy, state agencies face a number of conflicting concerns. Thus the aim of state agencies in the transaction is maximum possible leeway to pursue their own separate goals with the federal money. Because each participant values settlement, neither is anxious to cause conflict if it can be avoided. For instance, federal agencies are unlikely to embark upon enforcement practices that they anticipate will bring them little support and much criticism. Similarly, when the returns to a state are substantial and certain, and the state interest sacrificed is small, the state is likely to accede to federal requirements. The result is a process of implementation that is a complex succession of bids and counterbids between the state and federal levels during which the initial aims of each are substantially modified.

Bargaining at "Arm's Length"

Much of what goes on in grants bargaining is based upon anticipated reaction; in plotting their actions, federal and state bargainers implicitly take each other into account without explicit exchange. The federal system introduces a remoteness in grant bargaining that is not at all like the close contact logrolling and compromise that occur in legislatures.[2] Most of the contexts within which federal and state officials operate are different. The states are just one part of a federal agency's political environment, which also includes departments and other agencies, OMB, congressional committees, interest groups, and the like. By the same token, individual states have their own distinctive political culture and the federal government is viewed as an outside force. Certain prevailing attitudes and prejudices that federal bureaucrats and state agency people have about one another perpetuate separation and encourage independence. The ideology of states' rights is very strong, and federal officials wish to avoid the appearance of interference. Consequently, federal administrators sometimes wait for a formal document to be submitted rather than participate in the writing of proposals. States are frequently reluctant to deal face-to-face with "Feds" because they dislike feeling dominated and outclassed.

Resources in Bargaining

What either the state or the federal government wins or is forced to concede in the grant process is determined by the distribution of resources. Federal strength is often more apparent than real. On the one hand, money is a powerful incentive, and federal administrative agencies hold the grant purse strings. One would expect the competition between localities to be intense and state officials to be highly motivated to meet both the formal requirements and informal preferences of federal officials. Only a few states are able to compete with the national government in attracting outstanding professional talent, and state counterparts are often outclassed in negotiations. On the other hand, states can offset resources by controlling the context in which the federal government acts. Furthermore, states have other important resources of their own.

Precedent and prevailing expectations often give the advantage to states. Grant bargaining between the federal agency and the states takes place in the context of previous settlements that cause each to expect certain results and to limit or expand their aspirations. Phillip Monypenny concluded that when a loose coalition is too weak to secure its program in each individual state, it turns to Congress. Congress responds with a grant-in-aid program when a wholly federal program with specific requirements engenders too much opposition to pass, but the coalition is too strong to deny altogether.[3] The resulting legislation authorizing grants-in-aid reflects the political weakness of support among the states and perpetuates it into the future. Built into the authorizing statute are explicit or implicit promises that national uniformity will not be imposed and that individual states will not be made to pursue some unshared objectives. Federal agencies are aware of these promises and are consequently reluctant to exercise supervisory powers. Furthermore, once a grant program is underway, past practice has an enormous influence upon expectations. If states have routinely been given grants on the basis of a certain level of performance, then they are likely to project past experience into the future.

States have strength in numbers. Any state has the advantage of being only one among fifty, and federal grant offices are seldom capable of giving detailed supervision of each at once. . . . There is considerable state discretion to shop around among grants and avoid some that involve quantities of federal red tape.

States control essential information for the allocation of grants and for monitoring the impacts of grants. Unless the federal agency duplicates state efforts, it must depend on the accuracy and thoroughness of documents supplied by states. Because of state representation in Congress, states have easy access to the amending process if grant negotiations go against state interest. Administrative agencies are dependent upon the ongoing support of state recipients in the congressional budgetary process. The bargaining strength of states increases in time because the more state participation increases, the more the program is likely to continue and the less likely it will be amended against state interests.[4]

The bargaining framework set out above suggests a set of rules that follow logically and that may govern the extent to which federal policies can be implemented through the grant strategy in particular programs. These rules are stated in the next section of the paper and are quite different from those one would explore if the carrot model in which the federal government is dominant actually prevailed. . . .

Propositions Concerning Implementation and Impact of Specific Grants-in-Aid Programs

Establishing a Bargaining Context

The initial bargaining position of a federal administrative agency is likely to be undercut when Congress selects grants-in-aid as a means to build support and assuage opposition in the legislative process. Congress has available a range of techniques to implement its policy objectives. These mechanisms vary in the extent to which they rely on coercion. Some, such as the provision of information, are not at all coercive. Agricultural extension programs are an example. Others, such as the provision of a subsidy, tax relief, or a grant, are gently coercive. Only rewards are distributed, and the sole penalty is failure to share in the benefits. The establishment of specific rules and regulations is more coercive because penalties are imposed for noncompliance. The coercive force of government is even greater when the federal government itself takes action by establishing management entities that become involved in issues that were formerly state and local or private.[5]

Modern legislation is often a complex composite of goals and objectives to be achieved through a variety of more or less coercive techniques. In choosing various policy strategies Congress must attend, not just to possible effectiveness, but also to the support or opposition engendered. Subsidy techniques, such as grants, are sometimes chosen less for their supposed effectiveness than for their acceptability. Because participation is in principle voluntary, state governments need not accept grants unless it is to their advantage to do so. Congressmen see to it that for state governments the ratio of benefits to cost in the grant program is high enough to be attractive.[6]

Subsidy programs are often legislatively packaged with other more coercive programs to make controversial provisions more palatable. . . .

While it is possible for Congress to make real demands on states as conditions for grants and to authorize federal agencies to apply the use of significant sanctions to states that do not comply, the use of grant programs as "sweeteners" renders congressional demands less likely. The promise of money to come serves as a *quid pro quo* for immediate legislative support. . . .

When grant programs are included to make legislation more acceptable, there follows a tendency to be vague about objectives and indefinite about the conditions under which grants can be denied to states. . . .

Another reason for the weakness of federal requirements in some grant programs is that their legislative purpose is less to impose some federal objective than to improve state programs.[7] . . .

Federal administrators who must enforce programs containing "sweetener" grants have little in terms of legal mandate, legislative history, or public expectations upon which to base a tough line on state performance. Federal bureaucrats have little legitimacy in imposing their views. . . .

Broadly Distributing Benefits

In the grant bargaining process, federal administrative agencies are likely to place highest priority upon achieving broad support, even if this means refusing to terminate funds for reasons of noncompliance or poor performance, or failing to reward states that excel in program objectives. In a bargaining situation, participants can be expected to pursue a course of least cost and maximum benefit. It serves neither the interests of the federal granting agency nor those of the states to deny grant funds. Administrators of grants are supposed to spend money for a specified purpose, and not doing so is an obvious failure. Just as

Congress concentrates on grants-in-aid as a support-building device, so also do federal agencies see grants as a means of building a broad state constituency. Failure to give a state its allocation is bound to elicit a complaint from its congressional delegation and evoke the sympathetic concern of other congressmen who are made aware of potential threats to their own constituencies. Of course, states are anxious to get federal money and are willing to make some accommodation. In the process of intergovernmental bargaining, states do make concessions in order to meet some federal objectives.

It is not surprising that federal agency officials are likely to place the highest premium on maintaining support for the agency and its long-term welfare. This does not mean policy implementation is unimportant, just that there are limits to the organizational sacrifices that federal agencies will make for policy gains. As a result, the sanctions that federal agencies can impose by denying discretionary funds are exercised with caution and moderation. The threat to hold back funds is most effective as a potential resource. States cannot be completely certain that federal agencies will not, in fact, cut off the flow of funds. The leverage that comes from this potential power is most credible in the early stages of a grant program, before a routine and a pattern of expectations have been established.[8] In his study of grants-in-aid for public assistance, Steiner found that, over time, states were likely to win their battles with Washington. "In the long-run sense, the intensity of federal control of the public assistance program probably diminishes as the federal agency responsible for administration becomes less insecure, less of a novelty, and begins to establish quiet negotiation procedures that could serve as alternatives to noisy withdrawal of federal cooperation."[9] It is equally likely that during extended periods of intergovernmental bargaining, states have shifted somewhat toward federal objectives.

In some grant programs, even a federal agency's opportunity to apply early sanctions is foregone. Edner found that in the Southwest Region of the Environmental Protection Agency, no state has ever been denied funds. Instead, state program plans have been ranked, and marginal and poor ones have been cited, in an effort to persuade states to improve their applications.[10] Murphy found that Title V of the Elementary and Secondary Education Act has been implemented as general aid, accommodating all state applicants.[11] Of course, federal agencies have other coercive tools beyond the withholding of funds: delays are imposed, extra paperwork and particular procedures are required, and so on. These strategies, too, are conflict producing, and lose credibility if not eventually supported by imposition of financial penalties. . . .

Changing Organizations

Through the grant-bargaining process, federal administrative agencies are more likely to win improvements in state organizational infrastructure than to change state action. Through the grant-in-aid system the federal government becomes a participant in the state political system. It is, however, a peripheral actor because it has no legitimate role, no formal right to impose its decisions.[12] The federal government manipulates state actors indirectly by changing the atmosphere in which decisions are made and by increasing the benefits for acting in accord with federal objectives. In a bargaining situation states are likely to respond most positively to federal directives where the cost of compliance is small and the expected return is large. The greatest impact of federal grants is in their initial phase when it is attractive to states to establish an agency in order to be eligible for federal grants. Bitterman has noted that states acted quickly to set up organizations to receive grants from New Deal Programs. While only Wisconsin passed social security legislation before the federal government did, all states passed legislation within two years after federal funds became available.[13] In a more contemporary example, Derthick found that many local and urban organizations, especially those in urban renewal, public housing, and anti-poverty programs, have been created for the purpose of receiving and administering federal grants.[14]

State agencies established to receive federal funds are often favored by certain resources and advantages in state government. Cost-sharing arrangements for programs underwritten by federal grants augment the benefits of state appropriations, and consequently grants often induce state investment. More sizable staffing naturally goes along with larger expenditures. The Kestnbaum Report found that state legislatures are less likely to investigate and supervise state agencies administering federal funds, and that federal aid "requirements" are often used as an excuse to fend off state reorganization.[15]

While states may accept or even pursue federal grants that create independent agencies with their own resources, they may not agree that these agencies, once in place, are to implement mainly federal objectives. As Ira Sharkansky has observed, grants-in-aid can be turned to states' own ends by a variety of devices.[16] For federal grants actually to affect policy outputs of state agencies, there must be common interests. The values and objectives of the designated agency must be fashioned along the lines of federal objectives. Further, these aims must carry the day in the larger political processes of the state. . . .

Imposing Administrative Rules

Through the grant-bargaining process, federal administrative agencies are more likely to achieve efficient state management practices than to alter state policy-making processes. Federal agencies place a high priority upon keeping careful track of funds and avoiding scandals. Casual bookkeeping and accounting in grant programs can lead to very damaging investigations by congressional committees, the General Accounting Office, or others. Because of the stake that federal agencies have in their own institutional welfare, which goes beyond commitment to individual policies, states are likely to be held to strict financial account. These concerns produced a raft of procedural guidelines and generated a large amount of paperwork in the Model Cities program, for instance.[17] Furthermore, management requirements that relate to proper and efficient operation are relatively easy to impose. Such rules are attractive because they are cast in what seem to be value-free, neutral terms.[18] So long as the federal requirements are fairly simple and reasonably related to efficiency, economy, professionalism, or other generally respected criteria, the diversity of values that exists among states is not offended. If, however, the federal rules and regulations address the way state agencies communicate with one another or favor some actors over others, then peculiar state conditions are likely to become overriding. . . .

Facilitating Policy Change

As a result of grant bargaining, federal administrative agencies can facilitate change in a willing state. But in the absence of state commitment, the federal agency cannot compel state policy change. The federal government is at best a peripheral participant in the state political process. It depends upon the existence of a state counterpart agency for implementation of its objectives. State agencies are not blind surrogates of federal agencies and are likely to have their own independent goals and objectives. Their success in implementing federal goals and/or their own goals will depend upon their own organizational characteristics, leadership, and the broader political environment within which they operate. In short, federal agencies are heavily dependent upon the initiative of the state for program innovation. In an analysis of federal water pollution control policy, Sheldon Edner found that the influence of the federal program had been minimal in stimulating vigorous state counterparts. Of the two states he studied, California and Arizona, the former was much more effective in achieving federal goals because of its own initiative, not because of federal prodding. Arizona simply lacked interest in water pollution and reacted lethargically to federal incentives and sanctions.[19] . . .

Notes

1. Cited in Michael Reagan, *The New Federalism* (New York: Oxford University Press, 1972), p. 55. See also Earl M. Baker, et al., *Federal Grants, The National Interest and State Response: A Review of Theory and Research* (Philadelphia: Center for the Study of Federalism, Temple University, March 1974).
2. Lewis A. Froman, Jr., *The Congressional Process* (Boston: Little, Brown & Co., 1967), p. 22.
3. Phillip Monypenny, "Federal Grants-in-Aid to State Governments: A Political Analysis," in *National Tax Journal* 13 (March 1960), p. 15.
4. Edward W. Weidner, "Decision-Making in a Federal System," in *Federalism: Mature and Emergent,* Arthur W. Macmahon, ed. (New York: Doubleday & Co., 1955).
5. Randall B. Ripley (ed.), *Public Policies and Their Politics* (New York: W. W. Norton & Co., 1966), p. xi.
6. Martha Derthick, *The Influence of Federal Grants* (Cambridge: Harvard University Press, 1970), p. 197.
7. Reagan, *The New Federalism,* p. 67.
8. Derthick, *The Influence of Federal Grants,* p. 208.
9. Gilbert Y. Steiner, *Social Insecurity: The Politics of Welfare* (Chicago: Rand McNally, 1966), p. 84.
10. Sheldon M. Edner, "The Implementation of Federal Water Pollution Control Policy through Grants-in-Aid" (a paper delivered at the 27th Annual Meeting of the Western Political Science Association, San Diego, Calif., 1973), p. 13.
11. Jerome T. Murphy, *Grease the Squeaky Wheel* (Cambridge: Harvard Research Center for Educational Policy, 1973), p. 33.
12. Derthick, *The Influence of Federal Grants,* p. 201.
13. Henry J. Bitterman, *State and Federal Grants-in-Aid* (New York: Mentzer, Bush, & Co., 1938), cited in Baker et al., *Federal Grants, The National Interest and State Response,* pp. 56-57.
14. Derthick, *The Influence of Federal Grants,* p. 203.
15. Commission on Intergovernmental Relations, "A Survey Report on the Impacts of Federal Grant-in-Aid on the Structures and Function of State and Local Governments" (Washington, D.C.: GPO, 1955), pp. 4, 11.
16. Ira Sharkansky, *The Maligned States: Policy, Accomplishments, Problems and Opportunities* (New York: McGraw-Hill Book Co., 1972), pp. 30-33.
17. Lawrence D. Brown and Bernard Frieden, "Guidelines and Goals for the Model Cities Program," in *Policy Sciences* [actual citation: "Rulemaking by Improvisation: Guidelines and Goals in the Model Cities Program," *Policy Sciences* 7 (1976), pp. 455-488].
18. Derthick, *The Influence of Federal Grants,* p. 198.
19. Edner, "The Implementation of Federal Water Pollution Control Policy," pp. 18-19.

28. THE TECHNIQUES OF INTERGOVERNMENTAL REGULATION

U.S. Advisory Commission on Intergovernmental Relations

As was noted previously, an element of *compulsion* is one key feature of the new intergovernmental regulation that distinguishes it from the usual grant-in-aid conditions. The requirements traditionally attached to assistance programs may be viewed as part of a contractual agreement between two independent, coequal levels of government. In contrast, the policies which the new intergovernmental regulation imposes on state and local governments are more nearly mandatory. They cannot be sidestepped, without incurring some federal sanction, by the simple expedient of refusing to participate in a single federal assistance program. In one way or another, compliance has been made difficult to avoid.

A variety of legal and fiscal techniques has been employed by the national government to encourage acceptance of its regulatory standards. Four major strategies—direct orders, crosscutting requirements, crossover sanctions, and partial preemption—are described below and are summarized in Figure [2].

Direct Orders

In a few instances, federal regulation of state and local government takes the form of direct legal orders that must be complied with under the threat of civil or criminal penalties. For example, the *Equal Employment Opportunity Act of 1972* bars job discrimination by state and local governments on the basis of race, color, religion, sex and national origin. This statute extended to state and local governments the requirements imposed on private employers since 1964. Similarly, the *Marine Protection Research and Sanctuaries Act Amendments of 1977* prohibit cities from disposing of sewage sludge through ocean dumping. Court orders based on constitutional provisions, like those banning segregated schools, are similar in nature.

From ACIR, *Regulatory Federalism: Policy, Process, Impact and Reform* (Washington, D.C.: ACIR, February 1984), pp. 7-10. Reprinted by permission.

Figure 2 A Typology of Intergovernmental
Regulatory Programs

Program Type	Description	Major Policy Areas Employed
Direct Orders	Mandate state or local actions under the threat of criminal or civil penalties	Public employment, environmental protection
Crosscutting Requirements	Apply to all or many federal assistance programs	Nondiscrimination, environmental protection, public employment, assistance management
Crossover Sanctions	Threaten the termination or reduction of aid provided under one or more specified programs unless the requirements of another program are satisfied	Highway safety and beautification, environmental protection, health planning, handicapped education
Partial Preemptions	Establish federal standards, but delegate administration to states if they adopt standards equivalent to the national ones	Environmental protection, natural resources, occupational safety and health, meat and poultry inspection

For the most part, however, Washington has exempted subnational governments from many of the kinds of direct regulatory statutes that apply to businesses and individuals. Hence, although state governments may administer the *Occupational Safety and Health Act,* they (and local governments) are exempt from its provisions in their capacity as employers—as is the federal government itself. Politics often has dictated this course, but there also are some constitutional restrictions on the ability of Congress to regulate directly. The wage and hour requirements imposed on state and local governments by the 1974 amendments to the *Fair Labor Standards Act* were greatly circumscribed by the Supreme Court in *National League of Cities v. Usery* (1976).[1] The Court's ruling held that the law interfered with their "integral operations in areas of traditional governmental functions," and thus threatened their "independent existence."

In this respect, the relationship of the federal government with the states and localities must be contrasted with that of the states and their own local subdivisions. Because local governments are creatures of state law, state "mandating" through direct orders is both legally permissible and very frequent.[2]

Much more commonly, then, Washington has utilized other regulatory techniques to work its will. These may be distinguished by their breadth of application and the nature of the sanctions which back them up.

Crosscutting Requirements

First, and most widely recognized, are the crosscutting or generally applicable requirements imposed on grants across the board to further various national social and economic policies. One of the most important of these requirements is the nondiscrimination provision included in Title VI of the *Civil Rights Act of 1964,* which stipulates that

> No person in the United States shall, on the ground of race, color, or national origin, be excluded from participation in, be denied the benefits of, or be subjected to discrimination under any program receiving Federal financial assistance.[3]

Since 1964, crosscutting requirements have been enacted for the protection of other disadvantaged groups (the handicapped, elderly, and—in education programs—women). The same approach was utilized in the environmental impact statement process created in 1969, as well as for many other environmental purposes. It also has been extended into such fields as historic preservation, animal welfare and relocation assistance.[4] A total of some 36 across-the-board requirements dealing with various socio-economic issues, as well as an additional 23 administrative and fiscal policy requirements, were identified in a 1980 OMB inventory.[5] . . . Of the former group, the largest number involve some aspect of environmental protection (16) and nondiscrimination (9). Two-thirds of the 59 requirements have been adopted since 1969.

Crosscutting requirements have a pervasive impact because they apply "horizontally" to all or most federal agencies and their assistance programs. In contrast, two other new forms of intergovernmental regulation are directed at only a single function, department or program. Thus, both can be described as "vertical" mandates.[6]

Crossover Sanctions

One approach relies upon the power of the purse. It imposes federal fiscal sanctions in one program area or activity to influence state and local policy in another. The distinguishing feature here is that a failure to comply with the requirements of one program can result in a reduction or termination of funds from another, separately authorized and separately entered into, program. The penalty thus "crosses over."

The history of federal efforts to secure the removal of billboards from along the nation's major highways illustrates the use of the traditional financial "carrot" along with this new financial "stick." [7] Beginning in 1958, the federal government offered a small bonus in the form of additional highway funds to states that agreed to regulate billboard advertising along new interstate highways. By 1965, however, only half of the states had taken advantage of this offer—not enough to suit the Johnson White House.

A dramatic change occurred with the adoption of the *Highway Beautification Act of 1965.* The bonus system was dropped, and Congress substituted the threat of withholding 10% of a state's highway construction funds if it did not comply with newly expanded federal billboard control requirements. Despite the bitter opposition of the outdoor advertising industry, 32 states had enacted billboard control laws by 1970, though only 18 of these were judged to be in full compliance. Nearly all of the rest of the states fell quickly into line when Congress made appropriations to compensate for part of the cost of removing nonconforming signs, and the Federal Highway Administrator stepped up his pressure on them.

A similar fiscal penalty subsequently was employed in a number of other programs. In the wake of the OPEC [Organization of Petroleum Exporting Countries] oil embargo, federal officials urged the states to lower their speed limits and the Senate adopted a resolution to that effect. Twenty-nine states responded to this effort at "moral suasion." But these pleas were quickly replaced by a more authoritative measure: the *Emergency Highway Energy Conservation Act of 1974,* which prohibited the Secretary of Transportation from approving any highway construction projects in states having a speed limit in excess of 55 mph. All of the remaining states responded within two months.

Partial Preemption

The crossover sanctions, like the crosscutting requirements, are tied directly to the grant-in-aid system. Federal power in these cases derives from the Constitutional authority to spend for the general welfare. A final innovative technique, however, has another basis entirely. It rests on the authority of the federal government to preempt certain state and local activities under the supremacy clause and the commerce power.

Yet, this is preemption with a twist. Unlike traditional preemption statutes, preemption in these cases is only *partial.* Federal laws establish basic policies, but administrative responsibility may be delegated to the states or localities if they meet certain nationally determined conditions or standards.

The *Water Quality Act of 1965* was an early example of this strategy, which one analyst describes as the "if-then, if-then" approach. The statute was the first to establish a national policy for controlling pollution. Although the law allowed each state one year to set standards for its own interstate waters, the Secretary of Health, Education, and Welfare was authorized to enforce federal standards in any state that failed to do so. That is,

> . . . if a state does not issue regulations acceptable to the U.S., then a federal agency or department will do so, and if the state does not adopt and enforce these regulations, then the federal level of government will assume jurisdiction over that area.[8]

This same technique—which others have called the "substitution approach" to federalism[9]—has since been extended to a variety of other areas. For example, the OSHA law asserts national control over workplace health and safety but permits states to operate their own programs if their standards are "at least as effective" as the federal ones.

The most far-reaching applications, however, are in the *Clean Air Act Amendments of 1970*. This path-breaking environmental statute set federal air quality standards throughout the nation, but required that the states devise effective plans for their implementation and enforcement. Its compass is great: for example, EPA can require states to change their own transportation policies (perhaps by giving additional support to mass transit) or to regulate private individuals (as in establishing emission-control requirements and inspection programs for automobiles).[10] Two close observers comment:

> Of all the intergovernmental mechanisms used to nationalize regulatory policy, none is more revolutionary than the approach first applied in the Clean Air Act Amendments of 1970. It is an approach minimizing both the voluntariness of state and local participation and the substantive policy discretion provided for officials in subnational governments. In fact, it is a mechanism which challenges the very essence of federalism as a noncentralized system of separate legal jurisdictions and instead relies upon a unitary vision involving hierarchically related central and peripheral units. . . . [I]t is an approach allowing national policymakers and policy implementors to mobilize state and local resources on behalf of a national program. As preliminary measures, these resources can be mobilized using technical, financial, or other forms of assistance, but underlying this mechanism is the ability of national officials to formally and

officially "draft" those resources into national service. We call this legal conscription.[11]

Applications and Combinations

These four techniques—direct legal orders, crosscutting requirements, crossover sanctions and partial preemption—are the major new statutory tools in the federal government's kit for the regulation of states and localities. Each has distinctive characteristics, and poses special problems of policy, law, administration, finance and politics.

. . . Among the major regulatory statutes examined, crosscutting requirements (18) and partial preemptions (13) clearly are relatively numerous, while crossover sanctions (6) and direct orders (6) are relatively rare.

It also should be noted that these devices have sometimes been combined. A good example is provided by the 1970 *Clean Air Act Amendments*. Basically, the law relies upon the technique of partial preemption. States must prepare State Implementation Plans (SIPs) which will control pollution to the extent necessary to achieve federal air quality standards. These must be approved by the Environmental Protection Agency. If the EPA judges a SIP to be inadequate, it must disapprove the SIP. In the event that a state fails to make necessary revisions, EPA is required to promulgate an adequate SIP.

This, however, is not the only sanction imposed by the act. More teeth are added by Section 176(a), which bars both the EPA and the Department of Transportation from making grant awards in any air quality control region which has not attained primary ambient air quality standards and for which the state has failed to devise adequate transportation control plans. This, of course, is a tough crossover sanction. Furthermore, Section 176(c) prohibits any agency of the federal government from providing financial assistance to any activity which does not conform to a state SIP. This provision uses the crosscutting requirement approach to strengthening SIP implementation.

Fund termination, as in crossover sanctions, also is used to enforce compliance with a number of the crosscutting requirements relating to nondiscrimination. Discriminatory actions can result in the cutoff of aid, not only in the program area in which discrimination was found, but to an entire institution or jurisdiction.

Notes

1. *National League of Cities v. Usery,* 426 U.S. 833 (1976).
2. For a discussion of state practices, see Advisory Commission on Intergovernmental Relations, *State Mandating of Local Expenditures,* A-67 (Washington, D.C.: U.S. Government Printing Office, 1978).
3. PL 88-352, title VI, section 601, July 2, 1964.
4. See ACIR, *Categorical Grants: Their Role and Design,* A-52 (Washington, D.C.: U.S. Government Printing Office, 1978), chapter VII.
5. Office of Management and Budget, *Managing Federal Assistance in the 1980s, Working Papers, Volume I* (Washington, D.C.: U.S. Government Printing Office, 1980).
6. Catherine H. Lovell et al., *Federal and State Mandating on Local Governments: An Exploration of Issues and Impacts* (Riverside, Calif.: Graduate School of Administration, University of California, Riverside, 1979), p. 35.
7. See Roger A. Cunningham, "Billboard Control under the *Highway Beautification Act of 1965,*" *Michigan Law Review* 71 (June 1973), pp. 1295-1374.
8. James B. Croy, "Federal Supersession: The Road to Domination," *State Government* 48 (Winter 1975), p. 34. Emphasis added.
9. Frank J. Thompson, *Health Policy and the Bureaucracy: Politics and Administration* (Cambridge, Mass.: The MIT Press, 1981), p. 240.
10. Congressional Budget Office, *Federal Constraints on State and Local Government Actions* (Washington, D.C.: U.S. Government Printing Office, 1979), p. 7.
11. Mel Dubnick and Alan Gitelson, "Nationalizing State Policies," in *The Nationalization of State Government,* Jerome J. Hanus, ed., (Lexington, Mass.: D.C. Heath and Company, 1981), pp. 56-57.

29. THE MANDATE MILLSTONE

Edward I. Koch

Over the past decade, a maze of complex statutory and administrative directives has come to threaten both the initiative and the
financial health of local governments throughout the country. My
concern is not with the broad policy objectives that such mandates are
meant to serve, but rather with what I perceive as the lack of
comprehension by those who write them as to the cumulative impact on
a single city, and even the nation.

I want to emphasize that my criticism is directed at the shortcomings of a system that has evolved over the course of many years. This is
not the fault of particular individuals nor of today's leadership; it is
rather an inheritance from the work of several administrations and
Congresses, including some in which I served.

The City of New York, as an example, is driven by 47 federal and
state mandates. The total cost to the city of meeting these requirements
over the next four years will be $711 million in capital expenditures,
$6.25 billion in expense-budget dollars, and $1.66 billion in lost
revenue.

On the federal level, the current crop of mandated programs is
really the second stage in the evolutionary process of activist lawmaking
exhibited by the Congress. First, in the 1960's came the Great Society
programs. The nation's cities could choose from a bountiful catalog of
federal grants which offered to foot 80, 90, or even 100 percent of the
cost of enormously ambitious programs. In a time of unprecedented
prosperity, with only higher expectations ahead, local governments
eagerly went after federal funds even, at times, at the expense of
comprehensive planning.

Left unnoticed in the cities' rush to reallocate their budgets so as to
draw down maximum categorical aid were the basic service-delivery
programs taken for granted by the Great Society architects. New roads,
bridges, and subway routes were an exciting commitment to the future,

From *The Public Interest* 61 (Fall 1980): 42-48, 55-57. Reprinted by permission of *The Public
Interest.*

but they were launched at the expense of routine maintenance to the unglamorous, but essential, infrastructure of the existing systems. Further, the enticement of federal aid drew cities into new social service commitments that were soon to monopolize their budgets.

The 1960's left a bitter legacy for cities in two respects. As prosperity fell hostage to inflation, and then stagflation, the bright promises of programs so boldly launched with federal aid collapsed under exponential cost overruns. Projects under construction, such as New York's Second Avenue subway, had to be abandoned, and the now-concealed but still-remembered excavation serves to remind the public of how easily government can fall victim to monumental folly.

Perhaps more damaging was the shift in the 1970's in the legislative approach, particularly in Congress, to the grand commitments of the 1960's. Sweeping solutions to social ills were still in vogue, but this time the public purse had a bottom to it, and its guardians became adept at fending off the claims of local governments. The result has been an ever-widening gulf separating the programmatic demands of an activist Congress from its concurrent fiscal conservatism. By the close of the 1970's, the cities found themselves under the guns of dozens of federal laws imposing increasingly draconian mandates. From the perspective of local government the mandate mandarins who write these laws appear to be guided by certain disturbing maxims, such as:

1. *Mandates solve problems, particularly those in which you are not involved.* The federal government, for example, has shown no reluctance in ordering sweeping changes, the impact of which it will never have to face since it does not hold the final service-delivery responsibilities in such areas as education, transportation, and sewage disposal.

2. *Mandates need not be tempered by the lessons of local experience.* Frequently a statutory directive will impose a single nationwide solution to a perceived problem, such as sewage treatment, that has been developed in the isolation of a consultant's office and rarely, if ever, exposed to real-world conditions in the affected regions.

3. *Mandates will spontaneously generate the technology required to achieve them.* Congress has shown a disturbing penchant for prohibitions on existing approaches to problems such as ocean dumping, for which no practical replacement has been developed.

4. *The price tag of the lofty aspiration to be served by a mandate should never deter its imposition upon others.* Statutory commands are rarely accompanied by adequate financial assistance. Most extreme in this instance is the accessibility mandate for transit systems and the requirements relating to the education of the handicapped.

I do not for a moment claim immunity from the mandate fever of the 1970's. As a member of Congress I voted for many of the laws which I will discuss, and did so with every confidence that we were enacting sensible, permanent solutions to critical problems. It took a plunge into the Mayor's job to drive home how misguided my congressional outlook had been. The bills I voted for in Washington came to the House floor in a form that compelled approval. After all, who can vote against clean air and water, or better access and education for the handicapped? But as I look back it is hard to believe I could have been taken in by the simplicity of what the Congress was doing and by the flimsy empirical support—often no more than a carefully orchestrated hearing record or a single consultant's report—offered to persuade the members that the proposed solution could work throughout the country. The proposals I offer address this problem by increasing the level of scrutiny applied to both the cost and feasibility of mandates directed at local governments.

Let me now turn to the case histories of some of the more onerous mandates faced by New York City. I use my city as an example because I know its problems best. The problems we face, of course, occur throughout the United States. The numbers may be larger in New York but these mandates have an equally significant impact on the budget and local autonomy of every city.

Transportation and Education for the Handicapped

An example of a mandate that may totally skew capital spending nationwide in the 1980's at all levels of government is the handicapped-access program required by regulations promulgated in response to Section 504 of the Rehabilitation Act of 1973.

No one would argue that we need not commit funds to make transit systems and buildings accessible to the handicapped. But one also has to deal with the limitations—both financial and physical—that exist in the real world beyond the printed page of the *Federal Register*.

The Departments of Transportation and Health and Human Services (the erstwhile Department of Health, Education, and Welfare) have issued regulations that set as a mandate total accessibility for the handicapped to transit *systems,* instead of dealing with the *function* of transportation: mobility. In rejecting numerous appeals for modest exemptions and waivers, these regulations impose a restrictive and inflexible interpretation of the basic mandate of Section 504. Ironically, in focusing on accessibility the regulations fail to benefit a significant portion of the severely disabled. Subways and buses may ultimately be made fully accessible, but a disabled person may not be able to get to the system to enjoy its accessibility.

In this instance, alternatives are available. New York City has a far more extensive and flexible bus system than subway system. Given the numbers of handicapped people affected—some 22,800 in wheelchairs and 110,000 semi-ambulatory for a system that carries about 5.3 million on a weekday—a more reasonable approach can be formulated to meet the transportation needs of the disabled. The City of New York has proposed making its buses accessible and providing a paratransit system for the most severely disabled. Paratransit will provide door-to-door service and can make the difference between a handicapped person being a prisoner in his or her home or a mobile member of the community. Similar paratransit services are in planning or underway in other cities.

The DOT regulations presently proposed do not accept the alternative of a bus and paratransit mix. Beyond bus accessibility, the regulations appear to demand accessibility in 53 percent of our subway stations within 30 years, at a cost in today's dollars of some $1.3 billion. Added to this will be at least $50 million in recurring annual operating expenses. And the regulations make no affirmative provision for meeting the handicapped community's myriad difficulties in getting to buses and subways.

It would be cheaper for us to provide every severely disabled person with taxi service than to make 255 of our subway stations accessible. Indeed, the Congressional Budget Office, in its report of November 1979 on "Urban Transportation for Handicapped Persons: Alternative Federal Options," estimated that the cost of implementing the Section 504 regulations, when spread over the limited number of wheelchair users and severely disabled passengers, will be $38 per trip. In contrast, transit trips by the general public cost, on the average, about 85 cents.

Should we somehow achieve the prescribed level of systemwide rapid transit accessibility, I believe that even the most courageous will test it only once to satisfy themselves that they are able to ride the subways and that few will ride them on a regular basis.

The history of this mandate points up a basic fallacy in the process leading to its promulgation: unrealistic projections by federal agencies of the cost of realizing mandated goals. When the Department of Transportation issued its preliminary nationwide regulations for public review and comment in early 1978, it used a figure of $1.8 billion for the contemporary cost of making all transportation systems accessible. This was clearly an unrealistic estimate and implied an unwillingness by the Department to face up to the magnitude of the course they were proposing to require. The Congress acknowledged this credibility gap and in 1978 ordered the Department to submit by early 1980 a report on the costs of accessibility, based on a survey of all rail-transit operators.

Finally, the Section 504 regulations are crippled by the lack of available technology to achieve the mandated standard of accessibility. Bus lifts have yet to be developed that operate without frequent breakdowns; no American bus manufacturer would even bid to build the Transbus; and people are just starting to think about devices that can span the distance between a rapid-transit vehicle and the passenger-boarding platform.

The issue of transit accessibility is one that the Department of Transportation must deal with quickly. If an affirmative policy decision is not made to bring the demands of Section 504 in line with the practical limits on compliance efforts, transit subsidies in the 1980's will be severely distorted—making systems accessible to several thousand people, while forsaking improvements needed on the total system. The cost in operating reliability will very likely reduce the quality of service available to both current users and those who should benefit from improved accessibility. We may, in fact, build a system under the Section 504 mandate which most handicapped people won't be able to use because of the barriers still remaining, and which, if they do manage to board, breaks down far more frequently.

While the Congress may have been thoughtless or arbitrary in compelling universal access for the handicapped without sufficient consideration of the real world constraints on localities, it has been almost cynical in its implementation of the directive that all handicapped children be provided "a free and appropriate education." It is impossible to attack the virtues of this objective. Yet the structure of the program enacted to accomplish it not only dooms the compliance efforts of local school districts but also jeopardizes the overall quality of education that can be offered to all children.

The federal law contains three fundamental defects. First, the formula by which accompanying federal assistance is measured looks to the national average cost of educating a non-handicapped child and thus completely overlooks the far broader scope of services that are needed to bring the promise of the mandate to the actual population it was designed to benefit. The formula contains a second fallacy in its use of a single nationwide average cost. It deprives school districts with high education costs and high concentrations of handicapped pupils of any recognition of the greater costs and special problems they face in designing compliance programs. In New York City we have had to budget $8,180 per handicapped pupil, nearly three times the cost of educating a non-handicapped child. This compares to the national average figure of $1,400 per non-handicapped child employed by the federal government to determine the level of assistance for educational programs for the handicapped. Third, and most disturbing, has been the consistent failure by Congress even to appropriate the full measure of assistance authorized by an already restrictive formula. Here we have the Congress implicitly reneging on the delivery of an already meager federal share of the cost of meeting its own national mandates. The shortfall in appropriations has grown over the past two years to the point where less than half of the authorized amount has been distributed to affected school districts. The act authorized an appropriation in fiscal year 1980 of 20 percent of the understated federal calculation of national costs; the appropriation, however, was only 12 percent. In short, first they underestimate the costs and then they underfund the underestimate. New York City is receiving only $8.5 million in federal aid while spending an estimated $221 million in tax-levy dollars for special education in fiscal year 1980. Our commitment will grow to at least $278 million in fiscal year 1981 and we can only hope that the Congress will keep pace.

This mandate, combined with an inadequate level of federal funds for its fulfillment, has compelled the diversion of increasingly scarce local resources from the education of the rest of the school population. And as in Section 504, the absolute terms of the mandate discourage any efforts at the local level to develop alternative approaches to the statutory objective—such as the use of special facilities providing intensive attention to the needs of handicapped children—which might ease the enormous financial burden imposed by the program.

[Koch discusses other examples: programs for disposing of sewage sludge in the ocean, the federally imposed ceiling on the use of restricted public assistance payments, and mandates flowing from federal courts. Then he turns to an overall appraisal.—Ed.]

Needed Remedies

By cataloging these arbitrary, restrictive, or counterproductive mandates, I hope to have demonstrated both the complex demands confronting an urban chief executive today and the need for comprehensive revisions to the process by which such directives are formulated. A new mandate may appear to its authors to be a bold experiment in behavior modification for a worthy goal. But I do not think they view themselves as accountable for the hardship they may inflict on a particular locality. A superior level of government cannot, they would argue, be expected to anticipate every nuance in a far-reaching policy initiative. Indeed not—here lies the very reason why federal mandates must be flexible enough to accommodate local circumstances.

As the Mayor to whom those who must endure the hardship of irresponsible mandates look for relief, I can no longer accept the monotonous refrain that "it's up to Washington to correct its errors." It is long past time for the system to become responsive to the needs of those it purports to regulate, and for effective controls to be placed on the mandate machinery.

I do not claim to offer more than a rough outline for a modest measure of protection from the kinds of excesses now faced by a city like New York, but urge that prompt and careful consideration be given to the following proposals:

1. All mandates should include waiver provisions that afford an appropriate measure of recognition to a locality's efforts to address the objective through alternate means, or to integrate the required program with competing or complementary policies. New York, in several instances, commenced negotiations seeking administrative relief only to be met with an almost reflex hostility to allowing the slightest relaxation or modification of the mandate. This attitude may reflect a natural bureaucratic concern that the first variance breeds a collection of exceptions that will carve the underlying statute into an unworkable patchwork. But the administrators of these laws must be directed, by statute or Executive Order, to accommodate requests for waivers authorizing additional time or modified procedures from communities who offer reasonable evidence of an unfavorable impact.

2. Special consideration should be given to cities whose local revenue-raising and expenditure powers have come under the control of external authorities. It may be some years before we can measure the success of current efforts by all three levels of government to insulate the American metropolis from the twin cycles of declining revenues and spiraling costs. It makes absolutely no sense for the federal and state authorities to nullify their own ambitious urban assistance programs through the inflexible application of arbitrary mandates and the horrendous price tags they carry.

3. Action on any proposed mandate should be deferred until a report has been prepared on both the potential impact it would have on local government expenditures and the state of existing or proposed technology available to achieve timely compliance. Agencies such as the Congressional Budget Office and the Office of Technology Assessment are already in a position to perform an objective analysis of this nature, which could be summarized in the reports that accompany legislative proposals brought to the floors of Congress. Such a procedure would assure that the mandate makers are fully informed of the potential shock waves their action may send throughout affected communities.

4. No mandate should be imposed unless alternative methods of compliance are offered, with the final selection left to local option. In the exceptional case, in which mandates' authors are convinced that a single standard and procedure must be imposed, they should authorize

variations in the timing of and approach to compliance within appropriate parameters, proportional to the degree of hardship or potential program failure among affected communities.

5. Finally, it is of overriding importance that every mandate be accompanied by financial aid sufficient to achieve compliance. The aggregate tax-levy resources which must be committed to all of the federal and state mandates presently imposed on the City amount to $938 million at a time when we must identify $299 million in net-expense budget reductions for fiscal year 1981.

Throughout its history, this nation has encouraged local independence and diversity. We cannot allow the powerful diversity of spirit that is a basic characteristic of our federal system to be crushed under the grim conformity that will be the most enduring legacy of the mandate millstone.

30. THE FAILURE OF FEDERAL ENFORCEMENT OF CIVIL RIGHTS REGULATIONS IN PUBLIC HOUSING, 1963-1971: THE CO-OPTATION OF A FEDERAL AGENCY BY ITS LOCAL CONSTITUENCY
Frederick Aaron Lazin

... During the 1960s both the President and Congress acted to ban racial discrimination in Public Housing. Executive Order 11063, Title VI and Title VIII of the 1964 and 1968 Civil Rights Acts, respectively, made it illegal for a local agency to operate its federally funded Public Housing program in a racially discriminatory manner. Yet these Acts did not end racial discrimination in Public Housing.[1] A recent study by this author of CHA [Chicago Housing Authority] site selection and tenant assignment policies from 1963 through June 1971 found that CHA operated its federal programs in a racially discriminatory manner. A careful examination of CHA operation of the programs, the federal role and regulations and *Gautreaux v. CHA* yielded the following findings.[2]

First, the CHA administered regular (for families), elderly and Section 23 (leasing) Public Housing to keep blacks from living in white communities of Chicago. It placed Regular Public Housing in black ghetto-areas to reduce the number of black persons displaced by slum clearance and related programs being relocated in white areas. Quotas kept the number of black tenants at zero or at a minimum level in the four projects located in white neighborhoods. In Public Housing exclusively for the elderly, tenant assignment policies insured that projects in white neighborhoods had mostly white tenants. Only blacks chose to live in ghetto projects. Consequently integrated projects, that is, those with the second racial group constituting more than 10%, were found only in racially changing neighborhoods. In the latter cases both the neighborhoods and the projects eventually became all black. The same pattern existed with leased housing. CHA delegated its authority to select tenants to the landlords. It gave them the right to reject tenants on the basis of "undesirability." Moreover CHA permitted landlords to

Author's note: Prepared for delivery at the annual meeting of the American Political Science Association, Washington, D.C., September 8, 1972. Copyright © 1972, The American Political Science Association.

From *Policy Sciences* 4 (September 1973): 264-271, Elsevier Science Publishers, Amsterdam, The Netherlands.

choose tenants outside the almost all-black waiting list. As intended, most units in white neighborhoods were leased to white elderly tenants. Most blacks in the leasing program were placed in ghetto-rehabilitation projects.

Second, federal civil rights laws and regulations were meaningless. HUD officials were fully aware that CHA operations violated HUD regulations designed to implement and enforce constitutional executive, legislative and judicial bans on racial discrimination.[3] In these matters HUD chose to serve rather than regulate the local constituency. The few cases of federal intervention on civil rights matters were exercises in public relations. HUD would hold up funds and investigate. Upon receipt of an official commitment from CHA that it would desist from discrimination, it would release the funds. Unofficially, however, HUD would agree to let CHA continue its original discriminatory practices.[4]

Third, judicial redress proved equally ineffective. Having realized the futility of administrative redress, opponents of CHA policy filed a suit in U.S. District Court in August 1966 charging CHA with intent to discriminate against blacks.[5] In February 1969 the judge found the CHA guilty. Five months later he issued an order designed to foster integration and construction of Public Housing in white areas. But CHA refused to abide by the court's directives and HUD refused to use its resources to enforce compliance.

How and why the civil rights legislation proved so ineffective a curb on discrimination in Public Housing is worth considering in more detail. Central to the entire case is the fact that HUD operates within a federal system: it is responsible to Congress, which represents local interests. Consequently the administrative ideology of HUD holds that administrators must get local support to administer their programs successfully. Accordingly they are encouraged to serve rather than regulate. Both the Johnson and Nixon administrations reinforced this ideology.

Regardless of the attitudes of federal administrators toward Civil Rights and racial discrimination, the President and Congress forced them to confront the issue during the 1960s. President Kennedy's November 20, 1962, Executive Order 11063 and Title VI of the 1964 Civil Rights Act required federal agencies to issue regulations banning racial discrimination in site selection and tenant assignment policies.[6] While these acts provided the basis for challenges through administrative and judicial redress, they did not lead to federal enforcement. Instead HUD established a system of discretionary justice in which the administrator (the "judge and jury") was already committed to the principle that in matters of race, the program would be run locally without federal interference.

The Civil Rights Orders and Acts are very general and do not define key provisions and terms.[7] Executive Order 11063 and Title VI prohibit racial discrimination in Public Housing without defining what constitutes "racial discrimination." Title VIII of the 1968 Civil Rights Act directs the Secretary of HUD to affirmatively administer his programs to foster the goals of non-discrimination on the basis of race.[8] The Act does not define "affirmative action" and "racial discrimination." While HUD regulations established to comply with these Acts might be expected to clarify the terms, they do not.

Moreover most HUD regulations issued to bring about local compliance with Executive Order 11063 and Title VI are not binding. They permit exemptions which are not explicitly defined. The revised HUD site selection regulations issued in February 1967 are a good example.[9] They were designed to provide greater choice to minority families and to prevent concentration of Public Housing in the ghetto areas. The regulation reads in part:

> Any proposal to locate housing only in areas of racial concentration will be prima facie unacceptable and will be returned to the local authority for further consideration and submission of either (1) alternative or additional sites in other areas, so as to provide a *more balanced* distribution of the proposed housing, or (2) a clear showing *factually substantiated,* that *no acceptable sites are available outside the areas of racial concentration. . .* (emphasis added) [10]

The regulation may make ghetto concentration of Public Housing sites *prima facie* unacceptable, but it does not make it unlawful. If the local housing authority made "strenuous efforts" to build in non-ghetto areas and failed, it could concentrate sites in the ghetto.[11] All of the above emphasized words and phrases are not defined.

Therefore a federal administrator investigating a complaint against a local housing authority is not in a position to regulate even if he wants to. There is no explicit regulation or binding rule to enforce. The process of enforcement becomes arbitrary with primary responsibility placed on the individual administrator who must make a discretionary judgment. He must first determine what constitutes a violation in each particular case, and then whether the practice in question violates the newly established conditions. Most important, this system of enforcement provides the federal administrator with the legal option of non-enforcement.

In addition the Acts and subsequent regulations encourage informal bargaining rather than regulation and enforcement. In the case of a complaint or dispute the laws and regulations call for informal resolution between HUD and the local agency. Legal action where provided for is suggested only as a last resort.[12] Therefore HUD regulations instruct the administrator not to use his legal authority and power in dealing with alleged violations. A more arbitrary and discretionary arrangement is preferred.

A further element in the mechanism of civil rights enforcement was HUD's standard for compliance by the local authority. As proof of compliance HUD required that the local authority submit a resolution passed by the Board of Commissioners stating compliance. HUD's concern was with this formal evidence and not with actual CHA practices. Accordingly CHA passed appropriate resolutions stating compliance with Title VI. HUD accepted this despite its knowledge that CHA practices violated the law, HUD and even CHA regulations.[13]

This concern for formal compliance made several cases of federal intervention in local matters ludicrous. Typical incidents were the proximity rule in elderly Public Housing and the controversy over tenant assignment—"freedom of choice versus first come first served." In the first, CHA granted neighborhood residents a priority in tenant assignment over applicants on the waiting list. PHA held that this practice was unlawful. However, PHA wanted CHA to remove the rule from its regulations and nothing more.[14] In exchange for a promise to do so, it let the CHA continue to operate the rule which it had previously argued violated HHFA regulations and Executive Order 11063. In the second example HUD carried on a two-year battle with CHA to have it adopt a "first come first served" tenant assignment policy in the interest of integration. CHA eventually complied by formally adopting the recommended policy.[15] However, it continued to operate its program in violation of the federal guidelines and its newly adopted policy. HUD knew of this but remained satisfied that the approved policy was officially adopted. Therefore the only effect of the regulations was to place CHA practices in violation of official CHA policies.

Another aspect of civil rights enforcement was the response of HUD to complaints charging the CHA with racial discrimination. HUD's commitment to support CHA and HUD's lack of concern with actual practices resulted in justification for CHA policies. There was no real investigation in response to complaints.[16] This was evident in a complaint in 1965 charging that CHA's 1965 sites violated Title VI, 11063 and HHFA regulations.[17]

PHA did not investigate the charges.[18] Instead it defended CHA's actions. It justified CHA's choice of ghetto sites by arguing that CHA complied with federal regulations implementing Executive Order 11063, "... affording the greatest acceptability to eligible applicants." [19] Moreover it supported the CHA position that it could find no alternative sites outside the ghetto because of City Council opposition. PHA knew that the City Council rejected other sites because of racial considerations.[20]

Finally PHA's argument that CHA did not discriminate but operated with discriminatory boundaries made Title VI ineffective.[21] Therefore the West Side Federation (WSF) complaint bolstered CHA's choice of sites in the ghetto *vis-à-vis* the 1964 Civil Rights Act and Executive Order 11063. After receipt of PHA's letter absolving it, CHA publicly announced that the federal government in two separate legal opinions had "concluded that CHA had not violated the Civil Rights Act." [22]

In summary, HUD chose to supervise CHA using its own discretion. In doing so HUD supported the local constituency whenever it deemed propitious regardless of civil rights laws and federal regulations. In the light of HUD's ideology of supporting the local constituency, this was most of the time.

This same position persisted throughout the Gautreaux case almost without exception. While HUD did not defend CHA, it sought to retain its authority to determine what constitutes a violation rather than have the court set down guidelines. It preferred to negotiate with the CHA rather than to enforce a spelled-out order.

During the negotiations over the final order from February to June 30, 1969, HUD and the U.S. Department of Justice participated.[23] The important issue at this time was whether HUD would commit itself to the judge's final order.

In late April a Washington conference was held between HUD and the Justice Department. Jerris Leonard (Justice) and [Richard C.] Van Dusen (HUD) recommended a federal commitment to an order along the lines of the plaintiff's proposals which would require CHA to build a percentage of future units in white neighborhoods. HUD General Counsel Sherman Unger opposed this position. He did not want to establish a precedent (for HUD in court) order to integrate.[24]

Several times in May and June the judge asked HUD for its comments on the proposals. HUD stalled until the judge had already reached a decision.[25]

HUD delivered its brief on the proposed order the evening before the judge issued the final binding order. It was too late to be of considerable aid and too late to make HUD a party to it. While supporting the principles of the judge's February decision, the HUD-Justice brief was critical of many of the proposed elements of the order. Many of the doubts and criticisms were of a technical nature.

One participant in the HUD-Justice negotiations said of the HUD-Justice document that it allowed all sides to read into it what they wanted. He interpreted the document as committing HUD to the order. Therefore, he suggested that HUD would comply with it and even aid in its implementation. Yet most significantly, it was not HUD's order. HUD did not write it. HUD was not an official party to it. The memorandum had put HUD on record as being critical of parts of the decree. Therefore HUD retained its powers of discretion. To have supported the order would have denied it this course of action.

The July 1969 final order in the Gautreaux case was both similar to and different from previous federal regulations banning racial discrimination in Public Housing. While it too banned discrimination, it defined and made exclusive its key terms and requirements. It was designed to prohibit the future use and to remedy the past effects of CHA's unconstitutional site selections and tenant assignment procedures. It required CHA to build 700 family units in the white areas of Chicago. The order defined white and non-white areas of the city as follows: Non-white areas (LPHA) are areas lying within "census tracts of the U.S. Bureau of the Census having 30% or more non-white population, or within a distance of one mile from any point on the outer perimeter of any such census tract" and white areas (GPHA) as all others.[26] Thereafter for each unit built or leased in the LPHA, CHA had to build and lease three in GPHA.[27] The order permitted the placement of units in the suburbs; of three units constructed and leased after the original 700 not more than one-third of the regular and one-third of the leased required for the white areas of the city of Chicago may "at the option of the CHA, be located in the white areas of Cook County provided that the units are available to Chicago residents who applied to CHA for housing."[28]

Several provisions were designed to win community acceptance for Public Housing to be built in white communities. One limited project size to 120 persons.[29] Another prohibited the placement of additional Public Housing in a census tract if Public Housing would constitute more than 15% of the total number of apartments and single residences on the tract. A third prohibited the placement of families with children above the third story except in the case of leasing.[30] A later court-approved tenant assignment plan gave neighborhood residents a priority over applicants on the waiting list for 50% of the new units.[31]

Despite the definition of key terms and the specific and explicit requirements, HUD had no statutory directive to enforce the order. Again the question of whether or not to enforce was an arbitrary one— one of discretion. In light of its past record, CHA critics sought in a companion suit filed against HUD to direct the courts to order HUD to desist from support of CHA's racially discriminatory policies.[32] In the spring of 1968 the judge stayed the suit pending outcome of *Gautreaux v. CHA*. In October 1969 the plaintiffs filed for summary judgment in *Gautreaux v. HUD*. They asked the judge to issue an order to involve HUD in enforcement of the Gautreaux order.[33]

HUD opposed this. It held that such an order would infringe on its legitimate constitutional right to discretionary powers. It argued that the 1968 Civil Rights Act enjoined the Secretary of HUD, not the courts, to:

> administer the programs and activities relating to housing and urban development in a manner affirmatively to further the policies of this title.[34]

The Secretary could do it best and not the court. It was clearly within his legal realm:

> The determination of which powers and programs to bring to bear upon the admittedly unsatisfactory housing situation in the City of Chicago belongs to the defendant (HUD) (and not to the court).[35]

Moreover, the objectives of the plaintiffs, HUD argued, would be "more readily achieved by the *voluntary* efforts of the defendants than by the coercion of a judicial decree." [36] Finally HUD emphasized that by congressional design "maximum responsibility for the administration of the program must be vested in the local authority." [37]

When the judge ruled on September 1, 1970, that "the government must be permitted to carry out its findings unhampered by judicial intervention," he foreclosed on possible HUD enforcement of the Gautreaux order.[38] In effect he freed HUD to practice its own system of discretionary justice designed to serve the political interests of its constituency.[39]

In June 1971 HUD released Model Cities funds for Chicago in exchange for the Mayor's commitment to provide low-income housing. Significantly many of the Public Housing units involved violated the Gautreaux order. HUD had *decided not to enforce* the order.

Notes

1. National Committee Against Discrimination in Housing, *How the Federal Government Builds Ghettos* (New York: NCADH, 1968).
2. *Gautreaux v. CHA*, 296 F. Supp. 907 (N.D. Ill., 1969).
3. Throughout this paper the term "HUD officials" refers to personnel of the U.S. Department of Housing and Urban Development and its

predecessor agencies before 1965—the Housing and Home Finance Agency (HHFA) and the Public Housing Administration (PHA).

4. See discussion below on the Elderly Proximity Rule.

5. *Gautreaux v. CHA.*

6. Executive Order 11063 "Equal Opportunity in Housing"; Title VI (1964) Public Law 88-352, 78 Stat. 241, 42 U.S.C. 20002; Title VIII (1968) Public Law 90-284, 82 Stat. 73.

7. "Otherwise they might not have been passed," Alexander R. Polikoff, Esq., Interview, Chicago, Ill., April 1971.

8. Title VIII Sec. 808 (e) (5).

9. U.S. Department of Housing and Urban Development, Housing Assistance Administration, *Low Rent Housing Manual,* Transmittal Number 490 (Washington, D.C.: mimeograph, February 28, 1967).

10. *Ibid.,* p. 7.

11. *Ibid.* According to the *New York Times,* the intent of this directive was to change the disposition to place sites only in the ghetto.

12. Title VI, Secs. 602, 603.

13. Chicago Housing Authority, Resolution 65 CHA 50 (April 22, 1965), and Resolution 68 CHA 232 (November 14, 1968). HUD Regional Office, Chicago, Ill.: Interviews with several staff members, 1970-1971.

14. PHA feared that other local housing authorities, especially in the South, would adopt similar policies to insure segregation. Also it charged CHA with adopting the policy, which would give white-neighborhood residents priority over blacks on the waiting list in order to get City Council approval for sites. CHA policies had the effect of making tenancy in projects for the elderly in white areas all-white. Interviews with Marie McGuire, U.S. Public Housing Commissioner (Washington, D.C., January 1971); Charles Swibel, Chairman, Board of Commissioners of the CHA, 1970-1971. Letter and Supporting Brief from PHA to CHA December 11, 1963.

15. CHA Resolution 68 CHA 232 (November 14, 1968).

16. A qualified exception to this was HUD's pressuring CHA in November 1966 to drop several of its 12 ghetto sites on the grounds that they violated Title VI and they caused considerable neighborhood opposition. HUD conducted an investigation independently of CHA assistance. A compromise package was arrived at. However the compromise sites were also in violation of Title VI. HUD probably took this action because of suits filed in August 1966 (see below).

17. Letter from the West Side Federation to HHFA, August 26, 1965. The complaint was filed by the West Side Federation, an umbrella group encompassing black organizations in the West Side Ghetto of Chicago. The Chicago Urban League originally decided to appeal to HHFA. Urban League Staff wrote the letter to HHFA and had the WSF submit it.

18. Letter from PHA Commissioner McGuire to PHA Regional Administrator Bergeron, September 8, 1965.

19. Letter from PHA to WSF, October 14, 1965.
20. *Ibid.*
21. *Ibid.* PHA argued that the CHA was the sole recipient of funds and not the City Council under the terms of Title VI. Therefore *only* the actions of the CHA were subject to administrative redress under Title VI. Also see Chicago Urban League Memorandum, Harold Baron to Edwin Berry, November 5, 1965.
22. Statement by CHA, September 1965.
23. The Justice Department provided counsel for HUD and the U.S. Government.
24. The U.S. Departments of HUD and Justice, Washington, D.C., Chicago, Ill., and Cincinnati, Ohio, interviews with present (and former) staff, 1970-1972. One former Justice official claims that the Civil Rights Division of the Justice Department supported the "commitment" to improve its Civil Rights image.
25. *Ibid.* Some argue that HUD-Justice did not intentionally delay submission of their comments. They suggest that negotiations over positions and wording took until late June to satisfy all parties.
26. *Judgement Order, Gautreaux v. CHA,* 304 F. Supp. 736 (N.D. Ill., 1969). Article I (D), III (B). In the interest of de-politicizing the order, the parties agreed to refer to white and non-white areas as General Public Housing Area and Limited Public Housing Area, respectively.
27. *Ibid.,* III (C).
28. *Ibid.,* III (E).
29. *Ibid.,* IV. If impossible to comply with and if in the interest of the order, a project can contain 240 persons. This is one of the few provisions providing for discretion in enforcement.
30. *Ibid.,* III (C).
31. Order approving CHA Tenant Assignment Plan, *Gautreaux v. CHA,* No. 66C 1459 (N.D. Ill. November 27, 1969).
32. *Gautreaux v. HUD.* Filed in U.S. District Court (N.D. Ill.), August 1966.
33. *Ibid.*
34. See Frederick Aaron Lazin, "Public Housing in Chicago, 1963-1971" (unpublished Ph.D. dissertation, University of Chicago, 1972).
35. *Ibid.*
36. Emphasis added.
37. Defendant's Answering brief at 18, *Gautreaux v. HUD.*
38. *Order and Memorandum Gautreaux v. HUD.*
39. The Plaintiffs appealed. In February 1971 "The U.S. Court of Appeals found that HUD violated the Civil Rights of Negroes by funding CHA construction of public housing almost entirely in the ghetto." *Chicago Sun Times,* February 2, 1971. See also *Gautreaux v. Romney,* 448F. 2 cl. 731 (1971); *Gautreaux v. Romney,* 21, 457F. 2 cl. 124 (1972).

31. THE MANDATE BLUES

Kathleen Sylvester

---

*All county courthouses must buy and display a state flag in clear
weather, to be paid out of county courthouse maintenance funds.—South
Carolina Code 4-17-40 (enacted 1910)*

Ask David Watson if he's gotten any mandates from the state of
South Carolina lately, and it takes him only a moment to come up with
one.

Reaching into his wastebasket, the Anderson County administrator pulls out a wad of paper that just happens to be the most recent
memo from the state's retirement system. It says, in essence, that
because the General Assembly voted this year to increase state pensions,
Anderson County owes the state an additional $23,319. Please remit
immediately.

Now, Watson is not an irritable man, but he admits he wasn't
happy to get that memo just a few hours before the third and final
reading of Anderson County's annual budget. What did he do? He
"found" the pension money by taking it out of a fund earmarked for
county employees' salary increases. It was not a good solution, but
Watson had no choice. He was confronted with a prime example of
what local governments dislike most about their state governments:
mandates without money.

State mandates are a time-honored tradition, going back even
before there were states. South Carolina, for instance, began mandating
to its localities in 1691 with a prohibition on "worldly work" on the
Sabbath except by those who observed Saturday as the Sabbath and
who resided in Charleston County.

But state mandates have recently begun to receive serious attention. After spending nearly a decade deliberating over the appropriate-
ness of federal mandates imposed upon the states, politicians and

From *Governing* 2 (September 1989): 26-30. Copyright © 1989 *Governing* magazine. Reprinted
with permission.

administrators are now focusing on the new tension between the states and their local governments.

The main reason for that tension, suggest Michael Fix and Daphne A. Kenyon, is the prospect of unending federal deficits. Kenyon and Fix, editors of a . . . book from the Urban Institute called *Coping with Mandates: What Are the Alternatives?*, note that this is an era in which there are few federal grants and no federal revenue sharing going to either the states or the localities. In times like this, they suggest, higher levels of government often rely more heavily on legislative and regulatory authority to compel lower levels of government to implement policies.

Several other factors, says Fix, contribute to the increasing concern about the state mandate issue. The first is the taxpayer revolt, which placed revenue restrictions, both legal and psychological, on local governments and made compliance with mandates more painful. Another is the growing prominence of state policies, as opposed to federal ones, at a time of federal retrenchment. And finally, he suggests that local governments learned how to complain about mandates when their state governments started complaining about federal mandates: "It hadn't occurred to them that it was a problem until it became a national issue."

They learned their lessons well. Local governments—increasingly sophisticated with the emergence of state-level versions of the federal Advisory Commission on Intergovernmental Relations [ACIR] and interest groups that lobby for them—are beginning to grapple with the issue.

Their grappling has resulted in a serious effort in many states to ease the mandate burden. The efforts range from simply cataloging mandates to requiring estimates of their costs to mandatory reimbursement of mandates. In the process, state officials are finding out that mayors and county executives are not all that unreasonable. They are not categorically opposed to state mandates; they just want to have some say during the process and some flexibility in coming up with funds to pay for them.

In cities with populations of 86,000, there shall be five-person boards of plumbing examiners.—South Carolina Code 40-49-30 (1957)

In a number of states, the examination process is beginning with an effort to find out just what mandates are on the books. South Carolina's list, one of the most recent, is also one of the most comprehensive.

Dan B. Mackey, executive director of the state's ACIR, says that before the agency produced that catalog and its companion report, local officials "used to go around complaining about them all the time, but they really couldn't quantify the problem. just the word 'mandates' would send their blood pressure surging."

Economist Janet M. Kelly, the author of the mandate report, began by talking to local officials. "I'd ask what the problems are so that we could address them; they would say 'mandates,' and when I would ask which ones, they would say, 'All of them.' " So Kelly decided to look at "all of them."

The results were staggering. At latest count, there are 695 administrative and legislative mandates in effect in South Carolina. Kelly defines several categories. The first is the "active" mandates— legal requirements that a local government undertake a certain activity or provide a service meeting minimum state standards. "Equally important and frequently ignored," adds Kelly, "are the mandates that prevent the local government from undertaking an activity or providing a service," such as the South Carolina mandate that bans local government from appointing its own fire commissions. "And finally," she says, "there are mandates that aren't mandates at all; mandates that exist in custom rather than law." Together, the combination of mandates can paralyze a local government, says Kelly.

By the time she finished, says Kelly, "I realized that the local officials were telling the truth; it *was* 'all the mandates'—the cumulative effect of all of the mandates."

Any property owned by the General Assembly Retirement System is exempt from state or local taxation.—South Carolina Code 9-9-200 (1962)

Mandates certainly have an impact on Anderson County. Located in the far western corner of South Carolina, the county has 150,000 people spread over 770 square miles. It has made a comfortable transition over the past decade from domination by textiles and agriculture to a diversified economy, it has a healthy tax base, and Watson says its biggest problem is trying to keep up with its rapid growth. Now, that doesn't sound like a government that would have difficulty paying its bills. But it does.

In South Carolina, local governments rely heavily on the real estate tax, their largest tax source. Watson says that of his $19.7 million budget this year, $7.5 million comes from real estate taxes. What

Anderson County wants, and South Carolina's legislature isn't ready to grant, is authority to impose a local option sales tax, as the laws of 31 states permit. While the county may raise property taxes, Watson says it has "already done that to a fault."

The state tells Watson to do a lot of things. And while many services, such as the courts and indigent care, are ones the county has traditionally provided, there are two reasons Watson says it's more difficult now: The state's shared revenues have not kept pace with demand for those services, and federal revenue sharing is gone.

The "one-two punch" from the feds and the state is making things tough in Anderson County. One of Watson's favorite examples is the state law granting local tax exemptions to new industry. Under a statute passed a decade ago, new industries pay no local taxes for five years except for property taxes imposed by the school districts.

Or take landfills. "We must put out staggering amounts of monies for landfills," says Watson. While landfills have always been a county responsibility, environmental regulations have quadrupled the cost of maintaining them. Watson acknowledges that most of the requirements originate with the federal Environmental Protection Agency, but he points out that the state's Department of Health and Environmental Control often embellishes them as they are passed through.

The requirement to put liners in landfills is an example of what he considers an expensive and unnecessary mandate. While state officials agree that Anderson County's soil conditions don't necessarily warrant all the environmental safeguards being imposed, Watson says that the county "will have to do it. . . . It's not a matter of whether it's bothering anybody or whether there's an alternate way to do it or whether you can pay for it. It just gets passed down."

In the days before the demise of federal revenue sharing, says Watson, his county could rely on some federal grant money to satisfy that kind of mandate. In fact, about 10 to 12 percent of the county's annual budget used to come from the federal government. This year, it will get only about $425,000 in funding for employment training programs and some payments in lieu of taxes.

Finally, there are the traditional mandates. For example, says Watson, the county pays for salaries, office space, and equipment for all state employees in the county, including the Department of Social Services, the solicitor's office and the magistrates. Watson says he griped one day about having to spend so much on these state services, and discovered that there is no legal requirement to do so. Today, the county is supporting a state bureaucracy—complete with computers, fax machines, and other sophisticated equipment—that county officials say may be costing them as much as $6 million a year to support. That bureaucracy is so big, in fact, that local officials have just been squeezed out of their own courthouse and have floated a $9 million bond issue for a new one.

Watson says the practice began in the 1930s, when the county provided desks and telephones for a few state employees. While the county might be able to challenge the practice in court, he adds, "we believe it is a public responsibility to take care of those items; it's only the level of service we'd like clarified." So far, that clarification hasn't been forthcoming.

Finally, there are the piddling little mandates that Kelly says local officials find most irritating: the general government mandates. "They appear very innocuous, but their cumulative impact is enormous. If you take the cumulative impact of a mandate that says you have to keep three copies of this particular document when it is filed, that mandate costs nothing, practically nothing, next to nothing." But when there are dozens and dozens of those mandates, the county may be compelled to go out and build a new building to store all the paper.

When roads or bridges are named by the General Assembly in honor of some person, the costs incurred by the state Highway Department for such naming must be reimbursed to the Highway Department by the county where the facility is located.—South Carolina Code 57-1-45 (1987)

There has been an attempt in South Carolina to make the state accountable for what it demands of localities. It just hasn't worked.

In 1983, the state followed a number of others in adopting "fiscal note" legislation that requires the financial impact of any mandate to be assessed before the legislature acts on it. It is an understatement when Janet Kelly calls it "flawed." Legislators can ignore the requirement: They agreed when adopting it that the lack of a fiscal note wouldn't keep a bill from passing. Or they often satisfy the fiscal note requirement by calculating only the state's costs. Dozens of entries in the ACIR's mandates catalog bear the notation "No impact on state general fund."

South Carolina's lack of seriousness about fiscal notes isn't unusual. Last year, the U.S. General Accounting Office examined the state mandate issue to see if Congress could learn anything from the way the states and localities handle the mandate-funding issue. Not much, the GAO concluded. It reported that none of the formal control mechanisms to keep states from burdening localities work very well.

While 42 states have some form of fiscal noting, and 14 of those require reimbursement of the costs of mandates, success is really a function of the legislature's intent. California's mandate reimbursement program, which has been in place since the early 1970s, is a case in point. While California will provide almost $200 million in reimbursements to localities this year, local officials still contend that the process doesn't really work very well. To begin with, cities and counties don't have any option about compliance. If they think a mandate causes an undue financial burden, they must comply while appealing to the Commission on State Mandates, which investigates their complaints and tries to assess their costs.

Robert Eich, executive director of the commission, acknowledges that the documentation process is tedious. "We make them go to a fair amount of work," he says. Local governments, he adds, win about 75 percent of their appeals to the commission, which can fund a few directly but sends most back to the legislature for funding. If localities lose, they can still go to court.

The state has successfully circumvented the reimbursement policy in several key cases by arguing that what applies equally to the private sector, such as employer funding of unemployment compensation, can't be considered a mandate, and by asserting that there must be an increase in the level of service, not an increase in cost, to constitute a mandate.

The localities have tried unsuccessfully to get the legislature to amend the process. Now, they are talking to Paul Gann, the promoter of many successful initiatives, including the granddaddy of them all, Proposition 13, about putting the issue on the ballot in 1990.

In Massachusetts, the state has not tried to avoid paying for many mandates, but that may be purely a function of economics. Massachusetts's mandate reimbursement program was enacted in 1980 as part of a voter-initiated tax limitation known as Proposition 2 1/2. Under the terms of the proposition, any city, town or group of 10 taxpayers can challenge any state law or regulation that costs a locality money. These challenges are first reviewed by the Division of Local Mandates. Thomas F. Collins, director of the division, says his office reviews about 150 complaints a year, and that $15.7 million has been returned to the localities since fiscal year 1984. In the absence of reimbursement, local governments can petition the courts to permit non-compliance with unfunded mandates.

Massachusetts officials, however, are quick to concede that the main factor in their program's success was the state's economy, which was robust until recently. Says Collins: "The rate of reimbursements clearly follows the size of the economy. When there were surpluses, it was easy to get a legislator to file a bill for reimbursement. Now that the state is facing huge deficits," he adds, "call me in six months and I'll bet there won't be so many enacted."

Even absent funds for reimbursement, says Collins, "our most influential role is not so much getting funding from the legislature, but cost estimation before the fact." The process has "sensitized legislators to the impacts of what they do on cities and towns." As a result, the money saved by mandates never enacted is more significant than the amount that has been reimbursed to cities and towns.

Florida localities recently won a hard-fought battle when their legislature agreed to a compromise solution to the mandate dilemma. Next year, voters will consider a constitutional amendment that requires unfunded mandates to be passed by a two-thirds vote of the legislature (federal mandates and those that apply equally to the private and public sectors would be exempted). Tennessee has a reimbursement requirement, but funds are returned to localities through general purpose funds, and local officials say they're not getting any more money than before the law was enacted.

Richard Horte, author of the recent GAO study, says there's a reason for that: "There is only so much money out there, and the localities are not going to get any more of it. The attitude that 'you ought to pay for everything you make us do' simply isn't going to fly." Horte adds, however, that all of this fussing about mandates in the states is having an impact. "When consciousness is raised, and there is up-front negotiating, there is progress."

The governing body of each county shall provide bedding for prisoners in county jails and each prisoner shall be entitled to at least two blankets.—South Carolina Code 24-5-80 (1842)

If local officials could get one message across to their state legislators, it would be this: They don't object to mandates per se. They appreciate the social and political value of statewide standards. "I would hate to be in a place that wouldn't fund indigent care," says Anderson County's deputy administrator, Rusty Burns. "I would hate to be in a place that didn't care about the environment. . . . Sometimes those people in the state capitol are removed from day-to-day politics, and they can set state standards and not have to be right in the midst of the slings and arrows. That's good." Watson agrees. "Most of these things are good and right and ought to be. The problem is we don't have the funding sources for them. If you've got the responsibility for providing those services, you've got to have the privilege of collecting the money too."

That almost happened in the past legislative session. The South Carolina House fell just two votes short of passing a local option sales tax bill that would have allowed localities to go to their voters for permission to impost a 1-cent sales tax for specified purposes.

That two-vote margin of defeat was a victory of sorts for the localities. The South Carolina ACIR's Mackey says that, year by year, "there are more and more legislators who are concerned and understand." He had hoped that the mandates study would ignite some kind of a groundswell in the state. It didn't, but there was a positive effect.

"What people are saying now is, 'Thanks, now we understand it,' " says Mackey. While South Carolina's local officials don't expect the state's 695 mandates to go away, they are pleased that the dialogue has begun.

32. THE GROWTH OF INTERGOVERNMENTAL MANDATES IN AN ERA OF DEREGULATION AND DECENTRALIZATION

David R. Beam and Timothy J. Conlan

Two developments in domestic policy were hallmarks of this past decade. Each was closely identified with the Reagan administration of 1981-1988, though both in fact were initiated during Jimmy Carter's presidency or before.

First was a generally very successful movement toward *deregulation*. Federal controls over air transportation and a variety of other areas of endeavor were reduced or (as in the aviation case) actually eliminated.... Applauded by many who expected greater economic efficiency and energy to result from increased free-market competition, the policy shift also attracted critics' warnings that a "rush to deregulate" in so many areas was (according to one book title) "dismantling America." [1]

These same years were also a period of *decentralization*.... President Reagan took office pledging to "curb the size and influence of the federal establishment and to demand recognition of the distinction between the powers granted to the federal government and those reserved to the states or to the people." [2] This, to many observers, was a second significant reversal of the historical trend toward national policy control....

These twin policy movements converged to produce the first comprehensive attack on federal intergovernmental regulation or "mandates" affecting state and local governments....

An inventory prepared by the U.S. Advisory Commission on Intergovernmental Relations [ACIR] assessed the legislative magnitude of the issue. As of 1980, it included some thirty-six pertinent federal

An earlier version of this analysis was presented at the Thirteenth Annual Research Conference of the Association for Public Policy Analysis and Management, October 24-26, 1991, Bethesda, Maryland. Published with permission of the authors.

Authors' note: Much of the information reported here draws upon a study being conducted for the U.S. Advisory Commission on Intergovernmental Relations, tentatively titled "A Decade of Change in Regulatory Federalism: Evaluating Regulatory Trends and Relief Strategies for the 1990s." However, the views expressed are solely those of the authors, and should not be attributed to the ACIR's members or staff.

statutes employing one of four newer and intrusive intergovernmental mechanisms for forcing state and local governments to comply
with national standards.[3] ... Nearly all of these thirty-six laws
were enacted after 1960, and twenty-two—almost two-thirds—had
been enacted in the 1970s alone, suggesting the recent origins
of the mandating movement. Most of the statutes involved the
nondiscrimination, environmental protection, or health and safety
issues that had been high on the governmental agenda during these
decades.

The Deregulatory Campaign

State and local officials were not, of course, the only complainants
about "excessive federal regulation." Well before 1980 business and
consumer concern had sparked a movement toward regulatory reform
in the economic sphere, bearing fruit with the Ford administration's
"Whip Inflation Now" (or WIN) program, later termed the Economic
Impact Statement process operated by the Council on Wage and Price
Stability. President [Gerald R.] Ford also established the Domestic
Council Review Group on Regulatory Reform, a body that laid much
of the groundwork for the later legislative action.[4] His successor in the
White House, Jimmy Carter, established his own process for internal
cost reviews of proposed regulations, overseen by the Regulatory
Analysis Review Group (RARG) within the Executive Office.[5] Of
more lasting impact, however, was statutory deregulation affecting
railroads (1976), airlines (1978), natural gas (1980), trucking (1980),
rail transportation (1980), and banking (1980).

To these initiatives, the Reagan administration added its own,
spearheaded by the Task Force on Regulatory Relief, a cabinet-level
body chaired by the vice president, George Bush. Some of its actions
can be viewed as strengthening and centralizing prior procedures. But
the tone was clearly different, as was indicated by the administration's
preference for the term "regulatory relief" instead of "regulatory
reform" to describe its program. The aim seemed to be to "get federal
regulators off the backs of" business and industry, or to simply reduce
the volume of regulation. In contrast, preceding administrations had
been primarily concerned with "rationalizing" and streamlining regulatory processes: making regulation better, not making it less. More
importantly for purposes here, the Reagan administration also differed
from its predecessors by specifically including in its regulatory relief
program various federal requirements imposing cost burdens (or
otherwise intruding) on state and local governments. Despite the
continuities with the past, then, President Reagan "was the first to give
[intergovernmental regulation] prominent attention by including na-

tional rules affecting state and local governments in his proposals for regulatory reform." [6]

Congress, too, evinced concern with the mandating issue, as demonstrated by provisions of the Paperwork Reduction Act (1980), and most particularly the State and Local Government Cost Estimates Act (1981), which established the "fiscal notes" procedure operated by the Congressional Budget Office (CBO). And the Supreme Court had served notice, with its 1976 *National League of Cities* v. *Usery* (NLC) decision, that federal actions might be constitutionally rejected for exceeding the limits of the commerce power and contravening the reserved powers clause of the Tenth Amendment.[7] As the 1980s began, then, all three federal branches seemed to have begun erecting barricades against excessive intergovernmental mandating.

Such efforts appeared to bear fruit. Looking at actions then under way, some analysts concluded that state and local governments were "the big winners" of deregulation.[8] The author of one study observed that "state and local governments quietly captured some of the most important and enduring victories of the president's regulatory relief campaign." [9]

So matters seemed while the deregulatory drive was under way. Considered from our present vantage point, however, the facts now appear quite otherwise, for new data gathered on legislative and executive actions suggest that—despite the restrictive policies in place when the decade began—the years after 1981 saw a further proliferation of new federal mandates and the continuation and expansion of many preexisting ones. All the evidence indicates that federal intergovernmental regulation continued to grow throughout the decade of the 1980s at about [the same] or even at an accelerated pace.

In sum, if the tide was going out for federal regulation generally, in the sphere of intergovernmental mandating, Congress, the executive, and ultimately also the courts all were swimming against the tide. This [article] documents the continuing growth of intergovernmental mandating during the 1980s, drawing from ongoing research concerning both legislative and executive regulatory activity affecting state and local governments during the Reagan presidency.

Legislative Mandating in the 1980s

As noted previously, some thirty-six federal "mandates" affecting state and local governments were identified in the ACIR inventory as of 1980. According to our similar tabulation, designed to update the earlier ACIR report, by the end of 1990 an additional twenty-five regulatory statutes and amendments with significant intergovernmental effects had [been] passed by the Congress and signed into law.

... Some statutes, like the Drug Free Workplace Act of 1988 (P.L. 100-690), represented new policy concerns for federal regulators. Others, like the Education of the Handicapped Act Amendments of 1986, built upon and expanded earlier federal initiatives. Certain regulations, like the 1988 Ocean Dumping Ban Act (P.L. 100-688), which prohibits any additional dumping of municipal sewage sludge in ocean waters, were relatively simple and direct. Others were lengthy and complex laws that imposed multiple new obligations and requirements on both public and private entities. For example, the 1990 Clean Air Act Amendments (P.L. 101-549) contained provisions affecting both the intergovernmental regulatory system for controlling urban smog and industrial pollution as well as direct limitations on emissions from municipal incinerators and power plants.

Some of these mandates are considered objectionable chiefly because of their intrusiveness into spheres of traditional state authority. This was the case for legislation requiring states to allow longer and heavier trucks on their highways and forcing them to raise their minimum drinking age. In both cases, the instrument employed was the "crossover sanction," under which states that choose to neglect or defy federal regulations are threatened with reductions in their highway construction aid. Indeed, during this period, there seems to have been a trend toward the greater use of these "tougher" and—from either the state or constitutional perspective—more questionable regulatory devices. The 1980s saw increased reliance on both direct orders and crossover sanctions, the two most openly coercive of the four intergovernmental regulatory techniques. [Reading no. 28 of this book explains the regulatory techniques.—Ed.] Although these two were once among the least frequently used devices, they are now the most common: 68 percent of the requirements enacted between 1981 and 1990 utilized one or the other. In contrast, only 28 percent of earlier intergovernmental regulations employed [one or the other of] these two instruments. At the same time, reliance on cross-cutting requirements, which are probably the least controversial of the four types, declined sharply in the 1980s in comparison with earlier decades.

Ever since the mandate issue first arose, however, the problem of unreimbursed costs has been the priority concern of state and local officials. It is clear that several of these new mandates, like many of their predecessors, created costly financial burdens for state and local governments. For example, the Safe Drinking Water Act Amendments of 1986 will impose estimated costs of $2 to $3 billion annually on public water systems.[10] The Asbestos Hazard Emergency Response Act of 1986 required schools to remove hazardous asbestos at an estimated cost of $3.145 billion over thirty years. Overall, approximately 100,000 schools were likely to be affected.[11] Finally, the fiscal tab for the 1986 reauthorization of the Education for All Handicapped Children Act—which expanded services for preschool-age children—has been estimated to be about $575 million annually.[12]

Measuring Legislative Output

. . . A simple count of legislative enactments implicitly assumes that all bills are equally important—but of course, they are not. While the number of substantive enactments *did* decline in the 1980s, the average length and complexity of the bills that were enacted increased considerably. The 1980s were notorious for enormous budget reconciliation and omnibus appropriations bills, which often rolled into one statute legislation that previously might have been enacted in dozens of separate bills.

One way to account for such changes in the style of legislation is to focus solely on trends involving "major" bills. How, then, does the level of regulatory activity of the 1980s compare to earlier decades if only the *most important* legislative enactments are considered?

Although judgments about what constitutes "important" or "significant" legislation are necessarily somewhat subjective, a defensible and validated set of prominent enactments has been compiled by one leading congressional scholar. David Mayhew developed an inventory of the most important legislative enactments in the post–World War II era by combining contemporaneous assessments of the most notable legislative achievements at the conclusion of each session of Congress with subsequent retrospective judgments by historians and policy specialists.[13] This methodology identified 267 items of significant legislation enacted during the period between 1947 and 1990. The list includes laws from all major policy fields—foreign and defense policy, taxation, government reorganization—as well as intergovernmental grants and regulations.[14]

To make this inventory of major legislation comparable on a decade-by-decade basis, the laws enacted in the period from 1947 to 1950 were disregarded. [This adjustment yields] a total of 243 significant laws that were enacted between 1951 and 1990; of this total, almost one-third were intergovernmental in nature. Thirty statutes—or 12 percent of the total—may be classified as intergovernmental regulations under the ACIR definition, while forty-five statutes (18 percent) were intergovernmental grants. The remainder addressed defense or foreign affairs or some other aspect of domestic policy.

Of the thirty intergovernmental regulations contained in this inventory, eight (27 percent) were adopted in the 1980s. This is roughly comparable to the number enacted during the 1970s, but it is less than the twelve (40 percent) major regulations enacted between 1961 and 1970. As noted earlier, however, there was less substantive legislative activity of all kinds during the 1980s. Eighty-seven "major" statutes were enacted in the 1960s, compared with seventy-three during the 1970s and forty-six during the 1980s. Thus, as a proportion of all significant legislative activity, the percentage of major statutes that were both "intergovernmental" and "regulatory" in nature was larger during the past decade than in any previous ten-year period since 1950. In sum, even if one considers only those laws that were deemed to be of lasting significance by contemporary observers and policy specialists, the 1980s still emerge as a decade of sustained or heightened regulatory activity in intergovernmental relations.

Furthermore, this same data analysis indicates that this past decade, like the 1970s before it, stands out from earlier [periods] in the degree of reliance on regulations rather than subsidies to accomplish national goals in the intergovernmental arena. Whereas intergovernmental grants outnumbered intergovernmental regulations nearly two-to-one during the 1950s and 1960s, grants and regulations were employed with equal frequency during both of the past two decades.

Regulatory Relief in the Executive Branch

Although measures of legislative output probably offer the most significant indicator of the scope of intergovernmental regulation in the 1980s, it also is the case that the principal focus of President Reagan's regulatory relief campaign was internal to the executive branch. Rather than risk disappointment at the hands of congressional Democrats, or jeopardize other legislative priorities, most of the administration's effort was spearheaded by White House units and directed at federal agencies through administrative officials.[15]

Significant steps for carrying out this program occurred early in the first Reagan term. The Task Force on Regulatory Relief was established just two days after Reagan became president. He charged it with reviewing both pending and existing regulations with the aim to "reverse the trend of recent years and see at the end of the year a reduction in the number of pages in the *Federal Register* instead of an increase."[16] One week later, on January 29, 1981, President Reagan ordered federal regulatory agencies to postpone the effective dates of all regulations scheduled to take effect by March 20 of that year, and also to refrain from issuing any final regulations until that date. This sixty-day freeze was intended to allow the new administration time to review the so-called midnight regulations issued during the final days of the Carter presidency. Shortly thereafter, a number of rules were withdrawn, rescinded, or postponed indefinitely.[17]

Perhaps most important, on February 17, 1981, the president signed E. O. 12291, setting forth new regulatory procedures and standards. It established a new methodology for measuring the benefits of proposed rules against their costs, directing agencies to determine the most cost-effective approach for meeting their regulatory objectives. And, in contrast to the more limited prior procedures, an unprecedented degree of responsibility for coordination and implementation of agency actions was fixed in the director of the Office of Management and Budget [OMB] and its Office of Information and Regulatory Affairs (OIRA), under the general supervision of the Presidential Task Force.

These formal actions were bolstered by other, less formal, but perhaps equally important, ones. Agency budgets were cut, regulatory staffing was reduced, and personnel were appointed with an eye toward their acceptance of the administration's regulatory agenda. Indeed, the vice president commonly argued that the character of Reagan's appointees was more crucial to the success of the regulatory relief program than the actions of OMB or the new executive order.[18] While some decried the inattention to legislative change, feeling that lasting reform would be impossible without it, the White House effort was substantial for, as Goodman and Wrightson observe, until Reagan, "no president had made a concerted effort to bring [their] formidable array of management powers to bear on regulatory policy." [19]

Although the principal focus of these regulatory relief initiatives was on rules thought to hamper American business and the nation's economic performance, cognizance was taken of the intergovernmental aspects of the regulation issue from the first. E. O. 12291 defined "major" rules to include those that might cause "a major increase in costs or prices for . . . State or local government agencies" as well as industry and consumers. The president's statement on "America's New Beginning," issued the following day, also pointed out the "costs to business, nonprofit institutions, and State and local governments of complying with regulations." [20]

Consistent with this orientation, state and local government jurisdictions and public interest groups like the National Governors' Association were actively solicited for recommendations on needed regulatory changes. This request produced some twenty-five hundred submissions identifying rules regarded as especially burdensome or inefficient,[21] and many such regulations became targets of federal review. Some actions were taken, too: for example, controversial and costly requirements in the area of bilingual education were among the first rules withdrawn by executive agencies. If left in place, these could have resulted in expenditures of up to $1 billion over the first five years of the program, the White House indicated, by requiring all school systems to offer bilingual education to each child whose primary language was other than English. Also modified in the first days of the regulatory relief campaign were EPA's noise-emission standards for garbage trucks that, EPA estimated, would have cost $25 million annually, with most of that amount borne by municipalities.[22]

The Task Force's work was ended in August 1983. But its final report,[23] as well as several interim reviews, suggested that much had been accomplished. By that time, many additional rules had been addressed. These ranged from the dress-code regulations (which put schools at risk for the loss of federal funds if they distinguished between boys and girls in their dress codes) to Department of Transportation handicapped-access provisions, estimated to impose capital costs on New York City alone of up to $1.6 billion. Projected cost savings for state and local governments *in toto* were about $4-$6 billion in capital investments and about $2 billion in annual recurring outlays.[24]

Measuring the Impact of Intergovernmental Regulatory Relief

Such self-assessments are naturally prone to be somewhat self-congratulatory. Therefore, to assess the impact of the Reagan administration's regulatory relief program on state and local governments in a more objective manner, data concerning administrative procedures for eighteen of the major federal mandates (or half the initial thirty-six) identified in the ACIR's 1982 *Regulatory Federalism* were gathered by the U.S. General Accounting Office (GAO). These previously unpublished data provide the most complete record of changes in intergovernmental regulatory programs affecting state and local governments during the 1980s. The following account is based on GAO's draft documents that were made available to the authors for use in the ACIR study.[25]

GAO examined changes in regulatory requirements for these programs during the period 1981-1986,[26] using the *Federal Register* and the *Code of Federal Regulations* (CFR). To bolster and help interpret conclusions suggested by these empirical data—and to obtain information on changes in the level of funding, delegation of regulatory decision making to states, and the intensity of federal administrative oversight—its staff also interviewed responsible federal agency officials, public interest group members, and state and local officials.

Overall, the data obtained suggest that, despite the Reagan administration's effort to restrain intergovernmental regulation by concerted executive action, the federal government's regulatory burden on state and local governments from these programs continued to increase during the 1980s. . . . In eleven of the eighteen program areas studied (or 61 percent of the total), [the evidence shows] a rising federal regulatory burden on state and local governments as measured by changes in program standards, administrative procedures, compliance costs and federal aid, state delegation, and enforcement patterns. Increasingly prescriptive regulations produced rising programmatic burdens and compliance costs, while federal funding to help states administer these programs generally declined. [Furthermore,] mandate burdens remained stable—that is, were not reduced by the regulatory relief effort—in two additional cases. Overall, then, reductions in regulatory burden occurred for *only five* of the eighteen statutes (or 28 percent of the total).

A total of 140 regulatory changes were identified, adding a net 5,943 requirements in the eighteen policy areas. Included were a net 4,702 additions to program standards and a net 1,241 changes in administrative procedures. Many of these had far-reaching effects on state and local governments. For example, during the review period:

- An additional 7.7 million state and local employees were brought under the coverage of the Fair Labor Standards Act.
- Thirty-six states were affected by new visibility standards for federal park lands issued by the Environmental Protection Agency.
- Nearly 2,500 requirements expanding existing occupational safety and health standards for states were issued by OSHA [the Occupational Safety and Health Administration].
- [More than] 2,200 requirements were issued by several federal agencies under Section 504 of the Rehabilitation Act of 1973.
- About 250 animal and plant species were added to the endangered and threatened lists under the Endangered Species Act of 1973—an increase of over 150 percent since 1980.
- Approximately 415 new requirements affecting state and local governments were added by the National Park Service and Advisory Council on Historic Preservation under the National Historic Preservation Act of 1966.
- Among all programs studied, there was a net increase of 382 monitoring/oversight procedures and 238 financial management processes.

As these examples show, there was a considerable increase in both the stringency of program standards and in the specificity of administrative procedures. And, in many cases, the increase in the "burdensomeness" of mandates occurred in programs that had been at the center of this intergovernmental controversy. . . .

As regulatory requirements of these kinds mounted and the costs of state and local compliance also generally rose, federal assistance to aid in the performance of regulatory tasks was reduced, consistent with the general decline in federal aid expenditures during these same years. In nine of the eighteen programs studied, where states serve as "partners" in assuring compliance with national standards, federal agencies do provide grants to support state administrative operations, such as technical assistance and oversight. However, this federal grant support declined between FY 1981 and 1988 for all nine of these programs. . . . Aid cuts ranged from $1.9 million for Flood Disaster Protection to $12.2 [million] under the Clean Air Act and $15.5 [million] for Handicapped Education. On a percentage basis, Endangered Species and Historic Preservation programs were most greatly affected.

In the other nine programs, state and local governments are regulated directly by the federal government and no federal funds are generally available to comply with program standards. Increased state and local costs were anticipated in several of these. Most important, the Urban Mass Transportation Administration estimated that local transit authorities would need to spend up to an additional $79 million annually to provide services, such as wheelchair lifts and extended service hours for handicapped persons, not previously required under more lenient interim regulations.

In sum, the record concerning "deregulation" through executive action during the 1980s is fully consistent with that obtained by examination of congressional output. Sometimes because of constraints imposed by legislative or judicial activity, or for other reasons, executive agencies added to, rather than subtracted from, the mandate total. In the intergovernmental sphere, if not in other areas, this past decade has been one of increasing federal regulation, with new requirements being added to those already present—and found objectionable either individually or in the aggregate—at the start of the decade.

Conclusion

The evidence presented in this paper suggests strongly that highly visible efforts to deregulate and decentralize intergovernmental relations over this past decade were, however prominent, also largely ineffective. By two separate and independent measures, federal mandating was shown to have continued apace during the 1980s, growing in terms of statutory adoptions by the Congress as well as in the promulgation of rules by executive agencies. Consequently, the intergovernmental regulatory system in place in 1980, when the mandating issue first arose, had become "bigger, broader, and deeper" by 1988, when President Reagan left office, and by the start of the new decade in 1990.

[Among the materials from the authors' original essay that are omitted here for reasons of space is coverage of a few "success stories" in mandate reform. The paper resumes here with the final subsection.—Ed.]

What of the Future?

The factors contributing to the continued activism of the 1980s were many and complex, and identifying and weighing them is a task well beyond the scope of the research undertaken here. Nonetheless, some contributing causes may be noted.

First, one suspects that the fiscal constraints imposed on new federal spending programs by large and chronic budget deficits throughout the decade, along with popular opposition to new taxes, were an important stimulus. Because regulatory programs generally impose greater costs on the regulated third parties than on the federal government, they represent—in federal budgetary terms—a "low cost" method of responding to issues and problems. Consequently, their popularity might be expected to rise as fiscal resources decline. Just this dynamic lay behind the rapid growth of regulation during the economically troubled 1970s. As one former member of the Johnson administration observed in the middle of that decade:

> Congressmen see themselves as having been elected to legis-
> late. Confronted with a problem . . . their strong tendency is to pass
> a law. Ten years ago, money was Washington's antidote for
> problems. Now, the new fiscal realities . . . mean that Congress
> provides fewer dollars. Still determined to legislate against prob-
> lems, Congress uses sticks instead of carrots.[27]

Continued legislative activism has probably also been sustained by the erosion of once-powerful legitimacy barriers to federal regulatory action. Viewed over the long sweep of history, opposition to federal involvement in a new field of policy activity was usually very strong. Once this opposition was overcome through the enactment of a landmark piece of legislation, however, it usually proved very much easier to enact subsequent program expansions in that same area.[28] This pattern of "breakthrough politics" was an important element in the expansion of federal aid and regulatory programs in the 1960s and 1970s.[29]

Its legacy continued to shape politics in the 1980s. Although various regulations came under renewed scrutiny in the 1980s, the techniques of regulatory federalism had become commonplace. Given this acceptance for what have now become established regulatory approaches, Congress's extension of such methods to new or recently identified problems can be readily understood. Furthermore, many of the new requirements enacted in the 1980s could be viewed as "only" expansions of existing regulatory programs and missions. Even where they were very significant expansions—imposing substantial new costs and responsibilities on affected states and localities—they were clearly built on an established regulatory foundation. And their legitimacy was further enhanced by political popularity. For example, the sweeping Clean Air Act Amendments of 1990 were strongly supported by the nation's governors and state air pollution officials despite—and in some cases because of—their expanded federal controls. This seems to reflect public approval of tougher air pollution requirements. One recent survey found that 80 percent of respondents agreed with the strongly worded statement that "Protecting the environment is so important that requirements and standards *cannot be too high* and continuing environmental improvements must be made *regardless of cost.*" [30]

Considerations such as these seem to have made intergovernmental regulation acceptable to adherents of both political parties and major ideologies. Despite public platforms espousing deregulation and new federalism, few of the new regulations were enacted over the determined opposition of either the Reagan or Bush administration. Indeed, on important cases ranging from uniform trucking standards to "baby doe" requirements to the Americans with Disabilities Act, administration officials assumed a leadership role in advancing the new requirements. Throughout the Reagan administration, the "conservative" politics of decentralization often found itself playing second fiddle to, or even in conflict with, "conservative" social or economic policies. The latter generally proved paramount. As one intergovernmental lobbyist observed: "When our problems are business's problems, then we get action. . . . When we are business's problem, then we feel the heat." [31]

What must be concluded, then, is that the continuing tendency to use intergovernmental mandates to accomplish national goals throughout the 1980s may force a reappraisal of the basic dynamics of contemporary federalism. Just as the growth of grants-in-aid from the 1930s through the 1960s encouraged the replacement of the traditional "layer-cake" metaphor of "dual federalism" by marble-cake "cooperative" analogies, the continuing regulatory shift ought to prompt similar reconceptualizations. This will be no small task, for the growth of regulation proceeded apace with a notable strengthening of state and local governments as policy innovators and independent actors. If damage to the balance of federalism is being done, it has surely not yet been fatal! Both of these seemingly contradictory trends must be accounted for.

Still, the evidence presented here suggests that fundamental questions about the political status of state and local governments in the contemporary federal system do need to be raised. If the movement toward centralizing intergovernmental regulations could not be reversed or even slowed when it represented the self-proclaimed policy objective of a popular administration, at a time when the "tide" seemed to be shifting toward decentralization and deregulation, when state and local interest groups were unified in their concern about a new threat to their legal autonomy and fiscal well-being, and in a period in which the Supreme Court itself had put the other branches on notice that their actions must not infringe too greatly on traditional state functions—if not under these very favorable conditions, what then are the regulatory prospects facing state and local governments in the future? To be sure, there are counterexamples where mandates were limited or lessened; these merit closer examination. And surprising policy developments can occur, as the case of the 1986 tax-reform legislation, adopted against seemingly impossible odds, shows.[32] Nonetheless, given the overall trend of this past decade, even the most optimistic forecaster would have to say that "more of the same" is certainly the likely prognosis.

Notes

1. Susan Tolchin and Martin Tolchin, *Dismantling America: The Rush to Deregulate* (Boston: Houghton Mifflin, 1983).
2. Ronald Reagan, Inaugural Address as Fortieth President of the United States, Washington, D.C., January 20, 1981. For a thorough insider's account of the Reagan program, see Richard S. Williamson, *Reagan's Federalism: His Efforts to Decentralize Government* (Lanham, Md.: University Press of America, 1990).
3. See U.S. Advisory Commission on Intergovernmental Relations, *Regulatory Federalism: Policy, Process, Impact, and Reform*, A-5 (Washington, D.C.: GPO, 1984), 6, 19-21.
4. See Marshall R. Goodman and Margaret T. Wrightson, *Managing Regulatory Reform: The Reagan Strategy and Its Impacts* (New York: Praeger, 1987), 30-32.
5. Executive Order 12044, issued March 1978.
6. Goodman and Wrightson, *Managing Regulatory Reform*, 89.
7. *National League of Cities* v. *Usery*, 426 U.S. 833 (176).
8. Molly Sinclair, "Reagan Helps State, Local Regulators," *Washington Post*, June 17, 1984.

9. Michael Fix, "Regulatory Relief: The Real New Federalism," *State Government News,* January 1985, 7.
10. See Arnold M. Kuzmack, "The Safe Drinking Water Act: A Case Study," in *Coping with Mandates: What Are the Alternatives?,* ed. Michael Fix and Daphne A. Kenyon (Washington, D.C.: Urban Institute Press, 1990), 73.
11. 52 *CFR* 210, October 30, 1987, 41844-41845.
12. U.S. General Accounting Office, *Legislative Mandates: State Experiences Offer Insights for Federal Action,* HRD 88-75 (Washington, D.C.: GPO, 1988), 48.
13. David R. Mayhew, *Divided We Govern: Party Control, Lawmaking, and Investigations, 1946-1990* (New Haven: Yale University Press, 1991), table 4.1.
14. Mayhew's listing included some, but not all, of the intergovernmental regulatory statutes compiled [for this paper], as well as many of the regulations examined [in] the original ACIR *Regulatory Federalism* volume. . . . Prominent examples include the Clean Air Act of 1970, the Clean Water Act, the Occupational Safety and Health Act, and the Civil Rights Act of 1964.
15. This emphasis on an "administrative" rather than a "statutory" strategy is a theme of Goodman and Wrightson.
16. "Remarks by the President," January 22, 1981, in *Materials on President Reagan's Program of Regulatory Relief,* June 13, 1981, 37.
17. See Office of the Press Secretary, the White House, "Fact Sheet: President Reagan's Initiatives to Reduce Regulatory Burdens," February 18, 1981, 2-4.
18. Tolchin and Tolchin, *Dismantling America,* 85.
19. Goodman and Wrightson, *Managing Regulatory Reform,* 27.
20. Both documents are included in *Materials on President Reagan's Program of Regulatory Relief,* June 13, 1981, 45-50, 55-59.
21. Goodman and Wrightson, *Managing Regulatory Reform,* 103.
22. See Office of the Press Secretary, the White House, "Fact Sheet on President Reagan's Initiatives to Reduce Regulatory Burdens," February 18, 1981, 3, included in *Materials on President Reagan's Program of Regulatory Relief,* June 13, 1981, 61-66. The bilingual education rules were withdrawn by the secretary of education on February 2, 1981, while the EPA asked the D.C. Court of Appeals to remand to it the rule setting noise-emission standards on February 9.
23. See Presidential Task Force on Regulatory Relief, *Reagan Administration Regulatory Achievements,* August 11, 1983.
24. Presidential Task Force on Regulatory Relief, *Reagan Administration Achievements in Regulatory Relief for State and Local Governments: A Progress Report,* August 1982, 1-2.
25. Though the report was never released in final form, the General Accounting Office made its preliminary findings available to ACIR.

26. Although comparable, detailed data are not available for the last two years of the Reagan administration or the first years of the Bush administration, it is reasonable to believe that findings for 1981-1986 reflect overall trends for the entire decade of the 1980s. The years studied went well beyond the period of the most extensive administrative action in this area. They followed expressions of congressional concern with regulation and mandating and embraced the period in which President Reagan championed his most far-reaching new federalism reform proposals, 1982 and 1983.

27. Samuel Halperin, "Federal Takeover, State Default, or Family Problem," in *Federalism at the Crossroads: Improving Educational Policymaking,* ed. Samuel Halperin (Washington, D.C.: Institute for Educational Leadership, 1976), 19.

28. See James Q. Wilson, "American Politics: Then and Now," *Commentary* (February 1979).

29. See U.S. Advisory Commission on Intergovernmental Relations, *The Federal Role in the Federal System: The Dynamics of Growth,* vol. 2 of *The Condition of Contemporary Federalism: Conflicting Theories and Collapsing Constraints,* A-78 (Washington, D.C.: GPO, 1981), chap. 3; and U.S. Advisory Commission on Intergovernmental Relations, *Regulatory Federalism,* chap. 3.

30. Quoted in Stephen Klaidman, "Muddling Through," *Wilson Quarterly* (Spring 1991): 73. Emphasis added.

31. Quoted in Goodman and Wrightson, *Managing Regulatory Reform,* 108.

32. See Timothy J. Conlan, Margaret T. Wrightson, and David R. Beam, *Taxing Choices: The Politics of Tax Reform* (Washington, D.C.: CQ Press, 1990).

Part IV

REVIEW QUESTIONS

1. Ingram indicates that federal administrators, in dealing with their counterparts in the states, cannot and do not simply give orders. She claims that under some circumstances, however, federal policies are likely to be administered straightforwardly by the states. When? Why?

2. Ingram's model of intergovernmental administration suggests that, relatively speaking, the states have impressive advantages in dealing with the national bureaucracy. Apply her model (modified for federal-local relations) to the case of the Chicago Housing Authority described by Lazin. What empirical support does the case contain for Ingram's propositions?

3. Ingram claims that in intergovernmental bargaining, neither party wants to cause conflict: "Federal agencies are unlikely to embark upon enforcement practices that they anticipate will bring them little support and much criticism." Is this argument still valid in a time of federal budget cuts and strained intergovernmental fiscal relations? Would one expect even more conflict to develop with today's shrinking pie? Consider in your response the types of regulatory devices increasingly employed by the national government since the 1970s, and evaluate Koch's comments on this subject.

4. Many of the early advocates of public administrative reform argued that politics should be separated from administration; in fact, this idea is still voiced today by some advocates of good government. If by "politics" one means the conflict about and determination of public goals, do you think that administration and politics in intergovernmental relations can really be separated? Be specific and use examples in your response.

5. How, if at all, is the direction of recent Supreme Court rulings on federal relations with state and local governments (see, for instance,

the readings by Howard and by Wrightson in earlier sections of this book) likely to influence the actual implementation of intergovernmental mandates?

6. The articles by Sylvester and by Beam and Conlan seem to suggest by implication that fewer intergovernmental mandates would be a good thing. Can you critique such an assumption? Can you find any defensible justification for the extent of intergovernmental regulation witnessed in recent years?

7. Koch claims that national bureaucrats adopt and advocate regulations that extend far beyond what they might reasonably need or expect to accomplish. Does Ingram's model, when combined with other views included in this book (such as those of Pressman and Derthick), indicate that this bureaucratic behavior may have a rational basis?

8. Many observers of the American legislative process claim that lawmakers often design ambiguous, even contradictory, policies and leave tough decisions to those who implement them. What would be some reasons for such an approach? Why might this tendency be magnified on intergovernmental matters? How does the Chicago housing case support this argument?

Part V

THE POST-REAGAN ERA, THE EMERGING
RESPONSIBILITIES OF THE STATES, AND THE
FUTURE OF THE INTERGOVERNMENTAL SYSTEM

The readings presented thus far have documented the persistent salience of intergovernmental matters in American public life. A number of recent developments have raised the topic of intergovernmental relations to a very prominent position in domestic policy discussions today.

Since the mid 1970s, for instance, the federal aid system has altered considerably, both responding to and stimulating political and administrative shifts. A fiscal network of hundreds of narrow categorical programs has been broadened and made more complex by the compression of numerous categoricals into block grants and, for a time, by the experiment with revenue sharing. Fiscal constraints have heightened tensions. And intergovernmental regulation has increased, despite reform efforts.

The Reagan era, in particular, saw attempts at dramatic change in the system. By suggesting a relaxation of national administrative controls in a variety of policy areas, a further shift toward the block-grant method of intergovernmental finance, a clearer separation of responsibilities between the states and Washington, a devolution of many responsibilities to the states, and a major reduction in the total amount of federal financial support for states and localities, the "new federalism" initiatives established a lengthy and controversial agenda for the Reagan years.

During his terms in office, these issues were joined by many of those who have a stake in their resolution. As several of the readings in this section explain, Reagan was by no means fully successful in effecting a drastic redirection in intergovernmental matters. However, on a number of issues (especially deregulation, the creation of new block grants, and the enactment of aid cutbacks) there were major developments. Furthermore, although his most radical proposals went nowhere, the tightened budgetary circumstances of his administration and that of President Bush have effectively encouraged additional developments originally endorsed by Reagan. The most obvious and important example here is the states' increasingly active role in addressing important policy issues in the intergovernmental system.

The post-Reagan years have seen no diminution in the importance of these issues and developments. Most of these dilemmas, cast as major themes during the Reagan years, continue unresolved but no less important today. Indeed, during the Bush administration proposals for block grants, efforts to trim intergovernmental regulation, and budget cutbacks have largely echoed the major points of emphasis from the 1980s. Yet clear breakthroughs or resolutions seem distant.

In this context, stern challenges face the states and their localities. The policy challenges of poverty and homelessness, health care and drug addiction, AIDS as an especially severe manifestation of these other social problems, economic development, educational revitalization, racial tensions, environmental degradation, and scores of other issues are pressing on nonnational governments everywhere. Yet these heavy demands for public services and public programs confront the specter of citizens' revolts against the tax burdens of many jurisdictions (witness, as an example, the David Duke phenomenon in the early 1990s), constrained budgets, difficulties in stimulating additional intergovernmental assistance, increased responsibilities from burgeoning regulation, and today's ever more complex administrative arrangements.

Of course, earlier selections have addressed many of these contemporary issues and controversies, including the role of courts in the system, the plight of many of the nation's cities, the prominence of "printout" politics in policy making, and the rise of heavy intergovernmental regulation. Certainly, the impact of many of the Reagan efforts has already been alluded to frequently. Part V provides a more focused look at the importance and impact, intended and unintended, of the Reagan era and beyond. Special emphases are placed on understanding the approach undertaken in the Reagan years, the resurgence of and challenge to the states in the current period, and the important tensions in the intergovernmental system likely to be especially important through the 1990s.

Because of the continuing importance of the Reagan efforts, the first three readings in this section (nos. 33-35) focus on intergovernmental developments and issues stimulated during the Reagan presidency. The first selection, from Reagan's 1982 State of the Union address, constitutes his most explicit statement of intentions and proposals for the intergovernmental system. As indicated in other selections here, only a few of these proposals were implemented directly. However, the reading constitutes a fairly clear summary of the approach taken by Reagan and, less forcefully, Bush.

The essay by Samuel Beer (no. 34) was written not for a scholarly audience, as were many of the readings in this book, but for a well-known journal of opinion, *The New Republic*. Beer explicitly challenges the viewpoint of Reagan (in general and as explained in his first inaugural address) and others who hope to "return" the American system to an era in which the United States was less consciously a nation, and during which there was significantly less interdependence. Beer's argument remains timely because he challenges premises that continue to form prominent parts of political debate in the 1990s. Beer places today's disputes against the sweep of American history and political thought, demonstrating the link between some of the most enduring concerns and the policy issues on the front pages of today's newspapers.

The third article in Part V (no. 35) is a careful study by Timothy Conlan comparing the intent and achievement of the Reagan administration on intergovernmental reform. Conlan's assessment of the conflict between Reagan's intergovernmental proposals and his other policy preferences is especially illuminating. He argues that the Reagan administration was far less consistent in and supportive of intergovernmental reform than rhetoric would suggest. His more tentative general conclusion may be even more significant: *all* recent presidents have been less than faithful in practice to the goal of a vital intergovernmental system. The complexity of the pattern, the political costs of reform, and the salience of immediate policy problems temper any efforts to make major changes from the center—that is, from Washington.

Although Conlan wrote his essay while Reagan was still in office, the interpretation he offers still stands as valid.[1] Yet, for us to understand more fully the implications of this period for the future of the intergovernmental system in the 1990s requires more than this retrospective analysis. Therefore, the final three readings in Part V (nos. 36-38) focus more on what has been wrought by the Reagan efforts, the continuation during the Bush years, and the longer-term impact of years of financial cutbacks.

In the first essay of this trio, David Beam marshals considerable evidence that the states have already become the prime locus of economic-development policy in the United States. In Beam's view, the national government will continue to assume a very significant place in policy decisions, especially those requiring attention to redistribution and equity. However, states in the post-Reagan period can serve as laboratories for innovation and can help to stimulate economic vitality in ways that have been only dimly understood in the past. Although some state and local development activities have been widely criticized for their parochial and ineffective features, other initiatives away from Washington may hold the key to making the United States more competitive in the world arena. Beam's argument is especially intriguing to those interested in intergovernmental relations for many reasons. He offers a very contemporary justification for preserving a vigorous federal arrangement. In addition, when read in conjunction with Beer's essay on the idea of the nation, this piece stimulates thinking on the question of what level can most appropriately be considered the center of national vitality.

The reader may also want to consider whether Beam's provocative analysis may paint too rosy a picture of the states' actual or potential role. Is competition among the states for economic development likely to be an important force *limiting* the potential sketched so vividly by Beam? In their efforts to attract commerce are states likely to find themselves emphasizing the interests of business rather than the health, environmental, and welfare needs of their most vulnerable citizens? It is more obvious now than ever, then, that the shape of the intergovernmental system is linked to some of the most important policy issues at the center of public debate.

Morton Keller (no. 37) also focuses on the emergent role of the states, but his perspective is substantively broader: he assesses the place of the states today not only on economic development but also in various other sectors. By considering the emergent state agenda in historical context, he conveys a sense of both continuity and challenge as the intergovernmental system confronts the dilemmas of the coming years.

Finally, another essay by Timothy Conlan (no. 38) provides a fitting close for this section of the book. His point of view here is explicitly prospective, as he considers the question of what can be expected from the American intergovernmental system in the 1990s. Conlan clearly delineates two contrasting trends that have each been documented elsewhere in the present volume as well: a nationalization of *political* trends, counterpoised to increasing expectations for heightened state-level *governmental* activity and responsibility—along with "economic megatrends favoring decentralization." A careful reading of political, governmental, and economic tendencies, therefore, seems to suggest heightened levels of tension and frustration in the interdependent and complex network. In this eventuality, then, intergovernmental issues are likely to remain central to the nation's agenda in the years ahead.

Note

1. A more detailed version of his analysis of the Reagan approach to issues of federalism, and Nixon's as well, is his volume *New Federalism: Intergovernmental Reform from Nixon to Reagan* (Washington, D.C.: Brookings, 1988).

33. THE STATE OF THE UNION

Ronald Reagan

... Now that the essentials of [the administration's economic program] are in place, our next major undertaking must be a program—just as bold, just as innovative—to make government again accountable to the people, to make our system of federalism work again.

Our citizens feel they've lost control of even the most basic decisions made about the essential services of government, such as schools, welfare, roads, and even garbage collection. And they're right. A maze of interlocking jurisdictions and levels of government confronts average citizens in trying to solve even the simplest of problems. They don't know where to turn for answers, who to hold accountable, who to praise, who to blame, who to vote for or against. The main reason for this is the overpowering growth of Federal grants-in-aid programs during the past few decades.

In 1960 the Federal Government had 132 categorical grant programs, costing $7 billion. When I took office, there were approximately 500, costing nearly a hundred billion dollars—13 programs for energy, 36 for pollution control, 66 for social services, 90 for education. And here in the Congress, it takes at least 166 committees just to try to keep track of them.

You know and I know that neither the President nor the Congress can properly oversee this jungle of grants-in-aid; indeed, the growth of these grants has led to the distortion in the vital functions of government. As one Democratic Governor put it recently: The National Government should be worrying about "arms control, not potholes."

The growth in these Federal programs has—in the words of one intergovernmental commission—made the Federal Government "more pervasive, more intrusive, more unmanageable, more ineffective and costly, and above all, more unaccountable." Let's solve this problem with a single, bold stroke: the return of some $47 billion in Federal programs to State and local government, together with the means to

---

From the address delivered before a joint session of Congress, January 26, 1982.

finance them and a transition period of nearly 10 years to avoid unnecessary disruption.

I will shortly send this Congress a message describing this program. I want to emphasize, however, that its full details will have been worked out only after close consultation with congressional, State, and local officials.

Starting in fiscal 1984, the Federal Government will assume full responsibility for the cost of the rapidly growing Medicaid program to go along with its existing responsibility for Medicare. As part of a financially equal swap, the States will simultaneously take full responsibility for Aid to Families with Dependent Children and food stamps. This will make welfare less costly and more responsive to genuine need, because it'll be designed and administered closer to the grassroots and the people it serves.

In 1984 the Federal Government will apply the full proceeds from certain excise taxes to a grassroots trust fund that will belong in fair shares to the 50 States. The total amount flowing into this fund will be $28 billion a year. Over the next 4 years the States can use this money in either of two ways. If they want to continue receiving Federal grants in such areas as transportation, education, and social services, they can use their trust fund money to pay for the grants. Or to the extent they choose to forgo the Federal grant programs, they can use their trust fund money on their own for those or other purposes. There will be a mandatory pass-through of part of these funds to local governments.

By 1988 the States will be in complete control of over 40 Federal grant programs. The trust fund will start to phase out, eventually to disappear, and the excise taxes will be turned over to the States. They can then preserve, lower, or raise taxes on their own and fund and mandate these programs as they see fit.

In a single stroke we will be accomplishing a realignment that will end cumbersome administration and spiraling costs at the Federal level while we ensure these programs will be more responsive to both the people they're meant to help and the people who pay for them.

Hand in hand with this program to strengthen the discretion and flexibility of State and local governments, we're proposing legislation for an experimental effort to improve and develop our depressed urban areas in the 1980's and '90's. This legislation will permit States and localities to apply to the Federal Government for designation as urban enterprise zones. A broad range of special economic incentives in the zones will help attract new business, new jobs, new opportunity to America's inner cities and rural towns. Some will say our mission is to save free enterprise. Well, I say we must free enterprise so that together we can save America.

Some will also say our States and local communities are not up to the challenge of a new and creative partnership. Well, that might have been true 20 years ago before reforms like reapportionment and the Voting Rights Act, the 10-year extension of which I strongly support. It's no longer true today. This administration has faith in State and local governments and the constitutional balance envisioned by the Founding Fathers. We also believe in the integrity, decency and sound good sense of grassroots Americans.

34.   THE IDEA OF THE NATION

Samuel H. Beer

I have a difference of opinion with President Reagan. We have all heard of the President's new federalism and his proposals to cut back on the activities of the federal government by reducing or eliminating certain programs and transferring others to the states. He wishes to do this because he finds these activities to be inefficient and wasteful. He also claims that they are improper under the U.S. Constitution—not in the sense that the courts have found them to violate our fundamental law, but in the larger philosophical and historical sense that the present distribution of power between levels of government offends against the true meaning and intent of that document.

In justification of this conclusion, he has relied upon a certain view of the founding of the Republic. In his inaugural address he summarized its essentials when he said: "The federal government did not create the states; the states created the federal government." This allegation of historical fact did not pass without comment. Richard Morris of Columbia took issue with the President, called his view of the historical facts "a hoary myth about the origin of the Union," and went on to summarize the evidence showing that "the United States was created by the people in collectivity, not by the individual states." No less bluntly, Henry Steele Commager of Amherst said the President did not understand the Constitution, which in its own words asserts that it was ordained by "We, the People of the United States," not by the states severally.

We may smile at this exchange between the President and the professors. They are talking about something that happened a long time ago. To be sure, the conflict of ideas between them did inform the most serious crisis of our first century—the grim struggle that culminated in the Civil War. In that conflict, President Reagan's view—the compact theory of the Constitution—was championed by Jefferson Davis, the president of the seceding South. The first

From *The New Republic*, July 19 and 26, 1982, 23-29. Reprinted by permission of *The New Republic*, © 1982, The New Republic, Inc.

Republican President of the United States, on the other hand, espoused the national theory of the Constitution. "The Union," said Abraham Lincoln, "is older than any of the states and, in fact, it created them as States. . . . The Union and not the states separately produced their independence and their liberty. . . . The Union gave each of them whatever of independence and liberty it has."

As stated by President Lincoln, the national idea is a theory that ultimate authority lies in the United States. It identifies the whole people of the nation as the source of the legitimate power of both the federal government and the state governments.

The national idea, however, is not only a theory of authority but also a theory of purpose, a perspective on public policy, a guide to the ends for which power should be used. It invites us to ask ourselves what sort of a people we are, and whether we are a people, and what we wish to make of ourselves as a people. In this sense the national idea is as alive and contentious today as it was when Alexander Hamilton set the course of the first Administration of George Washington.

Like the other founders, Hamilton sought to establish a regime of republican liberty, that is, a system of government which would protect the individual's rights of person and property and which would be founded upon the consent of the governed. He was by no means satisfied with the legal framework produced by the Philadelphia convention. Fearing the states, he would have preferred a much stronger central authority, and, distrusting the common people, he would have set a greater distance between them and the exercise of power. He was less concerned, however, with the legal framework than with the use that would be made of it. He saw in the Constitution not only a regime of liberty but also, and especially, the promise of nationhood.

He understood, moreover, that this promise of nationhood would have to be fulfilled if the regime of liberty itself was to endure. The scale of the country almost daunted him. At Philadelphia, as its chief diarist reported, Hamilton "confessed that he was much discouraged by the amazing extent of the Country in expecting the desired blessings from any general sovereignty that could be substituted." This fear echoed the conventional wisdom of the time. The great Montesquieu had warned that popular government was not suitable for a large and diverse country. If attempted, he predicted that its counsels would be distracted by "a thousand private views" and its extent would provide cover for ambitious men seeking despotic power.

One reply to Montesquieu turned this argument on its head by declaring that such pluralism would be a source of stability. In his famous Tenth Federalist, James Madison argued that the more extensive republic, precisely because of its diversity, would protect popular government by making oppressive combinations less likely. Hamilton did not deny Madison's reasoning, but perceived that something more than a balance of groups would be necessary if the more extensive republic was to escape the disorder that would destroy its liberty.

Hamilton summarized his views in the farewell address he drafted for Washington in 1796. Its theme is the importance of union. But this union does not consist merely in a balance of groups or a consensus of values, and certainly not merely in a strong central government or a common framework of constitutional law. It is rather a condition of the people, uniting them by both sympathy and interest, but above all in "an indissoluble community of interest as *one nation*."

Hamilton's nationalism did not consist solely in his belief that the Americans were "one people" rather than thirteen separate peoples. The father of the compact theory himself, Thomas Jefferson, at times shared that opinion, to which he gave expression in the Declaration of Independence. The contrast with Jefferson lay in Hamilton's activism, his belief that this American people must make vigorous use of its central government for the task of nation-building. This difference between the two members of Washington's Cabinet, the great individualist and the great nationalist, achieved classic expression in their conflict over the proposed Bank of the United States. Jefferson feared that the bank would corrupt his cherished agrarian order and discovered no authority for it in the Constitution. Hamilton, believing that a central bank was necessary to sustain public credit, promote economic development, and—in his graphic phrase—"cement the union," found in a broad construction of the "necessary and proper" clause of Article I ample constitutional authorization. Looking back today and recognizing that the words of the Constitution can be fitted into either line of reasoning, we must sigh with relief that President Washington, and in later years the Supreme Court, preferred the Hamiltonian doctrine.

Hamilton was not only a nationalist and centralizer, he was also an elitist. Along with the bank, his first steps to revive and sustain the public credit were the full funding of the federal debt and the federal assumption of the debts incurred by the states during the war of independence. These measures had their fiscal and economic purposes. Their social impact, moreover, favored the fortunes of those members of the propertied classes who had come to hold the federal and state obligations. This result, while fully understood, was incidental to Hamilton's ultimate purpose, which was political. As with the bank, that purpose was to strengthen the newly empowered central government by attracting to it the interests of these influential members of society. Hamilton promoted capitalism, but not because he was a lackey of the capitalist class—indeed, he once wrote to a close friend, "I hate moneying men." His elitism was subservient to his nationalism.

In the same cause he was not only an elitist, but also an integrationist. I use that term expressly because of its current overtones, wishing to suggest Hamilton's perception of how diversity need not always be divisive, but may lead to mutual dependence and union. Here again he broke from Jefferson, who valued homogeneity. Hamilton, on the other hand, planned for active federal intervention to diversify the economy by the development of commerce and industry. His great report on manufactures is at once visionary and far-seeing— "the embryo of modern America," a recent writer terms it.

Hamilton is renowned for his statecraft: for his methods of using the powers of government for economic, political, and social ends. But that emphasis obscures his originality, which consisted in his conceptualization of those ends. His methods were derivative, being taken from the theory and practice of statebuilders of the seventeenth and eighteenth centuries, from Colbert to Pitt. Hamilton used this familiar technology, however, to forward the unprecedented attempt to establish republican government on a continental scale. In his scheme the unities of nationhood would sustain the authority of such a regime. By contrast, those earlier craftsmen of the modern state in Bourbon France or Hohenzollern Prussia or Whig Britain could take for granted the established authority of a monarchic and aristocratic regime. They too had their techniques for enhancing the attachment of the people to the prince. But in America the people were the prince. To enhance their attachment to the ultimate governing power, therefore, meant fortifying the bonds that united them as a people. If the authority of this first nation-state was to suffice for its governance, the purpose of the state would have to become the development of the nation. This was the distinctive Hamiltonian end: to make the nation more of a nation.

The national idea, so engendered, confronted three great crises: the crisis of sectionalism, culminating in the Civil War; the crisis of industrialism, culminating in the Great Depression and the New Deal; and the crisis of racism, which continues to rack our country.

In the course of the struggle with sectionalism, John C. Calhoun defined the issue and threw down the challenge to nationalism when he said: ". . . the very idea of an *American People,* as constituting a single community, is a mere chimera. Such a community never for a single moment existed—neither before nor since the Declaration of Independence." This was a logical deduction from the compact theory, which according to Calhoun's system made of each state a "separate sovereign community."

His leading opponent, Daniel Webster, has been called the first great champion of the national theory of the union. If we are thinking of speech rather than action, that is true, since Hamilton's contribution, although earlier, was in the realm of deeds rather than words. Webster never won the high executive power that he sought, and the cause of union for which he spent himself suffered continual defeat during his lifetime. But the impact on history of words such as his is not to be underestimated. "When finally, after his death, civil war did eventuate," concludes his biographer, "it was Webster's doctrine, from the lips of Abraham Lincoln, which animated the North and made its victory inevitable." Webster gave us not only doctrine, but also imagery and myth. He was not the narrow legalist and materialistic Whig of some critical portraits. And if his oratory is too florid for our taste today, its effect on his audiences was overpowering. "I was never so excited by public speaking before in my life," exclaimed George Ticknor, an otherwise cool Bostonian, after one address. "Three or four times I thought my temples would burst with the gush of blood." Those who heard him, it has been said, "experienced the same delight which they might have received from a performance of *Hamlet* or Beethoven's Fifth Symphony." Poets have been called, "the unacknowledged legislators of the world"; this legislator was the unacknowledged poet of the young Republic.

To say this is to emphasize his style; but what was the substance of his achievement? Historians of political thought usually, and correctly, look first to his memorable debate with Senator Robert Hayne of South Carolina in January of 1830. Echoing Calhoun's deductions from the compact theory, Hayne had stated the doctrine of nullification. This doctrine would deny to the federal judiciary the right to draw the line between federal and state authority, leaving such questions of constitutionality to be decided—subject to various qualifications—by each state itself.

In reply Webster set forth with new boldness the national theory of authority. Asking what was the origin of "this general government," he concluded that the Constitution is not a compact between the states. It was not established by the government of the several states, or by the people of the several states, but by "the people of the United States in the aggregate." In Lincolnian phrases, he called it "the people's Constitution, the people's government, made for the people, made by the people and answerable to the people," and clinched his argument for the dependence of popular government on nationhood with that memorable and sonorous coda, "Liberty and union, one and inseparable, now and forever."

These later passages of his argument have almost monopolized the attention of historians of political thought. Yet it is in an earlier and longer part that he developed the Hamiltonian thrust, looking not to the origin but to the purpose of government. These initial passages of the debate had not focused on the problems of authority and nullification. The question was rather what to do with a great national resource— the public domain, already consisting of hundreds of millions of acres located in the states and territories and owned by the federal government. Large tracts had been used to finance internal improvements, such as roads, canals, and schools, as envisioned by Hamilton and ardently espoused by the previous President, John Quincy Adams.

When Webster defended such uses, citing the longstanding agreement that the public domain was for "the common benefit of all the States," Hayne made a revealing reply. If that was the rule, said he, how could one justify "voting away immense bodies of these lands—for canals in Indiana and Illinois, to the Louisville and Portland Canal, to Kenyon College in Ohio, to Schools for the Deaf and Dumb." "If grants of this character," he continued, "can fairly be considered as made for the common benefit of all the states, it can only be because all the states are interested in the welfare of each—a principle, which, carried to the full extent, destroys all distinction between local and national subjects."

Webster seized the objection and set out to answer it. His task was to show when a resource belonging to the whole country could legitimately be used to support works on "particular roads, particular canals, particular rivers, and particular institutions of education in the West." Calling this question "the real and wide difference in political opinion between the honorable gentleman and myself," he asserted that there was a "common good" distinguishable from "local goods," yet embracing such particular projects.

In these passages the rhetoric is suggestive, but one would like a more specific answer: what *is* the difference between a local and a general good? Suddenly Webster's discourse becomes quite concrete. His approach is to show what the federal government must do by demonstrating what the states cannot do. Using the development of transportation after the peace of 1815 for illustration, Webster shows why a particular project within a state, which also has substantial benefits for other states, will for that very reason probably not be undertaken by the state within which it is located.

"Take the instance of the Delaware breakwater," he said. (This was a large artificial harbor then under federal construction near the mouth of Delaware Bay.) "It will cost several millions of money. Would Pennsylvania ever have constructed it? Certainly never, . . .

because it is not for her sole benefit. Would Pennsylvania, New Jersey and Delaware have united to accomplish it at their joint expenses? Certainly not, for the same reason. It could not be done, therefore, but by the general government."

Hayne was right to shrink from the logic of this argument. For its logic does mean that in a rapidly developing economy such as that of America in the eighteenth century, increasing interdependence would bring more and more matters legitimately within the province of the federal government. But logic was not the only aspect of Webster's argument that Hayne was resisting. In the spirit of Hamilton, Webster did perceive the prospect of increasing interdependence and recognized that it could fully realize its promise of wealth and power only with the assistance of the federal government. Moreover, he looked beyond the merely material benefits that such intervention would bring to individuals, classes, and regions toward his grand objective, "the consolidation of the union." This further criterion of the common good could under no circumstances be reconciled with Hayne's "system."

Like Hamilton, Webster sought to make the nation more of a nation. As he conceived this objective, however, he broke from the bleak eighteenth-century realism of Hamilton and turned his imagination toward the vistas of social possibility being opened up by the rising romantic movement of his day. By "consolidation" Webster did not mean merely attachment to the union arising from economic benefits. Indeed, he blamed Hayne for regarding the union "as a mere question of present and temporary expedience; nothing more than a mere matter of profit and loss . . . to be preserved, while it suits local and temporary purposes to preserve it; and to be sundered whenever it shall be found to thwart such purposes."

The language brings to mind the imagery of another romantic nationalist, Edmund Burke; in his famous assault upon the French Revolution and social contract theory, he proclaimed that "the state ought not to be considered as nothing better than a partnership agreement in a trade of pepper and coffee, calico or tobacco, or some other such low concern, to be taken up for a little temporary interest, and to be dissolved at the fancy of the parties," but rather as "a partnership in all science; a partnership in all art; a partnership in every virtue, and in all perfection."

A later formulation echoes Burke's words and phrasing even more exactly, as Webster sets forth the organic conception of the nation: "The Union," he said, "is not a temporary partnership of states. It is an association of people, under a constitution of government, uniting their power, joining together their highest interests, cementing their present enjoyments, and blending into one indivisible mass, all their hopes for the future."

Webster articulated this conception most vividly not in Congress or before the Supreme Court, but at public gatherings on patriotic occasions. There the constraints of a professional and adversarial audience upon his imagination were relaxed and his powers as myth-maker released. Consider what some call the finest of his occasional addresses, his speech at the laying of the cornerstone of the Bunker Hill Monument on June 17, 1825. As in his advocacy and in his debates, his theme was the union. What he did, however, was not to make an argument for the union, but to tell a story about it—a story about its past with a lesson for its future.

The plot was simple: how American union foiled the British oppressors in 1775. They had thought to divide and conquer, anticipating that the other colonies would be cowed by the severity of the punishment visited on Massachusetts and that the other seaports would be seduced by the prospect of gain from trade diverted from Boston. "How miserably such reasoners deceived themselves!" exclaimed the orator. "Everywhere the unworthy boon was rejected with scorn. The fortunate occasion was seized, everywhere, to show to the whole world that the Colonies were swayed by no local interest, no partial interest, no selfish interest." In the imagery of Webster, the battle of Bunker Hill was a metaphor of that united people. As Warren, Prescott, Putnam, and Stark had fought side by side; as the four colonies of New England had on that day stood together with "one cause, one country, one heart"; so also "the feeling of resistance . . . possessed the whole American people." So much for Calhoun and his "system."

From this myth of war Webster drew a lesson for peace. "In a day of peace, let us advance the arts of peace and the works of peace. . . . Let us develop the resources of our land, call forth its powers, build up its institutions, and see whether we also, in our day and generation, may not perform something worthy to be remembered." Then he concluded with abrupt and brutal rhetoric: "Let our object be: OUR COUNTRY, OUR WHOLE COUNTRY, AND NOTHING BUT OUR COUNTRY."

With his own matchless sensibility Abraham Lincoln deployed the doctrine and imagery of Webster to animate the North during the Civil War. Lincoln's nationalism, like Webster's, had a positive message for peacetime, and it was this message that set the course of the country's development for the next several generations. Much that he did derived from the original Hamiltonian program, which, long frustrated by the dominance of the compact theory, now burst forth in legislative and executive action. During the war years, not only was slavery given the death blow, but also an integrated program of positive federal involvement was put through in the fields of banking and currency, transportation, the tariff, land grants to homesteaders, and aid to higher education. In the following decades, an enormous expansion of the economy propelled the United States into the age of industrialism, which in due course engendered its typical problems of deprivation, inequality, and class conflict.

A Republican, Theodore Roosevelt, first attempted to cope with these problems in terms of the national idea. Throughout his public career, an associate has written, Roosevelt "kept one steady purpose, the solidarity, the essential unity of our country. . . . All the details of his action, the specific policies he states, arise from his underlying purpose for the Union." Like other Progressives, Roosevelt was disturbed by the rising conflicts between groups and classes and sought to offset them by timely reform. In this sense integration was T.R.'s guiding aim, and he rightly christened his cause "The New Nationalism." Effective advocacy of this cause, however, fell to another Roosevelt a generation later, when the failings of industrialism were raising far greater dangers to the union.

None of the main points in Franklin Roosevelt's famous inaugural of March 4, 1933, can be summarized without reference to the nation. The emergency is national because of "the interdependence of the various elements in, and parts of, the United States." Our purpose must be, first, "the establishment of a sound national economy," and beyond that "the assurance of a rounded and permanent national life." The mode of action must be national, conducted by the federal government and carried out "on a national scale," helped "by national planning." No other thematic term faintly rivals the term "nation" as noun or adjective, in emphasis. Democracy is mentioned only once in Roosevelt's address; liberty, equality, or the individual not at all.

Franklin Roosevelt's nationalism was threefold. First it was a doctrine of federal centralization, and in his Administration, in peace as well as war, the balance of power in the federal system swung sharply toward Washington. Roosevelt called not only for a centralization of government, but also for a nationalization of politics. In these years a new kind of mass politics arose. The old rustic and sectional politics gave way to a new urban and class politics dividing electoral forces on a nationwide basis.

The third aspect of Roosevelt's nationalism was expressed in his policies. Those policies do not make a neat package and include many false starts and failures and ad hoc expedients. Yet in their overall impact one can detect the old purpose of "consolidation of the union."

During the very first phase of the New Deal, based on the National Industrial Recovery Act, this goal was explicit. In its declaration of policy, the act, having declared a "national emergency," called for "cooperative action among trade groups" and "united action of labor and management" under "adequate government sanctions and supervision." Engulfed in red, white, and blue propaganda, the [NIRA], after a first brief success, failed to achieve that coordinated effort and had virtually collapsed by the time it was declared unconstitutional in 1935. The second New Deal which followed, however, brought about fundamental and lasting changes in the structure of the American government and economy.

The paradox of the second New Deal is that although at the time it was intensely divisive, in the end it enhanced national solidarity. The divisiveness will be readily granted by anyone who remembers the campaign of 1936. The tone was set by Roosevelt's speech accepting the Democratic nomination. In swollen and abrasive hyperbole he promised that, just as 1776 had wiped out "political tyranny," so 1936 would bring "economic tyranny" to an end. The "economic royalist" metaphor that was launched into the political battle by this speech expressed the emerging purpose of the New Deal to create a new balance of power in the economy by means of a series of basic structural reforms. The Wagner Act was the most important and characteristic reform. Utilizing its protections of the right to organize and to bargain collectively, trade unions swept through industry in a massive organizing effort. Despite bitter and sometimes bloody resistance in what can only be called class war, over the years not only practices but also attitudes eventually were altered. The life of the working stiff was never again the same.

The Rooseveltian reforms had two aspects. In their material aspect they brought about a redistribution of power in favor of certain groups. No less important was their symbolic significance as recognition of the full membership of these groups in the national community. Industrial labor and recent immigrants won a degree of acceptance in the national consciousness and in everyday social intercourse that they had not previously enjoyed. In Roosevelt's appointments to the judiciary, Catholics and Jews were recognized as never before. He named the first Italo-American and the first blacks ever appointed to the federal bench. As Joseph Alsop has recently observed, "the essence of his achievement" was that he "included the excluded." And with such high spirits! He once addressed the Daughters of the American Revolution as "Fellow Immigrants!"

Recently I had a letter from a friend who asked: Did not "the new social democracy, which arose with the New Deal, make popular sacrifice, not least for foreign policy, more difficult to obtain?" Just the opposite, I replied. And I went on to recall how during the war it often occurred to me that we were lucky that those sudden, vast demands being put upon the people in the name of national defense had been preceded by a period of radical national reform. An anecdote will illustrate my point. One hot day in the late summer of 1944 while crossing France we stopped to vote by absentee ballot in the Presidential election. "Well, Guthrie," I said to one of the noncoms, "let's line up these men and vote them for Roosevelt." That light-hearted remark was entirely in keeping with the situation. Most of the GIs were from fairly poor families in the Bronx and New Jersey. Politics didn't greatly concern them, but nothing was more natural to them than to vote for the man who had brought WPA [Works Progress Administration], Social Security, and other benefits to their families. Even among the battalion officers I can think of only two who did not vote for Roosevelt—the colonel and a staff officer from New York City named something or other the fourth.

None of these conflicts in nation-building is ever wholly terminated. Sectionalism still flares up from time to time, as between frost belt and sun belt. So also does class struggle. Similarly today, the cleavages among ethnic groups that boiled up with a new bitterness in the 1960s are far from being resolved.

The issue is not just ethnicity, but race. To be sure, ethnic pluralism is a fact—there are said to be ninety-two ethnic groups in the New York area alone—but this broad focus obscures the burning issue, which is the coexistence of blacks and whites in large numbers on both sides. That question of numbers is crucial. In other times and places one can find instances of a small number of one race living in relative peace in a society composed overwhelmingly of the other race. "Tokenism" is viable. But the facts rule out that solution for the United States.

Another option is the model of "separate but equal." In some circumstances this option could be carried out on a decent and democratic basis. It is, for instance, the way the French-speaking citizens of Quebec would like to live in relation to Canada as a whole. And, commonly, Canadians contrast favorably what they call their "mosaic society" with the American "melting pot." But in the present crisis Americans have rejected this option in law and in opinion as segregation. American nationalism demands that diversity be dealt with not by separation, but by integration.

For John F. Kennedy and Lyndon Johnson, the question was, first of all, civil rights. This meant securing for blacks the legal and political rights that had been won for whites in other generations. But the problem of civil rights, which was mainly a problem of the South, merged with the problem of black deprivation, which was especially a problem of northern cities. Johnson's "war on poverty" characterized the main thrust of the Great Society measures which he built on the initiatives of Kennedy. To think of these measures as concerned simply with "the poor" is to miss the point. The actual incidence of poverty meant that their main concern would be with the living conditions and opportunities of blacks, and especially those who populated the decaying areas of the great urban centers swollen by migration from the South to the North during and after World War II.

These programs were based on the recognition that membership in one ethnic group rather than another can make a great difference to your life chances. In trying to make the opportunities somewhat less unequal, they sought to bring the individuals belonging to disadvantaged groups—as was often said—"into the mainstream of American life." The rhetoric of one of Johnson's most impassioned speeches echoes this purpose. Only a few days after a civil rights march led by Martin Luther King had been broken up by state troopers in full view of national television, he introduced the Voting Rights Act of 1965 into Congress. Calling upon the myths of former wars, like other nationalist orators before him, he harked back to Lexington and Concord and to Appomattox in his summons to national effort. "What happened in Selma," he continued, "is part of a larger movement which reaches into every section and state of America. It is the effort of American Negroes to secure for themselves the full blessings of American life. . . ." Then, declaring that "their cause must be our cause too," he closed with solemn echo of the song of the marchers: "*And we shall overcome.*"

Considering where we started from some thirty years ago, our progress has been substantial. Still, few will assert that our statecraft—from poverty programs to affirmative action to busing—has been adequate to the objective. This problem still awaits its Alexander Hamilton. We may take some comfort from the fact that it is continuous with his great work. The Founders confronted the task of founding a nation-state. Our present exercise in nation-building is no less challenging. What we are attempting has never before been attempted by any country at any time. It is to create within a liberal, democratic framework a society in which vast numbers of both black and white people live in free and equal intercourse—political, economic, and social. It is a unique, a stupendous, demand, but the national idea will let us be satisfied with nothing less.

The federal system that confronts Ronald Reagan is the outcome of these three great waves of centralization: the Lincolnian, the Rooseveltian, and the Johnsonian. By means of his new federalism President Reagan seeks radically to decentralize that system. Does the history of the national idea in American politics suggest any criticism or guidance?

I hope, at least, that it does something to undermine the appeal of compact theory rhetoric. Rhetoric is important. Words are the means through which politicians reach the motivations of voters and by which leaders may shape those motivations. Both the compact theory and the national theory touch nerves of the body politic. Each conveys a very different sense of nationhood—or the lack thereof. My theme has been the national theory, which envisions one people, at once sovereign and subject, source of authority and substance of history, asserting, through conflict and in diversity, our unity of origin and of destiny.

Such an image does not yield a rule for allocating functions between levels of government. That is for practical men, assisted no doubt by the policy sciences. But the imagery of the national idea can prepare the minds of practical men to recognize in the facts of our time the call for renewed effort to consolidate the union. The vice of the compact theory is that it obscures this issue, diverts attention from the facts, and muffles the call for action.

Today this issue is real. A destructive pluralism—sectional, economic, and ethnic—disrupts our common life. It is foolish to use the rhetoric of political discourse to divert attention from that fact. I would ask the new federalists not only to give up their diversionary rhetoric, but positively to advocate the national idea. This does not mean they must give up federal reform. A nationalist need not always be a centralizer. For philosophical and for pragmatic reasons he may prefer a less active federal government. The important thing is to keep alive in our speech and our intentions the move toward the consolidation of the union. People will differ on what and how much needs to be done. The common goal should not be denied. We may need a new federalism. We surely need a new nationalism. I plead with the new federalists: come out from behind that Jeffersonian verbiage, and take up the good old Hamiltonian cause.

35. FEDERALISM AND COMPETING VALUES IN THE REAGAN ADMINISTRATION

Timothy J. Conlan

To a remarkable extent, President Reagan has made federalism a central concern in his administration. He speaks frequently of his deep commitment to revitalizing the federal system and of his desire to return government responsibilities to states and localities. As he told a conference of state legislators in 1981, "My administration is committed—heart and soul—to the broad principles of American Federalism." [1] Indeed, Richard Williamson, the President's former assistant for intergovernmental affairs, has argued that federalism rests at the very top of the President's policy agenda—higher than tax or budget cuts and higher than regulatory relief:

> President Ronald Reagan has a dream. His dream is not to cut the bloated federal budget.... His dream is not about tax cuts.... His dream is not about regulatory relief.... Rather, the President's dream is to change how America is governed.... He is seeking a "quiet revolution," a new federalism which is a meaningful American partnership. [2]

The Administration has taken major strides to translate such intentions into tangible results. With the passage of the *Omnibus Reconciliation Act* in 1981, the Administration achieved the consolidation of 77 categorical programs into nine new or substantially revised block grants—almost twice the number that had been enacted in the preceding 15 years. This same legislation also produced the first absolute decline in levels of federal grants to states and localities since the 1950s, dramatically accelerating the slowdown in federal aid expenditures that began in the late 1970s. [3] Similarly, the Reagan Administration gave new impetus to the regulatory reform movement

Author's note: I wish to thank David Beam, Cynthia Colella, Robert Dilger, Donald Kettl, Lester Levine, Ann Martino, David Walker, and Margaret Wrightson for their helpful advice on earlier drafts of this article.

From a paper prepared for delivery at the Annual Meeting of the American Political Science Association, Washington, D.C., August 30-September 2, 1984. Reprinted with permission of *Publius: The Journal of Federalism* 15 (1985) and the American Political Science Association.

that began in the mid-1970s, becoming the first to make intergovernmental regulation—those requirements that directly or indirectly focus on state and local governments rather than the private sector—a major target of reform. By late 1982, the Administration claimed to have reduced the federal paperwork burden on states and localities by millions of hours and to have saved such governments billions of dollars in one-time expenses and annually recurring costs. [4] Finally, and most importantly, the President placed a sweeping New Federalism initiative at the center of his 1982 legislative agenda. Indeed, the Administration's complex proposals to sort out governmental responsibilities and to turn back multiple programs and revenue sources to the states dominated intergovernmental debates in 1982 and attracted broad public and media attention.

The sources of the President's commitment to federalism are multiple. The small-town values of his childhood and his experiences as Governor of California both contributed to forming it. Moreover, Ronald Reagan possesses the most thoroughly developed and internally coherent political ideology of any President since Woodrow Wilson. His belief in devolution forms an integral part of this ideology and is often reinforced by other aspects of his conservative agenda: lowering federal taxes and domestic expenditures, reducing government interference in the marketplace, eliminating welfare dependency, etc.

In measuring the true depth of Reagan's commitment to strengthening federalism, however, it is instructive to examine his Administration's record on those occasions when the goal of rebalancing federalism, as the President defines it, *conflicts* with other deeply held values. How high does federalism rank on the President's scale of priorities when the truly difficult decisions must be made? When judged by this standard, federalism has not fared nearly as well under this administration. Devolutionary policies elsewhere deemed to be supportive of federalism have repeatedly lost out in the Reagan Administration when they have come in conflict with the sometimes competing goals of reducing the federal budget, deregulating the private sector, and advancing the conservative social agenda. Although a full listing would embody Administration policies and actions across the broad expanse of federal activities, from restricting local regulation of cable TV to preempting state usury laws, some of the most prominent examples include policies: urging reduced appropriations for most block grant programs; opposing the expansion of General Revenue Sharing; supporting national product liability legislation; preempting state laws regulating double-trailer trucks and establishing minimum drinking ages; overriding state objections to increased off-shore oil drilling and expanded use of nuclear power; requiring that states establish workfare programs; and regulating medical care for handicapped infants. Each of these policies is briefly described in the following three sections.

Budgetary Policy and Reagan Federalism

Domestic program budget cuts have long been an integral part of President Reagan's approach to federalism since they help to reduce the relative fiscal profile of the federal government while encouraging greater financial independence among state and local governments. All federal programs are not identical in their intergovernmental effects, however, and an intergovernmentally sensitive program of budget cuts could be expected to affect certain federal grants far more than others. In particular, narrowly prescriptive and intrusive categorical grants might be expected to bear the brunt of federal budget cuts, allowing more flexible programs such as block grants and General Revenue Sharing to be touched more lightly or not at all. Because they can be readily adapted to meet a range of diverse local needs, such programs formed the core of Richard Nixon's New Federalism agenda, and they have remained a top priority of state and local governments. Although they were also a major policy goal of his administration, block grants received very different budgetary treatment under Ronald Reagan.

In 1981, the President proposed enacting seven sweeping new block grants intended to consolidate 85 existing federal aid programs for state and local governments. Although most of these proposals were significantly modified by Congress, nine new or substantially revised block grants were created as part of the *Omnibus Reconciliation Act of 1981,* consolidating more federal grant programs in one stroke than all previous block grants combined.

Yet consolidation, with its attendant cuts in application, reporting, and paperwork requirements, was not the only important feature of these legislative changes. The new block grants also embodied large reductions in levels of spending. In his initial block grant proposals, the President had requested reductions averaging almost 25% below fiscal 1981 spending on the programs suggested for merger, far below the modest 10% reductions in federal aid the governors had offered to accept in exchange for broader program authority. In fact, the President recommended block grants for some of the deepest spending cuts of any segment of the federal budget—deeper than total cuts in federal aid—while entitlements and defense actually increased over 1981 spending levels (see Table 4). Although less severe, a similar pattern was evident in the actual block grants enacted in fiscal 1982 (see Table 5).

This spending approach marked a dramatic shift in federalism strategy from the Nixon and Ford administrations, which demonstrated

Table 4   Comparison of Reagan Budget Requests for F.Y. 1982 with
Actual F.Y. 1981 Expenditures on Comparable Programs
(Budget Authority, in Billions)

Program Category	F.Y. 1981 Expenditures	Reagan F.Y. 1982 Request	Percentage Change F.Y. 1981-F.Y. 1982
Total Block Grants	18.7	14.8	−21%
New block grant proposals/prior categorical spending	12.8	9.7	−24%
Existing block grants[a]	5.9	5.1	−14%
Total Federal Aid	105.8	86.2	−19%
Major Entitlements[b]	311.4	335.3	+8%
Total Domestic Spending[c]	511.2	546.1	+7%
National Defense	182.4	226.3	+24%
Total Federal Spending	718.4	772.4	+8%

[a] Not including public service employment programs.

[b] Including social security.

[c] Total federal spending minus defense and international affairs.

SOURCE: *Budget of the United States, Budget Appendix,* and *Special Analyses* for appropriate years.

a consistent willingness to accept higher spending levels for block grant programs as a means of enhancing political support for them in Congress. [5] As a result, much of the political debate about the Reagan block grant proposals focused on their budgetary features rather than on the merits or demerits of grant consolidation. Most liberals in Congress, and even many mayors and governors, viewed the block grant proposals mainly as a Trojan horse for cutting social program budgets. As former DNC executive director Eugene Eidenberg expressed it:

> The driving force behind the Administration's decisions about federalism is primarily a concern with the federal deficit. . . . At the bottom of the New Federalism is, I believe, the Administration's belief that the best way to cut spending is to eliminate the substantial support that the federal government currently provides for a variety of programs administered by state and local governments. [6]

Though significant, such political concerns about the budgetary impacts of the 1981 block grants were not sufficient to prevent their

Table 5 Comparison of Actual F.Y. 1982 Expenditures with
F.Y. 1981 Expenditures on Comparable Programs
(Budget Authority, in Billions)

Program Category	F.Y. 1981 Expenditures	F.Y. 1982 Expenditures	Percentage Change F.Y. 1981–F.Y. 1982
Total Block Grants	13.6	11.6	−15%
New block grants established/prior categorical programs	7.7	7.1	−8%
Existing block grants[a]	5.9	4.5	−24%
Total Federal Aid	105.8	91.9	−13%
Major Entitlements[b]	311.4	323.7	+4%
Total Domestic Spending[c]	511.2	545.9	+7%
National Defense	182.4	218.7	+20%
Total Federal Spending	718.4	779.9	+9%

[a] Not including public service employment programs.
[b] Including social security.
[c] Total federal spending minus defense and international affairs.
SOURCE: *Budget of the United States, Budget Appendix,* and *Special Analyses* for appropriate years.

enactment, principally because the normal patterns of block grant politics in Congress were temporarily overwhelmed by broader political and economic forces. Since that time, however, the Administration has made 23 additional proposals to expand existing block grants or to enact new ones. It succeeded only once, replacing the existing CETA [Comprehensive Employment Training Act] program with the *Job Training Partnership Act* in 1982. In most cases, the Administration advocated further budget reductions in connection with its new consolidation proposals, and rarely did it subsequently signal a willingness to sacrifice these budgetary goals in order to secure block grant enactments. The message to state and local governments remained consistent and clear: The President would continue to support the general goal of grant reform, but—in contrast to alternative objectives like national defense, tuition tax credits, and urban enterprise zones—he would not adjust his fiscal priorities to advance this cause.

A similar situation existed with respect to General Revenue Sharing (GRS). General Revenue Sharing was the crown jewel of Nixon's New Federalism and the single federal program most dear to state and local governments. President Reagan has not shared this affection, however, and holds a far more skeptical view of efforts to harness the federal tax apparatus to provide funds for state and local governments. Accordingly, the President on several occasions has proposed terminating or severely modifying the program or reducing its budget. In 1975 and again in 1982, Governor and later President Reagan advocated folding the GRS program into a broad package of federal program and revenue turnbacks to the states, while in late 1981 he proposed a 12% cut in GRS spending as part of a planned across-the-board reduction in federal domestic expenditures. [7]

Such proposals stirred great concern and significant lobbying by mayors and other local government officials anxious to maintain their favorite program. Their efforts succeeded in obtaining Administration agreement to retain the GRS program at existing funding levels when the program was renewed in 1983, but the Administration adamantly opposed increasing the program's funds—even to keep pace with inflation—or to reinstate funding to state governments cut from the program in 1980. Thus, the GRS program continued on uneasily, backed by a presidential commitment that, as one observer put it, "has always seemed lukewarm." [8]

Perhaps the sharpest conflict between the Administration's federalism and budget priorities occurred in the context of the President's 1982 Federalism initiative. Although the President's sweeping initiative served to underscore his extraordinary interest in intergovernmental reform, its ultimate failure to advance beyond discussions with state and local officials was due in large part to the President's unwillingness to make fiscal concessions sufficient to gain gubernatorial backing for the plan.

The structure of the Federalism initiative was complex, but in essence it had two parts: (1) a "swap" component in which the federal government would acquire full financial responsibility for the Medicaid program in exchange for state assumption of the AFDC [Aid to Families with Dependent Children] and Food Stamp programs; and (2) a "turnback" component in which the federal government would return to states full responsibility for approximately 40 federal programs, along with a variety of tax resources to pay for them. The Administration claimed that the ultimate fiscal tradeoffs between the federal government and the states would be neutral or even slightly beneficial to states, and it went to great lengths in the initial phases of its program to avoid economic winners and losers among the states. Nevertheless, this fiscal neutrality was premised on having Congress make a series of budget cuts in the affected programs prior to putting the federalism initiative into effect. Without such cuts, the Congressional Budget Office estimated that the turned back programs would cost $34 billion to continue, rather than the $30 billion estimated by the White House or the $28 billion provided for in the trustfund. [9] Similar budget cuts were anticipated in the AFDC and Food Stamp programs. Such actions tended to reinforce earlier perceptions that the New Federalism was mainly a vehicle for shifting budget cuts to the states, an interpretation seemingly supported by some officials' attempts—most notably David Stockman's—to utilize the Federalism package to help address the federal government's growing deficit problem. [10] As Rich Williamson, the President's assistant for intergovernmental affairs, later acknowledged, such attempts to use the Federalism initiative for short-term budgetary gains undercut political support for the proposal:

> In retrospect, the Administration could have taken steps that might have enhanced the prospects of reaching final agreement in sorting out. . . . First, and most importantly, we allowed ourselves as an administration to be trapped into an obsession over short-term budget considerations. The budget was allowed to dominate internal administration machinery and crowd out the Federalism initiative. [11]

Moreover, such actions heightened governors' concerns about the long-term fiscal and policy impacts of the federalism proposal. The Administration argued that, in the long run, states would benefit financially from the swap portion of the initiative because the federalized Medicaid program was growing much faster than AFDC and Food Stamps, which were slated for devolution. But many state officials worried that Medicaid benefits and eligibility in a nationalized program would be set so low that they would feel compelled to supplement the federal program in their states. Governors were equally concerned with establishing a viable benefit floor in the income maintenance programs. Although the Administration agreed in negotiations to retain federal funding for Food Stamps, it refused to decouple Food Stamp benefits from AFDC payments. As a result, states would confront a federal disincentive to establish higher AFDC allowances because such payments would reduce food stamp benefits to their citizens.

Despite these difficulties, negotiations on the Federalism initiative made substantial progress during early 1982, and some participants believed they came close to an agreement. [12] Agreement with the governors almost certainly could have been achieved if President Reagan had been willing to devote additional federal resources to ease their concerns, just as Nixon had done before him. This would not have guaranteed enactment by Congress, but such fiscal accommodation would have given the plan a fighting chance, securing strong gubernatorial support for the package and undercutting charges that the initiative was merely a cloak for further budget cuts. In the final analysis, however, the President was unwilling to make such adjustments for his federalism initiative. As Williamson observed, he simply could not bring himself to sacrifice his budgetary goals for the sake of federalism:

> As much as the president wanted to strike a deal with the governors, and walk in step with them to Capitol Hill, the philosophical gap proved to be too wide. To move state and local officials, the president needed a bigger carrot than in good faith he felt he could offer. [13]

Deregulation and the New Federalism

Deregulation, like federalism, has been a major policy focus of the Reagan Administration, and in many instances the two goals have tended to complement one another. Although significant regulatory reform initiatives were begun under Presidents Ford and Carter, this administration was the first to recognize and seek to reduce the distinctive regulatory burdens imposed on state and local governments over the past twenty years. The President's Task Force on Regulatory Relief, the new regulatory review procedures established in OMB [Office of Management and Budget], and individual departmental paperwork reduction efforts have all been employed at various times to help redress problems stemming from intergovernmental regulation.

Yet, as in the past, most deregulation efforts in the Reagan Administration continued to focus predominantly on government regulation of the private sector, and most responsible officials continued to frame regulatory issues almost exclusively in such terms. Moreover, it readily became apparent that deregulating the private sector can easily conflict with deregulating states and localities. When it comes to regulation, business generally prefers not only fewer requirements to more, but [also] uniformity to diversity. Yet states—like the federal government—have become increasingly active regulators in recent years in more and more policy areas—from consumer and environmental protection to occupational and product safety. Often such activity is built upon federal regulatory foundations, as in the case of environmental programs where states are required or strongly encouraged to enforce federal minimum regulatory standards but are permitted to supplement or exceed them. [14] In other cases, states have chosen to develop their own regulatory activities independently. In either case, private industry has sought repeatedly to have the federal government restrict state regulatory activities beyond minimum national standards or to preempt state regulatory authority in a given field entirely. As one business spokesman proclaimed, when it comes to regulation the "national interest cannot be subjected to the parochial interests of localities." [15]

Such concerns have not been ignored by the Reagan Administration. As increasing conflicts have arisen between deregulation and intergovernmental deference, the Administration has sided repeatedly with business interests. According to one recent study of proposed federal preemptions, for example, the Administration "supported moves to take regulatory powers from the states" in nine out of 12 cases studied. [16] Similarly, an analysis of Reagan Administration briefs to the Supreme Court concluded that:

> The Administration . . . does not hesitate to give states' rights a back seat. . . . In each instance [examined], the issue, broadly framed, concerned states' rights, and . . . the Administration argued that Federal regulation should prevail. . . . Cynics might suggest that . . . the Administration preference for big business is so strong that it will override conflicting concerns for federalism. [17]

Whatever the merits of this view, several cases involving transportation, energy, and product liability regulation illustrate the conflicts that have arisen in this area.

Product Liability

Reagan Administration support for national product liability legislation has been described as a case in which "result-oriented reformers [in the Administration] won out over those who would have adhered to . . . the [federalist] principles of the framers." [18] Historically, manufacturers' liability for injuries resulting from defective products has been governed by state laws. In recent years, however, mounting concern has been voiced by business spokesmen about the difficulties resulting from differing and often increasingly stringent state laws in this area, and many have called for preemptive federal legislation.

Backed by the Product Liability Alliance—a coalition of over 200 trade and business organizations—legislation to this effect was introduced in Congress in 1982 by Senator Robert Kasten (R-Wis.). The Kasten bill would supersede state product liability laws but, in order to avoid overloading already crowded federal court dockets, would retain state court jurisdiction to try liability cases and interpret federal law. Thus, in the words of one analyst, the bill "represents a new approach to centralization that borders on state conscription." [19]

Confronted with a difficult choice between the concerns of manufacturing interests and its own federalism proclivities, the Reagan Administration "agonized" for several months over whether to support national product liability legislation. Strongest support for endorsing national legislation came from Commerce Secretary Malcolm Baldrige and from regulatory reform advocates in the Administration. As one Administration supporter of preemption wrote, conflicting state liability laws have created "significant burdens on interstate commerce" and "tremendous uncertainty for manufacturers." [20] Others in the Administration, however, including Attorney General William French Smith and Labor Secretary Raymond Donovan, argued that such a position was hardly consistent with the President's recently announced federalism initiative. Moreover, opponents pointed to practical difficulties in the Kasten approach. For example, denying federal courts jurisdiction to resolve likely differences of statutory interpretation by 50 different state judicial systems was hardly a format designed to guarantee uniformity in the product liability domain. Nevertheless, when the issue was put to the President for resolution, "Reagan overrode the objections . . . that endorsement of federal legislation would run counter to the Administration's 'federalism' drive" and agreed to support the preemptive Kasten Bill. [21]

Two for the Road: Federal Regulation of Trucking and Drinking-Age Standards

In the last three years, two new and highly visible federal regulations have also been enacted in the transportation field with the support and encouragement of the Reagan Administration. Like several other pioneering intergovernmental regulations enacted in the 1960s and 1970s, both requirements threaten reductions in federal highway aid as levers to force state adoption of federal uniform standards on truck size and a minimum drinking age.

Preemption of varying state restrictions on truck length, width, and weight has long been a goal of the trucking industry, which has sought by this means to expand the use of highly efficient double trailer trucks. Although such trucks were permitted in most areas of the country by 1982, they were still prohibited by 14 states and the District of Columbia because of concerns about their safety and their destructive effects on highways. [22] Against a backdrop of concerns about crumbling infrastructure and deteriorating highway conditions, the Reagan Administration launched an initiative to alter this situation in May, 1982. To help fund additional highway renovation, Secretary of Transportation Drew Lewis proposed increasing the federal gasoline tax and raising truckers' fees, but he combined these new levies with provisions to establish higher, uniform truck size and weight requirements to appease truckers unhappy about the new rates. [23] Under this proposal, states that refused to comply with the new standards would lose Federal highway funds. Shortly after it was announced, however, the

President began to back away from the Lewis initiative, primarily because of his uneasiness with the sizable tax increases it contained but also because of opposition expressed by many truckers and several state governments. When the President again endorsed the need for new transportation revenues following the November 1982 elections, a lame-duck session of Congress enacted legislation along the lines of Lewis' proposal in the waning days of the 97th Congress. [24]

Having helped to write uniform truck standards into law, the Administration pushed preemption to its limits in its subsequent regulations. The Administration decided to permit the large new trucks not only on interstate highways but also on an additional 140,000 miles of primary and access highways—38,000 miles more than state highway departments had designated as suitable for large trucks. This action infuriated officials in many states, including some of those which had long permitted double trailer trucks on their major highways. In response to state criticism, the Federal Highway Administration eventually removed 17,000 miles of roads from its initial designation, but it added another 19,000 miles of highways to its list, and moved to quash outstanding lawsuits against its actions. [25]

In 1984, the Administration reversed an earlier position and, in the face of rapidly spreading popular pressure, endorsed a second major highway-related regulatory expansion. On July 17, 1984, President Reagan signed legislation designed to compel all states to adopt a minimum drinking age of 21 or face reductions by 1987 of 10% in Federal highway aid. Initially, the President had been reluctant to support such a heavy-handed approach to changing state drinking laws, preferring instead to continue an existing program of incentives for state actions against drunk driving. Indeed, stronger federal action on this issue appeared to be unnecessary, since 20 states had raised their drinking age since 1980 and only eight still permitted alcohol consumption at age 18. [26] Moreover, legislation in this area seemed firmly fixed within the sphere of state responsibilities—a tradition strongly reaffirmed by the wording of the 21st Amendment.

Yet, if raising the drinking age proved to be a popular cause in most state legislatures, it became almost irresistible in Congress. In the wake of emotional publicity and effective lobbying by families victimized by drunk drivers, strong support emerged in Congress for an immediate, uniform approach to the problem. Faced with the prospect that Congress might enact preemptive legislation despite his own misgivings about it, and urged to change his mind by Transportation Secretary Elizabeth Dole, the President reversed his position on June 13, 1984, and came out strongly for federal sanctions to enforce a national drinking age. [27] With this policy reversal, the legislation sailed through Congress and was signed by the President a month later. "The problem is bigger than the individual states," he proclaimed at the signing ceremony. "With the problem so clear-cut and the proven solution at hand, we have no misgiving about this judicious use of Federal power." [28]

Fueling Conflicts Over Energy

Two prominent controversies over energy policy illustrate the conflicts that have arisen when the Administration's goal of expanding domestic energy production has clashed with state environmental policies and concerns. In seeking to accelerate off-shore oil drilling and nuclear power production, the Reagan Administration has faced a series of lawsuits and Congressional action inspired by the affected states. In both cases, long-running disputes have ensued as deference to state concerns has been sacrificed to other policy objectives.

Both controversies began early in the Reagan Administration's term. Indeed, one of James Watt's first actions as Secretary of Interior was to open bidding on new off-shore oil and gas drilling leases. By this action, the Administration sought to rapidly expand domestic energy production, to reduce Federal restraints on oil and gas exploration, and to utilize the proceeds from stepped-up sales to diminish federal deficits. But Interior's February 1981 sale of leases off the California coast was quickly challenged by the state in federal court. State officials were concerned about environmental impacts from the sale and successfully challenged the federal government's lack of consultation as required by the *Coastal Zone Management Act of 1972* (CZMA).

Faced with this reversal in the courts but still determined to expand the sale of off-shore leases, the Administration undertook to rewrite the regulations. According to one report, officials from Interior—with the President's support—overcame objections by the Commerce Department to altering the regulations and played a major role in rewriting the rules, even though they were legally under Commerce's jurisdiction. [29] Critics charged that the resulting regulations "virtually eliminate[d] state participation in decisions concerning their coasts" and made "a mockery of Reagan's 'new federalism.' " [30]

Having laid the necessary legal groundwork, Secretary Watt subsequently announced a massive new leasing plan. Again ignoring state objections, the Administration proposed to make a billion additional acres available for gas and oil exploration—40 times more than all the acreage leased during the previous thirty years. Once again several of the affected states went to court in an attempt to block the long-term leasing plan. They also took their case to Congress where, over Administration opposition, they won legislative changes that for the first time gave coastal states a portion of the proceeds from federal off-shore lease sales. [31] Congress also limited the sale of leases off the coasts of several of the most severely affected states. [32]

A similar pattern of intergovernmental conflict emerged over Administration policies supporting the construction of nuclear power plants. In 1976, the state of California enacted a moratorium on the licensing of new nuclear power plants until an adequate method for disposing of long-term nuclear wastes has been developed. Two California utilities subsequently challenged the state's moratorium in federal court, arguing that state action in this field had been preempted by federal law. Having lost the decision in circuit court in 1982, the utilities appealed the decision to the Supreme Court. Their appeal was supported by the Reagan Administration, which asserted a broad interpretation of federal powers in this field and sought to overturn the moratorium as part of a broader policy of promoting nuclear power. [33] Despite the Administration's arguments, however, the Court upheld the ban as an expression of the states' historical function to regulate the economic activities of public utilities. [34]

Nationalizing Currents in Social Policy

Social policy historically has offered fertile terrain for intergovernmental conflict, and the Reagan Administration has not entirely escaped such frictions. Although most fields of social policy traditionally have come under state and local jurisdiction—thus permitting adaptations to the cultural and social diversity of the nation—issues that arise in this arena also tend to evoke fundamental principles and values. This linkage not only tends to make compromise difficult, it also creates strong temptations for policy advocates to seek a single national solution—a temptation that affects conservatives and liberals alike.

Both implicit and explicit tensions between its social policy and federal objectives have arisen in the Reagan Administration. Implicit conflicts have been most evident in education policy. President Reagan generally shares the view of many state and local advocates that the federal role in education has grown unnecessarily large and intrusive and that the federal government should focus its resources more carefully on areas of clear national responsibility, leaving most aspects of education to states and localities. Yet despite the recent flurry of state activity to reform and upgrade educational programs, the President has found it hard to resist using his office as a "bully pulpit" for advocating his own vision of educational reform, legitimizing in the process the basic concept of national strategies for educational improvement. Thus, the President has appointed and called attention to his own reform commission on education, has proposed and lobbied for the passage of tuition tax credit legislation, and, in a move that harkens back to the Sputnik era, has proposed new federal legislation for enhancing math and science instruction.

There have also been explicit conflicts between the Administration's social policies and its federalism objectives. Two cases illustrate the tensions in this arena: the Administration's efforts to mandate state-implemented workfare programs for welfare recipients and its attempt to regulate medical care for handicapped infants.

Many governors, economists, and welfare reformers have long urged that funding for the nation's income maintenance programs be nationalized, in order to promote greater equity and rationality in benefit levels. Ronald Reagan has never shared this view, believing instead that welfare programs should be shaped by community standards and carefully monitored by each locality. As he remarked in one 1975 speech: "If there is one area of social policy that should be at the most local level of government possible, it is welfare. It should not be nationalized—it should be localized." [35]

Yet the President also believes that the current welfare system should be trimmed back and that anyone who is able to work should be required to do so. Hence, his administration has sought repeatedly to require that states establish "workfare" programs for able-bodied welfare recipients. It helped get workfare provisions covering AFDC and Food Stamps written into law in 1981, at which time Congress authorized—but did not require—state utilization of three workfare approaches: Community service in compensation for welfare (favored by the Administration), employment supplementation through wage subsidies, and jobs training and services through the existing work incentive program. [36] Since that time, various states have experimented with all three, usually on a small scale, in order to evaluate their costs and effectiveness.

Dissatisfied with the limited progress being made, the Administration has attempted to force faster state action in this area. In an attempt to make the community service approach mandatory, it sought to require that states involve 75% of eligible AFDC and Food Stamps recipients in such programs or face fiscal sanctions for inadequate compliance. To date, however, the states have successfully resisted the imposition of such mandates. Concerned that workfare programs may significantly raise administrative and social service costs and provide few long-term benefits for recipients, they have sought to retain the flexibility necessary to experiment with and refine alternative approaches.

Another case of social policy prescription involved Administration efforts to promulgate new and intrusive regulations governing medical care to handicapped infants. Ironically, the Administration has been supportive of efforts to moderate costly regulations mandating handicapped access to local mass transportation systems. But under pressure from right-to-life groups and on the heels of a highly publicized "baby doe" case, the Administration issued interim rules on March 7, 1983, requiring all public and private hospitals receiving federal funds to prominently post information about a federal hotline for reporting suspected cases of discrimination in medical care and to permit federal investigators 24-hour access to hospital records. Failure to comply with these regulations would make hospital personnel liable for lawsuits with civil and criminal penalties and could result in funding cutoffs to the hospital. [37] These rules were promptly attacked by hospital and medical groups as unnecessary and intrusive, and the groups succeeded in blocking the new rules in federal court. Several months later, however, Administration lawyers went to court in an unsuccessful attempt to obtain the records of a severely handicapped baby who was not given surgery in a state university hospital in New York. [38] In 1984, however, modified regulations dealing with this problem were issued after extensive consultations with the medical community.

Policy Dilemmas and the Future of Federalism

In all ten cases examined in this paper, the Reagan Administration has been confronted with difficult policy decisions. Forced to choose between policies supportive of its federalist objectives—devolution, enhanced state autonomy, and balanced intergovernmental relationships—and those supportive of other presidential priorities—reducing federal domestic spending, easing regulatory burdens on the private sector, and pursuing conservative social policy objectives—the Administration chose, in each case examined here, a course that was openly or implicitly contrary to its stated intergovernmental goals.

Some of these decisions were reached reluctantly. Some may have been products of bureaucratic momentum or political compromise rather than the products of a calculated strategy. Others can be defended on their merits. Moreover, there have been certain cases that have gone the other way. In 1983, the Department of Transportation declined to preempt local airport noise restrictions despite calls for uniformity from the airline industry. [39] Although it ultimately relented, the Administration long resisted legislative efforts to preempt state pesticide regulations. And, in his federalism package, the President did agree to nationalize funding of the costly Medicaid program in his effort to achieve a comprehensive sorting out of intergovernmental roles. Nonetheless, when the truly difficult decisions were on the line, the overall thrust of policy by this administration seemed to bear little resemblance to the President's rhetoric on intergovernmental reform.

This pattern of policy making has important implications for understanding the current political status and future prospects of federalism in America. The point is not that Ronald Reagan is less supportive of strengthening federalism than other recent presidents have been. On balance, he has probably been more committed to this end. Nevertheless, President Reagan resembles his more liberal predecessors—perhaps more than either would care to admit—by his willingness to sacrifice federalism whenever it conflicts with his other deeply held policy objectives. With his administration as with others, when opportunities arise to use preemptive national action to advance desired policy goals, the temptation to do so has proven too great to resist. As former Nixon economic aide Herbert Stein has written, "Even conservative governments when in office do not want to limit their own powers." [40]

This tendency appears to be wholly consistent with popular attitudes toward intergovernmental activism. Most Americans continue to pay lip service to the ideals of federalism and decentralization, but they, like the politicians who represent them, appear to be generally unwilling to sacrifice specific policy goals to pursue this ideal. The situation is not unlike the philosophical contradiction in public attitudes discovered by Lloyd Free and Hadley Cantril in 1968. They found that in terms of abstract political values, a majority of Americans could be classified as political conservatives, voicing support for the Jeffersonian ideals of small, decentralized government and reduced public interference in the private sector and in the lives of individuals. Yet, when asked to focus on a series of specific issues of public policy, a substantial majority of the populace could be considered "operational liberals" who favored increased federal government involvement in nearly every aspect of the welfare state. [41]

In a similar way, it appears that virtually no one today—from the public at large to the public interest groups—believes that maintaining the integrity of the federal system is sufficiently important to justify sacrificing other important values to do so. This, of course, does not mean that federalism is irrelevant. Politicians and interest groups continue to use federalist arguments for tactical purposes, as a vehicle to pursue other policy ends, but fewer and fewer people view federalism as a worthwhile end in itself. Although this may be understandable, it is very different from the intellectual and emotional commitment commonly invested in other aspects of the Constitution. There are many passionate defenders of absolute adherence to the guarantees of free speech or to prohibitions on search and seizure, for example, who are willing to endure the dissemination of offensive or unpopular publications or to accept less effective law enforcement to pursue these larger goals. Once common, such tradeoffs on behalf of federalism are now increasingly rare.

Ultimately, this tendency may represent the most fundamental challenge to the federal system. It gives rise, not to a wholesale onslaught on the system or to a wellspring of support for a unitary system, but to a subtle process of erosion that eventually leaves an archaic, sterile structure bound together only by a web of mundane administrative relationships. As Laurence Tribe expressed it:

> No one expects Congress to obliterate the states, at least in one fell swoop. If there is any danger, it lies in the tyranny of small decisions—in the prospect that Congress will nibble away at state sovereignty, bit by bit, until someday essentially nothing remains but a gutted shell. [42]

Perhaps, given advances in communications, world economic integration and greater social homogeneity, this is what the public ultimately prefers. The United States can surely survive without a strong federal system just as many other countries do. But considering the prominent role that federalism was intended to play in our system of government, we ought not allow ourselves to simply slip quietly into a quasi-unitary form of government. We ought to carefully evaluate federalism's real and potential contributions to our political life and weigh the gains and losses resulting from its quiet diminution. We just might find that there is something worth an occasional sacrifice after all.

Notes

1. "First Phase in Revitalizing Federalism," *Alabama Municipal Journal*, September 1981, p. 4
2. Richard S. Williamson, "The Self-Government Balancing Act: A View from the White House," *National Civic Review* 71 (January 1982): 19.
3. ACIR, *Significant Features of Fiscal Federalism* (Washington, D.C.: Government Printing Office, 1984), pp. 11, 120.
4. Presidential Task Force on Regulatory Relief, *Reagan Administration Achievements in Regulatory Relief for State and Local Government: A Progress Report* (Washington, D.C.: Presidential Task Force on Regulatory Relief, August 1982), p. i.
5. See Timothy J. Conlan, "Back in Vogue: The Politics of Block Grant Legislation," *Intergovernmental Perspective* 7 (Spring 1981): 11, 12.
6. Eugene Eidenberg, "Federalism: A Democratic View," *American Federalism: A New Partnership for the Republic*, ed. Robert B.

Hawkins, Jr. (San Francisco: Institute for Contemporary Studies, 1982), p. 112.

7. For more details on these proposals, see David R. Beam, "New Federalism, Old Realities: The Reagan Administration and Intergovernmental Reform," Paper prepared for the Urban Institute Conference on Governance: The Reagan Era and Beyond, Washington, D.C., 15-16 December 1983.

8. Ibid., p. 30.

9. Timothy J. Conlan and David B. Walker, "Reagan's New Federalism: Design, Debate and Discord," *Intergovernmental Perspective* 8 (Winter 1983): 9.

10. For more on this, see Laurence I. Barrett, *Gambling with History* (Garden City, N.Y.: Doubleday, 1983), pp. 342-343.

11. Richard S. Williamson, "The 1982 New Federalism Negotiations," *Publius* 13 (Spring 1983): 31.

12. "New Federalism: A Special Story," *Governors' Priorities: 1983* (Washington, D.C.: National Governors' Association, 1983), p. 39.

13. Williamson, "The 1982 New Federalism Negotiations," p. 26.

14. For more details about such "partial preemption" programs, see ACIR, *Regulatory Federalism: Policy, Process, Impact, and Reform,* A-95 (Washington, D.C.: Government Printing Office, 1984).

15. Quoted in Daniel Gottlieb, "Business Mobilizes as States Begin to Move into the Regulatory Vacuum," *National Journal,* 31 July 1982, p. 1342.

16. Felicity Barringer, "U.S. Preemption: Muscling In on the States," *Washington Post,* 25 October 1982, p. A11.

17. Alan B. Morrison, "N*w Fed*ral*sm Holes," *New York Times,* 20 September 1982, p. A15.

18. Alfred R. Light, "Federalism, *FERC v. Mississippi,* and Product Liability Reform," *Publius* 13 (Spring 1983): 85.

19. Ibid., p. 96.

20. C. Boyden Gray, "Regulation and Federalism," *Yale Journal on Regulation* 1 (1983): 96, 97.

21. Caroline Mayer, "Product Liability Dispute Is Settled," *Washington Post,* 16 July 1982, p. D3.

22. Tom Wicker, "Welcome, Killer Trucks," *New York Times,* 1 November 1982, p. E14.

23. Ernest Holsendolph, "Lewis Offers Plan on Trucks as Exchange for a Tax Rise," *New York Times,* 5 May 1982, p. A20.

24. *1982 Congressional Quarterly Almanac* (Washington: Congressional Quarterly, 1983), p. 317.

25. Barbara Harsha, "DOT Sets Final Routes for Large Trucks," *Nation's Cities Weekly,* 18 June 1984, p. 2.

26. Steven Weisman, "Reagan Signs Bill Tying Aid to Drinking Age," *New York Times,* 18 July 1984, p. A15.

27. Douglas Feaver, "Reagan Now Wants 21 as Drinking Age," *Washington Post,* 14 June 1984, p. A1.

28. Weisman, "Reagan Signs Bill," p. A1.
29. Michael Lerner, "Coastal Mismanagement," *The New Republic*, 14 October 1981, p. 14.
30. Ibid., p. 12.
31. *1982 Congressional Quarterly Almanac*, p. 448.
32. *1983 Congressional Quarterly Almanac*, p. 462.
33. Morrison, "N*w Fed*ral*sm Holes," p. A15.
34. *Pacific Gas and Electric Co. v. State Energy Resources Conservation and Development Commission*, 51 LW 4449.
35. Ronald Reagan, "Conservative Blueprint for the 1970s," reprinted in *Congressional Record*, 94th Cong., 1st Sess., 1975, p. 31186.
36. Linda Demkovich, "The Workfare Ethic," *National Journal*, 26 February 1983, p. 453.
37. *Federal Register* 48 (March 7, 1983), p. 9630.
38. Felicity Barringer, "Decision to Pursue Baby Doe Case Born in Confusion at HHS," *Washington Post*, 13 December 1983, p. A19.
39. Randy Arndt, "DOT Sees Airport Noise as State, Local Problem," *Nation's Cities Weekly*, 4 April 1983, p. 4.
40. Herbert Stein, "The Reagan Revolt That Wasn't," *Harper's*, February 1984, p. 48. Similarly, William Barnes has argued that: "If the conservatives in Washington choose to govern, I think they will govern on behalf of their constituencies rather than on behalf of an abstract idea [of deregulation] or technical efficiency. I expect then ... that intergovernmental mandates will continue to sprout apace." See William Barnes, "Cities and Their Regulatory Milieu," Paper prepared for the 1982 Annual Meeting of the American Political Science Association, Denver, 3 September 1982, p. 22.
41. Lloyd Free and Hadley Cantril, *The Political Beliefs of Americans* (New York: Simon & Schuster, 1968).
42. Laurence Tribe, *American Constitutional Law* (Mineola, N.Y.: The Foundation Press, 1978), p. 302.

36. REINVENTING FEDERALISM: STATE-LOCAL GOVERNMENT ROLES IN THE NEW ECONOMIC ORDER

David R. Beam

It is the premise of this [essay] ... that federalism must be defended on grounds related to contemporary needs if it is to be defended successfully. Further, it is the argument of this paper that federalism *can and is* improving the nation's response to its most important challenge: that of strengthening its competitiveness in a now-global economy. To champion federalism, then, is to support a system of government which, whatever its historical origins and merits, appears well-suited for the key tasks that face the U.S. into the 21st century and beyond.

The Changing Agenda

Among the variety of factors that led federalism to be discarded as an American ideal, if not wholly in practice, two deserve special emphasis. First, ever since the Civil War the cause of "states' rights" has been identified with the social injustice of slavery.... Second, and more decisively, federalism was seen as associated with the values of a preindustrial society. Since the Great Depression, the national government, not the states, has been identified with improved economic conditions for most citizens. . . .

Yet times change. When the 1960s ended, economists were confident that the key task of assuring prosperity had been addressed and understood. The cycle of recession and recovery was declared obsolete in the face of the nation's continuous economic expansion since early in the decade.[1] The federal government, it was widely believed, possessed the expertise and tools needed to keep the nation's economic house in order.

This confidence was badly shaken quite shortly thereafter, however. Economically, the 1970s were a decade of drab and gray, marked by slowdowns in income and productivity growth.

A more extensive version of this paper was initially presented at the 1988 Annual Meeting of the American Political Science Association, Washington, D.C., September 1-4, 1988. Reprinted by permission of the American Political Science Association.

The period since the late 1970s is best understood as an effort by politicians, economists, and other analysts to identify the causes of these slowdowns and to devise an appropriate solution. With the unwinding of the Keynesian consensus that had been declared only a few years earlier, two major philosophies—each grounded to a considerable degree in the thought of prior decades—competed as potential foundations for national policy. On the one hand (the right), "supply-siders" argued that growth can be generated by freeing entrepreneurs from the oppressive burdens of government—especially the burdens of high marginal personal income tax rates, but economic and social regulation as well. Though often regarded as something "new," this supply-side posture is in fact rooted in the free market, tax-cut philosophy of Andrew Mellon, secretary of treasury throughout most of the 1920s.

During the Reagan years, this side won politically, though rising deficits during the interim period have now largely discredited what was always a "fringe" school of economic analysis. On the other hand (the left) were the political "losers": advocates of an overt industrial policy. In the early 1980s there were numerous proposals for New Deal-like planning and coordinating bodies, among them a National Industrial Development Board, a National Industrial Development Bank, a National Economic Cooperation Council, or a new Department of Trade and Industry. Yet, though they stirred much interest at the time, calls for such industrial policy mechanisms were grounded by fears that the American national government could not be trusted to make critical decisions about the prospects for different firms, industries, and regions. . . .

In the face of such criticisms, calls for a national industrial policy faded away. What remained was an agreement, from both ends of the political spectrum, that some new initiatives to stimulate productivity and improve competitiveness were essential. What was in doubt was their nature.

The States Respond

In sharp contrast—and quite astonishingly, given the historical record—has been the panoply of economic-development initiatives launched at the state and local levels over the past decade. States reacted to the pressures of stagnation and unemployment, the slowdown in federal aid growth after 1978, and the need to hold down taxes following the "Proposition 13" tax revolt by actively striving to improve the economic circumstances of their citizenry as well as their own revenue base. As David Osborne comments:

> While the Reagan administration was denouncing government intervention in the marketplace, governors of both political parties

were embracing an unprecedented role as economic activists. Over the past decade, they have created well over 100 public investment funds, to make loans to and investments in businesses. Half the states have set up public venture capital funds; others have invested public money in the creation of private financial institutions. At least 40 states have created programs to stimulate technological innovation, which now number at least 200.... Tripartite business-labor-government boards have sprung up, often with the purpose of financing local committees dedicated to restructuring labor-management relations. A few states have even launched cooperative efforts with management and labor to revitalize regional industries.[2]

Motivated by a spirit of pragmatic activism, unschooled in any existing ideology, governors and legislators as well as mayors of all political stripes brought the issue of economic development to center stage, where it influenced nearly every aspect of public operations. Like tabulations and catalogs of new state economic development initiatives, an analysis of gubernatorial "state of the state" addresses confirms that economic development has risen high on the agenda for action. In 1973 not a single governor mentioned economic development concerns in his or her message, but 43 percent did so in 1981.[3] If "what does it do for the poor?" had been the key issue of federal policy in the 1960s, "what does it do for development?" became the touchstone of state policy in the 1980s.

Thus it was state and local governments, but the states in particular, which took the lead in attempting to devise an American competitiveness policy, and not the national government....

This leadership in economic development was only part of a broader "resurgence of the states" demonstrated in a host of policy fields.[4] Beginning in the early 1980s, states began to gain recognition as "laboratories of democracy," as they had during the Progressive era. In doing so, they took advantage of greatly improved administrative and legislative machinery, as well as popular support for experimental initiatives and a new generation of political leadership.[5] As Ann O'M. Bowman and Richard C. Kearney observe, the states once again could be viewed as "responsive, responsible, and progressive political actors within the scheme of U.S. federalism and intergovernmental relations." They had "experienced a revitalization ... [making them] key elements in the American democratic system of the 1980s and beyond." [6]

Yet, although states moved into the forefront in addressing such diverse problems as corporate takeovers (Indiana), universal health insurance (Massachusetts), surrogate births and tuition prepurchase (Michigan), acid rain (Minnesota, New York, and Wisconsin), car-owner "lemon laws" (California and Connecticut), and dozens of other areas, many of the most notable actions have been in areas directly or indirectly related to the economic well-being of their citizens. For example, it was such southern states as Tennessee, Mississippi, Florida, Virginia, and North Carolina that initiated the nationwide wave of educational reform measures in 1982-84. Their governors had become convinced that their states' economic futures depended on improving levels of academic achievement and school performance.[7] The movement they launched took hold nationwide, and by July 1984 more than 250 state task forces on education were in operation and thousands of legislative initiatives had been introduced and adopted.

The movement for economic improvement has even pushed states and localities to play new diplomatic roles. In 1981 Connecticut's William O'Neill became the first governor to lead a trade mission to Europe, symbolizing . . . the new level of state concern.[8] Such efforts are now quite routine. Nearly all states are attempting to expand overseas markets for their firms, as well as to attract foreign investment. Mayors, too, have viewed expanded trade and investment as ways of increasing jobs for their citizens.[9] And the growing state awareness of the international context of all economic issues has led the National Governors' Association to press for improved instruction in foreign languages and geography at the elementary and secondary level.[10]

All in all, the new surge of economic development activity has been far-reaching enough to alter conceptions of the job of the state and local executives. Governor Jim Thompson of Illinois recalls that

> When I began this job 12 years ago, the governor was essentially a chief operating officer, simply managing the flow of state funds and running the government. But that's all changed. Now governors have become the economic salesmen for their states. We spend most of our time these days not green-eyeshading the departments of the state, but rather representing the economic interests of the state by helping to provide a good business climate and pushing [a state's] goods and services around the world.[11] . . .

From Destructive to Constructive Competition

. . . Mainstream practitioners of [political science and economics] act as if there is little state and local governments can or should do to alter their own economic fate. To the extent that the nation's economic competitiveness is subject to public influence, the levers are thought to be placed in Washington.

Although it is recognized that the states and localities have long attempted to improve their economic status, the manner in which they tried to do so is frequently deplored. Well-established approaches to industrial recruitment, which typically involved the provision of tax or other financial lures to attract firms from other states, may be viewed as a zero-sum game in which jurisdictions simply steal jobs and tax resources from one another.[12] . . .

Indeed, the results of such interjurisdictional rivalries can be worse than "zero sum" because the strategies used for industrial recruitment can impose costs on other elements of the community. If jurisdictions sacrifice needed tax revenues and thus the quality of public services, or allow the deterioration of air and water quality and other aspects of the environment, the long-run damage may be substantial. Perhaps it is fortunate, then, that most evidence suggests that such efforts have limited success in achieving their desired aim. Taxes, in particular, are a minor cost of doing business and both tax levels and special tax concessions exert minimal influence on industrial location, at least beyond the metropolitan level.[13] Indeed, if the factors included in traditional "business climate" ratings were major contributors to a state's economic well-being, then the two Dakotas and Nebraska—the top three in one prominent study—would be the nation's manufacturing powerhouses.[14]

However, these practices, and the allegations that followed them, reflected the economic character of earlier times. In an economy based on manufacturing and mass production, lower costs appeared to be the key to industrial expansion. As a consequence, state and local governments traditionally competed largely by initiatives aimed at reducing business costs.

Since the mid 1970s, in contrast, the most rapidly expanding sectors of the economy have been service, technology-based, and information-based companies. Furthermore, it now is smaller firms, and not the Fortune 500, that are responsible [for] most of the net job growth in the economy.[15] Economic advances in a particular locale now seem to depend chiefly on increasing the level of economic innovation and the "birth rate" of new companies.[16]

In response to these new economic patterns, many state and local governments have been shifting their emphasis from *industrial relocation* to *job generation*. As economic geographer Edward J. Malecki has observed, "Encouraging and nurturing new companies bears more fruit than trying to lure firms from elsewhere." [17] States and localities are learning to compete, not by robbing Peter on Paul's behalf, but by assisting entrepreneurial development and creating the foundation for innovations in product and production technology.

The factors associated with the creation and expansion of new businesses, particularly high-technology and service firms, are quite different from those associated with the siting of branch manufacturing facilities. In many advanced industries, company location follows residential preference—plants will be generated (or move to) areas where their "mindworkers" find it desirable to live, work, and play. . . .

Other analyses concur that simply holding down taxes (and, consequently, public services) is not wise policy. The "new consensus" among locational economists is that, while high tax rates can have a negative effect on growth if considered in isolation, "government expenditures have the potential to more than offset the negative impact of taxes. Infrastructure expenses such as education and transportation encourage economic development and should be considered along with taxes as an important element of economic development strategy." [18]

These lessons have been taken very much to heart. "We've been selling the wrong things," says former Mississippi governor William F. Winter, who led that state's educational reform drive in 1982. "This is what we were selling in Mississippi: cheap labor, cheap land, and low taxes. And we got exactly what we paid for." [19] The new southern strategy, he says,

> is not going to be based on attracting external businesses. It's going to be based on building a climate where we keep intellectually creative people at home. And out of that intellectual creativity [we can] develop new businesses and resulting jobs. . . . Now, these are not going to be the 400-, 600-, 800-employee plant that we used to stand in front of a television camera and proudly announce was going to McComb, Mississippi. The new businesses are going to start with five, six, eight, ten people, maybe in a storefront operation, or some little prefab building out somewhere. The point is, this is where most of the new jobs in this country are being created. [20]

Furthermore, the new orientation toward economic development is not incompatible with environmental improvements and other stringent regulatory policies. States with good records in job creation, like Massachusetts and California, also top the list in establishing and enforcing environmental programs, according to resource conservation groups. [21] Indeed, many state governments have stepped into the breach left by the federal deregulatory policies, with the result that business has encouraged national laws preempting tougher state policies in such areas as product liability, pesticide regulation, nuclear power evacuation processes, and other fields. At the same time, consumer groups, labor activists, and environmentalists find that they now often get a warmer reception in state capitals than in Washington. [22]

Thus, it appears that instead of a "race to the bottom," the new economic competition among the states is leading to upward pressure on educational standards and other public services, while moderating taxes and encouraging greater efficiency in their production. In Mississippi, which has ranked close to fiftieth on many social indicators, Governor Ray Mabus ran on a reform platform with the slogan "We may not be first, but we'll never be last again!" [23] Such efforts, of course, are of general benefit. As Malecki observes:

> Everyone wins when towns deemphasize the traditional lures of low taxes, low wages, and limited unionization and instead improve their airport facilities, schools, research infrastructure, local entrepreneurship, quality of life, and training for technical workers.[24]

Furthermore, the kinds of economic development strategies being pursued by many states and communities should be generative, rather than merely competitive, from the standpoint of the nation as a whole. Strong, more efficient local markets aggregate to a better economy overall. . . .

Federalism's Economic Virtue

To encapsulate the foregoing argument, it appears that state and local governments, under conditions of fiscal stringency and international economic competition, are engaging in development activities that are likely to benefit both their own citizens and jurisdictions and the nation as a whole. Much more than the national government, they are seeking to nurture the growth and development of new firms and enhance the competitive capacity of the business sector.

Observation of the vitality and diversity of these state and local responses to the difficulties indicated by America's declining competitiveness suggests that, at least in the late twentieth century, federalism is a source of strength, rather than a weakness, as it has often been viewed since the New Deal. Indeed, both observation and strands of theory drawn from the studies of economic development and other pertinent fields suggest the hypothesis that

Under conditions of global competition and rapid technological change, a large nation composed of multiple political and economic centers, each striving to secure its own economic advantage, will be better able to advance the welfare of its citizens than a large nation dominated by a single political and economic center.

Substantiating this proposition is, of course, no easy task. Yet the argument is inherently attractive from two general standpoints. First, from the broad perspective of organizational analysis, it is true that innovation in general is best advanced by networks of small units. New ideas usually develop "bottom up," not "top down"; organizational centralization and formalization have been found to be negatively correlated with innovativeness.[25] Consequently, not large but small companies seem to be the main source of economic innovations, and large corporations often attempt to decentralize their structures and relax formal controls in order to increase levels of "intrapreneurship."

Second, the trend toward the "internationalization" of the economy is proceeding so rapidly that there is reason to believe that the importance of the nation-state itself is being diluted. Once it could be said that city, county, and state boundaries were economically artificial; the same claim is now made concerning our largest jurisdictions. Thus, urban analyst Jane Jacobs has noted that

> Nations are political and military entities, and so are blocs of nations. But it doesn't necessarily follow from this that nations are also the salient entities of economic life. . . . indeed, the failures of national government to force economic life to do their bidding suggests that nations are essentially irrelevant to promoting economic success. . . . Most nations are grab bags of very different economies, of rich regions and poor ones.[26]

Furthermore, state governments (and their local subdivisions) would appear to possess . . . several inherent advantages for the task of fostering economic growth. It must, of course, be recognized that the major responsibility for America's economic improvement rests in private hands. Complacency and poor management, including an inability to make effective use of changing technology and human resources, contributed to the nation's relative economic decline; only improvements in these areas of business performance are likely to reverse the trend. Given this reality, however, it is the states and localities, not the national government, that are best positioned to provide meaningful assistance to entrepreneurs and managers.

1. First, *State and local governments are more responsive to economic changes in particular firms, industries, and regions than is the national government.* Discussions of federalism often include arguments over which level of government is "closer to the people," the state or national. Partisans of the states point to the smaller geographic distance; those of the national comment on the higher levels of media coverage, citizen awareness, and voter turnout. There can be no argument, however, about which is "closer to the factories" and workers. As DeWitt John comments,

> In a country as diverse as the United States, it takes a long time to achieve coherent national policies. . . A system of fifty state-designed policies is inherently more flexible, more able to take advantage of new opportunities and accommodate to new economic

conditions. As states compete for economic growth, they constantly scan the economy for new opportunities that can be turned to their advantage. This competition will ensure that public policies for economic development are responsive to changing conditions.[27]

2. *State and local governments have control over key factors influencing job generation.* Historically, these include physical infrastructure, transportation, employment exchange, land-use control, environmental protection, natural resources, and many types of regulation.[28] Now the main emphasis should be placed on state primacy for education and training. . . .

3. *Successful economic development depends on interactions that can only occur on a regional scale.* Economic development is a product, not only of the presence of certain key ingredients, but also of the process of interaction among them. Beneficial cooperative and competitive relationships between private firms, as well as with public-sector institutions, are much more feasible in geographically confined areas. . . . Appropriate coordination of relevant public services is difficult to contemplate except at the state or local level. Piore and Sabel argue that America may best make its way through what they term the "second industrial divide" by encouraging the kind of craft-based industrial districts like those that fostered the original industrial revolution. Such areas, of which both Silicon Valley and Boston may be considered contemporary high-tech examples, foster "flexible specialization" that offers agglomeration economies without the rigidity of standardized mass production. Thus, they conclude that

> Successful industrial reorganization in the United States will require reinvigoration of local and regional government—not its supersession in favor of an expansion of corporate autonomy. Industrial policy will have to be regional policy: to be effective, the coordination of training programs, industrial research, transportation networks, credit, marketing information, environmental protection, and the other elements of the infrastructure will have to be done on a regional level.[29]

4. *Growth policies must be developed to fit the unique conditions and circumstances of each particular area.* There is no single, easily and universally applicable formula for encouraging economic development. One of the lessons gained by examining the economic advances of Silicon Valley and the Boston area is that their own successes are unlikely to be simply duplicated elsewhere. . . . Effective strategies therefore must be tailor-made; they cannot be simply applied. This requires a decentralized policy development and administrative structure. As a consequence,

States have a comparative advantage over the federal government with respect to activities that are diverse, decentralized, and
characterized by the need for experimentation. When public
policies seek to promote innovation, the presumption should lie
with state and local action instead of with federal action.[30]

5. *The development of political support for economic competitiveness policies is more feasible on a regional than national basis.*
This seems to be true whether the issue is viewed from the public or
private side of the table. Though it is too much to brand developmental politics as "consensual," as has sometimes been done, observation confirms what Paul Peterson deduced, that the goal of economic
growth has broad appeal when pursued at the community level. As he
writes, "Cities seek to improve their market position, their attrac-
tiveness as a locale for economic activity." [31] Indeed, this drive
is so strong that such goals have been embraced even by minority
mayors (like Denver's Federico Peña and Detroit's Coleman Young)
whose election owed little to support from traditional business
interests. . . .

Just as public officials feel bound to business, more business
leaders are coming to recognize that the long-run well-being of the
firms that they head depends on the quality of the labor force and of
state and community services. Thus, it is at the state and local level that
the traditional schism in American society between governmental and
private-sector action seems most likely to be mended. Many productive
initiatives have resulted, especially in the area of education. With a
high-school dropout rate of 30 percent, corporate America feels it is
getting a poor return on its tax investment in schools, according to
Fortune magazine, and "is ready, finally, to take action. Threatened
with a severe shortage of talent, corporate America is becoming a
powerful new supporter of reform in the public schools." [32]

Conclusion

The proper relationship of the states to the nation, Woodrow
Wilson wrote, is the "cardinal question" of the American constitutional
system. Furthermore, he added, it cannot be resolved for all time by any
one generation because "every new successive stage of our political and
economic development gives it a new aspect, makes it a new question." [33]

If the foregoing analysis is correct, Wilson's assessment still has
merit, for the recent resurgence of the states seems to be rooted in the
need to strengthen America's economic competitiveness that is the
principal concern and major challenge confronting this generation of

leaders and citizens. Thus viewed, the recent blossoming of state initiatives should not be interpreted as simply a reaction to aid cutbacks in Washington or part of a cyclical swing from domestic activism to passiveness at the national level.[34] Rather, it results from a refocusing of the political agenda on economic development issues that these governments are, by inclination and capacity, better positioned to address than the national government in Washington. This new agenda—along with stronger state institutions and political leadership, and coupled with greater recognition of the administrative dilemmas of many earlier federally initiated programs—has encouraged state and local efforts to become the focal point of America's competitiveness strategy.

There's no reason to doubt that the national government was and remains the right one to look toward for the expansion of redistributive programs. Standard economic theory, contemporary political analyses, the views of past presidents from both parties, and those of state and local officials confirm that state and local governments are poorly suited to develop and finance such income-support programs. At least in principle, too, the national government alone possesses the jurisdictional authority to devise regulatory policies on many issues of moment for the entire national economy. Initially, these concerned transportation, banking, and communications, but they later came to embrace a variety of health, environmental, safety, and nondiscrimination concerns as well.

At this point in history, however, economic redistribution has necessarily become a subordinate concern, one among several, rather than the overriding national goal. This is certainly not because problems of poverty have been solved: indeed, as Sen. Daniel Patrick Moynihan comments, "In the War on Poverty, Poverty Won." [35] . . . Further, it is clear that locally generated economic revitalization is not a sufficient solution to the problem of poverty, as is indicated by the persistence of hardship in even the most booming metropolises and states. At the same time, the recent historical record suggests that, without general prosperity, neither potential job opportunities for the poor, nor the financial resources and political will required to support assistance programs, will be forthcoming. Thus, from every political and social perspective, developmental rather than redistributive objectives now seem to be paramount.

What seems dubious, however, is the widespread supposition that command of a campaign for increased industrial competitiveness need be entrusted chiefly, or even largely, to federal captains. It is unlikely that the national government possesses, or can develop, either the economic capability or the political capacity needed to devise effective strategies for America's economic revitalization. Neither the creation of a "national industrial policy" aimed at "sunrise" or "sunset" industries, nor the "hands off" free-market policies of Reaganomics visited on the nation during the 1980s, seem to hold the key for improving the nation's economic well-being.

Certainly, Washington has a role to play; that is well understood. But given the primacy of developmental concerns, the states and localities both can and should be recognized as more vital partners in the economic arena. At the very least, these governments will be the test-beds for policies that may be considered and adopted by later federal administrations. What seems more probable, however, is that an American industrial policy must, given the very nature of the problem addressed, be plural in character: the amalgam of policies pursued by 50 different states and their cities, developed to address local problems in concert with business, workers, and citizens, and institutions in each region. . . .

Indeed, if federalism did not now exist, it might have to be reinvented. One notes with some interest the shift in Japan from its earlier reliance on a centrally coordinated economic policy to the decentralized "technopolis" strategy being pursued to assure its innovative leadership into the twenty-first century. Observing this change in our foremost Asian competitor, Sheridan Tatsuno has concluded that

> Regional high-tech strategies, not new national industrial policies, may be our best solution. . . . A single, unified, national industrial strategy may not be possible or desirable. Despite years of debate over national industrial policies, we are as far away from a consensus as ever. Our primary advantage as a nation lies in our regional, corporate, and cultural diversity. We should not put all our eggs in one basket, but promote a variety of industrial strategies. . . . We should encourage companies to work with state and local governments in developing their own tailored responses to the Japanese challenge.[36]

Such recognition and acceptance of inherent state and local governmental primacy in improving America's economic competitiveness also would be consistent with the stated intent of the founders. Madison, it may be recalled, wrote in support of the proposed Constitution that "the powers delegated . . . to the federal government are few and defined." In contrast, he added, those reserved to the states extended "to all the objects which, in the ordinary course of affairs, concern the lives, liberties and properties of the people, and the internal order, improvement, and prosperity of the State."[37]

Notes

1. Arthur M. Okun, *The Political Economy of Prosperity* (Washington, D.C.: Brookings, 1970), 31-33.
2. David Osborne, *Laboratories of Democracy: A New Breed of Governor Creates Models for Regional Growth* (Boston: Harvard Business School Press, 1988), 1.
3. Thomas Anton, "Economic Development, Employment and Training Policy, and Federalism," *Policy Studies Review* 6 (May 1987): 729.
4. This phrase is from the title of Ann O'M. Bowman and Richard C. Kearney, *The Resurgence of the States* (Englewood Cliffs, N.J.: Prentice-Hall, 1986).
5. On institutional changes, see Advisory Commission on Intergovernmental Relations, *The Question of State Government Capability* (Washington, D.C.: U.S. Government Printing Office, 1985). On the states' new political leadership, see Larry Sabato, *Goodbye to Good-time Charlie*, 2d ed. (Washington, D.C.: CQ Press, 1983).
6. Bowman and Kearney, *Resurgence of the States,* ix.
7. A discussion of state educational reform initiatives appears in Denis P. Doyle and Terry W. Hartle, *Excellence in Education: The States Take Charge* (Washington, D.C.: American Enterprise Institute, 1985).
8. Kathleen Sylvester, "Exporting Made Easy (Or How States and Cities Are Selling Products Overseas)," *Governing,* January 1988, 36.
9. Carol Steinbach and Neal R. Pierce, "Cities Are Setting Their Sights on International Trade and Investment," *National Journal,* April 28, 1984, 818.
10. William K. Stevens, "Governors Assert Key to Prosperity Is a Global View," *New York Times,* July 26, 1987, 1.
11. Gov. James Thompson, "I Pulled Out a Road Map and Showed Him Rte. 51," *Crain's Chicago Business,* June 6, 1988, A50.
12. A strong statement of this position is presented in Robert Goodman, *The Last Entrepreneurs: America's Regional Wars for Jobs and Dollars* (Boston: South End Press, 1979).
13. See Advisory Commission on Intergovernmental Relations, *Regional Growth: Interstate Tax Competition* (Washington, D.C.: U.S. Government Printing Office, March 1981), and Edward Humberger, *Business Location Decisions and Cities* (Washington, D.C.: Public Technology, Inc., 1983).
14. Grant Thornton, *General Manufacturing Climates of the Forty-Eight Contiguous States* (Chicago: Grant Thornton, 1987), 9.
15. See David Birch, *Job Creation in America: How Our Smallest Companies Put the Most People to Work* (New York: Free Press, 1987).
16. *Ibid.,* 114.
17. Edward J. Malecki, "Hope or Hyperbole? High Tech and Economic Development," *Technology Review,* October 1987, 49.

18. Paul D. Warner, "Business Climate, Taxes, and Economic Development," *Economic Development Quarterly* 1 (November 1987), 389.
19. Quoted in Ferrel Guillory, "Mississippi's Elder Statesman Preaches the Gospel of Economic Reform," *Governing,* February 1988, 36.
20. *Ibid.,* 37.
21. "Group Ranks Anti-Pollution Efforts," *New York Times,* February 28, 1988, Y28.
22. Martha M. Hamilton, "On Second Thought, We'd Prefer the Feds on Our Backs," *Washington Post National Weekly Edition,* December 14, 1987, 32.
23. Neal R. Peirce, "Playing Catch-Up," *National Journal,* March 19, 1988, 741.
24. Malecki, "Hope or Hyperbole? High Tech and Economic Development," 51.
25. Everett M. Rogers, *Diffusion of Innovations,* 3d ed. (New York: Free Press, 1983), 360.
26. Jane Jacobs, "Cities and the Wealth of Nations," *Atlantic Monthly,* March 1984, 41.
27. DeWitt John, *Shifting Responsibilities: Federalism in Economic Development* (Washington, D.C.: National Governors' Association, 1987), 7.
28. For an assessment of relevant state policies, see Committee on Economic Development, *Leadership for Dynamic State Economies* (New York: Committee on Economic Development, 1986), esp. chap. 4 and app. B.
29. Michael J. Piore and Charles F. Sabel, *The Second Industrial Divide: Possibilities for Prosperity* (New York: Basic Books, 1984), 301.
30. John, *Shifting Responsibilities,* 22.
31. Paul E. Peterson, *City Limits* (Chicago: University of Chicago Press, 1981), 22.
32. Nancy J. Perry, "The Education Crisis: What Business Can Do," *Fortune,* July 4, 1988, 71.
33. Woodrow Wilson, *Constitutional Government in the United States* (New York: Columbia University Press, 1908; rpt. 1961), 173.
34. A cyclical explanation emphasizing state responses to national conservative policies and grant cutbacks is presented in Richard P. Nathan and Fred C. Doolittle, *Reagan and the States* (Princeton: Princeton University Press, 1987), 355-363.
35. Daniel Patrick Moynihan, *Family and Nation* (San Diego: Harcourt Brace Jovanovich, 1986), 61.
36. Sheridan Tatsuno, *The Technology Strategy: Japan, High Technology, and the Control of the 21st Century* (New York: Prentice-Hall, 1986), 232, 243.
37. *The Federalist Papers,* no. 45, ed. Clinton Rossiter (New York: Modern American Library, 1939), 303.

37. STATE POWER NEEDN'T BE RESURRECTED BECAUSE IT NEVER DIED

Morton Keller

Not too long ago, the experts wrote off the states as quaint remnants of the American past, all but useless in the age of the atom bomb, big federal government, a thoroughly national economy and lifestyles that seem to have less and less to do with where one lives. Typical was journalist Robert S. Allen's declaration in *Our Sovereign State* (1949): "State government is the tawdriest, most incompetent and most stultifying unit of the nation's political structure."

But suddenly the states are where much of what is vital, new, interesting and important in American politics is going on. Back in the 1940s and '50s, to be governor of a state, even to be a notable governor of a big state, was no steppingstone to the presidency, as Tom Dewey and Adlai Stevenson painfully discovered. But our presidents since 1976—first Jimmy Carter, then Ronald Reagan—went from state-house to White House. And in 1988, Michael Dukakis of Massachusetts bids fair to follow them. [Of course, Dukakis was defeated by George Bush. Note that in 1992 Arkansas Governor Bill Clinton won the Democratic nomination for president.—Ed.]

What is the significance of this upsurge of the states as a major setting for the drama of American public life?

Is it a quirk, an accident, a blip in the otherwise steady growth of the federal government?

Is it the first sign of a fundamental shift in American public life: the beginnings of a devolution of power to the states after decades of expanding national authority?

Or is this revival of federalism a familiar turn of the wheel, a shuffling of governmental roles between state and nation that is as old as our history? Is it a reaffirmation of Mark Twain's dictum that while history does not repeat itself, it rhymes?

The Constitution was clear enough on the respective rules of the states and the national government. The power to tax, make war,

From *Governing* 2 (October 1988): 53-57. Copyright © 1988 *Governing* magazine. Reprinted with permission.

regulate commerce and provide for the general welfare rested with the federal government. Just about everything else was lodged in the states. James Madison, who more than anyone set the tone of the Constitution, explained in the *Federalist Papers:* "The powers reserved to the several states will extend to all the objects which, in the ordinary course of affairs, concern the lives, liberties and properties of the people; and the internal order, improvement and prosperity of the state."

As things turned out, the national government, not the states, was the focal point of public affairs during the nation's first quarter-century. The United States was born into a world dominated by the great, decades-long struggle between England and France. The American Revolution was fought out—and in good part determined—by the fact of that conflict. And not until the War of 1812 ended in 1815 would the new nation be free of it.

The early years of the republic were dominated by foreign-policy issues: John Jay's treaty of 1794, perceived to have given away so much to England that it set off a political firestorm which led directly to the emergence of the Jeffersonian Republicans as an opposition party; Jefferson's 1807-1809 embargo on trade overseas; and the War of 1812 with England.

The primary domestic issues of the day also were national more than state or local. They had to do with the character and survival of the government: its fiscal soundness, the role of the suddenly emergent national political parties, the no-less-sudden rise of judicial review.

The Federalist and Jeffersonian Republican parties that emerged in the 1790s were the product of the maneuverings of national figures such as Thomas Jefferson, Alexander Hamilton and James Madison. They were cadre parties spreading from the top down, not mass-based parties growing from the bottom up.

As dramatic—and as surprising—was the way in which John Marshall made judicial review by the Supreme Court an unexpectedly important part of the system of American government. Major disputes over public power and individual rights, it appeared, were to be decided by the federal judiciary.

While these national issues and institutions took form, the states were relatively minor players in the governmental game. State legislatures were distinguished not by the scale and importance of their activity, but by how little of substance came from them. A session of the Connecticut House in the early 1800s was devoted primarily to the passage of a tax on dogs; the next session with equal dedication debated its removal. Virginia planter John Campbell wrote to his son David in 1811: "I have heard with much pain that you have not recovered your health yet. Would a session in the legislature be of benefit to you?"

The conditions of American life changed dramatically after 1815, and so did the balance of power between national and state government. The years between the end of the War of 1812 and the 1850s were the high point of American federalism as a system in which the states and the federal government were at the very least co-equal partners. The basic idea of the Southern Confederacy—that a group of semisovereign states could decide to leave the Union if they chose—was a logical (if extreme) climax to this golden age of states' rights.

An exploding post-1815 American economy led to growing demands on government. There was bold talk in the wake of the War of 1812 of an "American system" of national internal improvements. "Let us bind the republic together with a perfect system of roads and canals. Let us conquer space," declared then-congressman John C. Calhoun of South Carolina in 1816. But within a few years, Calhoun was the patron saint of states' rights.

The decentralized, varied character of American society dictated that both stimulants to and regulation of economic growth came primarily from the states. Between 1815 and 1850, thousands of state laws and local ordinances provided subsidies, eased the path of incorporation, and regulated the activities of the turnpikes, land companies, canals, railroads, corporations and banks that were creating a new American economy. Social policy too—the control of slaves, the financing and the curricula of the schools, regulation of marriage and the family—was made by state legislatures and courts, local and municipal authorities. As Alexis de Tocqueville observed in the 1830s, American democracy "is allowed to follow, in the function of the laws, the natural instability of its desires."

The political parties also underwent a sea change. The top-down politics of the Federalists and the Jeffersonian Republicans gave way to a new kind of mass-based politics built from the bottom up: the politics of the Jacksonian Democrats and the Whigs. A new breed of politicians, such as New York's Democrat Martin Van Buren and Whig Thurlow Weed, constructed state parties out of township committees, local newspapers, county organizations. It was from this rich, down-home political ferment that the new national political parties emerged.

Meanwhile, the federal government stagnated. Washington had only 2,199 federal employees by 1861. These were either party hacks or low-level government workers. The professional civil services taking form in 19th-century Europe had no place here.

The city itself became not the grand capital of the republic envisioned by its planners, but rather a squalid, parochial place where congressmen stayed as briefly as they could. L'Enfant's ambitious city blueprint fell into oblivion. When the new Treasury building went up in the 1830s, it was placed square in the path of what was supposed to have been a majestic Pennsylvania Avenue linking the Capitol and the White House—so far had the original scheme been forgotten.

The presidency lost its initial luster. Save for John Adams and John Quincy Adams, chief executives from Washington through Jackson served two terms. From Jackson to Lincoln, none lasted beyond a single term.

But the emerging American national character of the early 19th century—intensely individualistic, hostile to authority, absorbed in private, local affairs—gradually eroded the capacity of the states to govern as well. Universal white male suffrage and the election of judges and other officials went hand in hand with a profound suspicion of public power.

By the 1850s, a number of state constitutions forbade subsidies for railroads or other ventures; free incorporation and banking laws made the creation of new enterprises all but automatic. The New York state constitution of 1846—the "people's constitution"—abolished "all officers for the weighing, gauging, measuring, culling or inspecting of any merchandise, produce, manufacture or commodity whatever," except for those charged with protecting the public health or ensuring honest weights and measures.

Cities and towns, too, shared in the general decline of government power. It was in this period that the courts came to define incorporated municipalities as creatures, pure and simple, of the states. So began the long saga of urban dependence on often-hostile, rural-dominated legislatures, of parochial city bosses and machines, and too-often inadequate municipal services.

Everywhere, it seemed, American freedom and individualism were leading to the decay of government. As the political scientist Walter Dean Burnham put it, "The chief distinguishing characteristic of the American political system before 1861 is that *there was no state.*"

The Civil War might have been expected to change all of this. It is conventional wisdom that the war was the great divide between an agrarian, decentralized young republic and the industrial, nationalized United States of modern times. Indeed, the Civil War may be regarded as the American version of the mid-19th-century outburst of nationalism that in the same decade led to the unification of Italy and Germany.

This war for the Union, and ultimately for the eradication of slavery, seemed to herald the coming of a strong, active national state, and even of a new conception of national citizenship transcending race. Lincoln made his presidency an impressive instrument of power. He raised and equipped the most powerful army since Napoleon, used the courts and the military to suppress dissent, and rallied public support with compelling rhetoric. Congress meanwhile enacted a protective tariff and an income tax, a national banking act, a national paper currency. And postwar civil rights acts and the 14th and 15th Amendments appeared to initiate a new era in American government, in which national authority replaced the states as the protector of the rights of citizens, regardless of color.

The Reconstruction experience made it clear, however, that neither in the structure of government nor in the realm of race relations had the Civil War wrought fundamental change. True, it ended the possibility of secession and abolished the "peculiar institution" of human slavery. But the old federalism—in particular, the states serving as the major source of social and economic policy—persisted in the new urban-industrial era.

The dominant style of party politics in the late 19th century hardly added to the capacity of the national government to cope with change. The needs of the parties themselves—highly organized, expensive to run, based primarily on regional, ethnic and religious loyalties—dictated their public policies. This was unfertile ground for the cultivation of a national state equipped to deal with the complex economic and social problems.

Aside from tariff and monetary policy, the federal government of the late 19th century responded little, if at all, to the coming of an industrial, urban society. Race relations, too, rapidly disappeared from the national agenda, to be left to the none-too-tender mercies of the states and localities.

After 1900 a new generation, led by Presidents Theodore Roosevelt and Woodrow Wilson, began the slow, painful process of using the national government to deal with the problems of a modern society. The regulation of big business became a major responsibility of federal agencies and courts—though how effectively is open to debate. Laws were passed to foster the conservation of natural resources, to ensure pure foods and drugs, to prohibit child labor (although the Supreme Court of the time found this an unconstitutional use of federal power). This was a thin record. The United States badly lagged behind other major Western nations in welfare legislation. It is a revealing (and depressing) commentary on the national government of the early 20th century that its major social enactments were Prohibition and immigration restriction: policies designed more to preserve a mythical American past than to come to terms with the realities of the present.

As constitutional law expert Zechariah Chafee Jr. observed in 1920, "The health, comfort and general welfare of citizens are in the charge of the state governments and not of the United States." The half century between 1880 and 1930 saw a flood of state legislation: from corporation, labor and housing regulations to the control of prostitution, drinking and gambling. The courts upheld the vast majority of this outpouring as valid applications of the states' police power. State legislatures in 1905 alone enacted about 15,000 laws, 60 percent of them dealing with local or private matters. About the same total was produced in 1923. A 1927 estimate put the number of national, state and local laws and ordinances on the books at 10 million!

A bewildering array of state agencies, boards and commissions dealing with taxation, public health, public utilities, housing and a multitude of other concerns came into being. New York had 10 of them in 1800; 81 in 1900; and 170 in 1925. Georgia's governor complained in the mid-'20s: "We are board-ridden, commission-ridden and trustee-ridden in this state." Under the leadership of forceful governors such as Robert LaFollette of Wisconsin and Charles Evans Hughes of New York, states in the early 20th century became laboratories for experiments in legislative and administrative solutions to the problems of a complex urban-industrial society.

But as in the 19th century, effective statecraft constantly ran afoul of the machinations of vested interests and deep popular hostility to government power. Progressive reformer Frederic C. Howe gushed in 1912 that LaFollette's Wisconsin "is doing for America what Germany is doing for the world" in developing the instruments of government. But Finley Peter Dunne's comic character Mr. Dooley came closer to the prevailing national ethos when he wryly observed of the bureaucratic state: "I wisht I was a German and believed in machinery."

In money spent and results achieved, the proudest peacetime achievements of American government before the New Deal were the construction of a new highway system for the automobile age and the expansion of schooling to make public secondary education available to almost everyone (outside the South). These accomplishments, attained on a larger scale in the United States than anywhere else, were the work of the states and localities. Far from fading away, federalism in the early 20th century was as important a reality in American public life as it had been a hundred years before.

But surely this came to an end in the 1930s. Surely from the time of Franklin D. Roosevelt and the New Deal on, the states steadily, inexorably slid to a subordinate place in American government. Surely the public administration expert who announced in 1933; "The American state is finished. I do not predict that the states will go, but affirm that they are gone," knew whereof he spoke.

The benchmarks are familiar and impressive:

- The nearly 100 new agencies of the New Deal and the billions spent for relief, public works and welfare during the Depression.
- The enormous expansion of federal taxation, borrowing, expenditure—and power—during World War II, and the varying but never-again minor scale of defense spending and international engagement during the Cold War decades since.
- The constant appearance of new national enterprises large in cost and social consequence: the federal highway program; the space program; the structure of civil rights enforcement; and the welfare, medical and educational programs of the Great Society and after.

The conventional view is that this burgeoning of the American state occurred hand in hand with a shrinkage in the role and power of the American states. Certainly from the 1930s to the 1960s, state government declined in relative importance. Governors and state legislatures wallowed in mediocrity. Social and economic problems seemed to be susceptible only to national solutions. The states came to be widely regarded as historical anomalies, of no particular significance in a new, thoroughly nationalized society.

But even during this nadir of state power, federalism was far from dead—or dying. Much New Deal spending was funneled through the states rather than going directly from Washington to its recipients. This was true as well of later big-ticket programs, such as the federal highway system and Medicaid.

As Washington took on expanding tasks and powers, the states developed subtle but significant new complementary relationships to the national government. While the federal treasury came to rely more and more on personal and corporate income taxes, the states developed significant new revenue sources from sales and gasoline levies. The large number of Americans disturbed by the growth of federal power found ideological and political comfort in the rhetoric of states' rights, culminating in the opposition to the civil rights revolution. For all the growth of federal safety and health policies, much of the regulatory apparatus that most directly impinges on the lives of modern Americans—automobile registration, licensing and insurance; the harms produced by machines and crowded urban living, which are lumped together under the generic legal term of torts—remains primarily in the province of state authorities, state laws, state courts.

Now, during the final decades of the 20th century, it appears that the states if anything are expanding their place in the governance of modern America. Lyndon Johnson's block grants programs of the 1960s, Richard Nixon's state and local revenue sharing of the 1970s, Ronald Reagan's New Federalism of the 1980s have given new meaning to the concept of a federal-state partnership. Civil rights and civil liberties advocates who a generation ago depended almost entirely on national law and policy are beginning to look to state constitutional law as an underutilized resource.

Education, public health, the environment, crime: These are issues of prime and growing concern in the late 20th-century American polity. And they are areas in which state and local governments have a major, even an expanding, role. Education alone is chiefly responsible for the fact that the number of state employees rose from 63 percent of the federal civilian total in 1960 to 135 percent in 1986, and local employees from 200 percent to 326 percent. In recent decades, governors and state legislatures and agencies have become notably more efficient, competent and effective. Nineteen legislatures met annually in 1962; 43 did so in 1986.

Perhaps the best way to get a grasp on what is happening is to see modern American government as an expanding balloon. Not too long ago, there was much talk of an "imperial presidency." More recently, an "imperial judiciary" aroused concern. And now attention is turning to the rise of an "imperial Congress." The fact is that the role of each branch of the national government has been changing, growing. But their overall relationship to one another has not been fundamentally altered.

This may be the case as well with the other basic structure of our government: federalism, the relationship between the states and the nation. The growth of the federal sector has been obvious for some time. It is increasingly evident that the states too are taking on new life and meaning in response to the demands of modern society.

Americans are increasingly subject to national social and economic forces. The most obvious consequence has been the growth of demands on the federal government. But the tensions and discontents of modern life have increased the need—social, even psychological—for units of government with what has been called the "geographic capability" to govern effectively, but which are not so large as to be beyond the reach and comprehension of the average citizen. Gallup found in 1936 that 56 percent of those polled favored federal over state government. But when the question was asked again in 1981, 64 percent preferred the states. In 1987, respondents were asked in which government they had "the most trust and confidence." Thirty-seven percent chose the localities, 22 percent the states, 19 percent the national government.

Finally, what of the future? It takes no great leap of the imagination to believe that the fillip to federalism provided by the Nixonian '70s and the Reagan '80s will pass, and that in the long run, the federal government will tighten its grip on the nation's public life. But it is just as easy to see Washington as a tiger long in the tooth, perhaps soon to be toothless, while new approaches to the art of governing spring up in the states and localities.

Certainly, changes in the way federalism works are both possible and desirable. Recent experience has shown that state and local obligations can often be better met when there are federal standards, and national needs can often be more flexibly and creatively met if they are spurred by federal incentives.

But if the historical record tells us anything, it is that changes in the relationship of the levels of American government are likely to be slow and piecemeal. The substance of that relationship has undergone enormous transformations in the course of 200 years. But American federalism is as meaningful at the end of the 20th century as it was at the end of the 18th. The words and music of American government have varied greatly over our history. The original rhythm—the rhyme—of our system persists.

38. POLITICS AND GOVERNANCE: CONFLICTING TRENDS IN THE 1990S?

Timothy J. Conlan

American federalism enters its third century with a new framework for intergovernmental politics. In 1985, the U.S. Supreme Court formally abandoned its historic role as the arbiter of issues involving the commerce power and the Tenth Amendment. Consolidating what had been the predominant operational pattern since the late 1930s, in 1985 the Court declared in *Garcia* v. *San Antonio Metropolitan Transit Authority*, "State sovereign interests are more properly protected by procedural safeguards inherent in the structure of the federal system than by judicially created limitations on federal power." [1] Political representation within the elected branches of government, not judicial circumscription, offers the appropriate avenue of defense for state and local governments, said the Court's majority.

In part, the Court's reasoning reflected long-standing views of American politics. Traditionally, decentralization was the dominant feature of the nation's political system. E. E. Schattschneider went so far as to argue that once decentralization of power "is understood, nearly everything else about American parties is greatly illuminated." [2] Party decentralization not only defined electoral politics; it structured the conduct of intergovernmental relations as well. In the classic formulation of this relationship, Morton Grodzins wrote, "The parties ... disperse power in favor of state and local governments.... States and localities, working through the parties ... are more influential in federal affairs than the federal government is in theirs." Elsewhere, he declared that "the parties are responsible for both the existence and form of the considerable measure of decentralization that exists in the United States." [3]

Yet even as Grodzins was writing, the political system was on the verge of dramatic changes affecting party structures, nominating processes, and the conduct of campaigns. Although the changes have been complex and occasionally contradictory, the direction has gener-

From *Annals* 509 (May 1990): 128-138. Copyright © 1990 by Sage Publications, Inc. Reprinted by permission.

ally been toward a more nationalized and less mediated political
system, attenuating in the process state and local governmental representation in national politics.

As a result, the *Garcia* decision abandoned states and localities to
the political fray at the very time when their political resources were
eroding. This permissive political and judicial context, reinforced by
federal budget stringency, has created new opportunities for increased
federal regulation and preemption. Yet conflicting trends of decentralization in policymaking and governance are also evident, especially the
growing operational responsibilities and policy assertiveness of the
states. Resolving this paradox of intergovernmental power and governance may well dominate the politics of federalism in the 1990s.

Party Nationalization

Few institutions in American society have undergone more dramatic changes in recent decades than the party system. The parties once
had a virtual monopoly on many of the central functions of the electoral
system—the recruitment and nomination of candidates, the structuring
of debate on public issues, the organization and mobilization of the
electorate, the financing of elections, and the communication of candidates' positions to the voters. Today, they face stiff competition from, or
they have ceded functions to, other institutions in society, from the mass
media to political action committees (PACs) to professional campaign
consultants. Where parties have adapted to this new electoral environment, the national committees have led the way, undermining the
parties' historically confederal power structure in the process.

Just thirty years ago, virtually all authorities on American politics
agreed that "our state and local party organizations, taken collectively,
are far more powerful than our national party organizations." [4] The
national party organizations were dismissed as "politics without
power." [5] Such organizational conditions had important intergovernmental consequences. Presidents were nominated by—and subsequently
beholden to—governors, mayors, and state and local party chieftains who
controlled state delegations to the national party conventions. Senators
and congressmen, too, often owed their election to vigorous state and local
parties. Some members of Congress held important posts within those
organizations, while others were viewed as emissaries sent to represent
their local party's interests in Washington.

Today, circumstances are very different. National party conventions have become media events in which the parties ratify decisions
reached earlier by the voters in primaries and caucuses. Members of
Congress have also become more independent of their state and local
parties. Most are now independent political entrepreneurs who secure

their own nominating and electoral coalitions, campaign funding, and instruments of direct communication with the voters.

Yet the parties have not withered away. They have evolved and adapted to the new electoral environment, in part through a dramatic shift in the roles played by different levels of party organization. Two party scholars summarize the scope of the transformation:

> the American party system ... is a new animal ... based in Washington. ... The national party used to exist solely for the purpose of selecting the national nominee and was financed by the state parties, but now it provides the money (and not infrequently the candidates) to the states. Where there is an active county organization, it, too, is often dependent on the funds and programs emanating from the top.[6]

This transformation in organizational roles has many dimensions—candidate recruitment, campaign services, fund-raising, electoral communications, and party rules—but it can be seen most dramatically in the distribution of party resources. Consistent, comprehensive longitudinal data on party finances do not exist, but available data are illustrative. In 1974, the Republican National Committee (RNC) had a gross income of $6.3 million. By 1978, the RNC's income had more than doubled to $14.5 million, which generated an operating budget of $9.7 million and a staff of 220.[7] Data for subsequent years show continued rapid growth in the income of both parties' national committees (see Table [6]). In financial terms, 79 percent of the Democratic and 83 percent of the Republican Party's resources are now collected and expended by national party committees, and the percentage among Democrats continues to grow. Both parties now have large, professionally staffed headquarters in Washington, D.C., which provide substantial contributions and services to candidates and which engage in a variety of other party-building activities in states and localities.

This enhancement of the national parties generally has not been at the expense of state party organizations. Although state parties vary enormously in their competitive ability, since the 1960s most state party organizations also have expanded their staffs, resources, and activities. In an astounding reversal of historical roles, however, the revitalization of many state party organizations has been actively promoted by the newly invigorated national committees. According to a 1983 survey of state party chairs, at least two-thirds of all Republican state organizations received direct financial, fund-raising, management, and candidate recruitment and training assistance from the RNC.[8] Although Democratic state parties received significantly

Table 6 Political Party Income and Contributions, 1978-1986 (in Thousands of 1982 Dollars)

| | Party Income | | |
	1978	1982	1986
Democrats			
National committees[a]	18,470	28,613	36,298
State/local committees	11,183	7,568	9,446
Total	29,653	36,181	45,744
National committees' percentage	62%	79%	79%
Republicans			
National committees	76,145	191,061	177,203
State/local committees	26,976	23,985	36,071
Total	103,121	215,046	213,274
National committees' percentage	74%	89%	83%
Contributions and Expenditures for Congressional Candidates			
Democrats			
National committees	1,413	3,438	5,596
State/local committees	982	1,628	1,206
Total	2,395	5,066	6,802
National committees' percentage	59%	68%	82%
Republicans			
National committees	8,987	18,697	14,188
State/local committees	1,705	1,214	872
Total	10,692	19,911	15,060
National committees' percentage	84%	94%	94%

[a] Includes the national, congressional, and senatorial committees.

SOURCE: Calculated from Norman J. Ornstein, Thomas E. Mann, and Michael J. Malbin, *Vital Statistics on Congress, 1987-1988* (Washington, D.C.: CQ Press, 1987), pp. 99-101.

less help in virtually all of these areas, the gap between the two parties appears to be closing, especially in the area of voter mobilization. In the 1983-84 election cycle, for example, the Democratic National Committee committed $5 million to state parties to help register new voters, and it leveraged millions more from liberal foundations and interest groups.[9] The Republicans countered with their own multimillion-dollar voter registration drive in targeted states and with one of several recurring efforts to build up effective organizations in hundreds of key counties. Because of the intricacies of federal campaign-finance law, both national parties have redoubled their efforts since 1984 to finance party-building efforts in the states through the routing of so-called soft money to state party organizations and to candidates.

Notwithstanding these party-building initiatives, "state and local parties are indisputably weaker today" than in the past in terms of their influence over federal elected officials.[10] As Table [6] demonstrates, the vast bulk of the financial assistance given by political parties to candidates for Congress is provided by the national party committees, not by state and local organizations. Most state party resources are expended on gubernatorial and state legislative races. This has important implications for congressional behavior and intergovernmental relations. While successful congressional candidates must be skillfully attuned to local needs, "once in office, [they] feel little sense of obligation to their state and local parties" or, in many cases, to state and local elected officials.[11]

Interest-Group Nationalism

National party contributions are by no means the only element of congressional campaign finance that has become nationalized in recent years. Although national party contributions and expenditures have grown rapidly over the past decade, they have failed to keep pace with special-interest spending, notably by PACs. Although PAC receipts vary widely among members and between the two parties—a strong incumbent bias in PAC giving benefits Democrats, especially in the House—PAC contributions have risen sharply since 1974, both in absolute terms and as a proportion of all contributions. On average, the percentage of congressional campaign contributions received from PACs doubled in each chamber between 1974 and 1986, growing from 17 percent to 36 percent in the House and from 11 percent to 22 percent in the Senate.[12]

This expansion has important intergovernmental consequences because PAC giving, and the legislation in which PAC contributors have an interest, are heavily concentrated in Washington. Congressional fundraising has increasingly become a Washington phenomenon, supplemented by infusions of cash from national financial and media centers in New York and Los Angeles. In the process, the influence of state and local parties—and local contributors and interests generally—have become further attenuated. As one Iowa congressman complained:

> We're mainly rural and small business, but in elections the Republicans are largely funded by business . . . and the Democrats . . . by labor, much of which doesn't have anything to do with the state. . . . We're seeing regional politics and state and citizen politics become national. National groups determine outcomes, whereas local constituencies used to. . . . This is new.[13]

Campaign funding is only one element in a broader process of nationalization in interest-group politics. Although interest groups and voluntary associations have always been prominent in American politics, never have they been as numerous, entrenched, or politically active in Washington as they are today. Estimating the number of interest groups over time is a difficult task, but according to one study the number of groups represented in the nation's capital increased by 25 percent in the 1970s alone.[14] This includes both newly formed groups and previously established organizations that relocated to Washington.

Although many factors have contributed to interest-group formation and migration—from economic growth and specialization to rising levels of education—a critical stimulant has been the federal government. Many groups were formed in response to new federal programs, as clients and service providers banded together to share information and expand their resources. Indeed, some groups have benefited from direct governmental assistance to help them sustain or expand their operations. Still others have organized for defensive purposes, responding to the burdens imposed by governmental action.

Federal policies and interest-group nationalization generated an intergovernmental response—the growth and development of the public-interest groups. Following the well-worn path to Washington, organizations representing the full range of state and local officials—from the state house to the town hall—have either located or established major offices there. Especially when viewed in historical perspective, this trend has been striking. In 1957, the National Association of Counties had a professional staff of one and a budget of $18,000. Twenty-five years later its staff had swelled to 120 and its budget totaled $6.3 million.[15] Equally dramatic changes occurred in the case of the National Governors' Association (NGA), which did not open a Washington office until 1967. Fourteen years later, the NGA had a staff of 70, a budget of $5.7 million, and a Capitol Hill office building housing numerous individual states and affiliated organizations. Many individual cities and counties also expanded their Washington presence during the 1960s and 1970s by establishing independent offices or hiring a part-time national representative, while smaller jurisdictions, such as townships, joined together to create organizations for the first time.

At first, some observers interpreted this expanded organizational presence as a sign of growing state and local political strength and sophistication. Clearly it helped these governments play a leading role in enacting and shaping certain pieces of federal legislation, such as General Revenue Sharing and Community Development Block Grants.

Fundamentally, however, this organizational boom reflected erosion in the unique political role once occupied by these officials and their party organizations in the political system. Viewed from this perspective, it constituted a form of compensation for lost political influence rather than a sign of mounting strength. As Donald Haider expressed it: "For governors and mayors, individually and collectively, national party influence is generally declining . . . [creating] the political necessity of banding together to deal with their federal constituency." [16]

Although their direct channels of representation were enhanced in this process, state and local officials came to be viewed in Washington not as uniquely constituted cosovereigns but as a few more voices among a multitude of special-interest claimants. Certainly they were viewed in this way by officials in the Reagan administration, some of whom characterized them as "wily stalkers of federal aid." The local government groups in particular saw their federal training and technical-assistance grants slashed by 50 percent or more in the early 1980s, necessitating cuts in staff and activities from which some have yet to recover (see Table [7]).

Political Nationalization and
Intergovernmental Policy

The net effects of the foregoing changes—reinforced by the growing political influence of the mass media, particularly network television—have been strongly nationalizing. As Sorauf and Beck observe:

> Party electorates respond increasingly to national issues, to national candidates, and to national party symbols and positions. Attention now centers as well on the national parties in government; the president and the congressional leadership . . . are more than ever the preeminent spokesmen for their parties.[17]

Over the long term, states have responded to the nationalization of politics by moving to uncouple state elections from national races. Only a dozen states now elect governors in presidential years, compared with 34 in 1932.[18] Although this helps to insulate state politics from national influences, it does nothing to strengthen state representation in Washington.

Consequently, there is considerable, though fragmentary, evidence that state and local influence on federal policymaking has been diminished. It may be no accident that General Revenue Sharing, Urban Development Block Grants, and the Comprehensive Employment and Training Act were virtually the only large programs abolished since 1980, or that grants-in-aid to state and local govern-

Table 7 Budgets and Staffs of Public-Interest Groups, 1975-1989

	1975	1981	1983	1989
National Conference of State Legislatures				
Total staff	20	120	105	125
Total budget[a]	$0.08	$5.7	$5.4	$7.2
Percentage from the federal government	31.5%	50.1%	26.1%	NA[b]
National Governors' Association				
Total staff	NA[b]	70	70	108
Total budget[a]	$2.1	$5.7	$5.4	$9.5
Percentage from the federal government	40.2%	58.3%	43.0%	29.0%
National Association of Counties				
Total staff	87	120	58	63
Total budget[a]	NA[b]	$6.3	$6.4	$8.5
Percentage from the federal government	NA[b]	26.2%	11.7%	7.0%
National League of Cities				
Total staff	112	125[c]	56	73
Total budget[a]	NA[d]	$7.6	$5.2	$7.6
Percentage from the federal government	NA[b]	64.3%	5.8%	0.9%
U.S. Conference of Mayors				
Total staff	5	100[c]	55	45
Total budget[a]	NA[d]	$5.6	$3.2	$5.25
Percentage from the federal government	NA[b]	64.3%	32.4%	32.4%

[a] Budgets in millions of dollars.
[b] Not available.
[c] Figures for 1980.
[d] Data are unavailable, due to the combined operations of the National League of Cities and the Conference of Mayors at this time.

SOURCES: Data for 1975-1983 are from Charles H. Levine and James A. Thurber, "Reagan and the Intergovernmental Lobby: Iron Triangles, Cozy Subsystems, and Political Conflict," in *Interest Group Politics,* ed. Allan J. Cigler and Burdett A. Loomis, 2d ed. (Washington, D.C.: CQ Press, 1986), pp. 214-215. Data for 1989 were collected by the author from the groups' financial officers and annual reports.

ments have suffered the deepest cuts of any major segment of the federal budget, or that such grants were left relatively unprotected from sequestration under the Gramm-Rudman process.

Moreover, the policy challenges faced by states and localities in Washington extend far beyond declining federal aid. Recent decades have witnessed the rise of new and more intrusive forms of intergovernmental regulation. The U.S. Advisory Commission on Intergovernmental Relations counted 36 major requirements in 1981, three-quarters of which were enacted during the 1970s.[19] Despite Reagan's commitment to deregulation, the 1980s witnessed the enactment of intrusive new requirements to regulate trucking standards, the drinking age, asbestos removal, and municipal drinking-water and sewage systems; increases in federal paperwork burdens; and a 26 percent increase in the number of federal preemption statutes.[20]

Increased competition over tax sources has added a third front to the intergovernmental wars in the nation's capital. The pressure of persistent federal deficits and the Reagan and Bush administrations' refusal to increase income taxes have spawned intense scrambling for other revenue sources. Federal excise and gasoline taxes have been raised, and tax-exempt bonds have been under constant political and legal assault since 1978. The state and local income-tax deduction was targeted for elimination by the Reagan administration and the sales-tax deduction was subsequently abolished as part of tax reform. Further federal incursions on state and local tax room continue to loom on the horizon in the form of a value-added tax and/or sharply higher federal gas taxes. Combined with federal budget and regulatory actions, the result is often more than the public-interest groups can handle. As a lobbyist for the governors lamented, "The intergovernmental agenda is getting so long it would take all my time just to keep up the list of issues. We can't begin to respond to them all." [21]

The Paradox of Governance

Thus far, despite the constraints imposed by federal budget deficits, federal policy pressures on the states show few signs of abating. If the 1988 election was any indication, politicians and the public alike still expect national responses to the ever changing list of social and economic problems, from day-care and the environment to drugs and education. Wishing to respond but lacking funds to do so, the federal government may, if current trends persist, continue to turn increasingly to "low-cost" regulatory and preemptive solutions, together with a reshuffling of resources from existing grants to new initiatives.

Predicting the future by extrapolating current trends is inherently risky, however. Significant changes in policy direction are precluded, even though there is ample reason to believe that the current intergovernmental environment is ripe for change. Whether one considers the economic megatrends favoring decentralization, the renaissance of state policy activism, or the structural constraints on federal finances, continued federal policy leadership appears to be increasingly inconsistent with underlying social, economic, and fiscal developments. "No one expects a return to the days of overwhelming federal dominance," writes John Herbers, suggesting that the processes propelling political centralization may reverse themselves as politics begins adjusting to changing circumstances.[22]

Expressed in this way, the future of intergovernmental relations raises fundamental questions about the relationship between politics, governance, and society. Does the political system simply respond to changes in government policy and broad social trends, or is it an independent variable in its own right? This issue has a distinguished legacy in the scholarship on federalism: while Morton Grodzins was explaining the content of federal policy in terms of our decentralized party system during the 1950s, David Truman was elaborating the converse. American parties were decentralized, he argued, because governmental power was dispersed: "In a federal system decentralization and lack of cohesion in the party system are based on the structural fact of federalism . . . that it creates separate, self-sustaining centers of power, privilege, and profit." [23]

According to Truman's thesis, the nationalization of American parties has constituted a belated but unavoidable response to the centralization of functional activity and political power in Washington since the New Deal.[24] Now that states are becoming increasingly active and financially powerful vis-à-vis the federal government, should we not expect that the processes of political nationalization will begin to reverse themselves, with obvious consequences for federal policymaking?

There are some signs that this is beginning to happen. One study of interest-group responses to the budgetary and devolutionary policies of the Reagan administration found that many social-welfare groups "were making efforts to build up their state lobbying capacity. . . . Nearly all the groups we interviewed had state chapters and . . . have become more active in state capitals than they once were." [25] Business organizations, too, have responded to growing state activism with increased lobbying. "A decade ago, most corporate relations specialists gave state government precious little thought," observed one reporter. "As states have become more active, corporate America has been forced to pay more attention." [26] In the process, corporations have turned to a new breed of intergovernmental brokers to help them find effective lobbyists "in states they've never been in before." [27] There are even signs that politicians are beginning to respond to the new political environment, becoming frustrated with Washington and eyeing gubernatorial careers instead.

If these trends continue, it is possible that party organizations, nominating processes, campaign resources, and, ultimately, political power in the federal system will readjust accordingly. The 1990s may be the decade when this process becomes evident in an unambiguous way. On the other hand, it took forty years for political party structures to reflect the centralization of governmental power and resources that began during the New Deal. Assuming that this trend has been reversed—and not simply slowed or consolidated during the Reagan years—then the states may yet have a long and frustrating wait for the political fruits of their functional activity.

Notes

1. *Garcia* v. *San Antonio Metropolitan Transit Authority*, 469 U.S. 552 (1985).
2. E. E. Schattschneider, *Party Government* (New York: Holt, Rinehart & Winston, 1942), p. 129.
3. Morton Grodzins, "Centralization and Decentralization in the American Federal System," in *A Nation of States*, ed. Robert Goldwin (Chicago: Rand McNally, 1968), p. 9; idem, *The American System*, ed. Daniel J. Elazar (Chicago: Rand McNally, 1966), p. 254.
4. Austin Ranney and Willmoore Kendall, *Democracy and the American Party System* (New York: Harcourt, Brace, & World, 1956), p. 160.
5. Cornelius Cotter and Bernard Hennessey, *Politics without Power: The National Committees* (New York: Atherton, 1964).
6. Xandra Kayden and Eddie Mahe, Jr., *The Party Goes On: The Persistence of the Two-Party System in the United States* (New York: Basic Books, 1985), pp. 3, 4.
7. Ibid., p. 73; Cornelius Cotter and John Bibby, "Institutional Development of Parties and the Theory of Party Decline," *Political Science Quarterly* 95:5 (Spring 1980).
8. U.S. Advisory Commission on Intergovernmental Relations, *The Transformation in American Politics: Implications for Federalism* (Washington, D.C.: Government Printing Office, 1986), pp. 84-90, 118-22. See also Cornelius P. Cotter et al., *Party Organizations in American Politics* (New York: Praeger, 1984).
9. See A. James Reichley, "The Rise of National Parties," in *The New Direction in American Politics*, ed. John E. Chubb and Paul E. Peterson (Washington, D.C.: Brookings Institution, 1985), p. 193.
10. Frank J. Sorauf and Paul Allen Beck, *Party Politics in America* (Glenview, Ill.: Scott, Foresman, 1988), pp. 98-99.
11. Robert Huckshorn and John Bibby, "State Parties in an Era of Political Change," in *The Future of American Political Parties*, ed. Joel Fleishman (Englewood Cliffs, N.J.: Prentice-Hall, 1982), p. 91. See also Richard J. Fenno, *Home Styles: House Members in Their Districts* (Boston: Little, Brown, 1978), pp. 113-14.
12. Norman J. Ornstein, Thomas E. Mann, and Michael J. Malbin, *Vital Statistics on Congress, 1987-1988* (Washington, D.C.: CQ Press, 1987), pp. 92-93.

13. Representative Jim Leach, quoted in Elizabeth Drew, *Politics and Money: The New Road to Corruption* (New York: Macmillan, 1983), p. 34.

14. Calculated from Kay Lehman Schlozman and John T. Tierney, *Organized Interests and American Democracy* (New York: Harper & Row, 1986), p. 75.

15. These and the following data come from Timothy J. Conlan, "Federalism and American Politics: New Relationships, a Changing System," *Intergovernmental Perspective*, 11:43 (Winter 1985); Charles H. Levine and James A. Thurber, "Reagan and the Intergovernmental Lobby: Iron Triangles, Cozy Subsystems, and Political Conflict," in *Interest Group Politics*, ed. Allan J. Cigler and Burdett A. Loomis, 2d ed. (Washington, D.C.: CQ Press, 1986), pp. 214-15.

16. Donald H. Haider, *When Governments Come to Washington* (New York: Free Press, 1974), pp. 110, 111.

17. Sorauf and Beck, *Party Politics in America*, p. 133.

18. Barbara G. Salmore and Stephen A. Salmore, "The Transformation of State Electoral Politics," in *The State of the States*, ed. Carl E. Van Horn (Washington, D.C.: CQ Press, 1989), p. 186.

19. See David R. Beam, "Washington's Regulation of States and Localities: Origins and Issues," *Intergovernmental Perspective*, 7:8-18 (Summer 1981).

20. See U.S. General Accounting Office, *Paperwork Reduction: Little Real Burden Change in Recent Years*, PEMD-89-19FS (Washington, D.C.: Government Printing Office, 1989); U.S. Advisory Commission on Intergovernmental Relations, "Federal Preemption of State and Local Authority" (Draft report, Advisory Commission on Intergovernmental Relations, Aug. 1989), p. 2.

21. Interview with Jim Martin, 28 July 1986, Washington, D.C.

22. John Herbers, "The New Federalism: Unplanned, Innovative, and Here to Stay," *Governing*, 1:34 (Oct. 1987).

23. David B. Truman, "Federalism and the Party System," in *American Federalism in Perspective*, ed. Aaron Wildavsky (Boston: Little, Brown, 1967), pp. 92, 107.

24. David Truman, "Party Reform, Party Atrophy, and Constitutional Change," *Political Science Quarterly*, 99:640-47 (Winter 1984-85).

25. Harold Wolman and Fred Teitlebaum, "Interest Groups and the Reagan Presidency," in *The Reagan Presidency and the Governing of America*, ed. Lester M. Salamon and Michael S. Lund (Washington, D.C.: Urban Institute Press, 1985), pp. 313-14.

26. Tom Watson, "Dale Florio: A Lobbyist's Middleman Who Helps Business Navigate State Capitol Halls," *Governing*, 2:32-33 (Feb. 1989).

27. Ibid., p. 32.

Part V

REVIEW QUESTIONS

1. What values did Ronald Reagan seem to be pursuing in his intergovernmental reforms? Compare these values with those of the founders, as discussed in Part I. Was Reagan's effort a departure from American intergovernmental tradition, or a return to it? Can you make use of Beer's analysis in your assessment? How would you characterize the Bush administration on intergovernmental issues? Are there important similarities to or differences from the Reagan approach?

2. What were the political, fiscal, and administrative implications of Reagan's proposals for change in the intergovernmental system?

3. A successor to Reagan hires you as special assistant for intergovernmental relations. The president asks you for an assessment of Reagan's intergovernmental performance in office because many of the issues prominent in the 1980s seem to remain important in the 1990s. What do you say? In your answer, consider using the material in Conlan's study of Reagan's performance.

4. A governor in one of the nation's states hires you as special assistant for intergovernmental relations. The governor asks you for a status report on the system in the 1990s: What are the major intergovernmental problems that states currently face? What developments in the 1980s and 1990s, for instance in Washington and at the local level, are likely to matter as your state goes about its own business? What opportunities exist for states to exercise initiative and have influence on policy in the years ahead? What notes of caution are appropriate?

5. Compare Reagan's claims for federalism with Riker's critique in Part I, and explain how the evidence in this book supports one perspective or the other. Are there data to bolster both sets of

claims? Consider Conlan's concluding article in this part of the book as you respond.

6. What are the ideas of Webster, Lincoln, the Roosevelts, and Lyndon Johnson about the concept of the American nation (see Beer's essay)? How, if at all, do they bear on today's intergovernmental issues? Explain Beer's comment that "a nationalist need not always be a centralizer."

7. Describe an imaginary discussion between Ronald Reagan and Samuel Beer. How would Reagan respond to Beer's argument about the appropriate role for the national government in American life? Include an analysis of some specific issues, including racial tensions and economic development. Make use of your analysis from the preceding question in framing your response here.

8. Sketch the relationship between the nation and the states, both historically and at the present time. Utilize the insights and ideas presented in the essays by Beer, Beam, and Keller.

9. Referring to both of Conlan's analyses, argue that the federal government's budget problems may constitute both a stimulus and an impediment to intergovernmental reform.

10. How does Conlan's study of what happened to Reagan's efforts during his period in office demonstrate the importance of complexity and interdependence in the system? If you think it does not so demonstrate, explain why not. Use examples.

11. It is sometimes said that American conservatives desire to shift power to state and local governments. Use evidence from Reagan's administration to make a case that conservatives like Reagan can find themselves resistant to such shifts precisely because of certain elements in their perspective. Has some such shifting nonetheless occurred? Explain.

12. What does the experience in intergovernmental matters during recent administrations suggest about our ability to sort out national from state and local responsibilities?

13. Why would Conlan argue, in the final essay in this part, that American politics are becoming centralized while important aspects

of governance are moving to the states? How would you incorporate earlier materials in this book, for instance on the role of the Supreme Court and on the resurgence of the states, into this discussion? Which of Deil Wright's models of the intergovernmental system (in Part I of this volume) most closely depicts the current circumstances? Or can you offer another version that more accurately fits the pattern of the 1990s?

14. Part I of this book includes an essay by Morton Grodzins on the decentralized nature of American political parties and how these help to breathe vitality into the federal system. In the last article in Part V, however, Timothy Conlan documents centralization of party activities and raises critical questions about the relationship between politics and the intergovernmental structure of governance. If Conlan is correct about the centralization of important components of American politics in recent years, what are the implications? Is Grodzins's argument outdated? Do American politics now pose a threat to the federal system? Or do you see this tension as potentially productive? Consider the implications of the ideas of Beam and Keller in this connection.

AMERICAN INTERGOVERNMENTAL RELATIONS:
CONCLUDING THOUGHTS

Today a formidable set of intergovernmental issues and problems stretches ahead, yet it is important to realize that both the achievements and dilemmas of the contemporary scene are bound up with the choices made at the nation's founding. The framers of the American federal system made conscious decisions about the structure and relationships within and among American governments. To protect freedom, to stimulate diversity, and to foster civic virtues like active citizen involvement in the affairs of state, the founders established a basic framework that would facilitate, indeed stimulate, dynamic, vigorous intergovernmental relations. These early Americans were under few illusions about the character of the emerging nation. They realized that structuring the basic powers and relationships of the governments would not eliminate disputes or establish some neat, orderly, static pattern. Nor, however, would an absence of central authority serve legitimate interests. Instead, the founders crafted a system designed to provide a forum for the inevitable conflict and bargaining in the large and diverse new nation.

Although the intergovernmental system has changed tremendously from the earliest decades, the basic framework created by the founders continues to play a part in the perpetuation of vigorous intergovernmental relations. Historical and contemporary imperatives toward cooperation across governmental lines notwithstanding, the framework has allowed and even encouraged the rise of today's pattern, one of conflict and bargaining in a system characterized by complexity and interdependence.

The enormous complexity of a system composed of more than 83,000 governments suggests that it is impossible to have enough data to operate within it in a consistently rational fashion. There are too many other parties and sets of relationships, many of them highly dynamic. And in recent decades this complexity has been further increased by the addition of new elements in the makeup of the intergovernmental "mix": intergovernmental coordinating bodies, the PIGs, an active court system, lobbying groups representing myriad interests, the emergence of pressing policy issues at multiple levels in the system, more complicated fiscal instruments, a growing array of regulatory mechanisms, and manifold bargaining processes undertaken without the luxury of much budgetary flexibility to help inspire cooperation. A result of this complexity is that efforts to orchestrate dramatic change by any party, no matter how important in the pattern, are bound to fall short of expectations and may well complicate matters still further. We have seen how the efforts by one level of government to exercise control at another, the redesign of the federal government's grant structure, and the trimming of federal aid may produce unintended consequences.

A second important characteristic of the system—interdependence—fuels the complexity. This point is clearly demonstrated by the intergovernmental sharing of power, even within functions. Action by one unit requires support or at least acquiescence on the part of others, and participants can often halt or delay action they oppose. Thus, intergovernmental patterns do not fit a hierarchical, command-and-control pattern. Instead, different governments need each other, and bargaining of various types—even if not among or between equals—is the norm.

High levels of both interdependence and complexity in the system help to explain one of the most persistent dilemmas in the American network: the tension between generalists (whose responsibility is to a geographic area or general government) and specialists (who focus on specific functions that are parts of modern governments, perhaps at multiple levels). Frequently, efforts to modify the intergovernmental system are aimed at shifting the balance between these two groups or emphases. Reagan's new federalism initiatives, for instance, were motivated in part by a desire to take power from the specialists, with their influence over and preference for categoricals, and to give general-purpose executives more clout (for example, by increasing the influence of governors over the use of programs like the block grants). Indeed, the relative influence of these two groups *can* be altered at the margin— witness, for instance, the renewed activism of the governors as a group in numerous policy sectors in recent years. However, the perseverance of the tension is no accident, because the conflict derives from the original design of the system: its complexity generates a continuing need for specialists at all levels and its interdependence drives an imperative for coordination that generalists can facilitate.

The fiscal aspects of the intergovernmental system also reflect the characteristics of interdependence and complexity. Grants emerge from as well as create bargaining contests across levels of government and between specialist and generalist. Although the politics and administration of the various fiscal instruments can differ greatly, the grant system in general exhibits resistance to change, as can be seen in efforts to shrink the federal role or to reassign program responsibilities. This apparent intransigence to explicit redesign—as with the many other difficulties with the system—does not stem exclusively or primarily from intrusion, domination, or ill will on the part of one level of government in dealing with the others. Rather, the interdependence and complexity of the system mitigate against disentangling the several knots that hold the parts of the system together.

This observation is particularly timely today. In the more distant past (for instance, in the 1950s), efforts to induce "reform" to control specific programs, modify general characteristics of the intergovernmental system, or significantly alter the balance of roles among governments had been singularly unsuccessful. The fact of interdependence, along with the persistent sense among the American people that government should continue to be active in many fields to solve pressing and complex problems, had insulated the system itself from major reform. Two factors made, and continue to make, the task of consolidating majority coalitions in favor of systemic change of almost any sort nearly impossible: the multiple interconnections of participants built into the system, and the prospect of the significant dislocations—for agency functions and personnel, program recipients and other interested parties—often generated by reform.

Yet it would be equally mistaken to conclude from these cautionary comments that significant change in the system is not to be expected. Indeed, the historical development of the intergovernmental system in the United States documents repeated adaptations in the face of political, social, and economic events. The same holds true in the 1990s. In spite of the desire of both the citizenry and many officials to retain existing programs and the structural status quo, many observers lately have developed an acute sense of the problems of an "overloaded"—or perhaps underfunded—system. Public enthusiasm for new intergovernmental initiatives emanating from Washington seems to have waned. Massive federal budget problems are now a constant reminder of the apparent need to do *something* about spending and to scrutinize critically the worth and cost of each proposal. Meanwhile, newer forms of influence, like intergovernmental regulation, have become more prominent, more conflictual, and yet themselves highly resistant to reduction. Furthermore, while political trends in the nation have rendered state and local channels less significant than in an earlier era, the agenda for governmental activism at nonnational levels has become especially crowded. Thus, the American intergovernmental network has reached a stage where difficult decisions must be made. Characteristics of the system render major retrenchment unlikely and, many argue, unwise. Even Ronald Reagan was not consistently able to support a wholesale reform of the network. Nor has George Bush. But the status quo offers few signs of balance or resolution.

Lest one conclude that satisfying answers to such questions should be easy to discern, the examples readily visible in other parts of the globe are instructive. The 1990s have seen efforts within the European Community, among the new nations of the former Soviet Union, and in various parts of the old Yugoslavian federation to wrestle with the themes of partial sovereignty in the modern world. Issues like the globalization of the economy and the systemic nature of environmental problems vie with regional and ethnic pride, tradition, and competitiveness in many lands, not merely this one. As the century comes to a close, then, the themes of governance so prominent during more than two centuries of American experience are high on the global agenda.

Yet, as has been seen in this volume, the system of American intergovernmental relations is under increasing challenge. Can the basic framework continue to fulfill its essential function? Can the pragmatic bargaining often viewed as so much a part of the American intergovernmental arrangement be sustained in an era of resource constraints? Can the contrasting trends of politics and governance in the 1990s be brought into some reconciliation or creative dialogue? Can the American experience offer some guidance to those who face similar issues elsewhere in the world? Or, in turn, can some of the struggles over interdependence and complexity occurring abroad provide enlightenment and encourage creative action in the United States? The answer to these practical questions will go far toward determining whether we can resolve the difficult policy problems thrust on modern intergovernmental relationships.

INDEX